The English Novel and the Movies

EDITED BY

Michael Klein and Gillian Parker

WITH HALFTONE ILLUSTRATIONS

Frederick Ungar Publishing Co. / New York

Library of Congress Cataloging in Publication Data

Main entry under title:

The English novel and the movies.

"Selected filmography: film adaptations of English novels, 1719–1930s": p.
  Bibliography: p.
  Includes index.
  1. Film adaptations. 2. English fiction—Film adaptations. 3. English fiction—Film adaptations—Catalogs. I. Klein, Michael, 1939–   II. Parker, Gillian.

PN1997.85.E53   791.43′09′09357   80–5342
ISBN 0–8044–2472–1
ISBN 0–8044–6358–1 (pbk.)

The English Novel and the Movies

Ungar Film Library

Stanley Hochman, GENERAL EDITOR

For Daniel and Jessie

ACKNOWLEDGMENTS

We would like to thank Stanley Hochman of Frederick Ungar for his support, counsel, and patience; Jerry Peary and Ann Kaplan for their prudent advice on how best to go about organizing and editing a collection of essays; Richard Mc-Causland, who helped with research; Mary Corless of the Museum of Modern Art Film Stills archive, who guided us in the selection of photographs; the Reference Department of the Educational Film Librarians Association. And, of course, we would like to thank our contributors, without whom there would be no book.

Contents

Introduction: Film and Literature

Summing up his major intentions in 1913, D. W. Griffith is reported to have said, "The task I'm trying to achieve above all is to make you see." Whether by accident or design, the statement coincides almost exactly with . . . [Conrad's declaration] published sixteen years earlier: "My task which I am trying to make you hear, to make you feel—it is before all, to make you *see*." Aside from the strong syntactical resemblance, the coincidence is remarkable in suggesting the points at which film and novel both join and part company. . . . One may . . . see visually through the eye or imaginatively through the mind. And between the the precept of the visual image and the concept of the mental image lies the root difference between the two media.

—George Bluestone

Let Dickens and the whole ancestral array, going back as far as the Greeks and Shakespeare, be . . . reminders that both Griffith and our cinema prove our origins to be not solely as of Edison and his fellow inventors, but as based on an enormous cultural past . . . [on] literature which . . . is, in the first and most important place, the art of viewing— not only the *eye*, but *viewing*—both meanings embraced in this term.

—Sergei Eisenstein

The cinema should always be the discovery of something. . . . I try to plunge myself into a poetic development, which differs from a narrative development and dramatic development.

—Orson Welles

There is no need to regard the cinema as a completely new art; in its fictional form it has the same purpose as the novel, just as the novel had the same purpose as the drama. Chekhov, writing of his fellow novelists remarked: "The best of them are realistic and paint life as it is, but because each line is permeated . . . by awareness of a purpose, you feel,

1

besides life as it is, also life as it ought to be, and this captivates you."
Life as it is and life as it ought to be: let us take that as the only true
subject for film.

—Graham Greene

Too often discussions about adaptations from literature to film have
for some reason been clouded by categorical claims for the superiority of one of the two art forms, claims that seem not to be aroused
by other acts of adaptation. When, for example, Bandello's novella
Romeo and Juliet was transformed by Shakespeare into drama, and
later orchestrated into ballet scores by Tchaikovsky and Prokofiev,
the either/or controversy seldom arose. Yet it is customary for
articles about film adaptations of Shakespeare's play to evidence a
fair amount of discomfort about the legitimacy of transposing a
literary text into film. Because of this general assumption, and
because it may appear to be implicit in the very structure of the
present collection of essays, where the inclusion of a work is in the
first instance determined by the stature of the novel rather than that
of the film, some balancing of the scales seems called for here, in
this brief survey of the issues surrounding the metamorphosis of
literature into film.

The Range and Scope of the Language of Film

The relation of literature to film can be seen as part of a larger
question: the relation of literature to visual art. For example, the
eighteenth-century philosopher and critic, Gotthold Lessing, assigned the narration of sequential actions to literature and the
representation of objects and persons to painting and sculpture.
Each art form had its proper sphere and concerns. While Lessing's
divisions may seem overly strict, we normally do respond to painting
and novels in different ways, ways that assume that the two art
forms have very different properties. The case of film is somewhat
more complex. Robert Scholes, in a perceptive essay "Narration and
Narrativity in Film," has persuasively argued that film is capable of
combining the essential qualities of both narrative literature ("ver-

bal narrative") and visual art ("pictorial representation"), and that if Lessing "were brought back to life again today he would recognize in cinema the reconciliation of the parts of his divided world."[1]

Scholes's insight can be further extended: we may say that, insofar as film is an encyclopedic and synthesizing art form, it combines aspects of not only literature (that is, fiction, drama, and poetry) and painting, but also of photography, mime, dance, architecture, music, and holography.

Indeed film is capable of drawing upon most aspects of its artistic heritage to document, render, and interpret experience. It does so, however, through its own particular formal and signifying properties. Camera position, camera movement, framing, lighting, sound, and editing are, perhaps, the primary means by which a director may reproduce, shape, and thus express and evaluate the significance of a narrative. André Bazin has called attention to the ways in which the camera situates and frames action,[2] Bela Balázs to the iconic function of close-ups,[3] George Bluestone to the complexity of cinematic tropes,[4] and Sergei Eisenstein to the analytic and expressive possibilities of spatial, tonal, and cognitive montage.[5] A film of a novel, far from being a mechanical copy of the source, is a transposition or translation from one set of conventions for representing the world to another.

In addition to its distinct formal and expressive aspects, film also conveys a range of cultural signs—the facial expressions, gestures, dialects, dress, and style of its characters; the architecture, advertising, landscape, and common artifacts of its setting; the semiotic expression of a culture in a particular historical period. These signs

1. Robert Scholes, "Narration and Narrativity in Film," *Quarterly Review of Film Studies*, 1:111 (August, 1976), p. 290.

2. André Bazin, "The Evolution of the Language of Cinema ," *What is Cinema?*, 1, trans. Hugh Gray (Berkeley: University of California Press, 1971), pp. 23-41.

3. Bela Balázs, *Theory of the Film: Character and Growth of a New Art*, trans. Edith Bone (London: Dobson, 1952).

4. George Bluestone, "The Limits of the Novel and the Limits of Film," *Novels into Film: the Metamorphosis of Fiction into Cinema* (Berkeley: University of California Press, 1968).

5. Sergei Eisenstein, *Film Form* and *The Film Sense*, trans. Jay Leyda (Cleveland: Meridian, 1957), especially *Film Form* pp. 28-84.

or hieroglyphs are a kind of cultural picture language. They have a mimetic or almost documentarylike quality, and are thus a source of verisimilitude; they are also an index of the ideologies, values, and conventions by which we order experience and predicate activity.

Both the formal and semiotic qualities of film are an inherent part of the background or secondary field of a cinematic image and thus of the discourse of the work. In a sense, we may regard the total visual and aural configuration of a film (camera position and movement, lighting, editing, and music, as well as cultural or semiological material) as background, analogous to the novelist's devices of description or metaphoric and tonal language in prose fiction.

André Bazin touches upon some of these questions in his discussion of deep focus in "The Evolution of the Language of Cinema."[6] "Deep focus" or depth of field is more than a literal description of the results of technological innovations that enabled both the foreground and the background of an image to be brought together into clear focus. The fact of depth involves *simultaneity*, perhaps the most important synthetic quality of film: we, as viewers, perceive multiple objects, signs, codes, connections, and relations. By convention, the main narrative events are situated most often in the foreground and a configuration of secondary signs in the background—the latter noted in passing, or sensed subliminally. Both background (or subtext) and foreground may constitute distinct discourses. At times there may be a dialectical shift of emphasis: elements of the background may overdetermine (amplify, qualify, or supplant) the action in the foreground. The complex, simultaneous interaction—of foreground and background, of text and subtext, of discourse and containing discourse—mirrors the complex relations of experience that are the common subject of significant literature and film.

6. Bazin, pp. 23-41. He concludes: "The filmmaker is no longer the competitor of the painter and the playwright, he is at last, the equal of the novelist." Bazin, in his discussion of depth of focus, stresses the importance of multiple relations within a frame, while Eisenstein, in his discussion of montage, calls our attention to the importance of multiple relations and connections arising out of the juxtaposition of frames and scenes. Recently, Metz, in *Film Language*, and Eco, in *A Theory of Semiotics*, have extended our sense of the ways in which film and cultural codes interact in the cinema.

H. D. F. Kitto, in *Form and Meaning in Drama*, uses the term
"juxtaposition" to isolate a similar quality as the key to dramatic
construction and to our understanding of the way a play works:
"Aeschylus, like Pindar, Sophocles, Shakespeare and sundry other
poets sometimes uses sharp juxtaposition rather than words to
express his thought."[7] Drama is defined by Kitto as "the art of
significant juxtaposition,"[8] a definition perhaps better suited to film,
with its characteristic ability to encompass, and juxtapose for
meaning, a wide range of references in the brief space of an image.
Thus Sergei Eisenstein wrote, with respect to both reality and film:

> We never see anything isolated, but everything in connection with
> something else which is before it, beside it, under it and over it.[9]

If film can achieve the degree of complexity suggested in the
above statement, which Eisenstein culled from Goethe, what of the
criticism that film does not have the range or depth of prose fiction
because of its inherent limitations? It has been argued that because
the camera records the surface of actions, events, and objects, film
cannot be analytic or metaphoric; it cannot render complex internal
or psychological relations, or a sense of memory, or a sense of past
time bearing upon present time. While such objections can help to
highlight differences of stress between the two art forms, they seem
to suggest that film can only paraphrase a received literary text to
produce a kind of masterplot or classic comic rather than, as we
shall see, realize the work anew in terms of film form.

When a literary work is translated into film, it is metamorphosized
not only by the camera, the editing, the performances, the setting,
and the music, but by distinct film codes and conventions, culturally
signifying elements, and by the producer's and director's interpretations as well. Meanings that may have been lost when the text of
the narrative first became the screenplay, condensed and bereft of
some of its linguistic resources, may be resurrected subsequently by

7. H. D. F. Kitto, "Agamemnon," in *Form and Meaning in Drama* (London:
Methuen, 1960), p. 4.
8. Kitto, "Hamlet," p. 270.
9. Johann Goethe, quoted by Eisenstein in "A Dialectical Approach to Film
Form," *Film Form*, p. 45.

the new medium in different form and through a different kind of imaginative process.

When a filmed script comes alive on the screen and is experienced by an audience, the dialectic between film and viewer is not exactly the same as that between literary text and reader. Robert Scholes has observed that film is, for example, a more collaborative process than literature.

> In cinematic narrative, the spectator must supply a more categorical and abstract narrativity. . . . A well-made film requires interpretation while a well-made novel may only need understanding. . . . The cinematic world invites—even requires—conceptualization. The images presented to us, their arrangement and juxtapositioning, are narrational blueprints for a fiction that must be constructed by the viewer's narrativity.[10]

In response to signs and codes, to conventions that very much depend upon a shared cultural context or *geist*, the audience experiencing a film supplies the appropriate feelings, perceptions, and interpretations, and thus, in a sense, completes the film. This tends to occur whether cinematic meaning is conveyed primarily by dramatized action or by metaphor, or through rendition of states of mind or states of memory that relate past time to present experience.

Visual symbols and metaphors often contain the action of a film so as to enhance its meaning significantly. For example, in Hitchcock's free adaptation of the sources of *Foreign Correspondent* (1940), historical forces determining the onset of World War II are symbolized by an ominous windmill. At the surface level of the narrative the windmill is only the background, the setting within which the hero first learns about a Nazi plot that will provoke the end of peace in Europe. However the action is so visualized within the mill (the hero, hiding, pressed against the cogs and wheels of the machinery) that the espionage narrative is subsumed as merely an occasion for an intense expressionist metaphor: the inexorable wheel of fortune, the grinding millstones of history. The social context within which the film was viewed in 1940-1941 significantly height-

---

10. Scholes, pp. 291-293. Also see Wolfgang Iser, *The Implied Reader: Patterns of Communication in Prose Fiction from Bunyan to Beckett* (Baltimore: Johns Hopkins Press, 1978), for a detailed study of the interrelation of text and reader.

ened the intensity of the image; audiences, like the protagonist of Hitchcock's film, would have felt themselves about to be caught up in the machinery of history. A related example is Carol Reed's adaptation of Graham Greene's *The Third Man* (1949), a film set in Vienna at the end of the War. The action occurs for the most part in the streets, in front of the rubble of baroque architecture and down in the sewers below the city, while the cacophonous soundtrack reverberates with a multilingual babble, the voices of pursuing military police. The visual and aural background of the film becomes an apocalyptic objective correlative: Europe as Wasteland—culturally, spiritually, and economically exhausted by the war; occupied by foreign powers; sapped by internal corruption. Again, the narrative is contained by a series of visual and aural metaphors that function as discourse to clarify and extend its meaning, and that depend upon a shared cultural context for their power.

In addition to charging the 'surface of reality with significance, film may penetrate below that surface to express interior states of being. George Bluestone has observed that superimpositions and musical leitmotifs are "visual and aural substitutes" for "interior monologues" in John Ford's adaptation of Liam O'Flaherty's novel *The Informer* (1935).[11] Film can render or express subjective points of view in ways that range from first-person camera perspective (Robert Montgomery's 1947 adaptation of Chandler's *Lady in the Lake*) to visual or aural externalization of a character's state of mind (the use of color in Corman's adaptation of Poe's *Masque of the Red Death*, 1964, or of shadow and space in Welles's adaptation of Kafka's *The Trial*, 1962, or of music in Truffaut's adaptation of Roché's *Jules and Jim*, 1961).

At times film establishes multiple points of view: for example Hitchcock, in *Notorious* (1946), cross-cuts between two characters' subjective points of view so that we alternately see each one from the other's perspective. Antonioni, in *Red Desert* (1964), establishes a bifocal perspective somewhat analogous to limited omniscient point of view in complex narrative fiction: we experience the world as an industrial and spiritual wasteland from within the anomic,

11. Bluestone, p. 86.

alienated points of view of the main characters, and, often at the same time, perceive them from an objective historical perspective.

Like literature, film has the ability to represent multiple layers of time and consciousness: time past, time present, future time, imaginative time. This is often achieved through well-established conventions that signal a flash-back, a dream, or, in recent film, perhaps also a flash-forward. In early silent film a bubble superimposed over part of an image might enclose either a memory or the representation of a dream. Soon time shifts became implicit: D. W. Griffith developed techniques of cutting from a close-up of a face to action that was occurring either in a different location (temporal as well as spatial) or, for example in his adaptation of Poe's *The Tell-Tale Heart* (1912), to action taking place entirely in the mind or imagination.

John Ward has analyzed temporal fluidity, what he calls "Bergsonian" or "Proustian" time, in the films that Alain Resnais made from the novels of Alain Robbe-Grillet and in collaboration with the novelist Marguerite Duras.[12] Resnais's *Hiroshima Mon Amour* (1959) has a complex temporal structure: 1958, time-present in Hiroshima; 1945, time-past in Nevers, France; August 6th, 1945, time-past in Hiroshima. We may suddenly move back in time by means of objective references (photographs of the aftermath of the holocaust in Hiroshima), by cinematic tropes that fuse and thus interrelate past and present (the image of the two lovers' bodies in the opening of the film, 1958, are so photographed that they seem momentarily transformed into archetypal images of Hiroshima victims in 1945), or by entering the subjectivity of the main character (the woman's sight of her sleeping Japanese lover, in Hiroshima in 1958, evokes memory of her dead lover, in Nevers in 1945, and a flood of traumatic images of her youth in France at the close of the war). Resnais' film carries us back and forth in time, in and out of memory, defining the present in terms of the protagonist's recollection and reconstruction of the past.

Bergsonian time is conveyed through somewhat different means in Francois Truffaut's recent film *The Green Room*, adapted from Henry James's story "The Altar of the Dead." The film itself is self-

12. John Ward, *Alain Resnais or the Theme of Time* (London: Secker and Warburg, 1968).

reflective, a cinematic equivalent of James's prose: photographs of artistic figures from the past who have influenced the director, portraits of people whose lives expressed important values for him, images from the war and allusions to significant scenes in previous Truffaut films, all fuse in a central metaphor, the flickering candles on the altar of the dead, to convey a sense of collective memory, of common tradition from the past.

Adaptation of Fiction into Film

Studies of the adaptation of novels into film generally focus upon several interrelated questions: whether the film is a literal, critical, or relatively free adaptation of the literary source; whether significant cultural and ideological shifts occur when a novel that was written in a particular historical period is transposed into modern film; whether cinematic equivalents of the rhetoric and discourse of fiction extend the perspective of the literary source.

To begin with the first of these questions: the degree of correspondence between the adaptation and the source. There are, perhaps, three main approaches to the task of adaptation to be considered.

First, because of the expectations of the audience, most films of classic novels attempt to give the impression of being faithful, that is, literal, translations of the text into the language of film: for example, the film versions of *Tom Jones* (1963), *Pride and Prejudice* (1940), *A Christmas Carol* (1959), *Of Human Bondage* (1964), and *Sons and Lovers* (1960). There has to be a good deal of selection and condensation when a novel, which may take several days to read, is transposed into a film of roughly two hours: scenes have to be cut, minor characters simplified or eliminated, subplots dispensed with. But this need not exclude fidelity to the main thrust of the narrative, to the author's central concerns, to the natures of the major characters, to the ambience of the novel, and, what is perhaps most important, to the *genre* of the source. When the film genre matches the spirit and genre of the literary text the results can be very satisfying—for example, *Tom Jones* (a comic epic in film), *A Christmas Carol* (allegorical fantasy), or *Sons and Lovers* (formal narrative realism). If, however, while striving to be a literal recreation of a text, the film transposes it into a different genre, the result can be discordant: for example, *Wuthering Heights* (1939), a gothic romance, for the most part larger than life, becomes a well-made dramatic film about the personal relations of the main characters; Dickens's *David Copperfield* (1935), a novel structured to express a significant theme, becomes a filmed series of colorful vignettes and enjoyable character sketches.

A second and different approach to adaptation is one that retains the core of the structure of the narrative while significantly reinterpreting or, in some cases, deconstructing the source text: for example, the films of *Robinson Crusoe* (1952), *Barry Lyndon* (1975), and *A Portrait of the Artist as a Young Man* (1978). There a major director or auteur, having a particular perspective on a literary source, reinterprets it in order to make a new and significant statement, one that often in some way relates to the contemporary world: Bunuel subtly deconstructs *Robinson Crusoe* to reveal the negative aspects of Defoe's cultural assumptions while recreating the Crusoe myth to express his own vision of the world; Kubrick transmutes *Barry Lyndon* into a parable about modern class mobility and alienation; Strick contains Stephen Dedalus's alienated vision within a discourse that expresses the positive aspects of Irish national culture, so that the film becomes a portrait, as it were, of Joyce's *A Portrait of the Artist as a Young Man* (1914).

A third approach to adaptation is one that regards the source merely as raw material, as simply the occasion for an original work. Of the films studied in this collection of essays, only *Nosferatu* (1979) and *Apocalypse Now* (1979) apprroach this category, perhaps because well-known works of English fiction tend to command at least the outward appearance of fidelity.[13]

Cultural factors also affect adaptations in significant ways, especially when an English novel is transposed into an American film or a film primarily intended for an American audience. The novels

13. However, minor novels and short stories are often the basis of free interpretations since their brevity allows for imaginative expansion—for example, Bertolucci's historicized *The Spider's Strategm* (1970) based upon Borges's extremely compressed abstract fable "The Hero and the Traitor," or *First Love* (1970), Schell's modernist explication of Turgenev's understated short story. Bertolucci and Schell historicize their sources, whereas in *Apocalypse Now* fantasy displaces the history of U.S. involvement in Vietnam.

represented here were written in England in the eighteenth, nineteenth, or early twentieth centuries, but many have been filmed in accordance with the Hollywood codes and conventions familiar to the modern American market. Certain cultural distortions may occur when the English work is Americanized, even if the director intends to make a relatively literal adaptation, and then perhaps even more so as any disparities can be especially jarring. Thus if the children in the film of *Wuthering Heights* come across as types of American farm kids, and if the women in the film of *Pride and Prejudice* tend to be conventional midwestern smalltown daughters and matrons, we think of Hollywood first and Bronte or Austen second, the clash of styles being even more evident where, as in these cases, the lead performers are English and the dress of the characters is relatively authentic.

Apart from considerations of national differences, significant changes in interpretation are likely to occur when a literary text produced in one historical period is adapted in a later era, subject to the cultural and ideological preconceptions of the industry. For example, the latter part of David Lean's film *Great Expectations* (1947) diffuses Dickens's social criticism, and as a consequence the metaphors through which the novelist analyzed and illuminated the world are internalized and restricted: Dickens's nightmare image of Pip being trapped in the workings of nineteenth-century capitalist society becomes narrowed to merely an index of the character's crackup. Other examples of ideological shifts are similarly striking. In Hollywood, Thackeray's social satire, *Vanity Fair*, is inverted into a comic tribute to Becky Sharp's individualism, into a Horatio Alger myth for the Depression-period audience. *Jane Eyre* (1944), a feminist novel (the rebellious heroine is rendered in depth, with sympathy, and the world is seen from her point of view), becomes a vehicle for the expression of Hollywood's sexual codes, mystiques, and conventions.

Still within these examples there are some splendid moments, scenes in which feeling and thought are spatialized in imaginative cinematic equivalents of the verbal resources of literature. For example, in the early part of Lean's impressive film of Dickens's novel we see Miss Havisham's house from the child Pip's innocent and admiring point of view, at the same time being guided by the

director's *mise-en-scène* to see that the world of the house and, by
extension, the world of *Great Expectations* is out of joint. In a
striking scene in Mamoulian's *Becky Sharp* (1935), English society
disperses under the impending threat of Napoleon in a storm of
sound, color, and shifting space. In *Jane Eyre* the pervasive influence
of Welles's style (expressionism developing into *film noir*) external-
izes the inner conflicts of Rochester, the male protagonist, and
perhaps also those of the director faced with Bronte's material.

Often a director uses cinematic equivalents of the rhetoric and
discourse of fiction to either render or critique the perspective of a
literary source. In a climactic moment in Bunuel's *The Adventures
of Robinson Crusoe*, Friday picks up a rifle, lunges forward as if to
kill Crusoe, then, continuing the motion, stretches out his arms and
presents Crusoe with the gun, a gesture or sign of voluntary
subordination. The scene is set in a garden, an Eden-like or
Rousseau-like setting. It is a picture of a social covenant. In a single
image all the ambiguities and contradictions of Friday's democratic
servitude and of the colonial social covenant are manifested. The
gesture is worth a thousand words. In privileged moments like this
film attains the power and clarity of allegory and folk narrative, of
forms that centuries ago began to fuse and develop further within
the novel. It is also at moments like this that we fully appreciate
what Eisenstein, Conrad and Griffith meant when they said that
their art was designed to make us "see": that is, to make us perceive
and understand. Adequacy of vision and talent are, in the final
sense, the determining factors of the quality of an adaptation from
literature into film.

The films chosen for inclusion in this collection of essays could
form the basis of several courses or seminars in an English department or film program. As a planned second volume will focus on
films based on contemporary popular English fiction, we have
limited this collection to adaptations of English novels from Defoe
and Fielding to Lawrence and Joyce, and, with the exception of
Finnegans Wake, to films of novels that were written before 1930.

For the most part we have chosen as source texts representative
works of classic English novelists; however in some cases novels that
have become metamorphosized into cultural myths (*Frankenstein*,

Dracula, Dr. Jekyll and Mr. Hyde), in part because of the success of the film versions, have also been included. We have also included works by novelists who while not English are often included in English Literature courses (for example, Joyce). We have attempted to include as many films by significant directors as possible, not only film classics but adaptations made as recently as 1979.

Unfortunately, considerations of time, space, and the availability of prints have made it impossible for us to cover the following: *The New Gulliver* (1935), *Ivanhoe* (1952), *The Woman in White* (1948), *The Mill on the Floss* (1937), *Outcast of the Islands* (1952), *Lord Jim* (1965) and recent television versions of the novels of Charles Dickens (*Hard Times, Our Mutual Friend*), Robert Tressell (*The Ragged Trouser Philanthropists*), and John Galsworthy (*The Forsyte Saga*). We have included information on these and related works in the Filmography. The essays in this volume were chosen to illustrate a wide variety of critical approaches and with the general reader's and film student's interests and needs in mind.

—MICHAEL KLEIN

Robinson Crusoe (1719), Daniel Defoe

Luis Bunuel, 1953: *The Adventures of Robinson Crusoe*

Crusoe Through the Looking-Glass

GILLIAN PARKER

The name of Luis Bunuel commonly calls to mind two periods of filmmaking, linked by the director's consistent vision. There are the early works that emerged out of the surrealist avant garde of the 1920s—*Un Chien Andalou* (made with Dali in 1928), or *L'Age d'Or* (1930). Decades later came the recent works with their international reputation and rather milder rhetoric—*Belle de Jour (1966)*, say, or *Tristana* (1971), or *The Discreet Charm of the Bourgeoisie* (1972). Despite the gap in time and the shifts in style, the films make up a unified body of work: in one way or another they assault, from different vantage points, the mystifications that justify the status quo, and those who perpetrate them. Bunuel, perhaps having in mind his work in the lean years between his early and late successes, has insisted that "the need to eat never excuses the prostituting of one's art. . . . I have made bad films, but always morally acceptable to me."[1] *Robinson Crusoe* (1952) is then a surprising title to come upon in the list of Bunuel's films: the novel (1719) is a moral work, certainly, but hardly in the Bunuellian sense. *Wuthering Heights* (*Cumbres Borrascosas*, 1953), the other English novel adaptation Bunuel made at this time, during his years of comparative obscurity as a commercial director in Mexico, fits in well enough, with its defiance of the conventions in the name of *l'amour fou*. But the

---

1. Cited by James M. Wall in "Luis Bunuel and the Death of God," *Three European Directors*, ed. James M. Wall (Michigan: W. B. Eerdmans, 1973), p. 135.

14

only link between Bunuel and Crusoe would indeed appear to be the need to eat.

Defoe seems an uncongenial source for Bunuel. Neither the novel's famous realism, nor its sequential plot, nor its authorial point of view, so close to that of Crusoe the narrator as to be indistinguishable, seems likely to recommend the work to a filmmaker who characteristically juxtaposes surrealistic images in defiance of narrative sequence and whose distance from his characters often reaches beyond irony to parody. Even more of a stumbling block are the values implicit in the novel, which generations of critics have pointed out. Crusoe is *homo economicus*, the paradigmatic bourgeois hero who, in his concentration on the accumulation of capital, exemplifies Defoe's tradesman's ethos; an odd hero surely for Bunuel, whose films are ferocious raiding parties on the dignity of the acquisitive bourgeoisie. Then there is the moral-religious accompaniment to Crusoe's efforts: he begins as a rather obvious failure, washed-up and abandoned by God, but as his material goods mount his spiritual guilt is assuaged and replaced by an assurance of salvation—the Protestant Ethic in action. Further, there are the political overtones of the work: Crusoe as the embryonic imperialist, extending his dominion first over foreign territory, and then over the native population in the person of Friday—a fitting cultural hero for the early days of Empire, but not for Bunuel, whose nearest political position is anarchism. And finally there is Defoe's implied view of man's social relations, hostile and even wolfish as the island incursions of the representative cannibals and marauding English indicate; Crusoe's thirty-odd years of solitude are not finally relieved by a friendly face but broken by an unwelcome threat to his property.

At first glance the film appears to conform to the novel, and Bunuel to have given way gracefully in this instance to Defoe and the conditions of commercial production: the film won an award from *Parents* magazine (New York),[2] something of a backhanded compliment to one of Bunuel's outlook. As in the novel, Crusoe tells his story, here in voice-over, while the images, visual equivalents for the most part of Defoe's realism, decorously follow the sequence of

---

2. "Filmography," Francisco Aranda, *Luis Bunuel: A Critical Biography* (London: Secker and Warburg, 1975), p. 296.

his narrative. After a shipwreck in the tropics, Crusoe, the sole survivor, sets about providing for his needs: he builds a shelter and a storeroom, learns to herd his own animals and to produce his own crops and corn. After some twenty years cannibals arrive, from whom Crusoe saves Friday, and years later a band of mutinous English sailors appear. Crusoe routs them and so is at last taken off the island by the grateful ship's captain. As this outline shows, however, the sequence of events is in itself almost meaningless; there is no necessary correlation in an adaptation between the film's conformity to the novel's plot, and to its vision. Defoe used the experience of the island shipwreck to tell one story, Bunuel to tell another.

What Bunuel does is divide off from the original work its whole freight of implications—its economic, religious, moral, political meanings—either by simply omitting implications, showing the event but excluding Crusoe/Defoe's interpretation, or by including, for example, some of the religious or imperial overtones, but only for critical scrutiny and rejection. While Bunuel does add on scenes of his own invention, in which, on the whole, Crusoe's values are seen as representative faults, much of the film stays close to Defoe's action, and, like the original, celebrates its hero. In either case, however, what is being achieved in the film is not Defoe's commendation, but Bunuel's critique of the middle-class ethos of Crusoe's day and, by implication, of our own.

What is intriguing in the parts of the film that closely follow Defoe is the method by which the director shifts the original meaning. These are the scenes of Crusoe's building, wheat growing, bread making, pottery, and so on. Throughout this major part of the novel Crusoe exemplifies the virtues of the entrepreneur of his day, learning, after the ruinous slaving enterprise that has rendered him destitute or bankrupt, the arts of thrift, capitalization through delayed gratification, reinvestment, bookkeeping. His very survival (and indeed salvation) depends on his conforming to the ethos of the class from which he has precipitously dropped, and to which he returns, reformed after his youthful rebellion. Bunuel, however, creates a different hero in these scenes. He excludes their economic implications and presents Crusoe not as a representative but as an outsider, whose new skills, essential for survival, are those held to be of least value in society. As in the novel, Crusoe begins his story as a rebel against his father's control: "against the will, nay, command of my father I broke loose and went to sea," and while Crusoe has second thoughts about this, Bunuel does not; he shows Crusoe released from the closed world of his father into the more perilous but open world of nature.

This is made clear in visual terms early in the film. The wreck grounds on a reef following the first fearful night on the island, and Crusoe (Dan O'Herlihy) is full of joy as at the sight of home. However the visual rhetoric of the scene works against Crusoe's response. We see a vista of the island from a hilltop—an expanse of turquoise water and green foliage sparkling in sunlight. Crusoe spies the ship and rushes gladly downhill toward it. Leaving Crusoe and his point of view behind, the scene jumps ahead to the ship's interior, focusing first in the dank gloom on a cluster of gnawing rats, then drawing back to reveal the dark, constricted hold. Crusoe appears outside, still in the light with the golden island behind him, but now framed, imprisoned by the dark rectangle of the window. After the flowing lines of the island, all is angular, machine made, harsh. Crusoe enters down narrow, tilted, black passageways, his movements cramped by stark intersecting lines, the detritus of a slaving ship—an iron ladder, racks of upright guns, chains. The irony of the visual contrast affirms the island, for all its earlier threat, and denies the ship and the burden of civilization it carries.

Consequently whereas the novel catalogues with relish the great store of commodities Crusoe salvages from the wreck, the film ignores this, preferring to have him start a manifestly new life. Rats and bread come off Bunuel's ship; Crusoe drowns the former and soon finishes the latter, replacing it with bread of his own making. He does, however, salvage something of worth, tinder and flint, with which, Prometheus-like, he can steal fire from the civilization he has left, but only on condition he become a new man. At first he scrapes away helplessly—"how often had I seen my servants do this, but I, master of servants, couldn't even build my own fire"—but as he ceases to be a "master" his skills, including fire making, increase. In the novel, Crusoe's efforts increase his property and are seen as gradually leading to his regaining his class position, whereas Bun-

The Adventures of Robinson Crusoe (1953). Two expressive shots of actor Dan O'Herlihy show Bunuel's use of space. Confined space: society sinks with Crusoe's slave ship. Open space: the new pastoral world of Crusoe's island. (Photo courtesy of the Museum of Modern Art)

some years to present us with a strictly Bunuelian rendition of this. Crusoe, whom we see clad for the first time in his bizarre skin outfit, complete with parasol, is leaning with divine condescension over two beetles he has discovered on a stroll through his Eden. Addressing them in a hearty tone as "my little friends," he feeds them a living ant with an indulgent chuckle, "I'll feed you—here's a morsel for you—go on, get him!" then rubs his hands as at a task completed, "Well, goodbye." Now resembling his father in the nightmare, and speaking in a similar tone (Dan O'Herlihy plays both parts, to this end), Crusoe has ceased to be the rebel and has made himself over into the image of the patriarchal God—deranged and arbitrary, perhaps malicious—suggested by both his religion and his experience. The ant struggles hopelessly for a while and then is dragged down by the claws of the beetles as Crusoe takes off jauntily along the beach in a grotesque music-hall walk—knees bent, arms shooting out in great strides, crouched over under his hairy umbrella: God as an Englishman.

These added scenes of Bunuel's not only break disconcertingly into the narrative but are also in themselves fraught with tension, in contrast to the harmony of the pastoral sequences: the actor's motions no longer fit what he is doing; they become gestural or theatrical, his voice becomes inappropriately magisterial, the character's emotions clash with the setting or the occasion, what is done is at odds with what is said, and so on. In this way Bunuel cuts what he is presenting, indicates the shifts into criticism or satiry, and disorders the viewer's response to forestall conventional reactions. And where Defoe labored to unify contradictions, divides them with a flourish. In the last section of the film, makes full use of his rhetorical skills to convey the moral introduces into Crusoe's relationship with Friday and the ions of that relationship.

does not appear in the novel until about two-thirds of the ugh; he then appears not as an an afterthought, but as a on. Defoe's Crusoe has been extending his mastery over ent, and Friday comes on as the last proof of his control: ng assurance for a still insecure commercial class beginend its sway over England and Empire and to redefine

uel's hero gives up his middle-class identity to a great extent through his manual labor, and becomes a skilled artisan. The rhetoric of the scenes emphasizes his transformation from one who had "never before handled an axe or tool" and was "a very sorry workman" to a new man, one who through "constant hard labour" manages to survive by his own efforts. The film celebrates Crusoe's achievements—his house building, husbandry, pottery—with swift, coherent sequences of tactile images that give a rhythmic sense of his growing dexterity and physical competence. He raises wheat, harvests it, grinds flour, bakes bread; images of his nimble hands at work culminate in "the most delicious meal of my life . . . I could truly say I worked for my bread."

At one point as he goes about his tasks, Crusoe appears in iconic outline against the horizon, bearing a young kid around his neck, an unmistakably pastoral image. In telling his tale of a man who returns to nature, survives by gaining knowledge of its ways, and lives by satisfyingly earthy work, Bunuel taps into a modern version of pastoral, and to the form's built-in critique of the upside-down values of the outside world. It is a frame of reference that never comes to mind in discussing the novel because there the island is not the green world that stands in opposition to civilization, but on the contrary a confirmation of the commercial world. Where the film shows Crusoe simply herding his goats, the novel's corresponding description includes an analogy: "After I had thus secur'd one Part of my little living Stock, I went about the whole Island, searching for another private Place, to make such another Deposit,"[3] and here the goats are capital, their enclosures banks or joint-stock companies, and Crusoe is not so much herding as wisely splitting his investment.

The pastoral hero characteristically shows up the remoteness from reality of his superiors in the world of the court or the city. The film's Crusoe, whose daily survival depends upon his grasping the real workings of the material world, is then a fitting hero for Bunuel, whose fiercest attacks have always been directed against this remoteness, against the various forms of illusion or false consciousness that

3. Daniel Defoe, *Robinson Crusoe* (1719; reprinted in London: Oxford University Press, 1972), p. 164.

sustain the "discreet charm of the bourgeoisie."[4] However, this is only one side of Crusoe. Bunuel, never one to avoid contradictions, makes him also a representative of the other side, of the negative traits which the film is criticizing: after all, additional characters can hardly be brought on to serve this function as they sometimes are in pastoral works set in more accessible spots. Crusoe takes on this role, bringing into the pastoral world the faults of his, and our, society, in scenes which break discordantly into the rhythms of his practical life, and split him virtually into two figures, the competent workman and, eventually, the deluded "master."

The other side is presented largely by scenes that Bunuel either invents or radically alters from the original, and that he thrusts abruptly into the film's flow. Whereas the novel follows a rising curve through Crusoe's moral improvement to his eventual salvation, the film deliberately breaks this structure, with its providential implications, and follows instead a zig-zag of contradictions. The first time this occurs Crusoe's father is brought on as a representative figure, the root of error. Crusoe is progressing tentatively with his new life when suddenly Father appears, lecturing him in sonorous tones about his former recklessness and present abandonment by God. The speech has been moved from the opening pages of the novel, where it cast a seriously prophetic shadow of consequent disasters over Crusoe's leaving his station, to an altogether ironic setting by Bunuel. The elder Crusoe recommends the virtues of the family's middle station in life, which is "safe from the misery, hardship and labour of mankind's lower estate, nor yet embarrassed by the pride, luxury and ambition of the upper state." While he speaks he is scrubbing a pig—Bunuel's implication being perhaps that his words are a comparable clean-up job. His feverished son calls to him for water, but Father ignores him, tipping over a full cask. Crusoe dangles up to his waist in tantalizingly unreachable water, while Father pontificates on, making great show with his crown of authority, his black Puritan hat; he piously tenders his own forgiveness to his errant son, but warns that God will never forgive

4. Irving Louis Horowitz, "Bunuel's Bourgeoisie" in *The World of Luis Bunuel: Essays in Criticism*, ed. Joan Mellen (New York: Oxford University Press, 1978), pp. 397-404.

him. As Crusoe becomes enraged at his deviousness, Father shrugs indifferently, and backs carefully out of the doo[r] denied all help or comfort. For his part, Crusoe determine[s] out and gets his own water, maintaining the spiritual ind[ependence] of his new life. Bunuel opened the scene by cutting str[aight] shot of Father, without warning that what he was about[to] nightmare; the paratactic style of these inserted scenes counter movement with the abrupt jolt of a sudden co[ntradiction]

Although Crusoe ends the intrusion by running at [the image with] ax, his influence is not so easily dispelled; now in [sensibly cultivating his garden, great metaphysical [urges] grip Crusoe, causing him to swoop around the isl[and on strange] quests. With wild eyes and matted hair he dashe[s] over a canyon and bellows the twenty-third [Psalm] mocked by the sublime intimations of the sple[ndor] which, however, no divine voice sounds, while h[is own voice returns] to him as an increasingly desperate echo: "The [Lord is my shepherd,] I shall not want . . ." he asserts, despite th[e fact that the only] pastoral on the island is that created by a com[bination of nature and] his own hands. Or, he dashes into the sea b[earing a cross held] aloft, which matches the flaming sunset ar[ound him, an ironic] sign to explain his situation, but the sky s[tays] silently orange as his despairing arm droo[ps, finally extinguishing] his torch in the water. Thus whereas th[e novel insists on] interpreting his years on the island as [a providential design in] which he progresses from punishment b[y God to salvation,] the film reveals the absurdity of Crusoe[searching for a divine] design behind his adventitious fate, [the mere] workings of nature. Crusoe declares [he will] raise a crop of corn, as he marches [behind a] cross, but which turns out, rather m[ore like the arms] of a scarecrow; a visual metonymy [which] brings in the metaphysical world v[with a] materialist thump.

In the latter half of the nov[el, Crusoe is a different] figure. Now perfected in prud[ence, faith and his sense of] Providence, Defoe's Crusoe i[s in full] omniscient control of his kingd[om]

reality in its own terms. Crusoe is building up his creation, and, like God, he ends with man: Friday is brought inside the circumference of his order from the darkness without and given a social—"servant"—and religious—"convert"—place in the now complete schema.

Bunuel, as we might expect, shifts these implications radically. Crusoe's managing to cultivate land is admirable for its human competence but not as a metaphor of power. This Crusoe works in alliance with nature rather than in control of it as master, and it is this reciprocal relationship that will eventually be extended to include Friday, after the original implication of order-as-dominance has been dealt with and rejected. Further, the film's fragmentation of the novel's pattern of rising mastery, by disordered scenes of Crusoe's Kurtz-like descent into delusion, guarantees that the attempt to subjugate the natives, in the person of Friday, will not appear as the linchpin of order, and that analogies to divinity will be only mockeries both of the imperial stance and of its higher justification.

After saving one of the cannibals' victims Crusoe names him, in a drily Bunuelian moment, "Friday, " himself "Master," and adds, brightly oblivious to the contradiction, "Friends." While at first Crusoe beams through this and other unconscious hypocrisies, Friday (Jaime Fernandez) stares unsmilingly at this man who has evidently conquered him, unaware as yet of the nicer subtleties of patriarchal rule, although he will later develop quite a keen sense of irony. In the beginning Friday kneels and puts Crusoe's foot on his head, which Crusoe finds distressingly excessive, although he is well content to enjoy once again the privileges of the master—"how pleasant it was once more to have a servant"—and sits smugly smoking and reading while Friday pounds away glumly at the millet. However the lurking contradictions of this familiar situation soon emerge. Crusoe begins to fear for his life and his property, and starts to tighten up. He encloses himself at night in his cave, with the door barricaded, manacles Friday with the chains he had intended years before for slaves, and intimidates him by firing off his gun. These innovations of Bunuel's (in the novel the relationship is congenial throughout) show the master-servant imperial relationship not as a grand type of order, but simply as a situation of constriction and oppression. Interestingly, Bunuel also introduces a wild scene in which Friday dresses up as a woman, drawing out the parallel with the traditional form of male-female bond within the same system. Once again Crusoe is acting not as the rebel from, but as the representative of the culture, and again he looks and sounds hollow, like Father. The dark prison of the slave ship and the society it summed up, recalled by the chains and guns, have taken over the island.

However Bunuel does not leave the relationship between Friday and Crusoe in this emblematically hostile state, with Friday hopping around in manacles to do his work, and Crusoe waving his gun. Instead he reverses the contradiction and shows them developing into friends, not in order to whitewash colonialism, but to suggest, on the contrary, the possibility of other forms of human connection beyond the exploitative. In the film Friday also appears, as in the novel, as the culmination of an aspect of the plot: not, however, as the final object to be dominated by Crusoe's mastery, but as the final relief to Crusoe's awful loneliness. He enters the plot, then, not as a native to be made subordinate, but as a fellow human being, bringing companionship, the lack of which has driven Crusoe mad. The film has emphasized Crusoe's dreadful solitude, inventing a scene in which he imagines himself among friends in a tavern, only to reawaken to his ghastly isolation; the novel's Crusoe suffers far less from loneliness. This is because Defoe sees man as an island, entire unto himself. The novel's island is not so much as emblem of the isolation brought on by individualism as a sanctuary from competition. The often ferocious social relations of the eighteenth century come through in the novel as timeless manifestations of human nature—hence the cannibals. In Bunuel, however, man is not an island and connection is essential, although he also asserts, here as elsewhere, that given the nature of social relations, hell is very often other people. Hence he retains the cannibals and their far more dangerous counterparts, the all-consuming English muti-neers, voraciously searching for gold; but at the same time he leaves a free space for human nature, leaving it undefined by allowing for the possibility, under new circumstances such as the island presents, for community. Thus toward the end the island once again becomes the pastoral world, the measure of the outside world's shortcomings.

Gradually a situation of mutual trust develops between the two men. Both carry guns, and Friday learns how to shoot. Friday cuts Crusoe's hair but then they change places and Crusoe becomes the barber. They work side by side and take their rest together, instead of one sitting while the other labors. They discuss theology, and Friday, an ironic glint in his eye, gets the better of Crusoe and of the omnipotent but apparently malicious God he has tried to serve throughout his island stay: why does God give the devil leave to tempt us, but then hold us to blame when he succeeds, he asks. Both now smoke pipes, sharing the Promethean fire which earlier Friday had tried to steal and which Crusoe had denied him. Their comradeship is encouraged by the conditions of their life and labor—Crusoe notes that two working together is far better than one alone, or presumably, than one guarding his back while the other grudgingly slaves. Meanwhile in the background Bunuel enhances the landscape to celebrate this brief millennium, filling it with Edenic flowers and vines and playful animals, as unafraid of man as before the Fall.

Of course this cannot last. The outside world comes to the island, bringing its antagonisms with it. As has often been the case throughout the film, this is reflected not in Crusoe's commentary, thus not in his awareness, but visually: the images cast a larger ironic perspective on the reality of the situation. Crusoe tells the mutineers who are to remain on the island that they will have the one crucial thing he lacked for so long—community; but while he speaks the images of their habitually ferocious expressions cast doubt on their ability to maintain a peaceable commonwealth. Just before they leave, Crusoe asks Friday if he is not afraid to leave the island for civilization, to which of course Friday sturdily replies "no"; but instead of their old similar clothing, Friday is now wearing common seaman's dress, while Crusoe is attired as a gentleman in an outfit from his former life, complete with long lace ruffles, the main function of which was to denote that the hands they covered did no manual labor. Regardless of the words and conscious wills of the participants, the rules of class relations are asserting themselves again.

As an adaptation of a novel, Bunuel's version of *Robinson Crusoe* is less a straight translation from literary to film form than it is an active, at times critical, commentary upon the text. This deconstructive approach answers the needs of both director and viewer: Bunuel's unflagging determination to present his own vision of things in his films, and our need, when faced with a work by Defoe, for a more distanced perspective on his world. Both ends are served by the most basic change the film makes in the original, the drastic shift in point of view.

In the novel we look at the world solely through Crusoe's eyes; in the film we look at the world and at Crusoe, now a separate figure, situated within it. This is an essential difference. In the novel, because Defoe is not present as an authorial consciousness, there is no distinction made between an event and Crusoe's evaluation of it: Crusoe as narrator describes, that is, presents, the object or the event, and simultaneously judges it, fits it into his schema. In the film, however, the event is presented not in Crusoe's words but in independent images, and so it exists free of his definition.

This opens up the possibility of a significant discrepancy between the situation and Crusoe's view of it, a possibility which Bunuel needs in order to reveal the extent of the character's removal from reality: the illusions created by cultural or ideological assumptions which, here as ever, Bunuel is intent on demystifying. Words, the only guide to reality in the book, are unreliable in the film. Embedded with cultural values, they redefine and often falsify reality for Crusoe: "The Lord is my Shepherd"; "Friday—Master—Friends." In these as in other scenes, the image presents a more reliable guide to the situation, and, in showing that situation to be at odds with Crusoe's (or Father's) words, conveys Bunuel's point that such concepts and the words that give them form obscure rather than illuminate reality.

But what is perhaps finally more crucial, in terms of an adaptation, than the film's realizing the *auteur*'s vision, is the fact that the change in perspective resolves a problem that the original work itself creates, at least for the modern reader. Defoe made a considerable effort in his works to unify aspects of his culture which we can hardly avoid seeing, however, as contradictions. It is difficult to read *Robinson Crusoe* without contending quite often with the narrator's judgments: surely the original slaving trip is not only morally reprehensible, we argue, because it was an imprudent investment and ended badly, which is how Crusoe presents it. That is, we find ourselves somewhere outside the boundary of the work, attempting to evaluate Crusoe and his world from a separate vantage point, something of a contortionist's trick since our only knowledge of that world comes, inevitably, from what Crusoe tells us in the first place. What the film does is provide this perspective within the frame of the work itself, showing us not only the event, separate from Crusoe's evaluation, but also Crusoe himself; he is, as a result, placed in the physical and moral landscape, not himself the judge but instead subject to judgment. Sometimes Crusoe returns, in new and rather different terms, as an exemplary hero; elsewhere the film provides us with a detached, potentially ironic and critical point of view on Defoe's myth: *Robinson Crusoe* through a necessary perspective-glass.

Joseph Andrews (1742), Henry Fielding
Tony Richardson, 1978

Visualizing Fielding's Point of View

LAWRENCE F. LABAN

One of the most difficult aspects of translating fiction into film is capturing the tone, character, commentary, and point of view of the narrator. The unique advantage of film—its ubiquitous visual eye—can be its greatest disadvantage when it tries literally to adopt the narrative voice and tone of fiction. It is not difficult for the camera to replace a traditional, third-person, uncharacterized narrator whose major function is to "visualize" the action. But once the narrator takes on distinct personal characteristics, provides subjective commentary, or is a character in the story, difficulties arise.

Although a first-person narration by a character in the story is the most obvious case of difficulty (as witnessed by such film adaptations as *Frankenstein*, *Wuthering Heights*, *Robinson Crusoe*, and *The Lady in the Lake*), a third-person characterized narration can also be problematic. And when the tone of the narration is ironic or satiric, as it is in Henry Fielding's *Joseph Andrews* (1742), and the commentary is as important to the novel as the plot and characters, then it takes a creative filmmaker to provide cinematic equivalents to the unique narrative voice of the original. Tony Richardson captures the essence of Fielding's friendly guide-narrator in his film of *Joseph Andrews* (1978) because he translates the satire and narrative voice in ways that are accessible to modern audiences, rather than slavishly imitating the novel.

28

Joseph Andrews tells the tale of the mishaps that befall a young man who tries to preserve his virtue. Like his sister, Pamela Andrews (the heroine of the contemporary novel by Samuel Richardson that Fielding is mocking), the young servant Joseph rebuffs the advances of his betters, but his trials are designed to arouse amusement rather than indignant sympathy in the reader. Thrown out of the lustful Lady Booby's service as footman, Joseph wends his way back to his true love, Fanny, meeting his old mentor, Parson Adams, and experiencing many misadventures along the way.

Fielding's major purpose in *Joseph Andrews* was to expose the affectations of vanity and hypocrisy in his own time. He also parodied the simplistic moral view ("virtue rewarded") and pretentious literary technique ("writing to the moment") of Richardson's *Pamela* (1740), and, through his preface, attempted to perfect a new art form—the "comic epic poem in prose." Although the film casts brief glances at these two latter ideas, it is the satiric edge that Richardson hones the sharpest.

It is a commonplace that the function of satire—in our own time as well as in the eighteenth century—is to correct as well as to find fault. The satirist, Fielding claims, is "to be regarded as our physician, not our enemy." *Joseph Andrews*, in addition to exposing vanity and hypocrisy, suggests possibilities for human growth through the examples of Parson Adams and Joseph. Positive alternatives may have been easier to suggest in Fielding's day—when order and perfectibility were still possible in the universe, if not in mankind—but the film offers some modern alternatives to universal vices.

Fielding's age and the method of his satire required a clear center of moral vision with which the reader could identify. There could be no room for ambiguity or doubtful judgments. Most of the characters in the novel cannot serve as that center either because they only reach it during the course of the novel (like Joseph), or are incapable of ever achieving it (like Lady Booby), or are ineffectual in communicating it to others (like Parson Adams in his conversations with Lady Booby). The moral center requires a voice of authority that is both entertaining and instructive; a voice the reader can like, trust, and believe. The narrator—more knowing, more experienced, more sophisticated, more verbal than his characters—comments on and criticizes the specific foibles of his age while his characters act out their causes and effects.

In the film of *Joseph Andrews*, as in *Tom Jones* (1963), Tony Richardson captures Fielding's blend of criticism and hope, of entertainment and instruction. Unlike Stanley Kubrick (who adapts novels that are more sarcastic and negative, such as Anthony Burgess's *A Clockwork Orange* and William Thackeray's *Barry Lyndon*), Richardson is in accord with the tendency in satire to look for the good and true beyond the appearances of shallowness and vanity.

There are several major changes in the narrative and subtle shifts of emphasis in character and theme (other than the cuts and telescoping of characters and events necessary to condense the novel into two hours of film time, and the expansion of the character of the Peddler to provide narrative continuity) that make the satire of Richardson's *Joseph Andrews* meaningful to modern audiences.

One major shift is sexual. Although Fielding is hardly shy about the universal realities of human sexual desire, he distinguishes the love of Joseph and Fanny from the baser lusts of those around them. And if the film were merely a recreation of the novel, their intercourse before marriage would be a distortion of the novel's moral vision. Marriage, as both a formal business contract and a civilizing spiritual ritual, was an assertion of human and divine order in the eighteenth century. Marriage both sanctioned and controlled basic sexual instincts by imbuing them with a noble purpose (propagation of the species) and by creating rules and limits of decorum for their exercise. And because the age allowed the double standard ("reformed rakes make the best husbands"), Joseph's adherence to chastity is both a comic reversal of expected masculine behavior and a moral statement of the possibility of the individual controlling his desire: natural instinct subordinated to rational order.

In the film, however, the values are shifted. The natural instincts of Joseph (Peter Firth) and Fanny are still valued above the gross, carefully planned lusts of Lady Booby (Ann-Margret), Mrs. Slip-slop (Beryl Reid), and Beau Didapper, who are rejected for their artifice, not for their instincts. But Joseph's and Fanny's natural instincts are also valued above strict adherence to moral order when that order stands between two honest lovers. The film emphasizes Lady Booby's *plans* to seduce Joseph: she carefully arranges her boudoir and mourning costume before sending for him after the death of her husband; Didapper is all prancing and mincing when he first sees Fanny on the road—all preplanned show with no spontaneous instinct.

The love of Fanny and Joseph, though clearly sexual, is also clearly innocent. The film opens with close-ups of the pair at a country festival, dressed in earth browns and greens and decked with flowers. The camera then pulls back and we see that the festivities include a group of dull country wenches and young men, and the grotesquely made-up and arranged Lady Booby and Mrs. Slipslop in a carriage. As the camera pans, rather than cuts, we automatically mark the contrast between naturalness and artifice, the first of many such contrasts in the film. Later, Fanny and Joseph's lovemaking is shot in soft-focus, with lush music, amid tall grasses and blooming flowers. Thus the emphasis is shifted from the importance of *chastity* as moral control to the importance of *choice* as moral control. Fanny and Joseph choose to love rather than use each other. The novel and the film share the view that their love is pure and innocent, as compared to the affectation of the others, but the film includes explicit sexuality as part of that purity.

Religious hypocrisy is another satiric theme that the film treats differently from the novel. First, Richardson excludes the minor clerics who exemplify the flaws of the church. Secondly, he adds a long scene in the center of the film in which Parson Adams (Michael Hordern), Fanny, and Joseph are the victims of an outlandish gothic-religious kidnapping and attemped rape (a scene reminiscent both of Lord Byron's parties at Newstead Abbey and Roman Polanski's *Rosemary's Baby*), a commentary on modern preoccupations with sex and religion. And thirdly, he makes major changes in the character of Parson Adams.

It has often been noted that *Joseph Andrews* becomes more of a novel and less a parody of *Pamela* as Parson Adams fills the pages. The film, however, emphasizes the lovers not the parson. To make convincing the shift from chastity to choice we need to see more of the young lovers; to understand their love and the temptations (like Beau Didapper and Lady Booby) and dangers (like the rapists in the

Joseph Andrews (1978). Richardson captures the affectations of vanity and hypocrisy in a single image showing Sir Thomas Booby (Peter Bull), Lady Booby (Ann-Margret) and Joseph (Peter Firth). (Photo courtesy of the Museum of Modern Art)

woods) which they withstand before they consummate their love. Nor should we overlook the fact that love and sex sell better, at least in the movies, than an Aeschylus-toting-quoting parson. So both thematic and practical concerns dictate this character change.

In the film, Adams is less of a sage and more of a boob. Although there is a delicate balance in the novel between these two aspects of his character, Adams is ultimately more of the former. In the film, he literally swings toward the latter. His first scenes, swinging from the bell ropes in the chapel and then disrupting Lady Booby's tea party, with appropriately burlesque music, emphasize his buffoon nature. While he still retains the moral value of his childlike naiveté, it is undercut by the increase in Joseph's physical and moral strength, and by his own comic antics, such as forgetting his lines when reading the banns for the young lovers, and overreacting to the near drowning of his son, just after he has preached about the virtue of moderation.

Besides adapting its satiric stance, the film also shares the self-conscious narrative technique of the novel—the way it calls attention to itself as a work of art. There are a number of scenes in which Richardson alludes to earlier films and film genres: the parallel with *Rosemary's Baby* in the gothic scene, the battles à la Errol Flynn between Joseph and the kidnappers, and a series of rescue scenes reminiscent of old cliff-hanger serials. Richardson even alludes to his own *Tom Jones*: the scene in which hunting dogs attack Joseph and Adams; the use of silent film for flashbacks, and the suggestions of incest.

Silent flashbacks occur in two important sequences in *Joseph Andrews*. The first reveals the relationship of Mr. Wilson and Lady Booby (as the young actress, Belle, in London) and the fact that Joseph is their lost child. By combining these three strands, the film allows for a more satisfying climax. All the loose ends are tied and the possibilities of incest increased severalfold. The second flashback occurs at the end of the film with further revelations about the interrelationships of the characters. In both of these sequences Richardson distorts the images through wide-angle lens and slow film. The explicit artificiality of the visuals is in sharp contrast to the rest of the film and points to the artificiality of London; it serves as notice that we are watching a film and further parallels Fielding's use of inset stories. Unlike several of the inset stories in the novel, however, all of those in the film are directly related to Joseph's history.

Another flashback sequence, the Peddler's story, is used differently. Its purpose is to present expository information as quickly and visually as possible. There is no distortion of visuals and, in contrast to the silent flashbacks, here the Peddler provides voice-over song and narration, as he does during the titles of the film to explain Joseph's childhood.

Holding together all the elements of the film is the underlying sense of *contrast*, already mentioned above, between the artificial world of Lady Booby and the natural world of Joseph. A scene in Bath epitomizes this: as Lady Booby emerges from the Royal Crescent, from the edifices of progress and civilization, the frame includes a young woman milking a cow in the street. In this scene, Richardson's eye speaks as clearly as Fielding's voice: Dressed in her finest regalia, Lady Booby—with layers of pancake make-up that barely hide the filth of the world she moves in and only disguise the baseness of her moral values—seems more out of place than the simple woman milking her cow: the earthiness of natural people performing natural functions.

This contrast between the two worlds—or classes, if we choose to be political—is emphasized in the gothic rape scene as well. There is effective cross-cutting between the elegant young lord tying Fanny to an altar to rape her and the drunken whore in the kitchen (hired by the lord) attempting to do the same to the drugged Joseph. The purity of the instincts of Fanny and Joseph are marked against the artificiality of Lady Booby, the young Lord, and the whore he pays.

We finally come around, then, to politics and Tony Richardson. It may be surprising that Richardson, a man of outspoken and liberal political views, should choose so often to look to the past for the sources of his films. But it becomes clear that, as in *The Charge of the Light Brigade* (1968), a film more about the 1960s than the 1850s, in *Joseph Andrews* we are seeing the present reflected through the prism of the past. For when speaking of moral choice and moral action, especially in the rigidly class-structured world of

Joseph Andrews, we are speaking ultimately of political choice and action.

And what could be more akin to the spirit of Fielding than consistently making a point about the present age and its follies through the exploitation of the traditions of the past? And, at the same time, creating a unique and personal artistic vision that expresses the present-day concerns of the filmmaker without destroying the spirit of the original.

Tom Jones (1749), Henry Fielding
Tony Richardson, 1963

A Whisper and a Wink

ANNETTE INSDORF AND SHARON GOODMAN

Henry Fielding's *Tom Jones* (1749) recounts the enormously complicated adventures of its hero, a young man, originally a foundling, who is wrongfully turned out of his home by his deceived guardian, Squire Allworthy. Allworthy, virtuous but imperceptive, believes the lies of Blifil, his seemingly virtuous nephew, who continually plots Tom's downfall. Being warm-hearted, and lacking the prudence and calculation of his enemies, Tom subsequently finds himself, while en route to London and while in that metropolis, embroiled in a number of dubious intrigues and a series of sexual encounters (Molly Seagrim, Mrs. Waters, Lady Bellaston). In the end, Tom's easy-going but genuine goodness is vindicated and, having narrowly missed the gallows, he is restored to his country home, his rightful inheritance, and to his childhood sweetheart Sophia, while the hypocrisy of Blifil and his aides is unmasked.

The characters and events of the novel are presented, mediated, and ultimately controlled by the voice of an omniscient narrator: his playfully ironic tone self-consciously creates—rather than merely records—the tale. The film version of *Tom Jones*, directed in England by Tony Richardson in 1963 (who also more recently directed *Joseph Andrews*, Fielding's earlier novel), acknowledges, recreates, and occasionally transcends its literary source, not only by incorporating the voice of a narrator, but by using an array of cinematic techniques that substitute visual delights for verbal

36

flights. Richardson's *Tom Jones* thus emerges not merely as an entertaining adaptation but as a witty exploration of cinematic styles.

Fielding enriches his narrative with what he calls "poetical embellishments"—similes, metaphors, hyperboles, parodies, mock-heroic passages, and an abundance of quotations from both classic and contemporary writers. Richardson translates these verbal instruments into filmic processes, which serve to chronicle not only the story but also the development of cinema as an art form. As Fielding alludes to the early days of literature, so Richardson recalls the origins of film—first through a sequence presented as a silent movie, and later through slightly subtler stylistic flourishes. As the film opens, title cards announce the narration and dialogue. The soundtrack intensifies the archaic and nostalgic mood as a harpsichord assumes the function of the upright piano heard in movie theaters seventy years ago. (Since the action takes place in the eighteenth century, the harpsichord is more appropriate than the piano, which had not yet been invented at the time Fielding wrote his novel.)

This sequence masterfully condenses into five minutes of viewing time Fielding's long exposition of the events surrounding Tom's (Albert Finney) discovery and adoption by Squire Allworthy (George Devine). The fast pace and stylized technique propel the audience into the tale's comic spirit and announce Richardson's dual concerns by portraying the hero's infancy in the language of cinema's infancy. The use of another well-worn device, accelerated action, extends the tone of the opening sequence. Richardson speeds up the action at Upton Inn, recalling scenes from silent film comedy. Most of the major characters converge in this episode, leading to a great deal of chaotic activity à la Keystone cops. This device clearly diverges from the rhythm of the novel: Fielding's narrator relishes telling his tale, slowly unfolding details which the reader follows at his own pace, whereas the film acknowledges uniquely cinematic time—compressed, ceaselessly moving, imposing itself on the spectator as if he were riding a wild horse.

The pace is also quickened to the point of breathlessness for transitions between scenes. In the novel, Fielding frequently heralds a change with ceremonious words; the film marks such passages with an ornamental device, either a flip frame or a wipe. For example, when Tom and Molly (Diane Cilento) enjoy an amorous escapade in the woods, the narrator intrudes with the comment, "It shall be our custom to leave such scenes where taste, decorum and the censor dictate." At this point, a double vertical wipe closes in from both sides of the screen toward the center, like a pair of sliding doors. When the camera later returns to the lovers, a double wipe appears in reverse, as though the sliding doors were now opening again. This technique serves to acknowledge—albeit playfully—not only our voyeurism, but the controlling power of the author who determines the degree of delectation at every moment.

On two occasions, Tom actually covers the lens of the camera. The first time occurs after Allworthy's recovery at Paradise Hall: a jubilant Tom pulls the black draperies off the windows and throws them over the dour faces of Blifil (David Warner), Thwackum, Square, and Dowling; he then turns to throw one over the camera. Later, when walking to Upton with Mrs. Waters (Joyce Redman), Tom covers the camera with his hat, to protect his half-undressed female companion from the audience's "prying eyes." A less challenging example of the wipe occurs when Tom receives a new and sophisticated wardrobe from Lady Bellaston (Joan Greenwood): Richardson uses a spiral-shaped wipe to represent the hero's exhilaration. Content and form, meaning and process, all interanimate one another in a self-celebratory manner. An intrusive transition is also effective between Tom's proposal of marriage to Lady Bellaston and Lord Fellamar's attempted rape of Sophia (Susannah York). Richardson links these two episodes with wipes in the shape of a diamond, suggesting an engagement ring. Beyond the immediate story, of course, the director is pointing out how one shot engages the other in a continuous wedding of images.

This kind of self-consciousness is intensified toward the end of the film when Tom goes to Newgate prison: a wipe consisting of a row of vertical stripes descends like prison bars over the screen. Richardson implies that the hero is enclosed not merely by events, but the form by which they are related. The film itself follows and captures its hero according to its own conventions, and often widens the scope of Tom's freedom only to close in on him again. The most successful device in this context is the iris, which once again incorporates the awareness of silent film, or visual language. This

Tom Jones (1963). Fielding's comic vision is captured in the film version starring Albert Finney (Tom) and Joyce Redman (Mrs. Waters). In another mood Tom covers the camera with his hat to protect the duo from the audience's prying eyes. (Photo courtesy of the Museum of Modern Art)

gradual opening or closing of the camera eye not only directs attention to a significant detail, but comments on the character's possibilities in space: it can be expanded or contracted, freeing or isolating its subject. In silent films, the camera often irised in on the villain; *Tom Jones* irises in on Dowling, the lawyer. At Bridget Allworthy's funeral, he gives Blifil the letter which reveals Tom's true parentage. The iris cleverly signals to the audience the importance of Dowling while indicating his villainous nature. Through this literal focusing on a character, Richardson points not only to Dowling's power, but to the lawyer's own subjugation to the all-encompassing eye of the camera.

The enchanting display of narrative control that the camera transposes from the novel's voice is especially well served by freeze frames. By imposing a sudden stasis on the flow of images and holding a shot motionless on the screen, Richardson paradoxically achieves the effect of Fielding's nimble prose. Both artists treat the story as a plaything upon which to exercise their ingenuity. For example, Tom visits Molly and discovers his tutor, Square, in her bedroom; Richardson ends this episode with a freeze frame, depicting Tom and Molly laughing, and Square standing by in awkward embarrassment. The device shifts our attention from Tom's escapades to Richardson's, or the relationship of the artist to his material. This is heightened when Tom and Lady Bellaston later sit on her bed and come together for their first kiss; the discreet narrator proclaims, "With our usual good breeding, we shall not follow this particular conversation further," as a freeze frame literalizes the edict of the ultimately paternal voice. In fact, the rowdy and free-wheeling quality of the film is balanced by a sense of reserve and control, as the director reminds us that the film is a series of sanctioned glances.

Near the end of the film, when Allworthy takes Jenny Jones, and then Dowling, behind closed doors to uncover the truth about Tom's birth, Richardson does not allow the audience behind those doors. Instead, he shows Mrs. Miller and Partridge listening at the keyhole in a series of freeze frames. They can hear what takes place inside, but the audience cannot. Like Fielding, Richardson thus engenders an awareness of time, for he will not permit us to learn certain facts until the narrative is good and ready to spring them on us. Like a fickle lover, the film asks us to be patient while undercutting our expectations at every turn. Moreover, the film uses stop-motion photography, which fools the eye much as Fielding's prose occasionally plays games with the reader. This device structures the montage sequence of the romantic idyll during which Tom and Sophia fall in love. At one point, they appear to form a procession on horseback, each following the other in an apparently impossible sequence—but made possible by the stop-photographic technique. The humor of these moments provides an emotional counterpoint to the potential sentimentality of the scene (which is due, in large part, to the lyrical theme song on the soundtrack). In this sense, it remains faithful to Fielding's gentle mockery, which never allows the romance to become excessive:

> The citadel of Jones was taken by Surprize. All those Considerations of Honour and Prudence, which our Hero had lately with so much military Wisdom placed as Guards over the Avenues of his Heart, ran away from their Posts, and the God of Love marched in in Triumph.

Each of the techniques discussed above calls attention to the presence of the camera, and exploits the technical resources of this relatively young medium. Such self-consciousness is appropriate to this work, since the novel was just emerging as a new literary form when Fielding wrote *Tom Jones*. His style reflects a heightened awareness of the act of fashioning a tale, and of the audience to whom it is addressed. His approach is in effect quite direct: "Reader, I think proper, before we proceed any farther together, to acquaint thee that I intend to digress, through this whole History, as often as I see Occasion. . . ." The film complements this vocal address with the visual demystification offered by the characters themselves. They often turn directly to the camera and (while disrupting narrative continuity for the sake of a self-conscious veracity) engage us with a complicitous wink. When Tom asks Sophia to give his mistress Molly Seagrim a job as her maid, he turns to wink at the audience. He and the viewers both know about his special interest in the Seagrim family, but Sophia does not. The device becomes a vehicle for dramatic irony in which the audience is always playfully implicated.

Similarly, during the lyrical love montage in the first half of the film, Sophia turns to wink at the audience while Tom navigates the gondola. This little parenthesis undercuts the sentimentality of the episode in the same way as the stop-photography "procession" mentioned above, and underscores our identity as spectators to romance. The ironic effects of this device can be seen when Lady Bellaston receives Tom's proposal of marriage, and her maid reads the letter over her shoulder. When the Lady announces that she will not receive Tom if he calls, the maid winks at the audience while the narrator observes, "In London, love and scandal are considered the best sweeteners of tea." And towards the end of the film, when Partridge tells Jenny Jones that Tom is her son, she directs a bemused shrug at the audience. Here, the dramatic irony becomes more complex in retrospect. At first, we laugh because Partridge does not know that Jenny, as Mrs. Waters, slept with Tom at Upton. A few minutes later, however, Jenny informs the audience that Tom is not her son. Therefore, when she shrugged, she knew something that neither Partridge nor the audience knew. In a sense, Richardson is developing an intricate narrative structure in which revelations move not only forward, but skip back to color past events as well. (And how appropriate, therefore, to end the film with a wipe in the form of a clock, pointing to an overriding temporal play!)

Fielding declared his authority in the following manner:

> For as I am, in Reality, the Founder of a new Province of Writing, so I am at Liberty to make what Laws I please therein. And these Laws, my Readers, whom I consider as my Subjects, are bound to believe in and obey. . . .

Richardson, however, has at his disposal subtler means of authorial power. To call attention to the work of art through a smorgasbord of visual delights is also to call attention to the artist whose consciousness mediates and reforms the tale.

The playful relationship established between the characters in the film and the audience represents Richardson's resourcefulness in adapting Fielding's novel. The cinematic techniques mentioned above realize in visual terms the effect created by Fielding's engaging, digressive, and exploratory prose style. Rather than settle for technically straightforward narrative presentation, Richardson accepted the challenge of finding cinematic equivalents for Fielding's unique style. His *Tom Jones* therefore remains a model of inventive visual storytelling, and of a fidelity that is enriched by taking a few liberties.

Pride and Prejudice (1813), Jane Austen

Robert Z. Leonard, 1940

Pride but No Prejudice

GEORGE LELLIS AND H. PHILIP BOLTON

> . . . in the final analysis cinema is above all *physical adventure* more than *interior adventure*. Moral conflicts make sense only if they develop by means of physical oppositions. . . .
>
> —Jean Domarchi
> *Cahiers du Cinéma*, November 1963

As we pass from a literary to a cinematic age, we may note both losses and gains to the popular mind of passing from realms of printed discourse to realms of images and sounds. Fantasists—especially the young—are ceasing to read long narratives as much as formerly and are escaping instead into the movies and television. We can get some glimpse of the consequences to their sensibilities by studying how one great novel, Jane Austen's *Pride and Prejudice* (1813), has been made into a film.

Hollywood has long understood that the cinematic medium facilitates portraying physical adventure rather than interior adventure. Defenders of Hollywood may argue that the greatest films are basically visual works of art to which verbal language is simply one of several aural supplements. Detractors of Hollywood, accustomed as they are to literary notations of subtle psychological or spiritual states of characters, may argue that the modern cinema presents too often merely a mundane, basic humanity embodied in gesture, facial expression, movement, and music. As Robert Z. Leonard's *Pride and Prejudice* (1940) illustrates, the movie can very well present a varied series of facial expressions. Greer Garson and her director rely on this technique to present Elizabeth Bennet's "interior adventure." But despite this attempt to present Lizzy's inner life by movements of the eye and subtle smiles, the film is yet another case of Hollywood reducing a great novel to the external action of melodrama.

Jane Austen's *Pride and Prejudice* is both well and ill suited for Hollywood adaptation. It is well suited because it has an aspect of something like physical adventure. Austen appears to write in a dramatic, playlike manner—an impression confirmed by fifteen staged versions of Pride and Prejudice.[1] Yet unlike these stage adaptations, the motion picture can share with Austen's narrative the fluidity of time and space that the print and film media have in common. (Indeed, although the movie lists Helen Jerome's play on its credits, screenwriters Aldous Huxley and Jane Murfin have gone back to the book for most of their material, and have borrowed little of Jerome's narrative restructuring or dialogue.) The novel's comedy, while often largely verbal, comes also substantially out of Austen's ironic detachment from her characters as she reveals them to us through dialogue and third-person narrative.

As a novelistic comedy of manners, *Pride and Prejudice* emphasizes the outer social mores of its period. Though Austen's prose is short on explicit visual images, *Pride and Prejudice* is a remarkably good choice for Hollywood filmmakers because the "surface" of the novel so emphasizes the customs of British gentry in the late eighteenth century that a movie version would not trivialize the story by adding bows and curtsies aplenty—just as Helen Jerome's and Margaret MacNamara's stage versions have copiously used comparable gestures. The novel's subject is partly the trivial, superficial silliness in the tribes of Bennet and de Bourgh.

On the other hand, *Pride and Prejudice* is ill suited to Hollywood adaptation especially because Lizzy's is the novel's central consciousness. Her point of view dominates the narrative, and the reader enjoys her wit and sense of irony and fun. We experience

1. Andrew Wright, "Jane Austen Adapted," *Nineteenth Century Fiction* (Dec., 1975), p. 421.

with Lizzy her initial perception of Darcy as rude and arrogant; later, because we see things through her eyes so frequently, her change of attitude toward him directly accompanies our own. In Chapter Twelve of Volume II, Lizzy reads Darcy's letter explaining his reasons for discouraging Bingley's courtship of Jane Bennet. He also explains his relations to Wickham, whom Lizzy herself has briefly fancied. Now we must reevaluate Darcy and Wickham, just as Elizabeth must. We come to understand her fault of judging people too quickly, and thereby participate in her interior adventure. Upon such participation in the inner life of a character much of the power of the novel depends. Such participation is an effect difficult to achieve on celluloid.

Darcy's pride is easy to demonstrate visually. His clothing may display his wealth. His gestures may display his gentility. His posture and facial expression may display his vanity. But Lizzy's complementary fault—her prejudice—is internalized, subtle, difficult to dramatize. A novelist can portray it fairly easily by detailing her thoughts; a filmmaker (unless he resorts to obtrusive devices, like the voice-over) has far more limited access to the judgmental processes of a character like Elizabeth Bennet. Even the sophisticated audience to a fine performance, like Garson's, may find any interior adventure elusive at best. Lizzy is the heroine of the novel because she is a moralist in an opportunistic world. Her sister Jane is the only other character who at first seems to share Lizzy's concern for spiritual and intellectual values. The movie has no trouble portraying false values like Mary's ostentatious intellectualism, or Kitty's or Lydia's feather-brained pursuit of soldiers. But there is no easy visual means to present Lizzy's intellectualism, idealism, morality, spiritualism—in short, her inner life.

At its worst, therefore, the movie version resorts to totally unconvincing dialogue to express what it cannot easily visualize. Characters baldly tell each other what their spiritual states are. Consider the exchange between Lizzy and Darcy midway through the film: "At this moment it's difficult to believe that you're so proud," says the heroine. To this the hero replies, "At this moment it's difficult to believe that you're so prejudiced." These lines are not in the book, since in the context of Austen's careful character development they would constitute the mistake of stating the obvious. A more successful technique is Leonard's use of Garson's face to invite imaginative entry into Lizzy's inner world. Garson is arguably the wrong actress to play Lizzy, since she is probably more beautiful than Austen intended Lizzy to be (in the book Jane is the knockout), and since one cannot imagine any normal man being unwilling to dance with Garson because her looks were only "tolerable." Garson is too sweetly beautiful and has trouble putting into her performance the bite of acid skepticism that Austen locates beneath Lizzy's polite exterior. Nor do the scriptwriters help matters much when they give Garson lines worthy of Judy Garland. "What does it matter where we live as long as we're all together?" she says as the family is preparing to move away after the shame of Lydia's elopement with Wickham.

Nevertheless, despite Garson's beauty and despite the occasional dull ears of the scriptwriters, Garson gives a good performance and Leonard directs her with intelligence. He gives her more close-ups than anyone else in the film, which first of all serve to imply the existence of her strong inner life. We can and do stare into that beautiful face and wonder what goes on behind those sparkling eyes. In the second place, Garson's face is more consistently mobile than anyone else's. After Darcy's first proposal of marriage to Lizzy, which the latter declines, and after Darcy has left the room in dismay, Garson's face reflects a series of emotions, from complacent bemusement, to regret, to frustration. Her expressions are outer signs of the inner process which Lizzy goes through in Austen's novel as she examines, reconsiders, and ultimately modifies her judgments about Darcy and Wickham. Garson's performance has effort and care stamped all over it. It is almost too good. It calls attention to itself as artifice and tends to destroy our willing suspension of disbelief. Striking examples of this include Garson's expressions of anger and outrage at overhearing Darcy insult her at the ball, her glances as she flirts with Wickham, and her suppressed anguish at hearing Mary sing in public. Only rarely does Garson's range of facial expression falter. When she says "I'm so unhappy" to her sister Jane, near the end of the film as she recounts Darcy's

Pride and Prejudice (1940). The mind's construction is conveyed by Leonard in the faces of two of the Bennet girls—Elizabeth (Greer Garson) and Jane (Maureen O'Sullivan). (Photo courtesy of Museum of Modern Art)

first proposal, we don't believe the performance at all. We may even titter at such a simplistic formulation popping up so suddenly.

By contrast, Leonard gets performances from the other actors which are less emphatic in their use of facial expression and derive more from theatrical pantomime and gesture than Garson's close-ups. Laurence Olivier in particular communicates more through his body than through his deadpan face. He conveys pride and vanity (together with their positive counterparts, dignity and gentility) through posture and carriage, suggesting emotions through stylized hand movements. Otis Ferguson describes his "upward jerks of the hand, as though he were starting a salute first with the right, then with the left, and then thought better of both."[2] Coming as he does out of the British tradition of classical acting, Olivier still seems to be projecting emotion out across some imaginary line of footlights. Leonard only rarely puts Olivier in close-up. The acting styles of the two stars do not clash but give viewers the pleasure of variety and are appropriate to the materials at hand. Each actor's technique emphasizes the qualities of the respective character. Olivier gives us Darcy's pride as externalized and gestural. Garson gives us the best indication she can of Lizzy's prejudice as internalized and facial.

Though Leonard's is no great movie, his *Pride and Prejudice* captures even better than the book a convincing sense of the biological attraction between Garson as Lizzy and Olivier as Darcy. For the visual medium can easily convey the contradiction between their tart verbal repartee on the one hand, and the glances and gestures that on the other hand suggest the underlying sensuality of their relationship. Garson's face is exquisite, with a perfect smoothness of complexion and pleasing shape; Olivier's sideburns are combed forward over cheekbone and temple almost as if to suggest the horns of Pan. Garson's and Olivier's performances illustrate the enormous gain of sensuality in a story transformed from the narrative to the cinematic medium. As a result of this gain, the movie emphasizes scenes of dalliance between Darcy and Lizzy even when the book indicates nothing of the sort. But no moment in the film captures the flavor of Austen's original better than when Lizzy and Caroline Bingley walk in front of the fire while Darcy

2. *The New Reublic*, CVIII (August 19, 1940), p. 246.

suggests that he might indeed wish to admire Elizabeth's figure. Garson has a figure to admire. Here in the movie the Austenian verbal wit is unspoiled because the dialogue is very close to the original language, yet supplemented by the physical presence of the actors and by the inobtrusively smooth tracking of the camera that complements the movement of the ladies back and forth before the fireplace.

Elsewhere, however, the cinematizing of the novel results in attempts to visualize verbal wit which replace Austen's refined humor with slapstick. Collins's proposal to Lizzy is certainly fun in the book; but Austen's prose never suggests Melville Cooper's exaggerated foppishness or his hobbling on his knees to remain close to his intended as Elizabeth moves away from him in horror. High comedy becomes farce. Later, when Lady Catherine de Bourgh calls on Lizzy to protest her rumored engagement to Darcy, their encounter turns into a comic series of mishaps involving a kicked-over tea tray, a too-talkative parrot, and a sat-upon music box. The filmmakers apparently lacked confidence in the capacity of the verbal wit of the interview to hold the audience's interest. But the visual humor seems to violate the refined spirit of the novel.

Far more comfortable are the movie's several other moments of original visual invention. The carriage race at the beginning of the motion picture—between the Bennets and the Lucases—foreshadows the competition to come between the two mothers so eager to marry off their daughters to rich husbands. Later, at the garden party, Lizzy proves an expert archer, and Garson creates an indelible impression of the heroine's Diana-like qualities, much to Darcy's chagrin since he has condescended toward her skills as a sportswoman. The archery scene acts as a visual metaphor which suggests facets of Lizzy's character that are perhaps not fully enough developed elsewhere. It suggests how "on target" the heroine is, both verbally and visually. She is much more a real match for a man of pride like Darcy than would be a vulnerable child like Kitty or Lydia. Or again, in a later scene at the Rosings estate, Lizzy's reintroduction to Darcy is staged so that her playing of the piano provides a visual subtext for the dialogue. Darcy's inability to turn the pages of the score at the right moments, because Lady Catherine keeps interrupting his gesture, illustrates effectively the hero's inability to play the genteel and courtly role that would customarily be his.

Despite some vulgarization, the film *Pride and Prejudice* is an intelligent adaptation partly because it borrows from Austen qualities of her narrative and theatrical manner that suit the film medium. Yet the movie is simply a good adaptation, and neither a great rendering of a novel nor a great film. For missing from the audience's experience of the movie is the sense of revelation and relief that Lizzy should at last recognize the error of her prejudice and accept the suitability of her marriage to Darcy. Try as she may, Greer Garson cannot by means of facial expression convey that "interior adventure" with sufficient detail to become moving. She can only hint at the reflection and self-analysis that Lizzy sustains in the novel. Thus the movie loses the inner half of the power of the book.

And this loss suggests what our popular culture suffers as we change from a nation of novel-readers to a nation of movie-goers and television-watchers. Because of its verbal medium, the novel ideally suits the depiction of inner sensitivities. Habitual novel-readers are thus trained to imagine what other human beings' inner lives are like. By contrast, because of its essentially visual medium, the cinema ideally suits the evocation of enraptured (though restrained) sensuality. Habitual movie-goers are not trained by their habits to imagine that other human beings have much inner life at all. The gain in sensuality comes at the expense of a loss in sensitivity. A good illustration of this danger is how Leonard's version of Austen's novel successfully evokes Darcy's pride, for which external equivalents are easy to find, but only partly evokes Lizzy's prejudice, for which outer signs are more difficult to come by. Leonard's movie is about pride but not really about prejudice. The evidence of this particular novel and its derivative film suggests that spiritual states subtler than those accompanying "cardinal" or basic sins may tend to vanish from the communal presentations of art as the novel loses its competition with the movie for the popular audience.

The Blasted Tree

L E S T E R   D.   F R I E D M A N

In the "wet, ungenial summer" of 1816, a season filled with incessant rain that often confined her for days on end to her house in Geneva, Mary Shelley found herself in almost constant contact with one uncommon and two extraordinary men. However bad the weather may have been that year, it was nonetheless a period of unusual creative productivity for these four people. During the days in Switzerland Byron worked on "Canto Three" of *Childe Harold*, wrote *Prometheus*, and began Manfred. His friend Percy Shelley completed "Hymn to Intellectual Beauty" and "Mont Blanc" and undoubtedly began thinking about what would eventually become his masterful epic poem, *Prometheus Unbound*. Even the least accomplished of the quartet, the young physician John Polidari, wrote a tale entitled *The Vampyre*, which was eventually published (though wrongly attributed to Lord Byron).

Yet it was also a time of harrowing personal tragedy for the Shelleys. Mary still lamented the loss of her premature, two-week-old baby in February of the previous year, and the suicide of her half-sister, Fanny Imlay, in October was closely followed by that of Shelley's first wife, Harriet Westbrook, in December. It was within this churning cauldron of creativity and personal grief from June of 1816 to July of 1817, both in Switzerland and England, that the daughter of feminist Mary Wollstonecraft and radical philosopher

52

Willam Godwin wrote her now famous tale of Dr. Frankenstein and his immortal monster.

But none of those huddled around the fire telling ghost stories in Byron's Villa Diodati could possibly have imagined the success young Mary's story would have in the world. For thirty years of the nineteenth century, *Frankenstein* would reign as the most popular novel in the English-speaking world, would eventually be translated into at least twenty-nine foreign languages, and would remain in print from the day of its publication. Indeed, *Frankenstein* provided Mary with much more popular acclaim in her own lifetime than Shelley was accorded in his, and for over twenty-five years the public regarded her as a major novelist who had been married to a rather minor poet; the revenues from her work brought more in each month than her husband's writings did in a year. The novel inspired at least nine different plays while Mary was still alive, several twentieth-century productions (such as that by the Living Theater), as well as some loosely related parodies like *Frank In Steam or the Modern Promise To Pay* (1833). Generations of films based on her story, ranging from the Edison Company's lost silent version of 1910, to James Whale's classic of 1931, to the Andy Warhol/Paul Morrisey modern interpretation (*Andy Warhol's Frankenstein*, 1975), to the Mel Brooks comedy (*Young Franken-stein*, 1975), keep Mary and her monster alive today. It would seem that whatever Mary Shelley discovered "with shut eyes and acute mental vision" that rainy summer in Switzerland struck a responsive chord in her own day that continues to reverberate even more strongly in our own.

Most traditional *Frankenstein* criticism, whether of the book or of Whale's film, centers around the notion that Victor (Henry in the movie) has somehow transgressed God's moral and natural laws by attempting to create life from dead matter.[1] Yet a close reading of the novel reveals that this position represents, at best, a simplistic view, and at worst, a total misreading of the work. Mary Shelley

1. See: John Dussinger, "Kinship and Guilt in Mary Shelley's *Frankenstein*," *Studies in the Novel*, 8, No. 1 (Spring, 1976), p. 38. Paul Lewis, "The Artist as Satan and as God," *Studies in Short Fiction*, 14 (1977), p. 281. Robert Philmus, *Into the Unknown* (Berkeley: University of California Press, 1970), P. 82. Masao Miyoshi, *The Divided Self* (New York: New York University Press, 1969), p. 102. Drake Douglas, *Horrors* (London: John Baker, 1967), p. 102.

specifically refuses to make value judgments in *Frankenstein*, allowing both the doctor and his creation to state their cases with equal eloquence and effectiveness. Throughout the work she remains much more interested in presenting the tensions between the man of genius and his world, and between a creator and his creation, than she is in assigning good or evil to either one. It is precisely these points of greatest tension, never fully resolved in the book, that James Whale captures so brilliantly in his film; he, better than anyone else who adapted the story to a different medium, understood the tragic majesty of *Frankenstein*.

To understand the method by which Mary Shelley carefully develops the seemingly opposing sides of her fictive world—society versus the genius, creator versus creation—one must first admit something that seems very basic, but inevitably fails to be mentioned by most commentators: Frankenstein is successful. He has literally done the miraculous. Whatever deaths may occur in the rest of the novel, whatever grief his experiments occasion, nothing should blind us to his truly spectacular achievement. He has duplicated the "first principle of life . . . the cause of generation," and the desire to do so is in and of itself neither evil nor inglorious. Where Frankenstein fails miserably is not in the dream, but in his inability to integrate the dream with his social obligations. Even more importantly, it is his refusal to provide the parental responsibility due his "offspring" that seals his fate.

Frankenstein's isolation becomes a major reason for the tragedy that follows. In relying upon no one but himself, Frankenstein becomes concerned only with how the events will affect him, and not with how it may possibly affect the world beyond the sheltered boundaries of his laboratory. What Mary Shelley suggests to be positive forces are the very things Victor in his isolation rejects: manly friendship represented by Henry Clervel, and feminine love represented by Elizabeth. Victor's isolation inevitably leads him to blind egoism, ultimately dooming his family and closest friends; a union with a like spirit on either the sexual or nonsexual level is the only potential salvation offered in the novel.

One need not look very far for the sources of Mary's notion of the need to combine intellectual goals with human interaction, for both of her intellectual idols—her father William Godwin and her husband Percy Shelley—stressed the need for even the man of genius to integrate his personal quest for knowledge with the concerns of the outside world. In his *Enquiry Concerning Political Justice*, Godwin wrote:

> No being can be either virtuous, or vicious, who has no opportunity of influencing the happiness of others. . . . Even knowledge, and the enlargement of intellect, are poor, when unmixed with sentiments of benevolence and sympathy . . . and science and abstraction will soon become cold unless they derive new attractions from ideas of society.[2]

Shelley's long poem *Alastor*, published a scant six months before Mary began *Frankenstein*, contains an even more profound vision of the relationship between one "who seeks strange truths in undiscovered lands" and the society he rejects. Even more to the point, the poet in *Alastor*, much like Dr. Frankenstein, makes his bed "in charnels and on coffins" as he obstinately searches for "what we are." Though Shelley is poet enough to express deep admiration for the doomed protagonist of his work, he remains man enough to make his position clear in the preface:

> The intellectual faculties, the imagination, the functions of sense, have their respective requisitions on the sympathy of corresponding powers in other human beings. . . . Those who love not their fellow-beings live unfruitful lives and prepare for their old age a miserable grave.[3]

Though perhaps overstating his case in the heat of despair, Victor's warning to young Walton comes as no surprise to anyone familiar with Godwin and Shelley: "If the study to which you apply yourself has a tendency to weaken your affections and to destroy your taste for those simple pleasures in which no alloy can possibly mix, then that study is certainly unlawful, that is to say, not befitting the human mind" (p. 56).[4]

Frankenstein also stands as a good example of what Harold Bloom labels "the internalization of Quest-Romance," in that it presents a

2. William Godwin, *Enquiry Concerning Political Justice*, ed. K. Codel Carter (Oxford: Clarendon Press, 1971), p. 56, pp. 79-83.
3. Percy Bysshe Shelley, *Selected Poetry*, ed. Neville Rogers (Oxford: Oxford University Press, 1968), pp. 29-30.
4. All quotations from the text refer to: Mary Shelley, *Frankenstein*, ed. M.K. Joseph (Oxford: Oxford University Press, 1971).

Frankenstein (1931). Mary Shelley's philosophical novel was more than a century later turned into "the most famous horror movie of all time" starring Boris Karloff as The Monster. (Photo courtesy of the Museum of Modern Art)

turning away from an outward union of man with nature and a turning inward toward an internalization of the imagination that becomes overly self-conscious and destructive of the social self. Bloom notes that at the same time the Romantics strove to widen their consciousnesses, to intensify their intellectual awarenesses, they ran the inevitable risk of narrowing themselves to an acute over-preoccupation with the self.[5] Frankenstein mistakenly substitutes cold, abstract logic for the warmth of human friendship and love. Almost all the great works of the Romantic Age cry out for some sort of completion, for a union of like beings, and *Frankenstein* is no exception; Walton, Frankenstein, and the monster all long for companionship. If Frankenstein deserves punishment for his actions, it is not for mocking God but rather for ignoring the social order. Any endeavor carried out in such isolation can lead to nothing good for society; and the duties one owes to society, Mary argues, are as strong and as binding as that owed to any abstract principle.

Obviously, Mary is not saying that Promethean man must exchange his glorious dreams for the mundane pleasures of hearth and home, but the novel does yearn for a compromise between the two. To fail to achieve this compromise is to become a robot incapable of discerning right from wrong. Thus, Frankenstein becomes an irresponsible researcher, for he fails to take human consequences into account. His original dream was oriented toward humanity's good ("to render man invulnerable to any but violent death"), a natural outgrowth of his upbringing among a loving community of family and friends, but his vision becomes perverted by his isolation and denial of the very impulses that first motivated him. In his solitude, a new and more selfish desire arises:

> A new species would bless me as its creator and source; many happy and excellent natures would owe their being to me. No father could claim the gratitude of his child so completely as I should deserve theirs. (p. 54)

Thus, ambition overtakes humanitarianism; the dream becomes an obsession.

Victor Frankenstein errs, therefore, not in his dream, but in the

5. Harold Bloom, "The Internalization of Quest-Romance," in *Romanticism and Consciousness*, ed. Harold Bloom (New York: W.W. Norton, 1970), pp. 3-24.

method he selects to achieve it. But his blindness extends even further, to the very nature of knowledge itself, for he fails to grasp its essential paradox. It is precisely in relation to the entire question of the price of gaining knowledge that Mary reaches her highest tension point and, not coincidentally, when she speaks most directly to our own age. With its vast Miltonic framework, it comes as no surprise that *Frankenstein* presents knowledge and sorrow as inextricably bound up with each other because Edenic knowledge must inevitably contain cosmic sorrow. All the characters in the novel come to realize that "increase of knowledge" makes them wretched outcasts. Every step upward is an "increase in despair," as it further alienates the learner from those who do not possess his knowledge. Can the individual genius accede to the natural demands of society, thus avoiding the risk of dissipating his wisdom in an unproductive void of sterile solipsism and perpetual alienation, and still progress upward along the path of knowledge? Within *Frankenstein* there is no answer to this crucial question.

Though Mary presents no answer to this question, she does show that Victor's rejection of the heterosexual love offered by Elizabeth and the friendship offered by Henry lead directly to his most crucial error: the failure to take moral responsibility and provide parental guidance for his creation. Again, this idea has a contemporary ring to it. Given Mary's position in the novel, she might well have argued that those who worked on the Manhattan project must bear as much responsibility as those who decided to drop the bombs on Japan. Responsibility begins, not ends, with creation.

In the very act of the monster's "birth," we witness the ever-widening gap between Frankenstein's original dream and the reality with which he is forced to deal. Because the "minuteness of the parts formed a great hindrance to [his] speed," the doctor resolves to make the creature of gigantic stature. The resulting misshapen and hideously ugly creature appears so twisted and bizarre that he is forever doomed as an outsider. When Victor beholds his creature's "dull, yellow eye," he is "unable to endure the aspect of his being" and is filled with "breathless horror and disgust." The dream vanishes, but the creature remains, a harmless, love-starved being called to life by a creator who now rejects and abandons him. Victor assumes his one act of supreme creativity will be his final one, only to discover it occasions a dependence he cannot tolerate.

The monster's drive to revenge and murder results from his intense desire to obtain what Victor has so carelessly rejected: friendship and love. He tells his creator:

> Unfeeling, heartless, creator! You had endowed me with perceptions and passions, and then cast me abroad an object for the scorn and horror of mankind. . . . I am alone, and miserable; man will not associate with me; but one as deformed and horrible as myself would not deny herself to me. (p. 139, 144)

Whether or not Frankenstein errs by not creating a female counterpart for the monster remains, at least for me, an issue open to question, but surely his very refusal to do so is evidence of a lesson learned; in the past he gave no heed to the consequences of creative actions. Yet the failure of love at this point is not the creature's; it is the creator's, who rejects his own creation solely on outward appearances. The monster's initial crime is merely his physical repulsiveness, something over which he had no control. Indeed, at one point, the monster rises to a level of moral understanding unsurpassed by any other figure in the novel, lecturing his maker on the responsibilities of creation: "How dare you sport thus with life? Do your duty towards me, and I will do mine toward you and the rest of mankind" (p. 99).

Though Frankenstein may not have performed the required duties toward his creature, James Whale certainly recognized his responsibilities toward Mary Shelley's "hideous progeny." And, like the novel, the film attained a great level of success. Critics like Paul Jensen label it "the most prestigious horror film ever made," while Carlos Clarens calls it "the most famous horror movie of all time." In the collection of essays entitled *Focus on the Horror Film*, the editors begin their chronology with the publication of *Frankenstein* in 1818 and end with the death of Karloff in 1969. The film catapulted Karloff from minor roles to overnight stardom, and it is no wonder he always cited it as his best horror film while affectionately calling the monster "my best friend."[6]

6. See: Paul Jensen, "Frankenstein," *Film Comment 6* (Fall, 1970), p. 42. Carlos Clarens, *Horror Films* (New York: Capricorn Books, 1968), p. 65. Roy Huss and T. J. Ross (eds.) *Focus on the Horror Film* (Englewood Cliffs: Prentice Hall, 1972), pp. 11-12. Peter Underwood, *Karloff* (New York: Drake Publishers, 1972), p. 56.

Not only did Whale understand the elements needed to make a financially successful and critically well-respected film, but he intuitively grasped the significance and meaning of Mary Shelley's work in such a modern way that the film retains its power for successive generations of moviegoers. Furthermore, he comprehended something about the film/literature relationship that is gaining only slow acceptance even today. The best film adaptations seek the spirit rather than the letter of their original source, and in fact, transferring that spirit to the screen sometimes demands violating the letter of the work. Lewis Milestone stated the situation correctly when he observed:

> If you want to produce a rose, you will not take the flower and put it into the earth. This would not result in another rose. Instead, you will take the seed and stick it into the soil. From it will grow a rose. It's the same with film adaptation.

So, for example, if one judges Akira Kurosawa's *Throne of Blood* by how well it reproduces the outer events in Shakespeare's *Macbeth*, he might well conclude it is a rather poor adaptation. But once we examine the themes and moods of Shakespeare's drama and then analyze how Kurosawa uses cinematic devices to recreate those ideas and feelings visually, we can see that, far from being a weak adaptation, *Throne of Blood* (1957) remains extremely faithful to the spirit and meaning of *Macbeth*. Thus, a director can become not only an illustrator of the written text, but an artist in his own right, one who draws inspiration from original sources as Shakespeare himself drew inspiration from the Holinshed Chronicles. It is precisely in terms of his visual constructions, particularly image motifs and a sophisticated *mise-en-scene*, that Whale communicates the essential tension points in Mary Shelley's novel, giving us a work that rivals its source in complexity while conveying its essential themes.

Whale's sophistication is conspicuously evident in the intricate pattern of light and dark, both natural and man-made, that he weaves throughout the film, never subverting organic, contextual unity for a strained or baroque effect. The inspiration for this image pattern probably comes from the novel itself, for lightning in darkness first draws the young Victor to the power of electricity, and he later comes to view himself in terms similar to the "blasted stump" that first so overwhelmed him: "But I am a blasted tree; the bolt has entered my soul" (p. 160). Whatever its source, the light/ dark imagery dominates the film, functioning both as basic *mise-en-scene* environment via its almost perpetual contextual presence and as symbolic metaphor via its role in the overall abstract theme of knowledge versus ignorance.

Immediately after Van Sloan's theatrical and readily dismissible prologue, the film proper begins with a medium shot of a pair of hands lowering something into the ground. From here, and as a good example of Whale's fluid visual style, the camera starts a long pan rightward past a young boy, an old woman dressed in black, an old man with his arm around her, a man fixing his glasses, a priest holding a banner, another man, a large tilted cross, another priest, another mourner, a skeleton symbolizing death and leaning on a cross or sword, and finally to the ghoulish face trapped between the posts of an iron railing (Fritz). Immediately, another more aristo-cratic man yanks him down. Whale then cuts to a medium long short of this man (Dr. Frankenstein) along with the skeleton of death in the same frame, intimately linking the two together as they will be throughout the film. At this point an old gravedigger finishes his chores and searches around in his pockets for a pipe and some matches. Lighting the pipe, he gives us the first of numerous images of fire surrounded by darkness, or darkness penetrated by light, that the film offers as its central motif. Here, however, the fire is small and under control, harnessed by man to aid his fellow creatures.

The film's second fire image is similar to the first in that it represents the tremendous forces of natural light and energy con-trolled to aid rather than injure man. The lantern that Fritz (Dwight Frye) carries on his pole cuts out patches of light in the night so that he and Dr. Frankenstein (Colin Clive) can see the convict, whose brain they need, hanging on the post. Fritz gives the lantern to Frankenstein, who holds it aloft so that his assistant can see to cut the man down. The light proves insufficient, however, since the man's broken neck has rendered the brain useless.

Up to this point, the entire film possesses a dark, nightmarish quality illuminated only by the tiny lights of matches and lantern. With the next scene we are thrust into a brightly lit hall at Goldstadt Medical College, a room dominated by high-powered electric lights over an operating table. In fact, several shots illustrate the predominance and power of the lights in the frame, particularly when Whale positions the camera for low angle shots beneath the feet of the cadaver, making the ring of lights on the wheellike fixture seem like a protective circle.[7] Of course, when Fritz enters the school to steal the brain, the bright lights have been extinguished; he is a creature of darkness and of night.

The fade-out on the now dark and empty medical school is matched by a fade-in on a portrait of Henry (Victor in the novel) illuminated by candlelight; in fact, candles glow from all over the Frankenstein manor: on the piano, on chandeliers, to Elizabeth's (Mae Clark) right as she reads Henry's letter to Victor Moritz (John Boles). Troubled by the letter, Moritz and Elizabeth visit Dr. Waldman (Edward Van Sloan), Frankenstein's tutor at school, who warns them of the "mad dreams and insane ambitions" that have driven him from formal medical study. This scene takes place in a potentially eerie environment. Human skulls on Waldman's desk and bookcase surround the trio. Yet the scene's frightfulness is almost totally mitigated by the electric light gleaming over the doctor's desk. Here, Whale demonstrates Mary's idea that the study of human life and death is not in itself evil, and when carried out under the proper conditions—lighted, in the open, and surrounded by colleagues and friends—can contribute to the betterment of mankind.

The next use of lighting, and one of the most famous in movie history, brings us to the dark and isolated castle (it was originally to have been the same windmill where the last scene between Frankenstein and the monster occurs) lit only by a fierce lightning storm. No longer is light under human control. It remains beyond the realm of human knowledge. Frankenstein's outlandish *hubris* in these scenes, such as when he exults that "the brain of a dead man is waiting to live again in a body *I* made with my own hands," is not

7. Circular strctures are also an important motif in the film starting with this image and culminating with the gear mechanism in the windmill at the film's conclusion.

to be seen as research similar to that of Dr. Waldman's. The buzzing, flashing, sputtering lights in the laboratory seem under his control, but of course this later proves to be a scientific illusion. Fritz's comic parody of the porter scene in *Macbeth*, accompanied by a lantern, sets the stage for the film's most famous scene. Frankenstein sends up his being's body like some ancient, votive offering to the creative forces in the universe as symbolized by the lightning.

It would be possible, of course, to continue listing and interpreting all the various sources of light in the film, but this opening description should provide sufficient insight into the feeling of the film's images. Three different, major sources of light exist: the untamed natural light formed by lightning, the sun, and the moon; the light made subservient to man such as lamps, candles, and matches; and the light that exists somewhere in between, like torches, that can either illuminate or destroy. Throughout the entire film, Whale makes us aware that light in various contexts presents various meanings. Like the knowledge it comes to symbolize in the film, light is a double-edged sword that is capable of great harm or great good. Again, it is not a matter of rejecting fire (light), but of realizing its potential for both evil and goodness.

In addition to the pattern of darkness and light that infuses the film on both an imagistic and symbolic level, Whale is also clearly aware of the other two sins committed by Dr. Frankenstein which form the tension points of greatest interest in the novel: Frankenstein's isolation, both moral and physical, from the community of men, and his refusal to accept proper responsibility or provide sufficient parental guidance for his creature. Like Mary, Whale refuses simply to censure Frankenstein as a mad lunatic, making him an incredibly vulnerable figure in the person of Colin Clive and giving him the least mundane speech in the entire film:

Have you never wanted to do anything that was dangerous? Where should we be if nobody tried to find out what lies beyond? Have you never wanted to look beyond the clouds and the stars or to know what causes the trees to bud? And what changes the darkness into light? Well, if I could discover just one of those things, what eternity is for example, I wouldn't care if they did think I was crazy.

Clearly this is no deranged, stereotypically mad scientist, but a man whose dream is no less great and no less valid than that of his literary precursor.

But how does Henry go about accomplishing his dream? First, he secludes himself from the positive forces of love, friendship, and familial affection and replaces them with Fritz (a character not present in the book), who represents some sort of middle stage between human being and monster. Even though the actual "birth" is witnessed by a friend, a loved one, and a father-figure, none of these people have any influence in the process or before it. As in the novel, Frankenstein's dream becomes an obsession, and his concern is not for his creature but for his own experience of bringing life out of dead matter.

Frankenstein's rejection of his creation is strongly presented in the film. When informed that he has mistakenly used a criminal brain, Frankenstein puts out his cigarette (tamed fire) and tells Waldman the creature is "only a few days old . . . wait till I bring him into the light." And in the astonishing and poignant scene that follows he does just that, but in a way that forever seals his fate.[8] He reaches up and turns out the lamp (man-made light) and watches as the monster appears in what must rank as one of the greatest entrances in film history. First Karloff backs into the room, then we see him in a medium shot profile, then a full front medium shot that changes to a close-up, that changes to an extreme close-up from the middle of his forehead to his chin. Frankenstein seats the monster in a harsh-looking wooden chair, reaches over for a chain that slides back the hatch in the ceiling, and allows the sun to enter the darkened room. In a tender moment, the monster glances upward toward this new sensation, stands, looking directly up into the sun, and slowly reaches out with his oversized arms to capture it. "Shut the light!" screams Waldman unexplainably, and Frankenstein, for no apparent reason, obeys him. In the moving moment that follows, Karloff holds out his hands to his creator, mutely begging for more light, more knowledge, more love. It is, of course, refused, and when Fritz slams into the room with his brightly burning torch, symbolizing the harsh light that can destroy with its painful heat, the monster reacts in terror. This is too much light at one time, and

8. At least it id until audiences reacted badly to Frankenstein's death in advance showings, so Carl Laemmle ordered Whale to shoot a "happier" ending.

this combination of the refusal of natural light and the harsh imposition of man-made light enrages the monster and causes his imprisonment in the cellar below.

From this point until the film's conclusion, Frankenstein refuses to accept responsibility for his creative actions. Telling Fritz to "come away . . . just leave it alone," he abandons the being to the demented Fritz's inhuman tortures. He even allows Dr. Waldman to deal with the disastrous results of his experiments. The scenes with Henry and Elizabeth sitting lovingly on the patio of his father's house contrast in image, brightness, and feeling, to the dark and foreboding isolation of the laboratory. But the doctor's hiatus from terror is short-lived. Hearing his father toast to "a son of the House of Frankenstein," Victor embarrassingly recognizes the irony, that the House of Frankenstein already has a "son" who will soon make his presence felt throughout the countryside.

It is only after this "son" makes an overt attack on his creator's intended bride (his rival?) that Henry can once more find the moral courage to assert his position of ethical leadership by helping a search party, equipped with torches, to find the creature. "I made him with these hands," he tells Victor, "and with these hands I will destroy him." The parade of torchbearers sets off in three directions, with Victor leading those assigned to the mountains. There, protected by a sole torch which the monster unfearingly knocks to the ground, Henry confronts his beast amid the mountains of Universal's soundstage, and after being knocked unconscious, awakens in the windmill for one last battle. Here again Whale's visual sensibility becomes evident as the monster and his maker confront each other around a large gear mechanism that turns the windmill. Each is shot in an identical way through the mechanism, visually emphasizing that there is as much of the monster in Frankenstein as there is Frankenstein in the monster. The shot further underlines the inevitability of their fates being forever linked together, round and round each other. This shared entrapment and identity is highlighted when the Burgomaster (Lionel Belmore) screams and points to the windmill's platform where the creator and his creation grapple with each other, "There he is. There's the monster." At that point, we understand that Whale means us to take that remark as referring to both combatants.

Two actions occur then that conclude the film's major image

patterns of circular shapes and light and dark. The monster throws Frankenstein from the top of the windmill. He catches on one of the blades (which have been moving clockwise), changes its direction (counterclockwise) for a moment, then falls lifelessly to the ground, while the wheel returns to its original rotation. The townspeople plunge their torches into the windmill, trapping the monster by the flames. Finally, after a huge beam falls on him, the monster perishes (in the original version) amid the fire he has both sought and avoided throughout the film. For the monster, light is both death and enlightenment. As in the novel, the more knowledge he gains, the more despair he feels; the more torture he receives, the more crazed he becomes.

As this analysis of the film demonstrates, Whale viewed the *Frankenstein* story much in the same way as did Mary Shelley. Of course, the novel/film comparison cries out for additional study in various areas: the doppelgänger motif, the political overtones, the sexual tensions, the role of parental figures, specific biographical relationships in the novel, the allegory of the artist and his creation, to name just the most obvious. Furthermore, if Paul Jensen is right in saying that the scientist is the last potential tragic hero, since the grandeur of his aims makes possible the greatest of falls, then it is not too much to claim that we all live in a Frankensteinian age. Certainly, we have to deal with forces man has unleashed that now range out of his control. The potential destructibility of nuclear power, the possible uses and misuses of DNA, and the wonder and fear created by the space exploration program—just to cite some clear examples—give us all pause to contemplate the ramifications of scientific endeavors made in the name of mankind, yet having the potential to destroy it. Both Mary Shelley's novel and James Whale's film are crucial to thinking about these issues, for if Mary Shelley wrote the word, James Whale made it flesh. Within this context, *Frankenstein* raises problems that strike at the very heart of our culture, become central to our values, and speak to the very survival of our species.

Wuthering Heights (1847), Emily Bronte

William Wyler, 1939

Wyler as Auteur

JOHN HARRINGTON

Although "Forty-Take Wyler" lacks the genius to be placed in the pantheon of American directors, he was a meticulous and intelligent filmmaker. As A. Badsen points out in his biography, William Wyler worked for two years to persuade Samuel Goldwyn to let him make *Wuthering Heights*, based on a script by Charles MacArthur and Ben Hecht, and originally written for Sylvia Sidney and Charles Boyer.[1] The crew drawn together by Goldwyn and Wyler was a model of the competence and creative intelligence available in the Hollywood studio system of the late 1930s, with Gregg Toland, the cinematographer, as a prime example of the talent of those assembled for the project.

The result of this creative collaboration was one of the best adaptations to come from Hollywood's middle period, a film which still attracts serious film audiences. While it is not an example of the very best art to come from Hollywood, *Wuthering Heights* (1939) is certainly among the notable films produced there. As comparison with the more recent adaptation (by Robert Fuest, 1971) of the novel makes clear, the strength of the Wyler version is in the handling of the tools of cinema rather than in the verbal translation from print to screen. Although the use of sound is unsophisticated compared to today's films, the rhetorical handling of camera, especially moving camera, and *mise-en-scene*—the aura emanating

1. A. Madsen, *William Wyler* (New York: Crowell, 1973), pp. 182-183.

67

from details of setting, staging, and scenery—creates a work of complexity and sensitivity. In directing and filming *Wuthering Heights*, Wyler and Toland used cinematic rhetoric creatively to interpret and present the brooding world of Emily Bronte's novel. It is this aspect of the film I wish to pursue here, in particular some of the means by which the filmmaker conveys Bronte's thematic concern with the opposition between nature and society—usually between the emotional needs of the individual and the ways in which society orders and shapes lives by stressing social position— through the complex use of *mise-en-scène* and a camera which, at crucial times, becomes an active force, a participating spirit suggesting the forces of nature which must be recognized.

Wyler's adaptation tells only the first half of the novel, which is itself broken into two parts. (Indeed, many critics view the division of the novel as a weakness.) The film begins with Mr. Lockwood's visit to Wuthering Heights one stormy evening (an appropriate opening since the word *wuthering* is a local term describing the tumult of the atmosphere in stormy weather). The storm forces Lockwood to spend the night. He awakens to an unseen presence (the spirit of the dead Catherine, who had married Edgar Linton while loving Heathcliff). Heathcliff, an old man at the film's opening, comes to Lockwood's room after the latter's shout of alarm at the touch of an icy hand through a broken window pane. Heathcliff rushes into the night to search for Catherine, and Ellen Dean, a faithful servant who raised Heathcliff and Catherine, begins to tell Lockwood the story of the two lovers.

Ellen (Flora Robson) portrays the house as having been a lively, warm place in the old days, bustling with energy and good feeling. One day, when Catherine and her brother Hindley were small children, their father, Mr. Earnshaw, arrived home with a ragged child he had found abandoned: this is Heathcliff, who is brought into the household as an equal of the two young Earnshaws. However the death of Mr. Earnshaw brings bleak times, with Hindley in control of the house. Heathcliff (Laurence Olivier) is degraded to servant status, while Catherine (Merle Oberon), his inseparable childhood ally, is now supposed to become a young lady. Catherine urges Heathcliff to leave the farm and return to her a rich man; she wants both his love and a high social position. He eventually does run off, but only after overhearing Catherine tell Ellen that she plans to marry Edgar Linton (David Niven), the elegant son of a refined local family. Although Catherine recognizes that she has made a fatally wrong decision, she disregards her feelings and marries Linton.

Catherine's life with Edgar is outwardly good; they lead the opulent life of the country gentry at Thrushcross Grange. But Catherine's emotional needs are not met by the polite society she has joined, and the return of Heathcliff, now a wealthy "gentleman" who has secretly bought Wuthering Heights, jars her. Heathcliff woos and marries Edgar's sister, Isabella (Geraldine Fitzgerald), in order to be near Catherine, and to hurt her. Eventually, Catherine wills herself to die because of the irresolvable conflict between the choice she has made for social position through her marriage to Edgar and the wild and deep love she has for Heathcliff. Heathcliff calls for her spirit to haunt him, and spends the rest of his life absorbed with Catherine. We learn at the end that Heathcliff has, at the movie's beginning, rushed into the storm to join his beloved Cathy in death.

With considerable intelligence, George Bluestone[2] has explored and compared the conceptual frameworks of book and film, making clear the basic changes in translating the book to a script and then to the screen. However, Bluestone has been overly casual with the film's complex visual rhetoric and, therefore, has been overly harsh on the film because of changes made in adapting the script. Before turning to a detailed analysis of the ways Wyler uses moving camera and *mise-en-scène* to successfully realize his version of the novel, it is instructive to examine some of the issues of adaptation with which Bluestone is concerned.

Bluestone emphasizes what he sees as a conceptual shift from novel to screen through a change from Bronte's opposition between nature and society to a focus in the film on "mythopoetic tendencies" and "social ambitions": "What is the result of bestowing these twin attributes, romanticism and desire for aggrandizement, on

2. George Bluestone, *Novels Into Film* (Berkeley: University of California Press, 1968).

Cathy in the movie version? The effect is to force Emily Bronte's story into a conventional Hollywood mold, the story of the stable boy and the lady."[3]

Bluestone's casual dismissal of the film's theme is confusing. Do viewers perceive Wyler's film as a love conflict between "the world of the stable boy and the world of the gentry"? Those who have viewed the recent adaptation of *Wuthering Heights* know that there is a fundamental difference in the two versions' insights into Bronte's themes, and Bluestone's comments on the earlier film better describe the later version. The struggle between nature and what society can provide is central thematically to both the novel and Wyler's adaptation, although one must look beyond the script and at the film's cinematic rhetoric to grasp how Wyler achieved an interpretation much closer to Bronte's novel than was managed in the recent version.[4]

Bluestone further sees the film as omitting promising pictorial effects of the novel, as well as of the original script:

> As it stands, the film is overloaded with medium shots, relieved only occasionally by long shots of the "castle" or the Heights. In spite of storms and brooding moors, the physical set-ups of the landscape and the characters are only occasionally allowed to endorse the dramatic event.[5]

He grudgingly acknowledges that the *mise-en-scène* is part of the conception and that certain scenes work well: the storm scene renders Cathy's troubled emotions, and Peniston Crag furnishes a unified physical symbol for the fierce passions of the novel. However, Bluestone is uneasy with the coloring of the two families, expecting lighter Lintons and darker Earnshaws. Clearly, the script writers wanted to accomplish some of what Bluestone seeks, as descriptions of the opening of the film and of Heathcliff suggest:

3. Bluestone, p. 99.

4. It should be noted that the film chooses to explore the thematic implications of only the novel's first half, following what numerous critics have viewed as a novelistic structure bifurcated and weaker than a novel which would not switch directions midway.

5. Bluestone, p. 103.

A long view of the MOORS fades in. A violent storm fills the night. Snow has been falling for days. The road and the moors are blanketed deep. The immense, lonely moor looks white, devilish and forlorn. There is no sound but the wind, no sight but the swirl of snow. . . . [Heathcliff is] a dark-skinned, saturnine looking figure, his hair half white. He is a surly, slovenly appearing, half gypsy half gentleman character; and on his features is the stamp of an embittered arrogance.[6]

Richard Griffith, in his monograph on Samuel Goldwyn, offers a view different from Bluestone's on Wyler's efforts to visualize Bronte's novel:

The setting for the film was not the moors of Yorkshire, but a wilderness of the imagination. To have reproduced on the screen any large expanse of landscape would have been to chain the story and its characters to the actual. Instead, Toland and Wyler devised a close-in camerawork which, in every shot, seemed to show only a small part of the whole scene, in which roads, crags, housetops, and human figures were revealed in outlines against dense grays or blacks. Thus was created a chiaroscuro country of the mind in which the passionate Bronte figures can come credibly alive.[7]

Bluestone essentially seeks greater realism from *Wuthering Heights*, but it is questionable whether more realistic effects would enhance the film. Certainly much of Wyler's version seems artificial by contemporary standards, and, as with *Citizen Kane* (also filmed by Gregg Toland), the *mise-en-scène* of the interiors does much to create character through ambience in the manner of the German expressionists of the preceding decade. However, chiaroscuro, coupled with a variety of shots, keeps most viewers from conscious awareness of the artifice of the film, and that is a distinct part of the filmmaker's achievement. Realism is not missed because Wyler and Toland successfully move *Wuthering Heights* to a psychological level.

6. Ben Hecht and Charles MacArthur, "Wuthering Heights," *Twenty Best Film Plays*, ed. John Gassner and Dudley Nichols (New York: Crown, 1943), p. 294. It is worth noting that the scriptwriters suggested Olivier, though he was an unknown actor at the time, for the project once Wyler took it over.

7. Quoted in Leonard Maltin, *Behind the Camera: The Cinematographer's Art* (New York: New American Libary, 1971), p. 34.

We do not insist on realism in *Wuthering Heights* largely because the camera is so busily probing, examining, looking, and participating in what happens that we are made coinvestigators with and by the camera. The camera is itself a force in this film. (This will soon be examined in detail.) Otis Ferguson was ahead of his time when he observed, without developing his case, that the camera created a dimension of cinematic articulation crucial to realizing *Wuthering Heights*:

> But the closeness with which the story holds together is ultimately the result of the way director, photographer, and cutters have used what should be called the moving camera, the part of photography that goes beyond a register of things to the position from which they are seen, moved up to, led away from, to the value in tempo, and coloring of each strip of film with relation to that of all the preceding and following strips—the camera telling a story.[8]

Ferguson perceptively credits not simply the cinematographer, but rather the range of creators who made the film in such a way that the camera could be used extensively. An investigation of the major scenes of the film will reveal just how crucial the moving camera is in exploring the characters and the *mise-en-scène* in order to develop the film's theme.

Wuthering Heights opens with a series of shots emphasizing natural elements (stone, clouds), with the house in dominant position. Backlighting creates a strange, preternatural effect. The storm which then engulfs the house in the film's first narrative sequence is immediately striking for its lack of realism, its "staginess." The snowstorm, the artificial trees, the man stumbling through the storm in the jerky, exaggerated movements of a stage actor: all of these work against realism, but at the same time prepare for the apparently more realistic events which occur inside the house (and, metaphorically, inside the minds of the major characters). What goes on in the house, seen in fragments and mostly in midshot, assumes authority, though heavily psychological, from the overwrought storm scene. Further, the first shot of the camera

8. Otis Ferguson, "For a Picture," *The New Republic* (April 26, 1939), p. 336.

establishes the camera as a *watcher*, a fellow traveler moving with a person (Lockwood, for now), approximately the point of view of someone sharing the character's experience. The camera accompanies Lockwood, but it is also a part of the natural setting it inhabits. The camera is clearly more than an observer: it is a *participant*. The shot in the storm begins to identify the camera with some sort of natural force which is involved in and concerned with the actions it observes. It is a part of the wild nature which it inhabits as a moving, active participant in the film, and we must look carefully at the ways this moving camera is involved in the action to understand how Wyler and Toland created meaning in the film.

As Lockwood enters the Heights in a reverse-angle shot of the door, we get our first sense of the interior of the house with its heavy door, panels, shadows on both sides, and columns at a slight angle. The impression is one of chaos and disrepair. The house is dark, shadowy; plaster has fallen away from the stone behind; pictures hang at strange angles; and a baluster is missing from the stair railing. It is the *mise-en-scène* of a horror film : the house is large, dark, threatening.

The hostility of the *mise-en-scène* is immediately reinforced by action as Lockwood enters. Again in reverse-angle shot, a large dog attacks Lockwood, who is viewed in close-up. We have moved from a storm, to a forbidding house, to an attack by an uncontrolled animal. A sense of hostility, a place where the forces of nature are not at peace, has been created in this effective combination of *mise-en-scène*, action, composition, reverse angles of shots, and the quick editing rhythm of the scene. Lockwood adds to this sense with his muffler, high hat, and mysteriousness. After the dog's attack, his eyes stare hollowly toward the inner rooms.

Maintaining Lockwood's point of view, the camera peers at Heathcliff in the distance, by the fireplace. Accompanied by eerie music, the camera dollies slowly with Lockwood toward the bright fire in the center of the room, a fire surrounded and threatened by darkness and shadow. With a match cut from the dolly to the room, the scene seems somewhat brighter. Heathcliff stands by the fireplace, looking vacantly into the shadows. Despite the fire, the room is still not inviting from Lockwood's point of view.

The remaining events of the scene add to the sense of mystery and threat. Isabella's face makes a ghostly appearance around the side of a wingback chair. Although Lockwood is lit so that his face is bright, inviting, and open, his face contrasts with Heathcliff's appearance and with the heavy, dark, shadowy environment surrounding him. In a quick series of close-ups, Lockwood and Heathcliff regard each other: Lockwood's face is open, kind, uncertain, fearful, weak, and trembling like some pitiful lapdog; Heathcliff remains unexpressive, blank, dark, cold, and yet mysterious and unfathomable in his half-light.

As the camera dollies with Lockwood toward Heathcliff, the latter tells Joseph to open the upstairs room. The sound of wind and the shadowy lighting create an ominous, foreboding feeling. The room is dark and threatening as the two men enter through the door opened from darkness. The oddly styled bed, the beamed ceiling, and the windblown curtains extend the ominous sense of the scene. After Lockwood stuffs his hat into the open hole in the window, we hear Cathy's theme for the first time since the few strains played in the opening shots of the film. By using music at this point, the filmmakers help us share emotionally what Lockwood feels and fears. We are able to apprehend his point of view both intellectually and emotionally, something difficult to accomplish with the written word alone.

After the banging shutter is connected with Cathy's theme, the scene dissolves to the inside with the camera dollying, seeming to feel its way along as it stops to peer between the bars of the bed at the restive Lockwood. The camera now seems to help us enter the point of view of a spirit, or force, participating in the scene and affecting the action. Although the actions of the camera are like those of the moving camera in Lockwood's opening scene, the sense of the participating force is now much more pronounced. The movements of the camera are not stable; it moves several ways, searching probing, uncertain, with the haunting Cathy's theme played in high choral notes. Lockwood reaches out and hears a voice. Since we see both what he is going through and the authentic (not hallucinatory) spiritual experience, we also hear her voice and recoil with him at the touch of her hand. The filmmakers have recreated the spiritual/psychological experience so that we can share that experience with Lockwood. The moving camera and the dark, haunted *mise-en-scène* have been united for us early in the film.

It is also interesting to note that Heathcliff's presence does not essentially change the point of view. As the distraught Heathcliff reaches out to Cathy, the camera retains the viewpoint of the participating spirit. We watch Heathcliff from the position from which Cathy's spirit called out. He then runs onto the stark, snow-covered moor, trying to contact the spirit we know for its presence, but which remains only a creation of camera and sound.

As Heathcliff runs out, we are given our first close look at Ellen Dean, the ostensible narrator and the housekeeper for so many years at both Wuthering Heights and Thrushcross Grange. She clearly has considerable involvement in the lives of the main characters and cares deeply for what happens to them. She is the first to articulate the deep spiritual bond between Catherine and Heathcliff. The way she is filmed underscores her perception of the spiritual power of this sequence: she is top- and back-lit brightly, and her expression is ecstatic. Soon she dominates the image in low angle by the fire, while the weaker and more peripheral Lockwood is seen from high angle as she begins to narrate the story of Heathcliff and Cathy. Through the use of skillful camera work in this sequence, the powerful spiritual force governing the lives of residents of the Heights is created with very little dependence on words. The combination of moving camera and *mise-en-scène* creates a spiritual dimension which is emotionally valid.

As Ellen tells her story in voice-over, we move from the Heights seen in gray, in a storm, to steadily brighter key lighting as she talks about the house as "a lovely place." Lighting, like the dolly shot that begins her narration, is used to communicate the changes in the house and in the family's life. A dark, forbidding house has changed, simply with lighting, to a place of energy and happiness. Simultaneously, we have moved from mid-shot and close-up to long shot. The effect is one of space, and the audience feels more comfortable with the psychological distance provided by long shot. The combination of lighting and shot length communicates well, at a nonverbal level, the changes in life at the Heights.

At the same time, *mise-en-scène* also has a key role in changes.

The bright exterior dissolves to a bright interior, with maids bustling about and energetic children filling the house with their games. No longer is the house in disrepair, but tidiness and a sense of purpose and harmony govern the placement of objects. As the master arrives at home, the *mise-en-scène* and lighting combine to make the Heights seem an extraordinarily attractive place to live. The camera is steady in the brightly lit house, not a creature moving with, and affecting, the action. The inner and outer worlds seem in harmony.

With exposition established, the plot begins to advance with the growing bond between Heathcliff and Cathy, as the two children turn against Hindley and begin to build their world of fantasy at Peniston Crag (a symbol of their relationship made more prominent in the film than in the novel). The *mise-en-scène* remains bright for their early relationship, but after Cathy hears the sounds of the Linton party and the two head for the Grange, the scene turns unaccountably to night. We begin to see that our first shift from dark to light was only a prelude, that the film will increasingly assign meaning to these shifts in lighting and *mise-en-scène*.

As the young couple approach the Grange, the implications of the shift in lighting are underscored by the camera again becoming a searching, probing creature rather than a recorder of happy action; the camera becomes an active participant in the events. The camera prowls along the wall, like an intruder, probes through the leaves blocking the couple's view of the Grange, then cranes along through the garden and up to the window to see what they see. It reflects their cautiousness and wonder, but it also acts as something apart from them, a participant in spirit rather than simply a subjective camera.

What the children, and the camera, see is the opulence of the Linton household. Cathy and Heathcliff stand in shadows outside, staring into the brightly lit, cheerful house. The dress and manners of the guests contrast strongly to those of Cathy and Heathcliff. The guests, formally dressed in mid-Victorian fashion, seem gaudy and false in their elaborate clothing. Cathy and Heathcliff, on the other hand, are dressed in working clothes. The guests seem appropriately dressed in the Linton house, but, when they come onto the porch after the dog's attack, the guests seem inappropriately dressed as their whiteness and formality glare against the natural setting of the

Wuthering Heights (1939). Wyler's adaptation tells only the first half of the novel. Here he visualizes the triangle formed by Cathy (Merle Oberon), Heathcliff (Laurence Olivier) and Linton (David Niven). (Photo courtesy of the Museum of Modern Art.)

garden. Heathcliff and Cathy, though, blend well into the natural setting, while looking pitifully common and out of place when they enter the Grange.

When she finally returns to Wuthering Heights, Cathy has adopted the dress of the Lintons and has also assumed their affected manners. Although the *mise-en-scène* is bright and warm, Cathy now contrasts with her environment. She wears her hair tightly against her head with straight, formal ringlets down the sides, giving her a look that is artificial and cold compared to the softness and wildness of her hair and face through the early parts of the film. Her face is drawn and cold, with lips narrowed and lines hardened. Her dress is tight at the neck and molded by supports, unlike the open-throated dress of the moors which followed the smooth lines of her body. The contrast to her former self and to her home is underscored when Heathcliff enters in his tattered clothes.

The camera, again a participating spirit, dollies toward Catherine as she and Edgar quarrel over Heathcliff. Although her outward demeanor and her sharp comments have indicated up to this point that she is a changed person, she angrily refuses to abide any slight to Heathcliff, and the association of the moving camera with her defense of Heathcliff is appropriate. Tearing off her elaborate Linton clothing, Cathy returns to her natural dress and runs to the Crag and to Heathcliff, completing a cycle of events which recurs throughout the story. Her vacillation between a wild and natural love for Heathcliff and the civilized and ordered life of proper society will be developed in the remainder of the film.

The contradictory impulses tormenting Cathy are brought together in the key scene in which Cathy says, "He's more myself than I am. . . . Ellen, I *am* Heathcliff." The storm rages inside, lightening and darkening the room as Cathy sorts through her emotions. Much of the scene is shot in low angle, mostly in close-up and medium close-up, but with the camera dollying. The camera's movement, at the moment of Cathy's self-awareness, suggests the larger forces, within and without, which she must face. Although the camera held back and remained stationary when Cathy described her attraction for Edgar, it is clearly an active, engaged, participating force when Cathy realizes the awesome interconnection she shares with Heathcliff. The camera actively responds to that part of Cathy that struggles against society's beckoning and asserts her emotional needs.

The camera is again a participant in the wedding scene, undercutting the expected happiness of that event. As the bride and groom emerge from the church, the camera adopts an unusual vantage point, behind the villagers waiting at the gate. As the two emerge from the church, the camera drops down behind the carriage, watching like a furtive interloper and providing the same sense of anxious "peeking" we saw when Cathy and Heathcliff first visited the Grange.[9] As Cathy climbs into the coach, with her fears of what she has done expressed in her sense of doom (brought on by the cold wind crossing her heart),[10] the camera climbs with her, letting the audience share with her the sense that some sort of spiritual violation is taking place. The camera then dollies to Ellen's face as she narrates her own perception of the fears she has for her lady's marriage.

As Ellen describes her fears, the image fades to the camera probing the walls of the Grange, peering into the windows, just as it had probed the garden walls when the children first trespassed. The visual repetition of the moving camera lurking in the trees and reminding us of dark, natural forces undercuts the happiness of the seemingly bright and cheerful scene within the Grange. By combining the exterior *mise-en-scène* and camera movement, edited in juxtaposition to the brightness of the interior of the Grange, the threat to Cathy's new life is clearly established and extended from the wedding scene. Emphasis is placed on the darkness surrounding the house, rather than on the artificial light within. *Mise-en-scène* contradicts, while the moving camera disturbs our emotions since we already have so thoroughly experienced the camera as a natural force concerned with the relationship of the two lovers. The rational, controlled order and civilization of the Grange stand in clear, and threatened, contrast to the dark and uncontrollable forces of nature. The scene is set for Heathcliff to arrive, and after he does come and

9. This scene contrasts sharply with the verbal conception of the scriptwriters, who rely on children's comments and the villagers' responses to throw into relief Cathy's verbalized doubts. Hecht, p. 315.

10. Hecht, P. 315. This articulation of a force of nature inspiring a feeling is consistent with the use of natural imagery throughout the film.

reenter their lives the camera, at the end of the scene, dollies back, through the window, to the outside of the house. The sound of wind and blowing foliage, and the return to darkness, accompany the camera's movement. The spiritual forces attending the lovers' relationship clearly will not rest while Cathy inhabits the rational, ordered world of the Lintons.

The interplay of *mise-en-scène* (bright house/dark natural settings) and moving camera continues as Heathcliff comes to the Linton's party. Again the camera repeats the earlier scene of the trespassing children by struggling out of the darkness, over the wall, and up the stairs to the party. The movement is uncomfortably from darkness to light, and Toland beautifully captures the brightness of the party by panning the entire suite of rooms, beginning with the dance scene shot in a large mirror (echoing previous window images and ironically recalling the two previous entries of the camera through the window). Shortly, Heathcliff escorts Cathy to the balcony, a kind of halfway point between the civilized and natural settings which represent the struggles of the two lovers. She is in control in the bright house, but she must struggle to maintain control as she enters the darkness of the balcony and feels the wind—again an important natural force—blowing around her. She must leave the balcony and return to the house to regain her self-control. Throughout the scene, the camera watches the two from the bushes, maintaining the camera's identity as a natural force; as Heathcliff talks with Isabella at the end of the scene, the camera pulls back into the trees and resumes its wait outside as Heathcliff reenters the bright and civilized world of the Lintons.

Cathy cannot resolve her emotional struggle between the forces of nature and the civilized, but emotionally stultifying, forces within the house, and she is willing to die rather than to make her commitment in life. While Edgar is gone to find the heather she so desperately wants (a reminder of the natural love represented by Peniston Crag), Heathcliff enters her bright and perfectly arranged room. But this time Cathy wears loose clothing and has her hair flowing freely around her. Heathcliff will not forgive her, and he pulls her into darkness and rages at her. The lighting is distinctly dimmed as he accuses her and as his darkness affects her spirit. She clings to him declaring her devotion, and he carries her through the windowed doors to the balcony where she can share the wind and wildness of nature. She dies with her spirit released from the house. He puts her on the bed and, in semidarkness, puts his curse on her, asking to be haunted.

The image of Heathcliff holding Catherine in the windowed doorway of Catherine's balcony summarizes all of the images of windows and doors seen throughout the film. These images suggest the thin membrane between inner and outer worlds, between the world of facts and events and the world of the mind with its perceptions and needs, between the forces of nature and the civilized order of society, between the two parts of one person which struggle between seeking gratification and being a "good" member of society. The windows in the film visually portray the barriers the characters feel in their lives, and the camera emphasizes windows as constraints regardless of which side they are seen from or through: Heathcliff, agonizing over Catherine's dining with Edgar, thrusts his hands through the stable windows and into nature's violent (and suggestive) storm, trying to break the barriers that keep him from fulfilling his relationship with Catherine; the hand of Catherine's spirit grabs Lockwood's hand through a broken pane, crying from outside and seeking to reach through the barrier to those within; Catherine is shot against windows (from low angle) with a climaxing storm flashing through the windows and lighting her as she recognizes, "I *am* Heathcliff"; the camera lurks outside windows, a creature of the natural world, but fascinated and tantalized by the world within the Grange while threatening the very stability of that world; Catherine, as well as Isabella, is shot in mirrors (reflective windows to the self) while contemplating relationships with men.

The cinematic rhetoric of Wyler and Toland has effectively rendered the two worlds of the novel. The images of the film suggest not a love story between a stable boy and a lady, as Bluestone suggests (finding his evidence in the thin descriptions of the script), but rather the difficulty of resolving the forces of nature and society as they influence the lives of those in the two houses. The Wyler version of *Wuthering Heights* succeeds because of the skillful ways in which the purposes of both novelist and scriptwriter have been achieved with visual, rather than verbal, language. The combination of *mise-en-scène* and moving camera (which is, itself, one of the forces of the story) has rendered an adaptation that still moves an audience after forty years. Wyler's experiment in cinematic language, form, and style has created on film a sense of the complex theme of Bronte's novel.

Jane Eyre (1847), Charlotte Bronte

Robert Stevenson, 1944; Delbert Mann, 1970

Feminism in Bronte's Novel and Its Film Versions

KATE ELLIS AND E. ANN KAPLAN

Charlotte Bronte's *Jane Eyre* is the story of a woman who understands instinctively the inequities of patriarchal structures but who cannot, finally, move entirely beyond them. Published in 1847 at the height of the Victorian era, the book won immediate popular acclaim, along with some harsh criticism.[1] But it is the intense ambivalence toward male domination on the part of Bronte and her heroine that speaks so strongly to present day feminists, who have claimed Bronte as one of the "foremothers" of the contemporary women's movement.[2] Jane's strength comes to the reader through the clear, strong voice of the first person narrative as she describes her situations: analysing them, commenting on them, and giving us her thoughts and reactions at every point. Neither film version (1944, 1970) is ultimately able to retain the centrality of Jane's point of view, though there is, in Stevenson's 1944 version, a voice-over narration that is a very much watered-down version of Bronte's strong diction. This dilution of Jane's rebellious vision has partly to do with the limitations of film form, but mainly it is a result of a

1. For a favorable contemporary review see G. H. Lewes, "The Reality of Jane Eyre," *Fraser's Magazine*, December, 1847, pp. 690-93; the most famous hostile review is Elizabeth Rigby, *Quarterly Review*, 84 (December, 1848), pp. 162-176.

2. See Adrienne Rich, *"Jane Eyre*: The Temptations of a Motherless Woman," *Ms.*, Vol. 2, No. 4 (October, 1973), pp. 69-73; Helen Moglen, *Charlotte Bronte: The Self Conceived* (New York: W. W. Norton and Co., 1976); Sandra Gilbert, "Plain Jane's Progress," *Signs*, Vol. 2, No. 4 (Summer, 1977), pp. 779-804.

reversion on the part of the two directors, Robert Stevenson and Delbert Mann, to accepted patriarchal structures so that Jane is seen, for the most part, from a male point of View.

In allowing Jane to narrate her own story, Bronte allows her heroine the complexity of a double vision. On the one hand, we see Jane chafe against the constrictions and inequities of the patriarchal spaces within which she is placed: Gateshead, Lowood School, Thornfield Hall, and finally Marsh End. She is "thrilled with ungovernable excitement" as she declares to her aunt, in words very close to those she will later say to Rochester, "You think I have no feelings, and that I can do without one bit of love or kindness; but I cannot live so" (chapter 4). This declaration will be, in fact, the motif of Jane's life, drawing her away from the Reeds, away from Lowood, toward and then away from Rochester and the ascetic St. John Rivers, until she finally finds, at Ferndean, a love and kindness that do not patronize her. On the other hand, when she discovers that she might have "some poor, low relations called Eyre," she will not leave Gateshead to go to them.

> "Not even if they were kind to you?"
> I shook my head. I could not see how poor people had the means of being kind; and then to learn to speak like them, to adopt their manners, to be uneducated, to grow up like one of the poor women I saw sometimes nursing their children or washing their clothes at the cottage doors of the village of Gateshead: no, I was not heroic enough to purchase liberty at the price of caste.   (chapter 3)

Again at Lowood, we see Jane raging against the submissiveness of Helen Burns, but also learning from it. When Miss Scratchard pins the word "Slattern" on Helen, Jane tells us:

> I ran to Helen, tore it off, and thrust it into the fire: the fury of which she was incapable had been burning in my soul all day, and tears, hot and large, had continually been scalding my cheek; for the spectacle of her sad resignation gave me an intolerable pain at the heart.   (chapter 8)

At the same time she has her first real experience of love and kindness there from Miss Temple and Helen, and this causes her to declare: "I would not now have exchanged Lowood with all its

privations, for Gateshead and its daily luxuries." Therefore she stays
on there for two years as a teacher (a post she rejects in both film
versions) and only leaves when her "motive" for staying is taken
away by the marriage and removal of Miss Temple.

Bronte gives us the same juxtaposition of need and contempt in
Jane's view of Thornfield. Explaining why she does not want to
leave in the wake of her master's purported marriage to Blanche
Ingram she says:

> I love Thornfield—I love it because I have lived in it a full and delightful
> life—momentarily at least. I have not been trampled on. I have not been
> petrified. I have not been buried with inferior minds, and excluded from
> every glimpse of communion with what is bright and energetic, and
> high. I have talked, face to face, with what I reverence; with what I
> delight in—with an original, a vigorous, an expanded mind.
>
> (chapter 23)

But she sees the necessity of leaving, acknowledges that this place
that has given her her first real experience of a home is an
appropriate setting for the kind of life Rochester will have with
Blanche Ingram. But "I would scorn such a union," she says,
"therefore I am better than you—let me go!" When Rochester
offers her a form of "union" that in her view is just as debased as
this one without love, she does scorn it. Finally, she scorns Rivers's
offer of marriage based not on mutual affection but on dedication to
a higher cause. Jane extricates herself from this temptation, yet it is
only because Rivers insists on marriage that she refuses. While she
lives under his roof she notices that "I daily wished more to please
him: but to do so, I felt daily more and more that I must disown
half my nature" (chapter 34). She sees that she cannot give her body
as well as her soul to him, yet she freely consents to go with him as
his fellow missionary. Clear-headedly she reasons: "I should suffer
often, no doubt, attached to him only in this capacity: my body
would be under a rather stringent yoke, but my heart and mind
would be free." Yet she is not immune to the attraction of heroic
action. It was she, after all, who in her first months at Thornfield
looked out at the skyline and "longed for a power of vision that
might overpass that limit; which might reach the busy world, towns,
regions full of life I had heard of but never seen" (chapter 12).

The question is: does she relinquish this restless side of her nature when she gives up her independent life and career to care for a blind, dependent man? In some ways, Bronte is simply following the narrative demands of her genre, which imitate the dominant bourgeois code. She brings the lovers safely back together, the woman firmly back in her place caring for the man. Yet Rochester's blindness suggests a fundamental weakness in men that belies the original harsh, invulnerable, controlling exterior that Rochester presents. Ultimately he is terribly dependent on Jane, needing her more than she, with her newly inherited income, needs him. She, on the other hand, turns out to be the stronger, thus fulfilling the symbolism of their first meeting where she helps him up after a fall from his horse. Yet this strength of hers is little more than the strength that mothers have in caring for their children: one wonders if this was the only alternative model that Bronte had to the traditional "he for God only, she for God in him" paradigm of male-female relationships. That is to say, Bronte offers only the alternatives of women feeling subordinate and vulnerable to men, living with them "as sisters" or without them altogether, or undertaking a nurturing, mothering role that gives them all the control. Here we see Bronte's ambivalence about the institution (as opposed to the experience, to borrow a distinction from Adrienne Rich) of marriage that becomes increasingly unmistakable in her later work. Then again, perhaps she is simply saying that it takes rather drastic events (blindness on the male side, a large inheritance on the female) to equalize, even in a place as far from "society" as Ferndean, the drastic sexual inequalities with which her age presented her.

What is interesting, from our point of view, about the film versions, is the ways in which Stevenson in 1944 and Mann in 1972 liquidate Bronte's ambivalence toward patriarchy. The Stevenson film was made in the post-World War II period when *film noir* was dominant. Having played active roles in the public sphere during the war, women were now being told to go back into their homes and care for their husbands and children. It is thus not surprising to find Joan Fontaine playing a very meek, docile, and submissive Jane in the second half of the film. Interestingly enough, the first half of the film, prior to Orson Welles's appearance as Rochester, sticks close to the novel in showing Jane's rebelliousness and defiance, first toward the Reed family and then at Lowood. Stevenson uses expressionist, nonrealist cinematic techniques to show the monstrosity of the Reed family and the vulnerability of Jane by using high and low angles. Mrs. Reed and John lower over her menacingly, or we see her small, pathetically cooped up, in the Red Room. But Jane fights back against these looming figures, putting up a brave, if pointless, fight. The camera angles thus express some of the Gothic terror that emerges from Bronte's description.

The use of high contrast in this black and white film also brings out the gothicism of a book in which the room where a man died is filled with secrets and a mad woman is confined to an attic. In this film, as in the novel, a sadistic Mr. Brocklehurst enjoys piling hardships on his pupils in the name of religion, and has no remorse even when Helen Burns (Elizabeth Taylor) dies as a result of harsh rules carried out by an equally unrelenting Miss Scratchard. The one mitigating female presence in the novel, it is important to note, is replaced by an added character, the kindly Dr. Rivers whose name is taken from the novel's stern St. John Rivers who does not appear in the film. Dr. Rivers tries to circumvent Brocklehurst's insane regulations and to explain their danger for the girls. But even though he is a man confronting another man, he is powerless to effect a change. While he comforts Jane, his role is essentially to teach her her place, to beg her to conform, to submit to the will of God. Like the Rivers of the novel, this essentially virtuous male figure sees no possibility for changing the omnipresence of male domination, and he tries to undermine Jane's independent spirit. In the novel it is Miss Temple who objects strongly to the rules and sometimes breaks them. Her warm, nurturing presence offsets the horror of Lowood for Jane. But even more importantly, she provides a powerful model for both Jane and Helen of a principled and intelligent, if ultimately powerless, woman.

One can only speculate on the reasons for a change like this: balancing the hateful Brocklehurst with the kindly Rivers mitigates an absolute condemnation of male authority that might be implied. Rivers is the good father to Jane cancelling out the bad one. Yet Bronte had been more interested in Miss Temple as the good

Jane Eyre (1944). A scene from the education of Jane (Peggy Ann Garner) as a young girl. Joan Fontaine was the adult heroine and Orson Welles was Rochester. The film also featured the young Elizabeth Taylor. (Photo courtesy of the Museum of Modern Art)

mother balancing out Mrs. Reed, the bad one. The film, in removing one side of this balance, represses the mother who in the novel brought about Jane's growth. Male authority is thereby left supreme.

While Jane's point of view is given prominence in the Lowood section of the film, the tension comes from the way it shows male authority trying to silence it. But once Joan Fontaine replaces Peggy Ann Garner, as Jane arrives at Thornfield Hall, the directing consciousness becomes Rochester's, in a complete reversal of the situation in the novel. This is partly because Orson Welles, who plays Rochester, always dominates whatever scene he is in. But it also has to do with the camera work, about which Welles may possibly have had some say. Cinematically, Jane is placed as Rochester's observer: she yearns for him, waits upon him, watches him from the window, the stairwell, a corner of the room, hiding her tears from him behind closed doors. We retain Jane's point of view, but her gaze is fixed on Rochester as object of desire, an odd reversal of the usual situation in film where the male observes the woman as object of desire in such a way that the audience sees her that way too. Interestingly, the reversal of the look does not give Jane any more power: Rochester comes and goes, commands and manages, orders Jane's presence as he wishes. Jane's look is of a yearning, passive kind as against the more usual controlling male look at the woman.

Jane's subordination and passivity are particularly marked in the scenes where Blanche Ingram and Rochester's other guests come to Thornfield. Jane then skulks around with Adele, shot often behind the guests, in the rear of the room, glimpsed behind a door, or through the richly dressed, loud party. Rochester places her in the impossible position of forcing her to be present, and then ignoring her and relegating her to the status of an observer of his love affair with Blanche. Since her voice-over commentary is silent at this point, we do not get her thoughts and analysis or the contempt for the situation that Jane's point of view in the novel so strongly registers. When the pain is intolerable she does of course ask to leave and, as in the novel, thus precipitates the marriage proposal. But overall we see Jane as passive and long-suffering, putting up with this treatment without complaint.

Jane's passivity is heightened by the naturally subservient and self-effacing style of Fontaine the actress. While this manner may have suited her role in Hitchcock's 1940 film *Rebecca*, it is quite unsuitable for Jane. But reinforcing this is the equally natural bombast of Welles, who dominates his costar in a way that Olivier did not in *Rebecca*. Yet Welles's baroque sensibility is in many ways suited to the gothic elements in the original novel, and on this score Stevenson's version does much better than the later one, largely due to Welles's influence. While he sometimes overplays his hand in an embarrassing manner—for instance, by the macho riding-off into the snow-swept landscape, storm blowing, and huge mastiff at his side (Jane meanwhile looking on passively from a window with a diminutive Margaret O'Brien as Adele, one sewing, the other painting)—he *has* caught the tenor of Bronte's image, the swash-buckling Byronic overtones of her male character. Anachronistic as is the medieval castle that constitutes the set for the Thornfield section, it again fits Bronte's gothic imagination. And while the film cannot reproduce the symbolism of Bertha in the novel, where she embodies the repressed parts of Jane, in not letting us see her properly, Stevenson surrounds her with mysterious and sinister elements.

The omission of the St. John Rivers sequence in this film seems to fit in with the subordination of Jane's point of view. In the novel, it is through her experiences away from Rochester that Jane learns to be strong and to function effectively on her own. The delay between the romantic passion and its fulfillment enables her to mature and return to Rochester as an equal. Stevenson deals with the necessity of sending Jane somewhere, after she has left the still-married Rochester, by moving forward the brief return to the Reed house-hold that Jane in the novel makes prior to Rochester's proposal. In the novel Jane comes as a result of this visit to pity her former tormentors, and the freedom from them that she thereby acquires is a necessary prelude to her ability to understand and express her feelings about Thornfield and its owner. But in the film Jane falls into the same passive, observing, subordinate role that she had at Thornfield. Dr. Rivers appears again as the emissary between herself and Rochester, and as a storm swirls around her she hears the voice of Rochester that calls her to his side. It is significant, we think, that they meet in the burned shell of the castle, the charred remnants surrounding them menacingly. Welles limps through the ruins but is hardly the mellowed, chastened Rochester (could Welles ever appear chastened?) of Bronte's closing chapters. Their coming together simply represents the typical lovers' reunion, with male and female traditionally placed. Jane is overjoyed to be back with Rochester and he is relieved at her return to take care of him. One has no sense of real change having taken place in either of them.

Delbert Mann's 1972 made-for-television version of *Jane Eyre* makes an interesting contrast to the 1944 film. The dominance of *film noir* as a film form in the postwar period enabled Stevenson to recreate quite effectively some of the gothic aspects of the novel: *film noir* looked back to expressionism, which in turn drew on the gothic revival and romanticism for its themes and style, so that the line from Bronte's novel to 1946 film aesthetics was reasonably direct. On the other hand, the ideology of the same postwar period in relation to women was partly responsible for the omission of Bronte's feminist leanings. But Mann's version, made in the period when the new wave of feminism was in its most exuberant, optimistic phase, humanizes Rochester and Bertha Mason, and removes much of the conflict from the relationship between Rochester (George C. Scott) and Jane (Susannah York). In doing this the characters become much more human and familiar, or at least familiar as film characters. But by the same token, the theme of personal growth through struggle and hard-won self-knowledge, which makes Bronte's novel an important document for feminists still, is swept away in a tide of rich, sensous film images.

To begin with, the lush, colorful photography is completly at odds with the gothicism of the original. All is bright, colorful, and unmysterious. Mann has a strong feeling for textures as well as colors, and on this level the film appeals strongly. The inmates in Lowood wear uniforms and nightgowns that could have been designed for the pages of *Vogue*. Thornfield is now an elegant mansion fitted out with magnificent eighteenth-century objects, furniture, and a stunning staircase. George C. Scott's Rochester is a humane, sympathetic character: instead of the charismatic, blustering Welles we have a tired, jaded, and aging man worn out by a life of too much easy pleasure, seeking in Jane the freshness of a young, innocent woman. His grief about Bertha is stressed, and to make this convincing, Mann lets us into Bertha's prison after the aborted wedding, as Stevenson did not. A desperate Rochester insists that the priest, Jane, and Bertha's brother Mason follow him to see the wife now preventing his happiness with Jane. Bertha is beautiful but catatonic, in contrast to the violent, "unchaste" creature described in Bronte's novel and implied in Stevenson's film. Rochester sits wearily down beside her and asks what they should do that night, making it clear that it is her incapacity for companionship that has driven him away in despair. His words thus highlight not only his utter loneliness but also her total isolation. Bertha has a strange kind of magnetism, and Rochester's words to Jane that he loved Bertha once as he now loves her gives the relationship a compelling dignity. Similarly the separation between Jane and Rochester after the marriage is realistically and touchingly done. We have a sense of two equal people, each determined to press for what he or she wants and thinks is right.

Having omitted the Reid family at the beginning, Mann includes the Marsh End section of the novel, and this enables him to show a different, more charismatic type of man. Black-haired and starkly handsome, Rivers represents a force that Jane must learn to withstand, and it is when she does so that she hears Rochester's mysterious call. The final reunion is extremely real and touching in this version. Rochester is humbled, not expecting anything, and fully supposing her to be married already. When he realizes she wants to stay with a blinded, crippled man, his pleasure is quietly expressed in their embrace. Fittingly, the reunion happens not in the gothic ruin Thornfield but in the peace and quiet of Ferndean, and here Mann is closer to Bronte than Stevenson was, conveying that sense of peace and transcendence with which Bronte ends.

In humanizing Rochester, Mann comes closer to portraying an equal relationship, but the camera still favors Rochester and shows Jane looking up to or being looked down upon by a male observer. Structurally Rochester is still in command, and it is significant that the equality comes not from Jane's rebellion or her questioning intelligence, but simply from the fact that Rochester's weaknesses are on the surface right from the beginning. While Welles made Rochester's anger at Jane's departure come from a defensive wounded pride, Scott makes us see the utter loneliness and loss that Rochester experiences—a loss that seems equal to Jane's in a way that it does not in either Bronte or the Stevenson film. Mann allows us to see more of Rochester's pain than Jane sees (she is not there when he tries to converse with Bertha, for instance) so that we become sensitive to his view of things, which thereby becomes the dominant point of view in the film.

It is worth dwelling a moment on the significance of the humanizing of Rochester in the Mann version in terms of what it does to the original gothic pattern. The gothic is premised on the father's being distant, unknown, unapproachable, commanding. Once he is known, his threat diminishes and the premise for gothic emotions is removed. Patriarchal structures are premised on the mysterious father's defining woman's place for her. Once he is no longer mysterious, once he enters into the structure as a human entity, his power is lost and the woman has room to interact, to enter the sphere from which she has been excluded. Scott's Rochester is thus (to answer Freud's question) what women want: a vulnerable, open, accessible father who is not afraid to reveal his weakness or the depth of his needs. A daughter may not have the same power in the world that a father has, but if they are equal in their need for one another, and can express this equally, then the differences in age and experience (which are the only ones Rochester insisted on in the novel) are not oppressive. The fantasy of "marrying daddy" comes out from behind its gothic trappings in Mann's film, but it is there in Bronte too, as well as in the innumerable contemporary "drugstore gothics" on the market today. Behind this gruff, male exterior, it says, lies true love, unable, for the most part, to express itself, but there nevertheless. He may seem distant, dazzled by charms that are beyond your reach, and bound to another, but in fact it is really you that he has loved all along.

A much more blatant departure from the Brontean gothic is the fact that Susannah York's Jane is in no way the plain heroine conceived by an author who, Mrs. Gaskell tells us,

once told her sisters that they were wrong—even morally wrong—in making their heroines beautiful as a matter of course. They replied that it was impossible to make a heroine interesting on any other terms. Her answer was, "I will prove to you that you are wrong; I will show you a heroine as plain and small as myself, who shall be as interesting as any of yours.[3]

Bronte lived in a society that rewarded pretty women but not plain ones; so do we. Fathers have become more casually accessible to their children since the Stevenson movie was made, and certainly since Bronte wrote. And for a brief time in the late 1960s and early 1970s, feminists were caught up in a belief that the world they wanted was right on the horizon: that the fate of pretty women in this culture could be distributed equally, that men could throw down their burdensome defenses, and that age-old struggles could be done away with through a change of consciousness. Fortunately for us now, Charlotte Bronte knew better.

3. Elizabeth Gaskell, *The Life of Charlotte Bronte* (London: J. M. Dent, 1960), pp. 215-16.

Barry Lyndon (1844), W. M. Thackeray

Stanley Kubrick, 1975

Narrative and Discourse
in Kubrick's Modern Tragedy

MICHAEL KLEIN

> Even inept films sometimes carry with them a certain mesmerizing
> authority. Stanley Kubrick's *Barry Lyndon*, a flawed work based upon a
> rather uninspiring novel, can be enjoyed, for instance, for its visual
> effects: sheer photography. And the background music is superb.[1]

> The music offputtingly classical under the titles . . . might as well be
> embalming fluid. . . . Even the action sequences in *Barry Lyndon* aren't
> meant to be exciting; they're meant only to be *visually* exciting.[2]

The quotations are typical of a good deal that has been written
about Kubrick's film, *Barry Lyndon*. Joyce Carol Oates, writing in
TV Guide, liked the "visual effects" and found the music "superb."
Pauline Kael, in *The New Yorker*, more antagonistically found the
classical background music "embalming" and "offputting," the
images merely "visually exciting" and hence meaningless. Both
critics responded to the music and the images as ends in themselves,
as either too beautiful or as too tendentious, but anyway as too
decorative to be functional. Hence they dismissed the film as a
rather overblown historical pageant.

There seems to be an expectation, virtually prescriptive, that the

1. Joyce Carol Oates, "A Private Dream Flashing onto an Enormous Screen," *TV Guide* (October 7-13, 1978), p. 6.
2. Pauline Kael, "Kubrick's Gilded Age," *The New Yorker* (December 29, 1975), p. 50.

core of the film should reside in the narrative, in the sequence of events and point of view of the main characters. However Kubrick's modernist perspective is somewhat different. While the events do shape the characters' lives, they are relatively neutral, incomplete signs. The characters are devoid of self-consciousness. The total configuration of visual and aural signs (including the music and the voice-over), that is the discourse, defines and determines our response to and comprehension of the events.[3] The discourse is ironic and analytic (places the characters and events in a larger perspective); it also engages our sympathy (defines value and meaning).

It is generally understood that Kubrick's science-fiction films are parables about life in present society, works that gain intensity when they are situated in relation to our contemporary experience. *Barry Lyndon* is not so much an historical epic as a parable about the modern condition. Redmond Barry is doubly alienated, from his class and from his nation. The rise and fall of Barry Lyndon (his name changes with his identity) is an emblematic tale of class mobility and lost roots. Redmond Barry (Ryan O'Neal), Irish and of relatively modest origins, becomes a rootless cosmopolitan, an expatriate wandering across Europe during the Seven Years War, finally settling in England (the colonial power that governs Ireland), where he marries into wealth and attempts to achieve a further rise in class by securing a peerage. It is a tragedy of class mobility: Barry is finally left maimed and destitute. Ironically, Barry fails because at several key junctions in the plot he acts in accordance with the best

3. "A discourse . . . includes all these items, aesthetic, semantic, ideological, social. . . . It is to be distinguished from point of view in that the latter is attached to a particular character or authorial position, while a discourse stretches across a text through a variety of different articulations of which character is only one; it need not be coherent but can be broken by a number of shorter or longer gaps or silences." Christine Gedhill, in E. Ann Kaplan, ed., *Women in Film Noir*, (London: British Film Institute, 1978), p. 13. I have used the term in a similar sense here and in a related article "Strick's Adaptation of Joyce's *A Portrait of the Artist*: Discourse and Containing Discourse," in Conger and Welsch, eds., *Narrative Strategies* (Macomb: Western Illinois University Press, 1981). A discourse is a configuration of Signs. Containing discourse is a discourse that overdetermines the narrative. The process of discourse is rhetoric as the process of narrative is diegesis.

values of the class to which he aspires, cultural values that the dominant class itself, in its decadence, regards as merely convenient mystifications. However the actions that are the cause of his undoing redeem him in our eyes. We are guided to a sense of pathos, a kind of affirmation.

To create an adaptation that conveys the director's vision, Thackeray's original text has been both compressed and expanded. Kubrick has altered the narrative of the novel in at least four significant respects:

He has made a large number of deletions. Often historical details and personages have been excised from the original, journalistic details and documentary incidents that would have overly particularized the story, fixed it immoveably in the eighteenth century. The result is a more universal parable.

Significant scenes have been added to the film. For example: Barry's son Bryan's birthday party and procession and later, set in parallel, Bryan's funeral procession; the climactic duel between Barry and his stepson Lord Bullingdon (the *peripety* of the film); the concluding scenes in which Lady Lyndon (Marisa Berenson) hesitates, then seals Barry's fate, while Lord Bullingdon looks on, with mingled guilt and apprehension.

Equally important, a number of scenes have been focused by condensation. For example: Barry's courtship of Lady Lyndon is compressed and heightened in intensity (four chapters of word-play and intrigue are rendered in an intense scene only several minutes in duration); the scene in which Barry thrashes Lord Bullingdon for his impudence is, in the film, directly linked to Barry's loss of the peerage for which he has striven. (Kubrick fuses two incidents from the novel, the events and a letter that Lord Bullingdon subsequently writes before departing to America, and instead has Lord Hallam and Lord Neville Wendover, Barry's primary patrons, witness the brawl.)

These changes also alter the proportion of the narrative, shifting our attention to scenes in which Barry is a victim and hence more sympathetic. Although less than a tenth of Thackeray's novel is devoted to Barry's downfall, Kubrick devotes more than a quarter of the film to his "misfortune and distress." In Thackeray's text Barry encounters Lady Lyndon three quarters of the way through the narrative; however half the film is devoted to the consequences of Barry's marriage of convenience and rise in class.

Finally Kubrick, in adapting Thackeray's text, has made a significant alteration in point of view. Thackeray's novel is presented to the reader in the first person. The point of view is consistently ironic. For example if Barry Lyndon tell us "I assure you it was a very short time before I was a pretty fellow of the first class," we recognize that he doth insist too much. We read "I was always too much a man of honour and spirit to save a penny of Lady Lyndon's income," as a sign that he is, with scant honor, squandering the family fortune. Phrases like, "and I, as tipsy as a lord," are especially damning. In case we miss the point Thackeray provides footnotes: editorial commentary, or a few revealing facts that italicize the parody.

Although Kubrick has got rid of the first person narration and the authorial footnotes (the rhetorical signposts of Thackeray's text) neither the sequence of events nor the perspective of any one character is developed in the film as substitutes for Thackeray's indicators. The film is not a text but a performance, an experience. Kubrick guides our responses or establishes a discourse by other devices: the voice-over, which is not the same as commentary in the novel, because it coexists with an image and thus may modify it and/or be modified by it; the camera style (panoramic and ironic in the first half of the film, often scenic and affirmative in the latter half); the music (both ironic and affirmative). The totality of these visual and aural signs in their interrelation are at once both discourse and rhetoric: they subsume and define the narrative or any particular point of view within the narrative; they guide and define and generalize our responses to the action.

In the rest of this chapter I shall deal in turn with each of these elements in the film.

The voice-over is an integral part of the discourse of the film. An unidentified gentlemanly voice provides information to the audience on perhaps thirty occasions, providing the necessary information to bridge gaps between shifts of time or place and thus to

ensure hypotactic continuity. At times the voice-over simply reinforces or clarifies the primary message of the image (for example,
the criticism of the scenes of looting and pillage during the Seven
Years War). Often it provides ironic perspective upon the action
(the mocking future obituary read during Lord Lyndon's heart
attack). On two occasions the voice-over provides a kind of prolepsis,
giving significant information about future events (Bryan's death
and Barry's decline are foretold to heighten the tragedy), or
providing advance information that guides our sympathy in relation
to future dramatic conflicts (by letting us know early in the film that
Lord Bullingdon is overly attached to his mother or that Barry is
justified in perceiving malice in Bullingdon's attitude toward him,
the voice-over prepares us to side with Barry in his conflict with
Bullingdon later in the film).[4]

Although the speaker is often a reliable guide he is by no means
definitive. Often within a general orientation our sympathies momentarily shift from one character to another. Also, at times, the
ironic position of the voice-over is significantly negated by a
dramatic situation (Barry's brief wartime romance with the German
woman), or by the intensity of the music and the camera style
(Barry's first view of Lady Lyndon in the Marienbad-like formal
garden), or by the beauty of the image.

The voice-over is only one element in a discourse that is especially
complex and heterogeneous, lifelike, but not without guidelines. In
the first half of the film there is an abundance of beautiful images,
images that are, however, incomplete signs. In this part of the film
the camera continually distances us from the image, imposing
perspective, increasing the detached tone of the voice-over. The
camera distances us in a double sense: we are placed at a physical
remove from the action and this occurs in a self-conscious way so
that the style of distancing soon in itself becomes a rhetorical signal.

At times we are given a distanced or ironic perspective on images
that appear to be replicas of eighteenth-century paintings—land-

---

4. The information defines Barry in a favorable light in contrast to the apparent
justice of Bullingdon's claim. Yet at the moment we receive the information
Bullingdon seems sympathetic, in part because he is a child without power or
capacity to do harm. This changes as the film unfolds: then our moral and emotional
sympathies converge.

scapes, family portraits, salon scenes, heroic military spectacles. The images often allude to paintings that would have been commissioned by wealthy patrons, and thus represent the dominant codes and ideals of the society: they portray people in the manner in which they would have wished to be seen. In the film they are demystified by the ironic discourse. In this way Kubrick situates a critique of his characters in a general critique of the culture in which they act out their roles.

Most often Kubrick distances us from the image, literally, by the repeated use of reverse zoom shots which begin in a close-up but then pull back gradually to include more and more of the natural or social landscape, the human figures now poignantly located within their setting and objective limitations. For example, early in the film, we see a line of British soldiers marching in drill formation across a landscape, proceeding in our direction. The camera gradually pulls back to include the crowd of Irish villagers gathered to watch the drill, then further back until we are perhaps a hundred yards behind the crowd who are watching the soldiers now further away in the distance. The telephoto lens renders the landscape behind the soldiers abstract and painterly. The military drill has become a static painterly image, the soldiers reduced to a minor element in the panorama. We observe a spectacle of puppets, some performers, other spectators, native Irish joined in a nonantagonistic dialectic with their British occupiers.

The duel between Barry and Captain Quinn in the early part of the film is photographed in a similar manner. We begin with a close-up of two duelling pistols being prepared for use. The camera then zooms back several hundred feet distancing the duel and the participants until they are minor figures in a panoramic landscape. The distancing camera (the reverse zooms, the panoramic long shots) objectifies the scene, reducing a passionate duel to an ironic and theatrical ritual. We soon learn that the duel was faked (Quinn only pretended to be shot so that Barry would flee to Dublin, leaving Nora to him). So much for honor, romance, and the gentlemanly code of duellists.

Kubrick's vision has been presented in a film language that borders on the absurd:

the . . . long shot, which, when it attempts to present something dramatically, hopelessly looks like a florid awkward phrase . . . a "theatrical" *mise-en-scene* . . . which . . . dooms itself. . . .[5]

I am cribbing the quote by Eisenstein on the long shot from an article I wrote in 1966 on absurdist space in Godard's *Pierrot le Fou*. In *Barry Lyndon*, as in *Pierrot le Fou*, a romantic narrative situated in a lush and romantic landscape is distanced and set in ironic perspective by the camera.[6]

There are many aspects of the camera style of *Barry Lyndon*, rhetorical signs that are part of the discourse: for example the direction of lateral movement within the frame. In the spatial conventions of reading, movement from left to right indicates progress, from right to left retrogression, reversion, going backward in time. Kubrick establishes analogous visual patterns in his film.

Barry's rise in the world is often signified by a line of motion from the left to the right side of the frame: Barry fires from left to right in his duel with Captain Quinn; he makes his first approach to Lady Lyndon in a similar manner (he enters the frame from the outside left and walks very slowly across the screen to her) and, the next morning, walks with her from the left across an aristocratic garden, the camera moving with them toward the horizon, open space, infinite prospect; on the day of his son's birthday celebration, Barry leads the lambs of Bryan's birthday cart in a procession, walking from the left across the frame.

The major scenes of Barry's decline are often structured parallel to the scenes of his rise, with the important distinction that now the line of motion is from the right to the left side of the screen. Where formerly he led Bryan's triumphant birthday procession Barry now follows behind Bryan's funeral cortege, walking slowly behind the hearse from the right to the left of the frame; where Barry fired triumphantly from left to right at Captain Quinn in his first duel, in his last he declines to fire, from right to left, at his stepson Lord Bullingdon, and is seriously wounded in return. In his final scene in

5. Sergei Eisenstein, *Film Form: Essays in Film Theory* (New York: Meridian, 1957), p. 250.
6. Michael Klein, "The Style of *Pierrot le Fou*," *Film Quarterly* (Spring, 1966), p. 48.

the film Barry exits across a courtyard, from right to left, estranged from Lady Lyndon, maimed and exiled.

The music is also an extremely important aspect of the discourse of the film. For the most part during the first half of the film it is a subordinate aspect of a complex and shifting ironic discourse, often the most ambiguous and therefore shifting aspect of the irony.

The ironic discourse ranges from affectionate undercutting to outright parody. There are certain moments when the music flows into the critical discourse without any ambiguity. For example Frederic the Great's *Hohenfriedberger March*, which is played over images of the Prussian army looting and pillaging. The music sounds gay and heroic but, given the extreme contrast between the sound and our sense of the scene, we reject the heroic implications of the music without reservation. Both the music and the image are perceived as negative. The critical vision is explicit and unqualified.

There are scenes similar in kind but different in degree in which the music fuses with a satiric trope, but the criticism is somewhat more complex, more detached, and implicit. For example Paisiello's *Cavatina* from his version of *Il Barbiere Di Siviglia*, which is juxtaposed to Barry's rise in class: Barry is a member of a "firm" of gamblers who operate in the decadent aristocratic resorts of Europe. Paisiello adapted his opera (in 1782) from Beaumarchais' play, which satirized the aristocracy of the *ancien regime* and heralded the rise of the innovative new classes. In *Barry Lyndon*, while at one level the music simply underscores the satire of the decadent aristocracy, at another level it serves as an ironic comment on Barry's aspirations, his class mobility, and thus by extension places Beaumarchais' democratic dream (in *Barry Lyndon* more a Gatsby quest for "life, liberty, and the pursuit of happiness" than "liberty, equality, and fraternity") in ironic perspective.

At other times in the film the discourse, although critical, is also somewhat ambiguous. Often in the early part of the film the music appears to be positive, although it is, in the final sense, subordinate to the general critical perspective. Yet even then it is not entirely lacking in appeal, in part because the surfaces of the images have a similar ambiguity. As a result there are moments in the film that in their mixed quality are an extraordinary imitation of life.

The clearest examples of this are the early scenes set in a lush Irish pastoral landscape, and accompanied by lyrical folk tunes: Barry's youthful romance with Nora Brady (who, however, is untrue); Barry's duel with Captain Quinn (formal, heroic, set in a beautiful landscape, but finally revealed to be a ruse). The tunes—*Women of Ireland, The Sea Maiden*—are parodied by the action and certainly are in the final sense ironic. Yet the beauty of the music and the images tugs against our objective assessment. Thus the Irish section of the film is at once critical and poignant.

In the latter half of the film there is significant change in the discourse. The music (especially Schubert's *Piano Trio in E* and Handel's *Sarabande*) engages our sympathy with minimal qualification; and at the same time the camera style shifts from distancing to engaging our sympathy. When these two elements fuse there is a shift from irony to pathos and tragedy. Let me briefly illustrate this with respect to several scenes in the latter part of the film.

When Barry first sees Lady Lyndon, the basic stylistic pattern of the film is inverted. We are not distanced from the scene by a reverse zoom or a long shot. Instead, for the first time, the camera zooms in a considerable distance without interruption, bringing us close to the beautiful object of Barry's attention. The scene is orchestrated by Schubert's romantic music. First a forceful and insistent piano trill—which heightens our awareness. Then the main theme, as the camera slowly moves toward Lady Lyndon. The music dramatically shifts into a major key when she comes into focus.

During the funeral of Barry's beloved child Bryan, both the music, the augmented chords of Handel's *Sarabande*, and the camera, engage our sympathy. The camera is placed close to the funeral procession. Bryan's white casket, drawn on a plumed carriage by harnessed lambs, the mourners, Barry and Lady Lyndon in deep black, move toward the camera eye until they fill the frame. Everything in the image is foregrounded in intense whites and blacks. Handel's music, familiar from being heard at repeated intervals throughout the film, is now transformed, punctuated by funeral drums, into a motif of fate. It evokes pathos and empathy. And as the scene draws to a close the sound of the funeral *Sarabande* merges with the words of the burial service ("We brought nothing into this world, and it is certain we can carry nothing out"), words that place Barry's life in a larger perspective, a perspective that Kubrick later echoes in secular form in the text of the epilogue with which the film concludes.[7]

Another example of the sympathetic (as opposed to distanced) mode in the film is the scene which occurs at the climax of Barry's attempt to secure a peerage. We are underdistanced by the discourse during this pivotal scene: Barry's public thrashing of Lord Bullingdon and consequent loss of the peerage he has sought in order to secure the tenure of his position. Lord Hallam and Lord Wendover, Barry's patrons, are present at a concert at Castle Hackton when Lord Bullingdon launches a verbal attack on his stepfather. The music (Bach's *Concerto for Two Harpsichords and Orchestra*) provides a gracious setting for Lord Bullingdon's oedipal trantrum: "Madam . . . it is not only the lowness of his birth and the general brutality of his manners which disgust me, but the shameful nature of his conduct towards your Ladyship." Lady Lyndon rebukes Lord Bullingdon and flees the room in distress. Barry, enraged, thrashes his stepson, venting all the contradictions of his situation in a cathartic, violent outburst. In an attempt to preserve decorum (an ideal of the society to which he aspires), Barry violates the code of that society, reveals his common origins, and thereafter is shunned and ruined.

The scene is photographed close-up by a hand-held camera that draws us into Barry's violence, draws us into the chaos of his situation while compressing the space so that there are no vistas of escape. A brief close-up of Lord Hallam's shocked expression signifies Barry's future ruin. Then Kubrick cuts to Barry standing alone on a stone terrace of the castle. The camera pulls back until he all but vanishes in the aristocratic tableau. His isolation is underscored by the melancholic chords of Vivaldi's *Cello Concerto in E-Minor.*

The camera and music further engage our sympathy in the final

7. The burial service is spoken by Reverend Runt, a satirical character for the most part of the film. However the discourse subsumes the traits of any given character, appropriates the ethic of the religious text and transforms it into a secular judgment. It is restated in secular form in the epilogue: all the historical (eighteenth-century) characters, rich and poor alike, are now dead, whatever their aspirations.

Barry Lyndon 1976. The contradictions between Barry (Ryan O'Neal) and
Lord Bullingdon (Leon Vitall) explode in Kubrick's parable about the
modern condition. (Photo courtesy of the Museum of Modern Art).

scenes of the film. Barry's duel with Lord Bullingdon (again the images are colored by the *Sarabande*) is rendered in a style antithetical to the distanced presentation of his duel with Captain Quinn in the opening of the film. In both scenes the establishing shot is identical: a close-up of the pistols. However in this final duel we are not distanced by a long zoom away from the guns. Instead, Kubrick renders the action by a hypotactic montage of close-ups, two-shots, and middle-distance shots that heighten the intensity. The setting, a ruined church, a closed and confining place in all respects unlike the open vistas of the Irish landscape that framed the first duel, is a sign of Barry's limited options.

As the duel begins Bullingdon's second asks, "Mr. Lyndon, do you know the rules?" Barry abides by the highest ideals of the code of the society he has aspired to enter. He declines to fire at Bullingdon after his stepson's pistol accidentally discharges. Lord Bullingdon, a secure member of the dominant class, interprets the rules of the game from his own perspective, and declaring he has not "received satisfaction" refuses to waive his second shot and conclude the duel. He fires again and Barry is maimed and ousted.

The final moments of the film are underscored by the insistently sweet and forward-thrusting piano trio that accompanied Barry's romance with Lady Lyndon and his rise in fortune. The irony here is a source of pathos. Barry exits, maimed, lonely, and baffled. Lady Lyndon hesitates for a second (her gesture is doubled by a bass tremolo) before blankly signing a document that seals Barry's fate. The epilogue tells us that all are equal in the grave. The *Sarabande* tolls.

In the final sense, the film unlike the novel has been a performance, one in which our sympathy has been distanced then engaged. We have been guided by the discourse to evaluate the characters and events in the film, signs that are insufficient when abstracted from the larger social and cultural configuration. The camera and the music, far from being extrinsic, have been essential—the source of consciousness, empathy, and value.

For the most part, nineteenth-century novelists defined meaning or truth in their fictive worlds, and by extension in the world of the times, primarily through plot, character, or direct address to the reader, it normally being clear whether the implied author or a significant character should be viewed as authoritative or ironic. In transposing Thackeray's novel into film, Kubrick shifted primacy away from these traditional literary elements, not to their dramatic counterparts in traditional film narrative but to other rhetorical and expressive cinematic equivalents.

The resulting discourse contains the action in a historical and cultural perspective and guides us to respond with irony or empathy. A double vision is established: Barry as a figure of modern alienation; Barry as an eighteenth-century character, a secondary aspect given the minimalist narrative. As a result the film adaptation precludes the danger of being perceived as a mere period piece or literal transposition of the original and speaks successfully to the modern audience. The discourse in placing the action in a larger perspective makes an esthetic and moral claim: esthetic because it appropriates the mantle of authority of the nineteenth-century author in twentieth-century cinematic terms; moral because like the work of the best nineteenth-century authors it affords insight into aspects of the human condition in bourgeois society.

Vanity Fair (1847), W. M. Thackeray

Rouben Mamoulian, 1935: Becky Sharp

Becky Sharp Takes Over

NOEL CARROLL

Becky Sharp is a film that warrants a place in world almanacs; it was the first feature-length movie to be shot completely in three-color Technicolor. Unlike other historic firsts of the medium, such as *The Jazz Singer*, *Becky Sharp* (1935) is not marred by the awkwardness of an experiment. Its use of color is various and assured. Its director, Rouben Mamoulian, had already completed seven films. He was brought onto the project in January, 1935, after the film's original director, Lowell Sherman, died while just beginning work on the production.[1]

Ostensibly the film is based on Langdon Mitchell's 1899 stage adaptation of W. M. Thackeray's *Vanity Fair*.[2] But examination of Mitchell's play quickly reveals that scriptwriter Francis Edward Faragoh, though using some of Mitchell's lines and ideas, returned to Thackeray's *Vanity Fair*, reinstating many of the scenes that the play had deleted: this is understandable since the pace of a 1930s film allowed for far more scene changes than a play did. The film owes more to Thackeray than to Mitchell and is rather an adaptation of the novel than of the play.

1. Tom Milne, *Mamoulian* (Bloomington: Indiana University Press, 1969), p. 91.
2. Mitchell's play is available in *Monte Cristo and Other Plays*, ed. by J. B. Rusak (Princeton, N. J.: Princeton University Press, 1941)

108

Adaptation

Thackeray's *Vanity Fair* (1847) is a novel on a scale and of a style that present imposing problems for film adaptation. Not only does it run over six hundred tightly printed pages of packed incident, but its emphasis is on comedy of manners rather than on visual description. The prospects for condensing all its dramatic (often digressive) details within the time frame of a standard-length feature film seem hopeless. *Becky Sharp* is only eighty-four minutes long. Obviously it involves a simplification of *Vanity Fair*. The important questions that this process of adaptation raises are: What is the nature of each of the major simplifications in the start in the film adaptation? Are the kinds of simplifications we find systematic? And, if they are systematic, what do they imply about the thematic, commercial, and ideological stance of the film?

A significant index of the type of simplication favored in *Becky Sharp* is the title itself. The move from *Vanity Fair: A Novel without a Hero* to *Becky Sharp* suggests that the novel without a hero has become a film with a heroine. Becky is certainly a prominent figure in the book, indeed the most prominent. But she appears only intermittently. She is first among a cast of equals, which includes Amelia, Dobbin, the elder Osborne, and others. In the film, Becky, played by Miriam Hopkins, is the central character, putting in an appearance in almost every scene and dominating most of them. The other characters are uniformly secondary and vaguely defined. If some strike us as particularly vivid, it is because several of the actors have produced witty, eccentric character studies. Generally, attention is focused on Becky and her motives, plans, attitudes, and adventures. In this respect the film is individualistic, rooted in a central character with whom the audience is invited to identify, whereas in Thackeray there are numerous characters, each of whom makes a play for our identification at different times. The use of shifting identification is part of what can be called Thackeray's perspectivism—his ability to represent situations from numerous points of view. By anchoring the film in Becky, not only is the ambiguity and complexity of the original reduced, but Becky and her associated values gain added rhetorical power since they are no longer in a context where alternative values seriously challenge them.

When Thackeray called his book *Vanity Fair*, the allusion to Bunyan marked it as a piece of social criticism. *Becky Sharp* is a title that befits the story of an individual. The novel is not only a description of social manners but of a social system. Through its wheel-of-fortune structure, it produces a multitude of repetitions and variations that suggest the relation of individual behavior and major narrative events to an underlying social system in which money and rank are coveted above all else. The narrative structure requires the reader to engage in a constant process of comparison and contrast that impresses us again and again with the recognition that what most people say and do in *Vanity Fair* is predicated on what they believe they stand to gain or lose in terms of wealth and prestige.

Becky's marriage to Rawdon Crawley and Amelia's marriage to George Osborne both meet strong opposition because both women are penniless. These marriages are implicitly contrasted to the unquestioned suits of George Osborne's sister and Rawdon Crawley's brother which are sanctioned by large dowries. Society's reaction to Amelia once she regains guardianship of little Georgy (the legatee of his grandfather's estate) contrasts with the way she was ignored when impoverished.

The structure of repetition and variation enables Thackeray to generalize his social criticism. He consistently treats his characters as admixtures of good and bad qualities while reserving the brunt of his moral judgment for the social system as a whole. What is monstrous about Becky and George Osborne, for instance, becomes intelligible within the context of the acquisitive society that spawns and nurtures them. The novelist is less concerned with the notion of individual villains as such than with the social institutions that produce them.

Becky Sharp, in the main, omits the comparative structure of *Vanity Fair* and in so doing brackets not only Thackeray's specific social criticisms, which admittedly by 1935 were out of date, but, more importantly, abandons the systematic viewpoint with which any serious social criticism begins. The result is that Becky's roguishness, or what remains of it in the film, is presented as an individual character trait rather than as the product of a social system. Likewise, the hypocrisy and vanity that typify so many of the characters are proposed as personal vices rather than as consequences of social ills.

The way the adaptation simplifies *Vanity Fair* is to recast its social criticism as questions of individual morality. Some characters are stupid, like Miss Julia Crawley, and some are willful, like Becky. But why the characters are as they are is ignored. The adaptation could have been otherwise. Perhaps, in the fashion of *Wuthering Heights* (the film), only half of the story could have been told, keeping the comparative structure intact. But since that is not how it was made, we must try to find some motive for the version we have. What is missing is Thackeray's emphasis on the ways that personal habits, attitudes, and decisions are determined by larger social forces. Note how the relation between parents and children is absent in the film. Mr. and Mrs. Sedley and Mr. Osborne, for example, have disappeared. This removes the action from the context of a social process. In *Becky Sharp* the fictional society is a collection of individuals, not a function of social institutions like the family. This, it seems to me, indicates part of the ideology of the film. In the mid-1930s *Becky Sharp* projects a view of society which obscures the potential for systematic social criticism in favor of a conception of the social world as fundamentally individualistic. Insofar as fictions can act as models for thinking about human events, *Becky Sharp*, unlike *Vanity Fair*, offers its audience history as a spectacle of individual effort, achievement, vice, and virtue. Although this was probably not the conscious intention of any of the makers of the film, the approach to society embodied in *Becky Sharp* does function to deflect and deny the possibility of social criticism in a way quite common in Hollywood film, and at a time when the need for systematic social criticism had particular urgency.

The adaptation also forgets several of Becky's worst deeds. In the novel Thackeray strongly suggests that Becky kills Joseph Sedley for his money, while in the film they seem destined to remain together playfully ever after. In the novel there is every indication that Becky conspires with Lord Steyne (Sir Cedric Hardwicke) in Rawdon's (Alan Mowbray) arrest so that the two can spend the evening together; nor, in the novel, does this seem to be their first tryst. But in the film, Steyne alone is responsible for the attempted arrest. Moreover, Becky's part is scripted to suggest that she hopes to charm her way out of Steyne's embrace. She is presented as a wife who is playing with fire but who is committed to staying out of the flame. In a way, her rendezvous with Steyne is connected with her dedication to Rawdon since it is the only way she can get the five hundred pounds that he needs. She is visibly and audibly depressed by her predicament. Listen to how her singing changes when Steyne places the money in her lap. And she attempts to turn the table banter about wolves and sheep into a plea for Steyne to release her from her promises. Not only is she not an adulteress, but she is working hard to avoid becoming one. This is not Thackeray's Becky but one laundered for an upright family audience.

In the novel, Thackeray spends a great deal of time establishing that Becky is a horrible mother. Her son hates her and her behavior is contrasted incisively with Rawdon's, Lady Jane's, and Amelia's (Frances Dee) attitudes toward parenthood. Becky only pays attention to her son when she believes it will impress people she is interested in winning over. But the whole mother/son relationship is dropped from the film. This is part of the overall tendency of the film to deemphasize Becky's ruthlessness. The omission of the murder, of Becky's callousness toward her child, and of her calculating infidelity makes her an easier character to identify with. Identification is basically a matter of empathy, grounded in an audience's recognition of the moral values that it shares with the characters. For an American family-oriented audience to identify with Becky, it was imperative to excise her crimes against the family, specifically her adultery and inattention to her son. What remains of her character is positive moral virtue—intelligence, drive, wit, and the joy of living. In Thackeray, Becky, as the symbol of selfishness in an acquisitive society, is the enemy of the family. But in the film, her selfish drive is framed in a way that the threat to the family (which would also constitute a threat to the audience) is hidden. This suppression does not merely soften Thackeray's point but rather negates it by making the attractiveness of selfishness stand out, without suggesting that it also has more destructive effects.

In the film, Becky's character is tinged with a blatant streak of dishonesty which may appear as a negative moral quality. Yet, for a 1930s audience, much of Becky's larceny may be excused because Becky is presented as a class heroine. Becky lies and cheats, but to a certain extent this is justified as the only means a member of an underprivileged class has for dealing with an unjust society that respects only money and rank, merit notwithstanding. The film begins with Becky's deflating Miss Pinkerton, whose pomposity marks her as extravagantly upperclass, ridiculous, and hypocritical. Note that the film lacks the Miss Jemima episode, thereby muting Becky's propensity toward cruelty. Instead, the image is of a brazen, clever, lower-class girl unafraid of her oppressively self-satisfied "betters." Characters like Miss Crawley, Pitt Crawley, and Joseph Sedley's offscreen parents similarly suggest that to a degree Becky's chicaneries are exculpable in the light of the exigencies of the conflict between rich and poor. Becky's loaded dice and thirst for success are chided within the film and duly punished. But these transgressions are not nearly as extreme as those in the book, and Becky remains essentially an exemplary figure, an emblem for members of aspiring social classes.

Previously it was claimed that the film's removal of Thackeray's comparative structures presents the values associated with Becky almost uncritically and, therefore, with more rhetorical seductiveness. What are those values? Clearly they are indomitable drive, the ability to "live by one's wits," and selfishness. As a class heroine, Becky gives value to enterprise and individualism. By downplaying her ruthlessness and by not contrasting her with fully developed moral alternatives, like Dobbin, the film effectively endorses her *modus vivendi*. Acquisitive self-interested individualism, exactly what Thackeray disdained, is presented as a positive moral virtue. More than that—as a role model for members of aspiring classes, Becky exemplified the attractiveness of individualism at a time in American history when individualism implied individualism-rather-than-collectivism. Needless to say, collectivism has nothing to do with *Vanity Fair*. But it was an issue that was relevant in the 1930s. And in this context it is possible for us to assess the unity of the simplifications in *Becky Sharp* as an ideological projection of a class heroine for a family-oriented audience—a heroine who celebrates spirited, self-interested individualism as the model for behavior in the conflict between rich and poor.

Stylization

As a Hollywood film of the mid-1930s, *Becky Sharp* is a very stylish production employing visual symbolism, clever scene transitions, a great deal of camera movement, and a deft manipulation of color. Some of this stylization is in the service of adapting *Vanity Fair*, whereas other elements are independent of the task of adaptation and contribute to the effect of the film as film.

Undoubtedly, Mamoulian's background in theater, as well as that of production designer Robert Edmond Jones,[3] are major factors behind the graceful, creative handling of color throughout the film. The range of ways color is used is quite rich. It directs attention—at Lady Richmond's ball our eyes jump ahead to the cluster of red uniforms from which Becky will emerge. It builds decorative patterns—the reds and the alterations of blacks and whites at the ball. At other times, it formally stresses dramatic contrasts—Becky in blue versus Amelia in pink; or it makes metaphoric comments— Miss Pinkerton costumed in the colors of Mademoiselle Harlequin. In the often cited flight from Lady Richmond's ball, color is coordinated with montage in order to express and release mounting tension, while on a purely formal level Mamoulian often composes medium long shots of British soldiers in which arresting, almost abstract, designs of redcoats leap at the spectator. Though these uses of color were not unprecedented in theater, their appearance in this first film of its kind established a high standard of sophistication for those who were to follow in Mamoulian's footsteps.

One key theme in the visual adaptation of *Vanity Fair* is that of theater, and especially acting. A central concept in Thackeray's vision of *Vanity Fair* is "artifice," a word he repeats innumerable times. In the film, this notion is visualized through constant references to theater. Throughout, there is a recurring use of

3. For information on Jones see *The Theater of Robert Edmond Jones*, ed. by Ralph Pendleton (Middletown, Conn.: Wesleyan University Press, 1958). Interestingly, Jones designed the sets for a production of Mitchell's *Vanity Fair* during the 1928-29 theater season.

drapery as an allusion to theater curtains. The action begins with the girls at Miss Pinkerton's school opening a curtain—the same curtain that figures prominently in the series of shots in which Becky hurls the *Dictionary* at the Grand Dame. Becky hangs on the blue satin drapery at the end of Lady Richmond's ball like a nineteenth-century diva. And in the scenes of the midnight dinner with Steyne and its discovery by Rawdon, the silken, diaphanous drapes at the entrance of the boudoir are stressed again and again. The curtains are a synecdoche for theater, which in turn stands for artifice and illusion—the hallmarks of Thackeray's *Vanity Fair*.

The theme of theater is also evoked in terms of overt acting, especially on the part of Miriam Hopkins as Becky. Thackeray suggests acting as a central metaphor for Becky in a number of ways. Becky's mother was an actress; Becky's ability to charm is based in large measure on her ability as a mime (as well as a singer, a musician, and an actress); and she briefly becomes a professional actress when her amateur standing in society fails her. Thackeray associates Becky with the arts of illusion, among which acting is her forte. Mamoulian takes the metaphor of Becky as actress and makes it the basis of Hopkins's role, directing her to adopt a very theatrical style when she is involved in deceiving other characters. Kneeling next to the trunk with plaintive, outstretched hands when defending her mother's memory to Rawdon's aunt is one of the many examples in the film of intentional overacting. This is meant to signal to the audience that Becky is playing a part and to represent her as an "actress" in the moral sense of the word.

Throughout, Mamoulian is careful to use Hopkins's gestures so that they convey rich connotations. She is a seductress as demonstrated by the almost supine positions she strikes when talking to men (for example in the couch scene with Joseph Sedley). Becky is as determined and as disciplined as a soldier in her quest for success—see how she marches to the balcony, strutting to the beat of drums at the end of the Waterloo sequence. Mamoulian repeatedly uses the hurling of objects as an act of defiance—including books, flowers, and a scrub brush—as a visual epithet for Becky's proud, rebellious mode of being-in-the-world. But of all the gestural symbolism, that of Becky's discernible acting is the most important. Other characters also display this tendency to a certain extent, and

Becky Sharp (1935). Miriam Hopkins as the heroine of Thackeray's *Vanity Fair* drives a good bargain. Throughout, Mamoulian uses her gestures to convey rich connotations. (Photo courtesy of the Museum of Modern Art)

Mamoulian directs some scenes so that the characters make what look like stage entrances and exits that are quotations of theater, rather than merely stagey, due to camera movements that constantly reframe the action.

The overriding significance of the metaphor of acting in the film is borne out by the addition of the scene of Becky's ill-fated performance, which is only a line in the book and which does not appear in the play at all. At one level this scene functions to complete the previous one since it fulfills Becky's dolorous prediction that "they'll laugh at me." This, of course, is what happens during the performance. Symbolically, Becky's failure on the stage also stands for the temporary dislocation of her ability to influence other people by acting. But that failure is only momentary, and in the final scenes—with wringing hands and feigned faints of virtually pantomimic dimensions—Becky is able to wrap Pitt Crawley and Lady Jane around her little finger. We leave Becky, the actress, triumphant.

Related to but distinguishable from the emphasis on theatrical acting is the use of fast transitions in character throughout the film. We see Becky contemptuously throw Joseph's rose away, while in the next shot she is graciously accepting another one from him and vowing that she presses all his flowers. The transition from crying to laughing, often marked by a cut, is an important motif; examples include Becky's exit from Miss Crawley's sitting room and the cutting that links Becky's interview with Dobbin to the one with Pitt. Becky changes her attitude with breathtaking speed. In the Waterloo sequence Becky moves from contempt for George, love for Rawdon, financial opportunism with Joseph, sympathy for the soldiers, casual compliance with Steyne, and hunger in the spate of a few minutes. The inconstancy of her character, her changeability, communicates her insincerity by representing her as an actress through contrast, that is, by juxtaposing her many different roles one on top of the other. This fast character transition captures part of the flavor of the novel where in one paragraph, as in the description of the early history of Becky's acquaintance with Miss Pinkerton and Jemima, Thackeray is able to change our moral perspective on Becky three or four times. Of course, in the film we are never completely appalled by what Becky does. However, her chameleonlike behavior does retain a residue of Thackeray's penchant for shifting, contradictory perspectives while at the same time supporting the central portrayal of Becky as the consummate actress.

Becky Sharp is an example of 1930s stylishness. The film employs a great deal of symbolism. Objects are given added meaning in order to make visual comments on characters and actions. The translucent dressing screen between Becky and Amelia, for instance, not only marks the contrast between the two, but Amelia, in silhouette, recalls a figure on a piece of bone china, thereby evoking connotations of refinement. At the same time, the screen also functions as a symbol of Amelia's blindness since George and Becky are flirting on the other side. The scrubwoman's brush is made to stand for the destiny of an adventuress so that when Becky hurls it out the door, the act visually expresses Becky's rejection of a fate similar to the char's. The book that beans Pitt at the end of the film recalls the one flung at Pinkerton (and, by extension, at her euphuistic elocution) so that the objects and actions become emblems of the refusal to be taken in by hypocrisy.

Mamoulian's treatment of objects is comparable to what is called, in another context, the Lubitsch touch—a talent for visual expression by means by the symbolic use of objects. The most elaborate example of this involves the exchange of flowers. The cut between Becky spurning and then accepting Joseph's roses signals her duplicity. Becky's compact with Steyne is sealed by the exchange of a flower which coincides with the exchange of the five hundred pounds—the passage of the flower amounting to a metaphor for prostitution. Finally, Becky's darkest hour, her disastrous performance, is represented by a battle of bouquets with Becky and the audience hostilely lobbing flowers back and forth. In each instance, an exchange of flowers indicates the state of Becky's fortunes.

The tendency toward visual symbolism extends to every aspect of the film. For example, camera movement at times functions metaphorically: the opening pans between Becky and Amelia present the opposite sides of the hall as spatial symbols of class. Mamoulian uses dissolves not only to make temporal transitions but to mount metaphoric asides. Through superimposition, the popular political metaphor of a dictator's specter or shadow falling over the land is literalized when Napoleon's shadow lingers and then fades out over the image of Lady Richmond's ball.[4] In terms of editing, Mamoulian transforms the flight from the ball into a symbol of frenzy by building the montage to the shot where the billowing red cloaks of the hussars predominate, provoking a chain of associations of excitement as the reds flap in the wind.

Besides symbols, Mamoulian uses emphatic juxtapositions, often achieved through editing, to make cinematic statements. Becky's and Amelia's reactions to Napoleon's escape are sharply contrasted in a lightning cut. Likewise, the aftermath of Waterloo is presented in terms of two rhyming dollies-back—the first from George's gravestone and the second at Becky's festive table. The similarity in the mode of cinematic articulation in these shots underscores the comparative disparity of the consequences of the war for honest Amelia versus ambitious Becky.

Becky Sharp, despite its theatrical trappings, is a very "cinematic" film: Mamoulian often underlines basic themes of the plot visually, rather than relying exclusively on their outright statement in the dialogue. By using the term "cinematic," however, I do not mean to argue that the film has a specific, transhistorical, quality-making feature that renders any film of any period good. Rather I mean that inscribed in *Becky Sharp* is an esthetic stance that is extremely relevant to films of the 1930s, when the advent of sound raised the danger of films that merely reproduced (or recorded) plays. Against this threat, directors like Mamoulian employed assertive visual stylization as a means of defending what they took to be the integrity of the film medium. *Becky Sharp* is a cinematic film by the standards of 1930s filmmaking; as such it bears the traces of an esthetic proclivity for strong visual stylization as an attempted hedge against canned theater.

Becky Sharp is not only very expressive visually; it also strives to be simply visual wherever possible. Mamoulian consistently dollies in and out of many of the talkier scenes not only to emphasize certain lines of dialogue but to inject some dynamism into the otherwise static theatricality. One can also see the clever scene transitions—the dissolve from the picture of the Prince Regent to the Prince in the flesh, or the tilt from the auction notice to the

4. In both the novel and the film, there are suggestions that Becky is to be understood as somewhat "Napoleonic."

playbill—as gestures that stress cinematic articulation as part of a commitment to the esthetic of film as film. Of course, to the eyes of a 1950s or 1960s filmviewer, whose prejudices about what is cinematic lean more towards realism, these effects may appear quite contrived. But in the 1930s, when the memory of the international style of silent film was tantamount to a yearning for a lost golden age, Mamoulian's stylization counted as an attempt to remain true to the medium through visual assertiveness.

At the same time, the artifice and stylization in which the film luxuriates has a holistic expressive effect on the audience. Its visual grace, wit, contrivance, and opulence appropriately correspond at the level of form to properties we associate with the *haute monde* the film represents. Like Lubitsch's *Trouble in Paradise*, there seems to be a fitting correlation between the panache, cleverness, and taste for splendor of both director and heroine. Becky's élan, for better or worse, is seductively incarnated in an "artful" cinematic idiom.

A Scrooge for All Seasons

LESTER J. KEYSER

When A *Christmas Carol* began its holiday run in New York City in 1951, the film played in Rockefeller Center, but not on the big screen of Radio City Music Hall. Instead, this black and white British import opened at the Guild Theatre, a small house memorable mostly for newsreels and other serious documentary works. American audiences did not flock to A *Christmas Carol*, and the reviewers were far from charitable in their assessment of this holiday fare from England. *Variety* sternly warned exhibitors that A *Christmas Carol* had only "a slight chance in the U.S. market," because it was "too grim for kiddies, too dull for adults," while Bosley Crowther of the *New York Times* found the film "spooky and somber . . . a bit on the overpowering side," and Otis L. Guernsey of the New York *Herald Tribune* judged the whole production "not quite on key."[1] Interestingly, all these critics acknowledged that director Brian Desmond Hurst and writer Noel Langley had been most faithful to their source, Dickens's most popular work, and they might well have concurred with Howard Thompson's later assessment that while the film may not be the generally accepted *Carol*, "It may be exactly what Dickens had in mind."[2]

1. *Variety*, 29 Nov. 1951; *New York Times*, 29 Nov. 1951; *Herald Tribune*, 29 Nov. 1951.

2. Howard Thompson, *The New York Times Guide to Movies on Television* (Chicago: Quadrangle Press, 1970), p. 47.

Writer Noel Langley and director Brian Desmond Hurst were just the sort of independent artists who would worry about preserving the spirit of Dickens in their cinematic adaptation. Both had worked in Hollywood, become disillusioned, and left, by choice, to do more intellectually challenging productions in England. Langley, originally a South African and a noted stage actor and radio announcer, had coauthored the screenplay for *The Wizard of Oz* and written *Ivanhoe, Florian,* and *Maytime.* Yet, as he told William Glynne-Jones in a syndicated interview, Hollywood "kicked the blazes out of me. They made me lose confidence. But they taught me my job. Now I can take it—and Hollywood—on my own terms." Langley's own terms included repatriation to England, where he threw himself into nationalistic projects, including *A Christmas Carol;* then *Pickwick Papers* (1952), which he also directed; and *Trio,* based on stories by W. Somerset Maugham. Langley's interest in Dickens was intense, and he told Mr. Glynne-Jones he did a lot of research on the author and his epoch, all of which convinced him that Dickens was a "fine commercial writer," who might, if he were alive today, have "cheerfully" adapted his own works for the screen.[3]

Langley's collaborator and friend, Brian Desmond Hurst, an Irishman who began his career as a painter but soon found himself working as a director in Hollywood, also rejected the California studios in favor of England. The two of them worked together on *Tom Brown's Schooldays* the same year they completed *A Christmas Carol.* Hurst always remained an artist by temperament, however, and many of his films, notably *Simba, Dangerous Exile, and The Playboy of the Western World,* are criticized for pictorialism and a static style. To prepare for *A Christmas Carol,* Hurst spent a great deal of time studying Victorian illustrators and especially *Punch* cartoonist John Leech, who did magnificent color plates for the first edition of *A Christmas Carol* (1843).

Leech's "look" is everywhere in this film, and it is no wonder that when Mrs. Alice Waley, a granddaughter of Charles Dickens, visited the set she declared "it seemed as if Leech's original and lovely

---

3.   The text of this interview is part of the Noel Langley file at the Lincoln Center Library for the Performing Arts, a research division of the New York Public Library

illustrations had come to life before my eyes."[4] Proof of Mrs. Waley's contention might be found in a consideration of the rare illustrations and sketches recently published by Michael Patrick Hearn as part of his laudable paperback, *The Annotated Christmas Carol*.[5] Pen sketches by Arthur Rackham, Phiz, Robert Seymour, and George Cruikshank obviously influenced Brian Desmond Hurst; and several landscapes of Clarkson Stanfield are carefully recreated in the film. The most striking influence of all, however, can be found in a comparison of John Leech's preliminary pencil and wash drawings with the composition and lighting of the film; Leech's preliminary sketches actually look like part of the story board for the film.

Director Hurst seems mesmerized by Victoriana in *A Christmas Carol*. His camera lovingly recreates the hustle and bustle of street scenes, the cold blustery snows of Christmas, the exciting dances, the bewitching shops, and the horrors of the Victorian underworld. One of the most chilling sequences in the film pictures the rag and bottle shop of Old Joe, a dark, gloomy, suffocating place reminiscent of Mr. Krook's shop in *Bleak House*. The rag and bottle shop is crowded with suffering children and street urchins, as the scrofulous merchants and avaricious customers coldly tally Scrooge's belongings. Even for seemingly mundane scenes of Scrooge at work, director Hurst demanded that the actual Royal Exchange be used as a backdrop. Such a request was unprecedented, and *A Christmas Carol* became the first movie ever filmed there, and only after insurance for five million pounds was posted.

Despite this large insurance policy, Hurst and his crew lacked the financial and technical resources to mount extensive special effects, so they frequently had to rely on clichéd transitional devices like twirling hour glasses, falling leaves, and ever thickening snow to suggest the convoluted chronology of Dickens's short fable, an odyssey in time often compared to Wells's *The Time Machine*. Hurst and his crew do manage, nevertheless, to be faithful to the tone, point of view, and themes that Dickens worked feverishly for

4. Quoted in the pressbook for the American release of *A Christmas Carol*.

5. Michael Patrick Hearn, *The Annotated Christmas Carol* by Charles Dickens (New York: Avon Books, 1976). Subsequent quotations from the text are from this facsimile edition.

six weeks to establish in this, his first major Christmas tale. If Dickens had, in large measure, written to remind his countrymen of the true meaning of Christmas and of the importance of simple joys in a complex time, Hurst and his crew remind their audience of the true meaning of Dickens's ghost story, emphasizing its origins as a gothic morality tale. The shadows of death so prominent in their filmic version echo Dickens's central insight that Christmas is the only time "when men and women seem by one consent to open their shut-up hearts freely, and to think of people below them as if they really were fellow-passengers to the grave, and not another race of creatures bound on other journeys" (p. 63).

Frequently this fidelity to the tone and atmosphere of the original tale pays off handsomely for director Hurst. Some of the finest footage in *A Christmas Carol* takes place on Hurst's recreation of one of the most famous staircases in all literature, the stairs to Scrooge's bedroom. Dickens's narrator was very taken by that stairway, its width, its darkness, and its echoes of the grave: "I meant to say you might have got a hearse up that staircase, and taken it broadwise with the splinter bar towards the wall, and the door towards the balustrade, and done it easy. There was plenty of width for that, and room to spare, which is perhaps the reason why Scrooge thought he saw a locomotive hearse going on before him in the gloom" (pp. 71-72). Brian Desmond Hurst creates much of the funereal and horrific in these dark stairs, which he introduces in dramatic high-angle shot, with his overhead camera placed to emphasize their length and width. Careful lighting forms sharp vertical shadows as Scrooge slowly ascends the stairs, and the camera tracks ever closer to him as he forms his familiar curse, a somewhat quavering "humbug." After Scrooge's reformation, Hurst returns to these steps, as Scrooge tries to quiet his frightened housekeeper; this time the stairs are well lighted and presented in an eye-level medium close-up so all the horror is dissipated.

Hurst's homage to Dickens actually begins in the very first shot of the film, a close-up of a shelf of leather-bound volumes all written by Dickens. From among *David Copperfield*, *A Tale of Two Cities*, *Great Expectations*, and *Pickwick Papers*, a hand chooses *A Christmas Carol*, at once establishing the primacy of the text, its exalted position as a classic, and the point of view of the film. Obviously, this is a fiction told by the noted author Charles Dickens, and all the words are his, especially those of the voice-over that begins the film with the death of Marley and ends it by bestowing Tiny Tim's blessing on us all. Recognizing the effectiveness of Dickens's dialogue, Noel Langley preserved as much of the original as possible. Dickens's contemporaries often observed that he heard the words in his own head before he wrote them down, testing them to see if they range true. The film *A Christmas Carol* provides interesting evidence of his fine ear for believable and enduring dialogue.

Some of Dickens's dialogues are shifted in position to heighten dramatic tension and effect. Noel Langley restructures, for example, the opening of the story, so that first Scrooge is seen negotiating the exchange, then dealing with a debtor, then dismissing carolers, offending solicitors, and finally chiding his nephew and his own Bob Cratchit (Mervyn Johns). The progression suggests that not only is Scrooge miserly in the world at large and to strangers, but he is also harsh with his family and intimates. Scrooge, at first seen as a crotchety and cantankerous old man, slowly emerges as a man who needs reclamation; he manages to seem loveless and yet lovable at the same time, brusque yet vulnerable, thanks both to this dramatic restructuring of revelations and the fine acting of Alastair Sim.

Once the ghosts appear, the film of *A Christmas Carol* is remarkably faithful to the narrative structure of the original text. The music of Richard Addinsell actually seems to divide the adventures into clear sections, paralleling Dickens's staves (so called to continue the music metaphor of a *Carol*). Especially notable, for example, is the dramatic handling of the two children, Ignorance and Want, whose appearance ends Stave Three, and the discovery of the Ghost of Christmas Yet to Come, which begins Stave Four. Dickens's inspiration for *A Christmas Carol* had come during a visit to a children's home, and he obviously centers all his themes on this unfortunate couple, the allegorical Ignorance and Want. The appearance of these two characters provides one of the emotional highpoints of the film, which is quickly followed by a shocking piece of camerawork and editing to introduce the character Death.

Dickens's description of his character the Spirit of Christmas Yet to Come might well be the very inspiration for Bergman's character

Death in *The Seventh Seal*: "It was shrouded in a deep black garment, which concealed its head, its face, its form, and left nothing of it visible save one outstretched hand" (p. 143). Director Hurst uses that one outstretched hand in a dramatic close-up, quickly edited into the film in a startling sequence. His childhood nurse's ghastly tales of hauntings and vengeance had deeply impressed the young Dickens; and his *A Christmas Carol* was, by his own admission, a "ghost" story, which he hoped would "raise a ghost of an idea" without putting his readers "out of humor with themselves, with each other, with the season or with me" (p. 56). Director Hurst highlights this theme and tinges it with the dark morality of *Everyman*. Hurst's death figure forcefully combines Dickens's ghost, Leech's spirits, Bergman's allegory, and horror film conventions in a chilling amalgam.

Hurst is similarly faithful and emphatic in regard to Dickens's economic and social theorizing. The specter of the poor laws, the work houses, and the prisons becomes one of the dominant motifs in the film. Scrooge's harsh prescriptions echo and reverberate on the soundtrack at the very moments he gains new insights into the need for humanity. *A Christmas Carol* is, after all, both on screen and in prose, as Angus Wilson so aptly put it, really "a sermon acted out in a dream."[6] All of Dickens's and Hurst's hell-fire and damnation serve largely as exempla for the larger message of humanism and charity.

To dramatize this social content, Hurst adds a critical new character, Mr. Jorkins, played by Jack Warner, who seduces the young Scrooge with a promise of "twice the salary" if he will leave Fezziwig's office and join a modern firm. Fezziwig had always taught Scrooge "there's more to life than money," but Scrooge couldn't understand, and through Jorkins, he meets Jacob Marley (Michael Hordern) "the wizard of accounts." Marley and Scrooge throw all their energies into the pursuit of wealth, operating under one new principle: "Don't be crushed with the weak and infirm." Ironically, it is Jorkins himself who is crushed by scandal, and as Marley and Scrooge gloat over their victories, their one-time mentor warns other businessmen to "Watch these fellows. They'd skin Jack

6. Angus Wilson, *The World of Charles Dickens* (New York: The Viking Press, 1970), p. 16.

Ketch alive and he'd never know it." Given this long history of Fezziwig and the old order crushed by Jorkins, and then Jorkins in turn crushed by Marley and Scrooge, the deathbed encounter between Marley and Scrooge holds a stunning lesson that the unredeemed Scrooge cannot understand. Marley warns Scrooge to save himself. Marley knows he was wrong, and he has to come to the revelation Dickens hoped all his readers would reach in reading *A Christmas Carol:* "Mankind was my business and common welfare was my business. Charity, mercy, and benevolence were all my business."

Hurst further reinforces Dickens's social theme by juxtaposing the rise of Scrooge's business fortunes with the collapse of his romance with Alice. The young Scrooge, when he clerks with Fezziwig, gives Alice an engagement ring, assuring her that he loves her because she is "plain and poor." As Scrooge moves into Jorkins's world, however, Alice realizes that money has become his new love, and she releases him from his promise, because he "weighs everything by wealth and gain." Alice leaves Scrooge with the wish that he be "happy in the life he has chosen." Scrooge's miserable life and joyless Christmas are then counterpointed with a vision of Alice ministering to the poor in a charity ward. She has retained her ties with her fellow men, and even in this impoverished quarter, she enjoys, she declares, "the happiest Christmas" of her life. The Spirit of Christmas Past then reminds Scrooge of his critical fault: "Did you not cut yourself off from your fellow creatures?"

The humanistic message of Scrooge's adventures has enchanted such diverse people as the novelist Tolstoy, who proclaimed the work one of the masterpieces of world literature most worthy of preservation; the filmmaker Sergei Eisenstein, who hailed Dickens as the master of montage and the first poet of industrialism and the urban experience; and Pope John Paul I, who, in an imaginary letter to Dickens, spoke of the author's love for the poor, his sense of social regeneration, and his humanity, all evidenced in *A Christmas Carol.*

Around this social motif in Dickens, director Hurst and writer Langley have embroidered a new psychological pattern, which is only implicit in the original text. To explain Scrooge's greed and introversion, they picture him as the pathetic victim of a loveless, motherless childhood, crushed by his vindictive father. In the film,

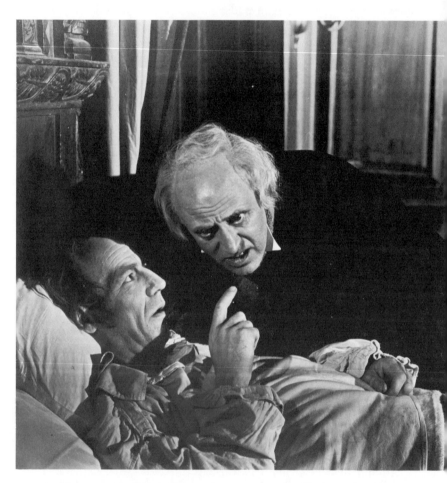

A Christmas Carol (1951). Too late, Marley (Michael Hordern) warns Scrooge (Alastair Sim). "Mankind was my business and common welfare was my business." (Photo courtesy of the Museum of Modern Art)

Scrooge's mother dies at his birth and his father exiles him to a bleak boarding school. Then Scrooge's sister Fan, whom he dearly loves, dies giving birth and asks him to care for her infant. Scrooge, like his father, cannot accept the death of a loved one and rejects both his nephew and, later, his nephew's wife (Olga Edwardes), a symbol of love, matrimony, and fertility. Director Hurst's inspiration for these striking variations on the theme of infant death and resultant trauma may well have come from a reading of Dickens's biography, for this Victorian author was quite familiar with infant mortality; and as the blacking factory episodes in his youth attest, he was well aware of traumatic experiences that terrify children and scar their development.

Brian Desmond Hurst's familiarity with Dickens's life and works might also have inspired his marvelous use of toys in the film *A Christmas Carol*. Charles Dickens was lavish in his gifts of toys for his children; and in his later Christmas book, *The Cricket on the Hearth*, illustrated by John Leech, he immersed his readers in the world of toymaker Caleb Plummer and the merchant Tackletown. Romance and illusion were important to Dickens, who never underestimated the importance of childhood fantasy and his youthful readings of *The Arabian Nights* in his development. In Hurst's film, Tiny Tim is introduced smiling dreamily through the picture window of Mrs. Burger's Toy Store. This crowded display is exotically rich and diverse: there are seductive snake charmers, grotesque rocking clowns, and elegant paddle boats. In this sequence, Hurst uses authentic Victorian mechanical toys and lavishes close-ups on them, capturing their mechnical motions and their more exotic effects. Tiny Tim is thus effectively identified with romance and fantasy, the very qualities Scrooge must master. When Scrooge is finally redeemed, he declares he is happy as "an angel" and "a schoolboy." Scrooge rediscovers the world of toys, and, as we see in his next scene with Tiny Tim's father, Bob, the world of practical jokes.

To bring his conception to the screen, Hurst had to depend heavily on his cast. In his introduction to the 1852 edition of *A Christmas Carol*, Charles Dickens admitted that the brevity of his tale placed severe restraints on his ability to develop character: "I never attempted great elaboration of detail in the working out of character within such limits, believing that it could not succeed" (p. 56). Noel Langley's script stays very close to Dickens's conception, so it is principally in individual performances that *A Christmas Carol* takes on new resonances in Hurst's cinematic adaptation. The large British cast works especially well at transforming small roles and little scenes into interesting characters and revealing episodes. Michael Hordern, for example, makes Marley's deathbed scene a stunning tour de force. As Scrooge listens timorously for Marley's faltering heart beat, Hordern as Marley opens his eyes slowly. Then Marley's palsied arm rises up to emphasize his message: "Save Yourself." Similarly, Ernest Thesiger expands a walk-on role as an undertaker into a major contribution, as he fiddles with his tape measure outside Marley's bedroom and apologizes for his somewhat unseemly punctuality with a classic understatement: "Ours is a highly competitive profession."

As Bob Cratchit, Mervyn Johns squeezes as much warmth as he can from Scrooge's meager stove and candles, and always manages to be in the way of Scrooge's scarf when he asks for a day off. At home, he is the perfect father, so gentle and humane that his Martha (Hermione Baddeley) cannot even play a mild joke on him. Roddy Hughes brings Mr. Fezziwig alive and Brian Worth admirably captures Fred's geniality.

In the middle of all these character actors, however, there is still the one hero of the work, Scrooge, skillfully played by Alastair Sim. Sim's performance so dominates the film that its English release was under the title *Scrooge*; and critic Hollis Alpert, in an uncharacteristic tribute, devoted his entire *Saturday Review* critique to the performance of "Our Mr. Sim."[7] As critic Alpert saw it, the film was "the basic primer of acting, as demonstrated by Mr. Sim. It is perfect; it is done up brown. Classic is maybe the word." Sim does have the vocabulary of terror down in his wide eyes, slack mouth, clawing hands, cowering posture, and crablike shuffle. Before his nephew and his employees, on the other hand, he is meticulous with the fitting of his gloves, imperious as he snaps his scarf against his neck, and unwavering as he strides out against pedestrian traffic.

7. Hollis Alpert, "Our Mr. Sim," *Saturday Review*, 1 Dec. 1951, p. 38.

Sim obviously enjoys the role; and if, as Hollis Alpert admits, he does ham it up, it is ham, in Alpert's words, "in the grand sense that all truly gifted actors understand it."

Neither Sim's acting skills nor the efforts of director Hurst and screenwriter Langley managed to escape *Variety's* prediction of commercial failure, and *A Christmas Carol* seems condemned to yearly reruns on television late on Christmas evening when few are watching. This commercial failure is a curious echo of Dickens's disappointment in his profits from his lavish first edition of *A Christmas Carol*. Dickens demanded such good bindings and such high quality color illustrations at a low retail price that even though the first edition sold out in one day, his profits were quite disappointing. Neither Dickens nor Hurst was to make his fortune from *A Christmas Carol*, but each has provided a powerful vision of Ebenezer Scrooge and his humbug.

David Copperfield (1849), Charles Dickens
George Cukor, 1935

Dickens's Narrative, Hollywood's Vignettes

WILLIAM LUHR

Charles Dickens considered *David Copperfield* (1849) his favorite among his novels and it has always been one of the most popular, but it has not received the critical attention given many of his other works, partly because it is often viewed as a trial balloon for *Great Expectations* and partly because it is frequently seen as thinly veiled autobiography. This remarkably complex and radically innovative novel deserves greater scrutiny.

The novel is commonly described as a *Bildungsroman*, one dealing with the formation of its hero, from his youth to his maturity. But it not only attempts to chronicle the milestones of personal growth from a fixed point of view, as is common with the form, it also attempts to deal with the subjective complexities of David's perceptual growth.

David well fits J. Hillis Miller's description of the "typical Dickens hero" as one "who has no given status or relation to nature, to family, or to the community. He is, in everybody's eyes, in the way, superfluous. . . . He will be totally responsible, himself, for any identity he achieves."[1] The novel is a first-person narrative in which the central concern of David, the narrator, is with the formation of

1. J. Hillis Miller, *Charles Dickens: The World of His Novels* (Bloomington: Indiana University Press, 1969), pp. 252-53. Future references will be designated "Miller" in the text.

a stable identity, and he perceives such an identity almost exclusively in familial terms. Nothing else has a comparable significance to him—he finds little consolation in religion, in his professional success, or in work itself.

David constantly seeks integration into a supportive familial unit. Since the novel presents domestic stability as a virtually nonexistent state, this is a nearly impossible task. The world of the novel is a debris of destroyed or severely threatened family units. As a child, David moves from one to another seeking an integration that is often corrosive and at best short-lived. As an adult he suffers a disastrous marriage. Only at the novel's end does he form his own successful family.

The novel deals not only with David's activities, but with his developing perceptions, and does so in a remarkable way. David records his experience not from a single cohering perspective but as an almost infinite cluster of separate experiences and responses to such experiences. He attempts to convey not only his past actions but also his past state of mind—his perception of those actions at the time they happened. To do this, he must often suspend what his future self knows, he must give his readers a sense of the progression of his life as he perceived it developing while it actually developed. He must describe it in the present and not in the past tense. At times he breaks in, stunning the reader with a perspective from the distant future vantage point from which he writes. He tells how, as a child, Em'ly (David's first love whose reputation is later ruined by Steerforth) terrified him when she recklessly ran out on a timber precariously balanced at a great height over the water. He describes his anxiety as a child, his fear for her safety, but suddenly places the incident into a radically different perspective.

> There has been a time since—I do not say it lasted long, but it has been—when I have asked myself the question, would it have been better for little Em'ly to have had the waters close above her head that morning in my sight; and when I have answered Yes. This may be premature. I have set it down too soon, perhaps. But let it stand.[2]

2. Charles Dickens, *David Copperfield* (N.Y.: Modern Library, 1950), p. 39. Future references will be designated "DC" in the text.

Here he leaps between radically different perspectives held upon the same event by the same man, but at different points in time. Neither of those points in time is the time of the narration, so a third or fourth perspective is possible.

David constantly indicates his realization that any single event or person, including himself, may be perceived in a multitude of ways. In his youth he is obsessed with his dead father; as he matures he becomes indifferent to him. David's maturation involves constant shifts in perspective upon other characters and events, as well as constant shifts in the ways other characters view him. David also realizes that one may hold contradictory views about a single object at the same time, as when, after Steerforth's death, David realizes that he never loved his school friend more than when he realized the full extent of his evil and the need to reject him.

The novel repeatedly indicates a lack of certainty, of stability—both about the family structures with which it deals and with the ability of the narrator to comprehend the significance of the experiences he relates. In the very first sentence of the novel, David indicates a significant reluctance to speculate upon his place in his own life: "Whether I shall turn out to be the hero of my own life, or whether that station will be held by anybody else, these pages must show" (DC, p. 1). His assumption that his history itself will tell more about him than any one point of view upon it, including his own, is borne out by the remainder of the novel. He repeatedly places more emphasis upon the "facts" as perceived contemporaneously than upon any single interpretation of them. Again on the first page, he says that neighborhood women predicted he would be unlucky in life: "I need say nothing here. . . . because nothing can show better than my history whether that prediction was verified or falsified by the result" (DC, p. 1). Once more he will let the events speak and let the reader judge. He presents much of the book in the present tense, especially in the four chapters (18, 43, 54, and 64) called "Retrospects." All appears as a stream of currently perceived experience, more reported than ordered.

David's periodic insertions of other points of view only underline his primary dedication to revealing the undigested experience. He is reluctant to make definitive statements, to select one solid base from which to view and then to evaluate experience. The implications of the events he relates suggest the wisdom of this, and the causes for it. Although he most avidly seeks a cohesive and continuous family structure within which to live, all of those he has known have been severely flawed, temporary, or even destructive. The world into which he has grown has been one in which traditional familial sustenance is more vestigial than real. Most parents, from David's mother to Mr. Murdstone to Mrs. Markleheim to Mr. Wickfield, among others, fail, in one way or another, to provide properly for their children, and most children barely have a sense of what such provision should comprise.

Elements and structures also change their significance. David's father and mother lose their importance to him; his deeply-felt youthful attachment to the Micawber family becomes a relationship of benign tolerance; his passionate love for his first wife, Dora, becomes almost paternal pity. David sees the world around him as in continual flux, as inconducive to fixed and sustaining structures. And as the elements of that world constantly reconfigure, so does he. As any single event or structure changes in time, so does he. As he changes, the coordinates of his perception change, placing his perspective upon experience in constant flux. David tries to avoid giving his perceptions and judgments a hierarchical order; he tries to avoid designating his perceptions at the time of writing as more valid than those at the time of the experience being related. He accepts the fragmentation, tries in the novel to present the experiences and their effect upon his contemporary perceptions, but they emerge as a collection of simultaneous impressions, not necessarily consistent, and important not for what they build to, but for what they are.

In reference to the "world" of Dickens's novels, J. Hillis Miller has written:

The "world" is the totality of all things as they are lived in by all human beings collectively. For Dickens the concrete embodiment of this totality is the great modern commercial city, made up of millions of people all connected to one another without knowing it, yet separated from one another and living in isolation and secrecy. . . . The most striking characteristic of his novels is their multitudinousness, the proliferation within each one of a great number of characters, each different from all

David Copperfield (1935). The youthful attachment of David (Freddie Bartholomew) to Micawber (W.C. Fields) and his family eventually becomes a relationship of benign tolerance. (Photo courtesy of the Museum of Modern Art)

the others, and each living imprisoned in his own milieu and in his own idiosyncratic way of looking at the world. . . . Though each individual reaches out toward a comprehension of the city, the essential quality of the city is its transcendence of any one person's knowledge of it. Each individual's knowledge is partial, baffled, askew. And yet it was the city as it really is, in all its unknowns and perhaps unknowable complexity, which Dickens wanted to know and to encompass in his work.

(Miller, pp. xv-xvi)

This city metaphor applies not only to the relations among the characters in *David Copperfield*, but to David's apprehension of his own life. His own experience has become too complex for him to interpret and, to deal with this problem, he attempts to present the experience with little regard for traditional concepts of consistency.

George Cukor's *David Copperfield* (1935) represents a relatively rare conjunction between the best of what the heyday of the Hollywood studio system had to offer and Victorian fiction. It was produced at MGM, the most successful studio of the 1930s, by the legendary David O. Selznick, and directed by the prolific and frequently acclaimed George Cukor. It was a pet project of Selznick's, and without him the film probably would not exist. He encountered a good deal of studio resistance to the project because it was a "costume" (therefore expensive) film, and one based upon "highbrow" fiction (therefore box-office poison). Defying most studio predictions, it enjoyed both critical and commercial success.

Both Selznick and Cukor wanted to preserve the "essence" of the novel in the film, and therefore attempted to include in *David Copperfield* as many characters and narrative incidents from Dickens's novel as possible. All of the characters and most of the events (the major exception is the theater sequence in which David, with Steerforth's aid, meets Dora) in the film have direct referents in the novel.

Such a task, preserving the "essence" of a novel in a film, is patently impossible; the forms are too radically different. On the simplest narrative level, innumerable incidents from the novel have no parallel incidents in the film's narrative—David's adventures at Mr. Creakle's or at Dr. Strong's schools, his career as a legal apprentice and as a parliamentary reporter, his trip to the continent, the emigration of many major characters to Australia, and so forth.

Similarly, major characters in the novel have no counterparts in the film—for example, Mrs. Steerforth, Rosa Dartle, Dr. and Annie Strong, Mr. Creakle, and Mr. Spenlow. But these differences do not begin to account for formal or thematic differences.

Films based upon novels are generally not based upon the novels but upon the filmmaker's (usually thematic) interpretations of those novels. Selznick's sense of Dickens's novel emerges in a memo discussing his *A Tale of Two Cities:*

> It is amazing that Dickens has so many brilliant characters in *David Copperfield* and so few in *A Tale of Two Cities*. There are twenty or perhaps forty living, breathing, fascinating people in *Copperfield* and practically none in *A Tale of Two Cities*, and herein lies the difficulty. The book is sheer melodrama. . . . The picture will be a job of which I will be proud—but is and will be entirely different from *David Copperfield*.[3]

The memo indicates that Selznick saw *David Copperfield* not as a carefully wrought narrative but primarily in terms of its distinctive characters. The film he based upon it bears this out in that its greatest asset lies in the often superb performances of its actors. In many ways, the film's chief structuring device lies in its presentation of character.

The *Variety* reviewer, "Chic," commented:

> Without derogation to the adaptors and producers, the chief factor in the success of *David Copperfield* is due more largely to those concerned in the casting than to the others. It is one of the most evenly good casts ever to have been assembled and it is due more to this than to any other factor that the picture probably will be a large grosser.[4]

Most contemporary reviewers similarly praised the cast, especially W.C. Fields as Mr. Micawber and Roland Young as Uriah Heep.

The film supports this. It is not tightly structured, and what structure there is comes from its interplay of dominant coherent characters. It is more a film of good scenes than a formally coherent

3. David O. Selznick, *Memo from David O. Selznick,* selected and edited by Rudy Behlmer (N.Y.: Viking Press, 1972), pp. 83-84.
    4. "Chic," "Review of *David Copperfield*," *Variety*, 22 January 1935.

whole. A significant element in this is a weakness at the center. David himself is poorly developed and never becomes a dynamic character in his own right. His existence in the film is less significant in itself than in its utility in providing the thread linking the other characters. His character in the novel functions as a growing perception, influencing and being influenced by the characters he encounters. He consciousness is a dominant element in the novel. In the film, however, he is simply another character, and not a very interesting one.

The film consists of approximately seventeen major sequences of which the first eight deal with David's life as a boy (played by Freddie Bartholomew) and the last nine deal with his life as a young man (Frank Lawton). Most of the sequences are dominated by a single character: the first by Betsey Trotwood (Edna Mae Oliver), the fourth by Mr. Murdstone (Basil Rathbone), the fifth by Mr. Micawber, and so on. Each half of the film has a dominant villain— Mr. Murdstone in the first half and Uriah Heep in the second half. The second-to-last sequence in each half deals with a dramatic confrontation between a dominant "good" figure and the villain. The first half climaxes when Betsey Trotwood confronts Mr. Murdstone and his sinister sister, denounces them for their cruelty, and takes custody of David. In the second half, Micawber gathers most of the cast together and denounces Uriah Heep. Significantly, most of the major events in the second half (except his marriage) have very little to do with David.

Much of the dramatic action in the narratives of both novel and film goes to characters other than David. This does not diminish David in the novel because the experiences all affect his developing consciousness; they make him what he becomes. The focus of the novel is primarily upon David's consciousness and not upon its incidents; his active participation in those incidents is not a primary factor.

David uses the other characters to find himself and, to an extent, those others become part of that self. His character has never been successful with dramatists, partially because the underlayer of self-formation incorporating the other characters is generally absent in the plays based upon the novel; they generally present a pack of lively characters surrounding a rather dull one. This is also the case with the film. The central self-fragmentation of the David of the novel is not central to the construction of the film. Further, the novel's specifically familial orientation—a dominant Victorian concern—is not a significant element in the film. What exists is what Selznick saw in the novel—a cast of interesting characters.

Selznick selected elements from his source that would appeal to his audience, and that selection omitted elements of predominantly Victorian concern. The novel deals not only with a fragmented self but with a fragmented family; it ends with a unified self in a unified family. The concern throughout is with self-definition and the establishment of a family. The film's David is not a fragmented character and is not obsessed with familial stability. It ends as he begins to court Agnes (Madge Evans) and not ten years after they have established a secure family.

In the novel, the ten-year postmarital leap indicates the solidity of the family unit David has established. The film is not impelled to show such a development because it is not as centrally concerned with domestic stability as is the novel. Its family units are less chaotic, and the giddy response of Betsey Trotwood and Mr. Dick to David's and Agnes's courtship indicates that there is no doubt in their minds that the courtship will ripen into a secure and fruitful marriage.

The sense of almost universal familial chaos is not nearly as strong in the film as it is in the novel. The families that remain unified do so under much less strain than their counterparts in the novel; the threats to domestic stability in the films are much less threatening, much more readily vanquished than those in the novel. The Micawber of the film is a much more benign, much less chaotic and improvident character than that of the novel. His family does not exist under the persistent and corrosive strain of imminent collapse as does the Micawber family of the novel. When the Murdstones are denounced by Betsey Trotwood, the triumph is complete—they never reappear. In the novel, they do. Miss Murdstone is Dora's chaperone and nearly thwarts David's marriage to Dora (Maureen O'Sullivan). Mr. Murdstone again weds and again destroys a woman's life.

The novel's David is more consistently alone than the David of the film. The film repeatedly provides sympathetic parental figures to buffer him from tragedy. The novel presents David's London life as grim and as virtually without succor. David must face the horrors and humiliations of factory work and poverty alone—Micawber is too inept at handling his own life to be of much help to David. When David goes to Dover, he goes alone—he has nothing to fall back upon; he has been rejected by his "family," Micawber is gone, and he has left his job . In the film, Micawber continually provides David with a sense of security; he continually acts as a buffer between David and the world.

The most indicative example of this pattern comes with the death of David's mother. In the novel, David feels hopelessly alone: "I had already broken out into a desolate cry, and felt an orphan in the wide world" (DC, P. 131). In the film, a comparable scene comes when David learns of his mother's death, not from virtual strangers at school, but from the kindly Peggotty. He says, "Oh, Peggotty, we're all alone now." The "we," the presence of a sympathetic person, as with Micawber in London, makes his plight not nearly as terrible as it is in the novel. He has someone with whom to share his misery.

David's successful marriage at the end of the novel and his virtual deification of Agnes provide a transcendent conclusion to the novel's constant pattern of familial inadequacy. It is the dominant emphasis of the final chapters because it was the dominant concern of the novel. The film, which has different concerns, eliminates it altogether. Agnes is not as much a figure of transcendent goodness, developed in opposition to the girls for whom David feels sexual attraction, as she is a girl-next-door whose worth is finally recognized. David does not "discover" his love for her at a moment of cosmic communion with the universe; he simply realizes her value and begins courting her at the film's end. The film is not as obsessively concerned with the difficulty of establishing family structures as is the novel and thus has no need to imbue the one person with whom David is able to establish a successful family with a quasi-religious, transcendental quality that, in the novel, is supposed to account for such a colossal accomplishment. Her superhuman qualities in the novel underline the difficulty of establishing a family; in the film she is not given those qualities and does not establish a family; she simply provides David with a companion.

The film is a good deal more optimistic than the novel. Its villains are vanquished with a finality that leads the viewer to assume that they will never reemerge. In the novel, however, they do reemerge, repeatedly. They are always there. Further, Dickens presents social institutions—schools, child labor, the courts—as destructive in themselves. The film deals only with individual villainy. Many of the characters who succeed in the novel do so in a curious context. Agnes is presented as a figure as much associated with heaven as with earth. The two family units to which David is most drawn in his youth, that of Mr. Micawber and that of Mr. Peggotty, both go to Australia at the end of the novel. One senses that familial sustenance in England is virtually impossible, that one needs heavenly intervention to achieve it, or that one must leave the country. Even David has to go to Switzerland to realize that he loves Agnes. In the film, no reference is made to places other than England (except for the Mediterranean town in which Em'ly was abandoned), and the general joy that reigns at the end of the film appears quite natural to the world of the film. The novel repeatedly undercuts its world.

The world of the film is one in which happiness can and frequently does exist; the world of the novel is one in which such happiness can exist only under the most extraordinary circumstances. Further, the world of the novel is one in which the family is an essential structure that is almost always debilitated. Happiness is presented in the novel as possible only through the establishment of a unified family. The film does not exhibit as central a fear about the impossibility of establishing a unified family and happiness, which, in it, is not nearly as difficult to achieve. It presents a less threatening society populated with less threatening people.

Great Expectations (1860), Charles Dickens

David Lean, 1946

Seeing the Book, Reading the Movie

JULIAN MOYNAHAN

One often hears that Dickens is the most "cinematic" of the classic English novelists, and by that a number of different things appear to be meant. There are the stunning atmospheric effects and the broadly environmental ones, from the evocation of London fog opening *Bleak House* (1853) to the description of the lowered-upon, storm-threatened churchyard, salt marsh, and distant river rendered in *Great Expectations* (1860), Chapter 1, which any ambitious cinematographer or director would be challenged to transfer to film. Then there is the intense dwelling on physical detail, the constant use of what has to be called visual metaphor, and Dickens's interest in conveying a complex of thematic meaning through such devices. There is a kind of Dickensian dumb show through which entire sequences and levels of dramatic and thematic implication are presented without any recourse to words, except of course those necessary words which merely describe the scene or action without adding either dialogue or discursive analysis. To oversimplify, these words can be thought of as the mere running on of the film, the camera eye lingering and scrutinizing while significance accumulates and the unspoken communication is made.

The above may sound as if I associate Dickens in some way with the overwhelmingly visual semiotic system of silent film. I certainly mean to do that. Major early directors like Griffiths and Eisenstein learned much, consciously and by osmosis, from "the Dickens theater," as Eisenstein himself acknowledged. Transmission of influence may even be indirect; for instance, we know that Dostoyevsky learned from Dickens's city novels how to project a claustral, nervous ("defamiliarized") atmosphere around the lives of his profoundly agitated characters in such St. Petersburg novels as *Crime and Punishment.* Something of the same atmosphere seems to have seeped into Eisenstein's *Ivan the Terrible, Part One*, where unfortunately it tends to work at cross purposes with the director's intent that we should take these larger-than-life historical figments seriously.

Some illustration of Dickens's visual semiotic is in order and it will be appropriate to draw the examples from *Great Expectations.* These crowd in upon us as soon as we open the pages of the book. When the child Pip hastens to his secret rendezvous at the churchyard with the convict, Magwitch, the village signposts, looming through mists, seem to be fingers pointing out his guilt, while the cattle on the marsh and even the marsh dikes and banks seem to rush at him crying "Stop thief!" Soon another convict, in process of being shifted from one place of confinement to another, pointedly stirs his drink with an iron file at the local tavern and Pip, looking on, recognizes uneasily that he is receiving a particular communication from "my convict," Abel Magwitch.

Much more elaborately, we have the living dumb show of Miss Havisham. She wears the tatters of her wedding costume, her bridal banquet rots under a heavy canopy of dust, rodent droppings, and spider webs, and the clock at the top of the brewery building adjacent to Satis House, her residence, is stopped at the precise hour and minute twenty years before at which she learned of her jilting by her false suitor, Compeyson.

That is Miss Havisham's way of telling the world that life and time ended for her with the cruel blighting of her innocent and romantic hopes. Yet Dickens's visual organization tells us more than Miss Havisham herself knows. She does change in the midst of her changeless woe, but only for the worse. The wilderness of weeds growing up unchecked in the brewery yard, the hideous condition of the banquet room, numerous other visual details of an unhygienic nature speak of Miss Havisham's psychological and indeed moral deterioration over the years of her willful self-confinement. It is this deterioration that permits her to play so negative a role in shaping the life of her ward, Estella, and Pip's life also, to a lesser extent. For a last illustration there is the matter of Pip's fascination with Estella's hands, which threads its way through the novel, eventually becoming the basis for Pip's solving one of the central mysteries of the plot, that of Estella's parentage. No doubt Pip first became conscious of Estella's pretty hands as he sat with her at Satis House, playing and losing countless games of Beggar My Neighbor under the brooding eye of Miss Havisham. Later on, when he was a young man of expectations resident in London, he went to meet Estella's coach as it came up to town from the country and felt a "nameless shadow" of presentiment pass over him as Estella waved her hand from the coach window. Something like this had happened once before, on a visit to Satis House for a reunion with Estella, when he had found that his eyes followed her white hand involuntarily while his mind groped after "a dim suggestion that I could not possibly grasp." Of course eventually he solves the enigma of these presentiments when he realizes that Estella's white, elegantly groomed hands closely resemble the scarred and powerful wrists and hands of Molly, the reprieved murderess who is the housekeeper of his legal guardian, Jaggers. From which follows the shocking but accurate inference that Molly and Estella are mother and daughter.

Though this revelation may seem melodramatic or adventitious, the visual clues leading to it are woven into the book with extreme subtlety. And of course it underscores one of the book's leading themes, the idea that on the surface of the Great Expectations world people are sharply segregated by class, fortune, degrees of respectability, privilege, and power; whereas beneath the surface these same people are linked by numerous invisible ties of blood, guilt, and creaturely need into a sort of stricken commonalty.

By hitching the cinema wagon to all this Dickensian visual richness, subtlety, and amplitude should it be easy, crass commercial pressures apart, to make a classic film out of a classic novel? Not at all. For one thing there isn't time. The most straightforward statement of the time problem is perhaps that given by Christopher Isherwood in *Prater Violet,* an excellent novel about filmmaking

which came out in 1945, just one year before the David Lean-
J. Arthur Rank production of *Great Expectations*:

> "The whole *beauty* of the film," I announced to my mother and Richard
> next morning at breakfast, "is that it has a certain fixed *speed*. The way
> you see it is mechanically conditioned. I mean, take a painting—you can
> just glance at it, or you can stare at the left-hand top corner for half an
> hour. Same thing with a book. The author can't stop you from skimming
> it, or starting at the last chapter and reading it backwards. The point is,
> you choose your approach. When you go into a cinema, it's different.
> There's the film, and you have to look at it as the director wants you to
> look at it. He makes his points, one after another, and he allows you a
> certain number of seconds or minutes to grasp each one. If you miss
> anything he won't repeat himself, and he won't stop to explain. He can't.
> He's started something, and he has to go through with it. . . . You see the
> film is really like a sort of infernal machine."   (New York: Avon-Bard,
> 1978, p. 43)

There are paradoxes in this state of affairs. The director may take
all the time in the world—all the time, that is, his budget will pay
for—to make the best use of the two to three reels of running time
which comprise the movie. The viewer, however, has no other
option than to submit to the certain fixed speed at which the story
unfolds according to the director's dictates and point of view. Films
are indeed infernal machines. Could it be that the machine shop
sequence in Chaplin's *Modern Times* is an allegory of movie going?
A second paradox entails the forcing of a novel of classic stature—to
which originally a director was attracted because of its richly visual
qualities, as well as its beguiling dramatic, narrational, and thematic
aspects—into that same infernal machine running on at fixed speed.
He can do it, of course, but only by means of relentless condensation, omission, oversimplification, and downright distortion. Could
it be that the machine shop sequence in *Modern Times* allegorizes
the attempt, nearly always unsuccessful, to adapt great literature to
film in a standard production format?

How David Lean's screen adaptation of *Great Expectations* struck
a reviewer as it ran by in the dark. From notes taken at the time.
The fourth (concluding) part of this essay will compare endings, as

between book and movie, to show that the screenwriters' changes are for the worse. It will also discuss the unfortunate consequences of the adapters' decision to eliminate a couple of apparently subordinate characters from their script. But first the movie "at a certain fixed *speed.*"

Begins with book pages turning by themselves, the voice of John Mills speaking Pip's first words ("My father's family name being Pirrup . . .")—boy running on dike, into graveyard, placing flowers at grave marker. INSTANTLY the convict, fearful to behold, pouncing! Abruptness, violence, pitifulness, all there just right.

Joe Gargery, the blacksmith, should be brawnier though Bernard Miles a fine actor. Mrs. Joe excellent—your blackavised, English village scold to the life. Pip's guilt over theft of food and file shown through menacing close-ups of looming adult faces and voices-off (both men and women). And then a human voice for the cow in the fog. Better left to the imagination.

The other convict has "a big scar on his face." In the book it is a "badly bruised" face. Lean is planting a detail for quick identification later on. Allowable. The film in this early part as good or better than CD at doing scenes in quick succession. The chase across the Marsh— Joe and Pip with the soldiers pursuing the convicts— particularly good. When Magwitch is caught, the touching face-to-face (Joe Gargery's "poor, miserable fellow-creature") is finely done.

"It was a year later"—Mills's voice, very good visual shorthand, semimontage effects ending in Pip's first arrival at Satis House all dressed up. Pip, boy and man, extra well cast, always believably of the village tradesman class until he goes to London. While Jean Simmons's performance of the young Estella is magical, enchanting, tour-de-force. She is the aloof fairy-tale Princess of Pip's callow dreaming, and a nastry brat to boot. Martita Hunt's Miss Havisham is a superb mixture of the imperious and the weird. She needs a touch more pathos.

Satis House: Pip's "Your clock's stopped, Miss," to Estella. Miss H.'s apartment a stage set of decay. Close-up of her prayer book, of all things. Part of the 19th-century wedding accouterment, no doubt. The pace here is quick like the opening. "Play!" They play cards and Miss H. bedizens Estella with her jewels. Sparkles in the near-dark. Very fine. Miss Havisham's greedy-eager "What do you think of her?" Children as erotic playthings and as instruments of revenge.

But it runs on too quickly to Pip hitting his head against the wall in misery and humiliation, to Estella slapping his face and calling him "Wretch!" *Viz.* Pip is a tough kid for all the yes, mum—no, mum stuff. While Estella is as enigmatic as she is bratty—to Pip, to herself, to Dickens. The sycophantic Pockets do appear on Miss Havisham's birthday, toadying away.

Arrival of Biddy at the Forge. Much too old an actress—looks three times age of Pip. Lawyer Jaggers brings the big news; actor is Francis Sullivan, fat, sly, clever: "Boys are a bad lot of fellows," and "You will always bear the name, Pip." which Miss H. wickedly repeats, presumably to confuse him about the source of his new fortune. Or is it only to misdirect the audience/reader?

No Dolge Orlick, no Trabb, and Trabb's Boy. These are shocking omissions. Wopsle's ham acting and most of Pumblechook's petty tyrannizing were cut out but that is allowable.

To London: (1) View of St. Paul's dome from low vantage point and then of Little Britain. (2) Jaggers's law office and his compulsive handwashing. (3) Introduction of Wemmick then of Molly the housekeeper *at the office.* Makes no sense but saves time and celluloid.

Reunion with Herbert Pocket at the lodgings in Bernard's Inn. Herbert's gentle lessons in table manners. Alec Guinness gently condescending in—and to—the part. The Joe Gargery visit is retained. Pip's snobbish embarrassment versus Joe's "simple dignity." A good scene well realized from the book.

Pip's unavailing courtship of the adult Estella (Valerie Hobson) in London. His rival, Bentley Drummle, the expected upper-class English brute—a living sneer. They live now in the Temple, near the river. Night of big storm, shots of rain pelting on rooftops and chimney pots. MAGWITCH HAS RETURNED

Great Expectations (1947). Magwitch (Finlay Currie) returns to Pip (John Mills). "The light of my lamps includes us both." (Photo courtesy of the Museum of Modern Art)

All that curious exultation of Magwitch's about "making a gentleman" is left in. Pip's ensuing visit to Miss H. to chide her for having misled him as to the source of his fortune finds Estella there. She knits and leaves first.

The fire scene. First Miss Havisham's contrite "What have I done?" He is halfway down the stairs when she combusts and he hears her screams. All wrong. In the book she ignites immediately after he gives her an angry-reproachful look at parting: "if looks could kill." Beating out the flames, tearing down the rotted drapes to cover her—terrific!

Brief scene at Walworth with Wemmick and the Aged P. Faithful, fine.

The river scenes. Magwitch first secreted at Limehouse, then downriver at a remote pub. Rowing practice with Herbert hampered by Pip's burnt hand. In the boat Magwitch tells of his lost daughter only briefly. The extended autobiography (of a "Varmint") is cut. The race to catch the pilot boat and the fight in the water between the same convict-antagonists as in Pip's boyhood. The film tells us so little about why they hate each other.

In court. Thirty-seven chained together—young and old, adults and children, men and women—as light streams in from high windows and the death sentence is pronounced on all. This important thematic scene is faithful to the book.

Concluding explanations don't explain enough. Jaggers shows off Molly as Estella's mother, the hand business being omitted. When Magwitch is dying in the prison sick ward Pip tells him of his daughter's survival and class elevation and "I love her." Magwitch goes out on a "Dear boy," practically touching his forelock.

Pip's illness: the fever delirium for which the book gives such stunning thematic imagery—the great machine clashing and grinding in a gulf of space, the toiling up great staircases, etc.—which imagery helps to define the vicious and predatory aspect of "great expectations" in a world of the condemned and abandoned, is a mere white blank until Joe Gargery's kind, overhanging face comes into focus. Pip wakes "at home" in the village house—just like that.

Brief picnic scene exhibiting Joe and Biddy's 'umble wedded bliss, then the windup at Miss Havisham's as Pip sadly revisits the apparently deserted and ruined Satis House, once the focus of his boyish dreaming.

At the gate a ghostly echo of little Estella's tart "What name?" "Pumblechook!" "Quite right." Lovely. The grown Estella is there! Attempting an abashed retirement like Miss Havisham's, for Bentley Drummle, always the gent, has divorced her upon hearing of her convict relations. Yet she retains the Magwitch fortune. Does Pip know she is in the chips as he pulls open the portieres and flutes, "Estella, come with me, out into the sunlight!"? Whether or not, the ending is bad and false—strictly movieland. And the heavy symphonic scoring, loaded with misplaced affect, merely underscores the falsity.

In sum, good camera work and even better actors' work in the film, but no movie masterpiece here.

The film's changed ending and also some of its omissions tend to rob the main characters, Pip in particular, of moral responsibility and autonomy and to blunt Dickens's probing analysis of the caste-ridden, ruthlessly competitive, and money-grubbing society in which Pip makes his rapid and undeserved rise. In the book Dickens's trick was to make Pip's good fortunes seem quite magical and uncompromised at first, and then to have him come slowly to understand, as a result of the most painful ordeals of acquired disillusioning knowledge and experience, that no one gets a free ride through life; or, rather, that no one gets such a ride without some one else paying for it in pain and torment.

At the end of the novel Pip and Estella meet briefly in a London street after a considerable lapse of years. Pip, a bachelor, has recently come from abroad, where he is a partner in a small English business firm, and he has Joe and Biddy's boy child, the second Pip, along with him. Estella has been married to Bentley Drummle, who used to beat her and then got himself killed while mistreating a horse. Then she married a physician and now lives childless with this second husband in the countryside. Pip and Estella contemplate each other sadly and wryly across a gulf of sundering experience and time. Pip's unhappy, obsessive love for her is a thing of the past. Estella asks Pip to hold up the little boy to her carriage seat so that she may kiss him. Then they part, presumably forever. This is the right ending for the searching, tough-minded book that Dickens wrote.

Yet Dickens made a new ending when his friend Bulwer-Lytton complained of the austerity of this one. Pip and Estella meet in the ruins of Satis House to which each by coincidence is paying a nostalgic visit after a lapse of eleven or more years. Other details are the same except that Estella has not remarried. She proposes their continuing as "friends apart" but Pip takes her firmly by the hand. They leave the "ruined place" together as the mists rise. Presumably they will marry and enjoy the combined income from Pip's business partnership and Estella's inheritance from Miss Havisham. This is the ending that most editions of *Great Expectations* print.

It tends to deny that Miss Havisham's severe conditioning of Estella—to be a heartbreaker and general scourge of the male sex—has had any long-range effect on her character. Time and Pip's absence have taught her to be submissive ("I took her hand in mine," says Pip firmly) as well as loving. Though Magwitch's fortune has been confiscated by the Crown, Pip gets the girl of his dreams and with her all those lucky bucks she inherited from Miss Havisham. The wisp of moral remaining is that you may have to wait a few years, as mild punishment for having been a rotten snob and something of a chucklehead earlier on, but you will get your great expectations in the end just as long as you happen to be a person named Pip.

In the movie ending there is no lapsed time while Pip makes good in business, and the once proud Estella is shown woefully reduced and passive, preparing to relive her patroness's life of neurotic withdrawal in the wreckage of Satis House. Of course she is really waiting for Pip to burst in, totally in command, to manhandle the drapes once again and draw her out into the sunlight. If there is a moral it is that women are weak and need a man to tell them what to do. Here Lean's 1946 version of a nineteen-century fable anticipates the "feminine mystique" of the 1950s. As for income, Pip and Estella can look forward to enjoying her inheritance from Miss Havisham plus the considerable fortune left by Abel Magwitch.

Why the scriptwriters changed the accurate legal detail of having Magwitch's property forfeited remains a mystery, unless they wished to suggest that, as the song says, the best things in life are free. In this ending, Pip learns nothing or very little about the world and about himself. It was all, or nearly all, a matter of fool luck.

The movie treatment eliminated—along with such details as the motif of Estella's hands, the death scene of Mrs. Joe and Magwitch's interpolated narrative, "The History of a Varmint"—the very important characters of Dolge Orlick and Trabb's Boy. Orlick was the blacksmith's villainous journeyman, the reader will remember. He was discharged by Gargery for threatening behavior, got away with a murderous assault on Mrs. Joe which left her paralyzed and psychologically shattered, turned up working as gate keeper at Satis House, and then as a spy and confidential servant for Compeyson. Orlick is always crossing Pip's path, competing with him, accusing him of motives as vicious as his own. Eventually he tries to kill him, only to be thwarted by the arrival of Trabb's Boy and some other local young men.

Through Orlick we grasp the aggressive potential and the uncouth power drive that underlie the career of "great expectations" in the bright, guilty, nineteenth-century world to which Dickens introduces us. In fact Orlick is a psychopathic version of Pip himself and is not completely wrong when he avers that Pip's motives will not bear much looking into. By bringing these two characters into confrontation Dickens deepens and complicates Pip's characterization. This extra dimension is entirely lost with Orlick's elimination from the script.

Trabb's Boy worked for the village haberdasher, Trabb and Co., where Pip bought his first expensive outfit after coming into his good fortune. Later, when Pip tried to play the London snob on the village high street, the Boy appeared and produced a hilarious public parody of Pip's acquired airs and graces of fashionable urbanity. Pip was so gravelled by this comic chastisement that he wrote Trabb saying he would give him no further business unless the "miscreant" was fired. From this point Trabb's Boy disappears, only to turn up in nick of time, stopping Orlick from flinging Pip, bound hand and foot, into a pit of fulminating quicklime.

We are indebted to Trabb's Boy for one of the funniest scenes in all Dickens but he has further value as representing a sort of norm and normalcy and irreducible integrity. He is the boy who does not rise in the world, does not depart his native place for the great city, does not get to play the class system as though it were a pinball machine, and probably would not if he could. He stays home, lives his life like his ancestors before him, joins the local rescue squad, turns up to do some good just when he is needed, then departs insouciantly into a life of privacy and guiltless self-containment. By eliminating the Boy from their script the screenwriters missed a large opportunity to point up through contrast the sheer abnormality and craziness of Pip's—and his century's—dream of a huge, unearned, undeserved success in the spheres of wealth, social status, power, and love to which Dickens gave the wonderfully cutting, ironic name of *Great Expectations*.

Hardy in Soft Focus

RITA COSTABILE

Certainly no one expects a film based on a novel to be entirely faithful to it, particularly since novels are comprised of rhetorical strategies for which there are no real visual equivalents. But while we do not expect films to imitate novels, we do hope for the kind of fruitful dialogue between novelist and director that distinguishes films like *Tom Jones*, in which the vocabulary and syntax of film are used to evoke the tone and spirit of the novel. Such is not the case, however, with John Schlesinger's *Far from the Madding Crowd* (1967). Following the plot scrupulously, if not relentlessly, Schlesinger makes, however, a film with little of the wit and ironic intelligence of the book. Frederick Raphael's screenplay lifts whole scenes from the novel, often with dialogue repeated verbatim, with no sense of their relative significance or symbolic value. Hardy's juxtaposition of action and imagery, his ideas about the ironic coincidence of human and natural history, and his use of natural imagery to foreshadow events are almost totally absent from the film.

An obvious instance of the film's difficulties is the problem it had with the hero of the novel, Gabriel Oak. As Bathsheba Everdene's guardian angel, Oak's influence must be felt even when he is absent. Hardy accomplishes this by referring to him indirectly, or by commenting on remarks that other characters make about him. Schlesinger, who does not enjoy the privileges of an omniscient

155

third-person narrator, must try to suggest visually that the absent Oak is really there. Lacking this, Oak virtually vanishes from the film after the crucial scene in which he and Bathsheba save her wheat crop from a lightning storm; he reappears only at the conclusion to marry Bathsheba after her husband, Frank Troy, has been murdered. As a result, he seems like any commonplace suitor, instead of the unseen protector and gentle influence that he is meant to be.

Schlesinger's difficulties derive directly from his failure to grasp the complex relationship between men and nature that is the principal theme of the novel. Considered by most critics to be Hardy's first "mature" work, *Madding Crowd* (1874) has all of the virtues of a first-rate melodrama, including a beautiful headstrong heroine, a profligate husband, and a suspenseful and macabre denouement complete with corpse. But at the same time, Hardy describes through action and imagery man's frustrated attempts to master his environment through laws, social institutions, and industry. Despite Hardy's claim that it is simply a "pastoral tale," *Madding Crowd* depicts relationships which Schlesinger does not acknowledge. As one reviewer wrote, "just as the desert was the real subject of the first part of *Lawrence of Arabia*, so the Hardy country is the real subject here."[1] Filmed in a succession of long shots which swoop in to focus on such details as the leaf on a tree, or a stalk of wheat, or a newborn lamb, the Wessex countryside is truly beautiful. Yet it seems curiously devitalized. The wheat is a little too golden to be real; water drips too precisely off a leaf; men are dwarfed by a cliff in a way too pretty to be convincing. The result is by turns pompous and ingenuous as, shooting for color and composition rather than vitality, Schlesinger overidealizes and sentimentalizes nature, misunderstanding its subtle, and sometimes destructive, encounters with man.

Hardy introduces Bathsheba Everdene as she sits on top of a farm wagon, surrounded by autumn foliage and admiring herself in a mirror. Replete with biblical, literary, and mythological resonances, the passage provides a classic example of Hardy's use of natural imagery:

1. P. Houston, *The Spectator*, October 27, 1967.

It was a fine morning, and the sun lighted up to a scarlet glow the crimson jacket that she wore, and painted a soft luster upon her bright face and dark hair. The myrtles, geraniums, and cactuses placed around her were fresh and green, and at such a leafless season they invested the whole concern of horses, wagon, furniture, and girl with a peculiar vernal charm.[2]

Such charm is peculiar because it is not spring, but winter, and the scene, although idyllic, is artificial. Bathsheba's own artifice strikes another discordant note:

What possessed her to indulge in such a performance in the sight of the sparrows, blackbirds, and unperceived farmer who were alone its spectators—whether the smile began as a factitious one, to test her capacity in that art—nobody knows; it ended certainly in a real smile. She blushed at herself, and seeing her reflection blush, blushed the more. (p. 54)

This is nothing if not an ironic pastoral. Not only are the flowers and plants out of season, but Bathsheba's own vanity is incongruous, spoiling the picture much as Eve's vanity spoiled paradise. Punning on the word "delicate," Hardy implies that Bathsheba has betrayed herself:

The scene was a delicate one. Woman's prescriptive infirmity had stalked into the sunlight, which had clothed it in the freshness of an originality. . . . A cynical inference was irresistible by Gabriel Oak as he regarded the scene, generous though he fain would have been. (p. 54)

Like the narrator, Gabriel Oak views the episode ironically. Bathsheba's wagon comes to a halt "just beneath his eyes," so that he is both apart from and above the action. Bathsheba too becomes an observer, as she recognizes her "sin" and blushes. Such images find their prototype in the myth of Narcissus and Echo, and readers familiar with their function as literary tropes recognize them as allusions to a fall.

Schlesinger dispenses, here as throughout the work, with such ironic readings, choosing to present this complicated imagery

2. Thomas Hardy, *Far from the Madding Crowd* (1874; rpt. London: Penguin, 1978), p. 53. All subsequent references are to this edition.

straightforwardly. He later makes a similar error by having Fanny Robin trek to Troy's barracks on a springlike evening, whereas in the novel she appears, as Bathsheba's less fortunate counterpart must, out of a raging snowstorm. Schlesinger does not read figuratively, a failure in interpretation which has serious consequences here, as he is working with a novel in which the sympathetic relationship between men and nature is paralleled by the ironic metaphorical relationships in the text.

For instance, readers who have predicted a fall are not surprised when Bathsheba falls passionately in love with Sergeant Frank Troy, a self-absorbed opportunist who has already impregnated and deserted Fanny Robin, and whose marriage to Bathsheba will bring her to the brink of emotional and financial disaster. Although Bathsheba has two other suitors—Gabriel Oak and the crazy Farmer Boldwood, who will eventually shoot Troy out of jealousy—she rejects both of them and marries Troy, the man with whom she is sexually infatuated. So deadly is this infatuation that she continues to cling to him even after learning of his affair with Fanny. When Troy rejects her, calling Fanny his "very, very wife" in the sight of heaven, she rushes from the house in a panic.

In Hardy's novel, Bathsheba awakens after a night in the woods to discover that what she thought was a forest glade is actually the edge of an oozing, fungus-ridden swamp. As in the wagon episode, Hardy uses natural imagery to make his point. Having been blind both to her husband's corruption and her own emotional vulnerability, Bathsheba has now awakened. This episode is critical, since it both recapitulates all that has already happened and signifies Bathsheba's present loss of innocence and the beginning of her regeneration. Hardy uses natural imagery to reiterate and elaborate the action, and expects the reader to realize this and to read accordingly. Schlesinger films Bathsheba in the woods. He even includes the small boy reading his catechism who awakens her. But he leaves out the swamp. Without the swamp the sequence is meaningless, and the few close-ups of leaves and reeds which Schlesinger offers instead do not compensate for the loss of a complex metaphor. Moreover, he has obscured Hardy's point that nature, including human nature, can be sinister and deceptive:

Bathsheba's excessive passion for Troy has contributed to her self-deception, and both have brought her close to disaster.

In another sequence, the camera moves in to focus on a leaf dripping water onto Fanny's coffin. But, in keeping with his misreading, the director invents this detail while ignoring Hardy's own strategy, which has Joseph, one of Bathsheba's farmworkers, drive the coffin to the Troys' home through a dense fog in which "The air was as an eye suddenly struck blind," and trees "stood in an attitude of intentness, as if they waited longingly for a wind to come and rock them." Why does Schlesinger choose to substitute for this evocative and seductive imagery such a trite metaphor as a crying leaf? Why does he show us Bathsheba waking up in the wood, only to omit the crucial detail that she awakens in a swamp? Certainly both fog and swamp have cinematic potential and afford him wonderful opportunities both to make Hardy's points about the sympathy between men and nature and to employ some of Hardy's own narrative techniques. But Schlesinger overlooks the fact that sympathy can be combative as well as harmonious and chooses to give us pretty plants precisely at the moment when we need some indication of the tensions that exist between nature and man.

For Hardy, human attempts to restrain nature represent a kind of artifice which nature resists by remaining capricious, erratic, and ungovernable. Men like Boldwood try to control their sexual desires; farmers domesticate animals and cultivate the land; modern farming techniques such as the threshing machine in *Tess of the D'Urbervilles* automate agriculture and turn farm workers into industrial laborers. But human efforts to achieve order and continuity are continually subverted by the unpredictable, senseless, and accidential quality of natural events.

Gabriel and Bathsheba are brought closer together by such natural disasters as the fire on the ricks, the illness of Bathsheba's sheep, and the lightning storm which threatens her crops. They marry because of one man-made disaster, Boldwood's murder of Troy. None of these events could have been foreseen, yet like Bathsheba's first meeting with Troy, in which he literally knocks her over in the dark, each has a whole string of consequences which may be disastrous for its victims. Each determines the course of

Far from the Madding Crowd (1967). The romance of the landscape provides a background for Bathsheba (Julie Christie). In Hardy, nature resists man and remains ungovernable. (Photo courtesy of Museum of Modern Art)

history, shaping human lives in a way that industry and free will cannot. Although characters like Gabriel Oak, whose "humanity often tore in pieces any politic intentions of his which bordered on strategy" (p. 86) are able to accommodate these twists of fate because they expect them to occur, Hardy suggests that most of us fall prey to the kind of strategizing and overformulation that lead to ruin. When Oak shoots his dog after the animal has accidentally herded an entire flock of sheep off a cliff, Hardy identifies the episode as

> another instance of the untoward fate which so often attends dogs and other philosophers who follow out a train of reasoning to its logical conclusion, and attempt perfectly consistent conduct in a world made up so largely of compromise. (p. 87)

Suggesting that knowledge and understanding require the kind of flexibility of which strategists are incapable, Hardy directs his irony at those philosophers who would attempt to foresee, if not to determine, events by systematic deduction from metaphysical or scientific dogma. In this novel, characters who survive are those who both recognize their bond with nature and reconcile themselves to the erratic and often disruptive consequences of this bond.

Each character must "read" nature in order to survive. Reading is, is fact, a principal metaphor for knowledge in the novel. Just as the reader "reads" the novel's natural imagery, Gabriel Oak reads nature, using what he learns to forecast the weather, rescue farm animals, and save crops. Boldwood's downfall is precipitated by a valentine which he misreads. Troy is unable to read nature's signs and is the only character in the novel who needs a watch to tell time. His blindness to the true nature of love between men and women is figured by his sleeping through the storm which threatens to destroy the wheat, while Bathsheba and Gabriel work together to save it in precisely the kind of cooperative partnership of which Troy is incapable. This is one scene which Schlesinger handles very well, intercutting shots of Gabriel and Bathsheba climbing the ricks with close-ups of Troy lying drunk in the barn. Later, he provides us with a few shots of water pouring out of a gargoyle's mouth, an image of sexual lascivity which is undercut by the pretentiousness with which it is filmed, as the camera swoops in, holds for a few seconds, and then quickly cuts away. This image is significant in the novel, as it follows a passage in which Troy's pathetic efforts to plant flowers on Fanny's grave are washed away by water from the overflowing gargoyle, whereas Bathsheba's attempts to replant the flowers succeed:

> Bathsheba collected the flowers, and began planting them with that sympathetic manipulation of roots and leaves which is so conspicuous in a woman's gardening, and which flowers seem to understand and thrive on. (p. 381)

In the film, however, the connection between the gargoyle and the grave is never made clear. Schlesinger does not exercise his directorial authority to make distinctions; he films everything as though it were equally important, diving in to focus on a rock with the same intensity, and often the same camera angle, as that with which he swoops down on a leaf or a rabbit.

Indeed, the cinematography is a serious problem in this film. Schlesinger overphotographs everything, lingering too long over insignificant details and employing a multitude of cinemagraphic techniques with no apparent concern for plot continuity. The cinematography calls attention to itself until it dwarfs even the vast spaces and rolling hills of Dorset. We drive up to a house which begins for no apparent reason to tremble and shake, until we realize that it is being filmed with a hand-held camera. Then, in a peculiar variation on Carl Dreyer's *Vampyr*, in which a funeral is filmed from the point of view of the corpse, Fanny Robin makes her last journey from the point of view of the drunken farmer who is driving her remains to the Troys' farm. And when Bathsheba and Troy rendezvous and marry in Weymouth, we see their mouths move but hear no dialogue. Such discretion is at best gratuitous and at worse annoying. Displays of technical virtuosity end up obscuring the very points that the film wishes to make about men and the world, as we become less conscious of nature than of the director's intention to film it.

Certainly humans and nature seem curiously indifferent to one another in this film, in which the intricate harmonies and dissonances which characterize the exchanges between men and the world in the novel have been blunted by an insistence on omitting the dissonances and either overdramatizing or prettifying the harmonies. Although Gabriel and Bathsheba are dutifully united at moments of natural crisis, we have no sense that these crises change their relationship, since Gabriel either disappears shortly afterwards, or continues to treat Bathsheba with the same insolent deference as he did before. Transforming Hardy's elegant lightning storm into what one reviewer termed "a Florida typhoon," Schlesinger also misses the point that Gabriel is not merely there whenever Bathsheba needs him, but that her needing him is closely tied to her need to understand both her own nature and the nature of the nonhuman world. She therefore recognizes her need for him precisely at those moments when the human and nonhuman worlds collide, at times of natural crisis. These are also the times when Troy always fails her. Thus the film overlooks one of the principal themes of the book.

The inattention to significant detail extends to the casting of Alan Bates and Julie Christie in the principal roles. Gabriel Oak was no innocent, but he nonetheless did not wander around the farm leering belligerently at Bathsheba, while she, in turn, did not bat her eyelashes at him and wear a granny shawl. Bates and Christie are a peculiar Oak and Everdene: Christie is much too sophisticated for the role, and Bates grins from the side of his mouth like a man with something up his sleeve, endowing the saintly Gabriel with a decidedly lascivious air.

Peter Finch, on the other hand, is superb as the obsessed and tormented Boldwood, who degenerates from the proud and aloof farmer to whom Bathsheba sends a valentine, to the pathetic madman who murders Frank Troy. His passionate and unyielding nature is chiefly responsible for his downfall, so that Bathsheba's valentine does not so much cause as trigger his insanity. Portrayed with great sensitivity by Finch, Boldwood is an explosion waiting to happen. He is the only character in the film whose development seems convincing and motivated, the only character who does not have to say, with Bathsheba, at the end of the film, "I've changed, you know."

While Hardy is a difficult and often baffling novelist to read, and

Far from the Madding Crowd a tricky novel to dramatize, the film version does not fail for these reasons. Nor does it fail because it echoes the novel too closely. It fails because of errors in casting and directorial excesses. Nature's only relation to human beings in this film is to dwarf them, and that point is made in the first five minutes. After that, all that countryside does nothing but provide a glamorous backdrop for a very ordinary love story. The film is not well integrated, either technically or thematically; ironic, when one considers that Hardy is concerned with nothing if not the kind of sympathy which Schlesinger does not achieve.

The film version of *Far from the Madding Crowd* was clearly an ambitious project, with everyone involved obviously hoping to produce more than just another technicolor spectacular. It is particularly unfortunate when a film like this one fails, since one can easily conclude that the novel is a genre which cannot be effectively dramatized, or that such dramatizations must sacrifice precisely those elements that make the novel unique. Films such as *Tom Jones* prove that this need not be the case. Recognizing that cinema is not a story told with pictures rather than words, but a distinct and different genre, a director can make a film that is both his own independent production and another, different, version of the novel on which it is based.

The Horrific and the Tragic

JANICE R. WELSCH

Robert Louis Stevenson's *The Strange Case of Dr. Jekyll and Mr. Hyde* (1886) is a mystery story that develops within an atmosphere of mounting gothic horror with characters molded by Victorian and Calvinistic values. Rouben Mamoulian's *Dr. Jekyll and Mr. Hyde* (1932), from a screenplay by Samuel Hoffenstein and Percy Heath based on Stevenson's novel,[1] develops within an atmosphere of increasing horror with characters similarly repressed. Both novel and film focus on the dual nature of their protagonist and on the question of the existence of good and evil within the individual; both rely heavily on animal imagery, on references to madness, and on landscapes of darkness, fog, and shadow. Yet despite these similarities each exists as a unique work of art, each seeks audience involvement in a distinct way and elicits a different reader/viewer response. While Stevenson's work focuses on the mystery involved in the Jekyll/Hyde phenomenon and plays on the reader's desire to learn exactly who Hyde is, Mamoulian's film emphasizes close audience identification with the person who is both Jekyll and Hyde

1. The structure and focus of Mamoulian's film suggests the director was influenced by earlier film versions of the novel and directly by T. R. Sullivan's play. Mamoulian credits only Stevenson as a source, however, and I will be referring only to Stevenson's novel and Mamoulian's film. For synopses of the play and other film versions, see William Luhr and Peter Lehman's *Authorship and Narrative in the Cinema* (New York: G. P. Putnam's Sons, 1977), pp. 221-80).

and elicits the viewer's sympathy for this ultimately tragic protagonist. Mamoulian, like Stevenson, relates the problem of good and evil within the individual to society at large, but the filmmaker shifts responsibility, motivation, and the manifestation of evil so that Stevenson's horrific but cerebral mystery becomes a more personal and immediate experience of human aspiration and failure.

Novel and film both do give us Dr. Jekyll, a practicing physician and scientist who, exploring the dual nature of man, succeeds in bringing forth a figure at once distinct from himself and integrally bound to him, "knit to him closer than a wife," as Jekyll says.[2] This figure is Mr. Hyde, presented by both Stevenson and Mamoulian initially as a primitive man, later as the epitome of evil, the dark side of Jekyll's civilized—and repressed—nature. Because he is associated with the primitive, or animal nature, in man, it is not surprising to find imagery which supports this association. Thus Stevenson describes Hyde (through a character and an omniscient narrator) as "the animal within Dr. Jekyll" (RLS, 446), a brute (RLS, 450), who growls (RLS, 446), roars (RLS, 443), and snarls (RLS, 365) his way through London. To show just how dangerous this uninhibited animal being is, Stevenson turns to imagery of hell. Hyde is "a really damnable man" (RLS, 353), perhaps initially "neither diabolical nor divine," but soon one who is wholly evil (RLS, 434-35) and a devil (RLS, 443).

Dr. Jekyll's image is associated with neither animal nor fiend. He is "a large, well-made, smooth-faced man of fifty, with something of a stylish cast perhaps, but every mark of capacity and kindness," who, after asserting that "the worst of [his] faults was a certain impatient gaiety of disposition" (RLS, 428), confesses also a commitment "to a profound duplicity of life": "I was no more myself when I laid aside restraint and plunged in shame than when I laboured, in the eye of day, at the furtherance of knowledge or the relief of sorrow and suffering" (RLS, 429). A man of science, Jekyll is depicted as civilized rather than primitive, but as his story unfolds his sanity is questioned with increasing frequency and seriousness.

2. Robert Louis Stevenson, "Strange Case of Dr. Jekyll and Mr. Hyde" in *The Works of Robert Louis Stevenson*, Vol. VII, Vailima Edition (New York: Charles Scribner's Sons, 1922), p. 452. All further references to this work (RLS) appear in the text.

After Hyde has killed a man, Jekyll's lawyer Utterson, knowing he has some connection with Hyde, and already thinking Jekyll's will (with Hyde as principal beneficiary) is madness (RLS, 358), asks Jekyll: "You have not been mad enough to hide this fellow?" (RLS, 382). Later, madness is briefly ascribed to Hyde (RLS, 386), but Jekyll's erratic behavior soon has Utterson again speculating on his friend's sanity: "So great and unprepared a change pointed to madness . . ." (RLS, 392). Jekyll himself convinces another friend and colleague that he is in danger of losing his reason (RLS, 416-19), but it is not until he recognizes the inevitability of Hyde's final usurpation that he acknowledges that he is mad, that he has become "a creature eaten up and emptied by fever, languidly weak both in body and mind." (RLS, 451).

Jekyll's appearance at the time of Utterson's last conversation with him suggested just such a wasted creature. Jekyll was sitting at a window, "taking the air with an infinite sadness of mien, like some disconsolate prisoner" (RLS, 395-96). His terror and despair are reflected in the black, cold, and windy landscape, in a London regularly engulfed in fog. There are occasional glimpses of fine, clear days such as a day in January when the air was "full of winter chirrupings and sweet with spring odours" (RLS, 446), and of interiors gay with firelight (RLS, 385-86), but the overwhelming mood is one of loneliness, isolation, and terror, just as the most dominant colors are black (the night with its shadows), brown (the fog that turned even the day "brown as umber"), and white (the pallid faces of those who encounter Hyde). Except for the rich red wine Utterson offers his head clerk (RLS, 385), even reds have sinister connotations through their association with blood, blood that not infrequently runs cold (RLS, 387, 423, 439).

Animal imagery in Mamoulian's filmed version of *Dr. Jekyll and Mr. Hyde* is at times evident in dialogue but is also part of the *mise-en-scène* and Fredric March's depiction of Hyde. A black cat ominously crosses the screen as Jekyll and his friend Lanyon discuss Jekyll's desire to separate the evil and the good aspects within man. It is in the very next sequence that we see Jekyll succeed in this. Later when Jekyll stops briefly in a park on his way to his fiancee's after having resolved to give up Hyde, a black cat again appears; this time it pounces on and kills a bird, thus triggering the first

Dr. Jekyll and Mr. Hyde (1932). Hyde (Fredric March) is the beast within Jekyll. In Mamoulian's filmed version animal imagery is evident in both the *mise-en-scène* and the dialogue. (Photo courtesy of the Museum of Modern Art)

spontaneous change of Dr. Jekyll into Hyde[3] and foreshadowing Hyde's attack on Ivy (one of two women characters Mamoulian adds to the work). Once released, Hyde's agility at times resembles that of a cat, at others that of an ape as he leaps over bannisters, stealthily makes his way through the night, or tries to elude the police as they corner him in the laboratory.[4] It is Hyde, not Jekyll, whose behavior most frequently resembles that of an animal and who is referred to as such: "He's a brute, that's what he is!" (RM, 105). As he usurps more and more of Jekyll's energy and asserts greater power over Jekyll as well as Ivy, he grows more hideous, more bestial. His initial appearance is that of Neanderthal man, the primitive, full of life and energy, exuberant, natural (RM, 74-77), but as his uninhibited drives are unleashed and, at times frustrated, his appearance deteriorates until at last his features are monstrously distorted (RM, 243). Underscoring this animal likeness are the terms of endearment with which Hyde brutally and sadistically assaults Ivy, for they emphatically point to her vulnerability as well as to his feral nature. Thus, Ivy becomes to Hyde "my little bird" (RM, 106, 117, 159, 161), "my dove" (RM, 161, 164), "my little lamb" (RM, 111, 161). There is no similar underscoring in Stevenson.

Hyde's brutality is such that Stevenson intertwines his direct references to it with allusions to evil and the devil. In this Mamoulian concurs, using Ivy to articulate Hyde's diabolical nature. When confiding in Jekyll she speaks of Hyde as a devil (RM, 142), and later, thinking her tormentor is gone forever, she curses him, saying, "Here's hoping that Hyde rots wherever he is. And burns where he ought to be" (RM, 154). Moments later, Hyde appears and when he reveals his knowledge of the conversation she has had with Jekyll, she can only respond with, "You must be the devil" (RM, 160). As he bends over her to strangle her the wings of a Cupid statue appear behind Hyde's head, visually becoming the horns which define him.

3. This scene has been deleted from most prints of Mamoulian's film, but it is described by Richard J. Anobile, ed., in *Rouben Mamoulian's Dr. Jekyll and Mr. Hyde* (New York: Avon, 1975), pp. 6-7. In prints currently available we see only the bird in the tree, not the cat.

4. Anobile, pp. 162-63, 166-71, 245-50. All further references to this work (RM), which is a reconstruction of the film in book form, appear in the text. Though a movie in book form is an impossibility, this reconstruction is useful in locating scenes efficiently and in refreshing one's memory of the movie experience.

He continues to follow his victim down to the floor, revealing the statue in its entirety, Cupid bending over Psyche. The scene provides a painful, ironic comment on the relationship Hyde has pursued with Ivy and emphasizes the opposing roles Jekyll and Hyde have played in Ivy's life. Just as Hyde became her devil, Jekyll was viewed as her angel: "You're an angel, sir" (RM, 142). Hyde uses this appellation to torment Ivy, declaring, just before he murders her that he is "the angel whom you wanted to slave for and love" (RM, 161).

Ivy's attitude of obeisance to Jekyll is shared perhaps by his charity ward patient, who through gesture and facial expression conveys her dependence and faith (RM, 22-23). Jekyll's fiancee (also a Mamoulian addition), Muriel, feels love, which is expressed through a desire to help and to understand (RM, 126-27, 201-02). The attitudes of Jekyll's colleague and friend, Dr. Lanyon, and of General Carew, Muriel's father, however, are more critical. Both accuse Jekyll of being indecent. This motif is repeated during Jekyll's first transformation into Hyde when Jekyll/Hyde defiantly recalls Lanyon's and Carew's accusations. Closely related is another motif which takes us back to Stevenson, that of insanity. Lanyon's reaction to Jekyll's theory of the dual nature of man is to call Jekyll a lunatic (RM, 21). Later, he tells Jekyll, "Oh, you are mad" (RM, 60). Jekyll's reply, "Mad, eh, Lanyon? Oh, we'll see. We'll see," takes us to Jekyll at work in his laboratory. Presenting, indeed, the image of the mad scientist, surrounded by multiple glass vials and tubes, coils and burners, so absorbed in his work that he forgets sleep, meals, and dinner engagements, Jekyll is intense, almost delirious with excitement and curiosity (RM, 61-69). As he is transformed into Hyde, Lanyon's judgment comes back, "Disgusting. You're mad, mad!" but the triumphant Hyde exuberantly dismisses it as he ventures forth.

The pessimism of Lanyon's judgment is reflected in the chiaroscuro lighting of Mamoulian's film. Stevenson writes of fog, of night, and of shadows to convey an atmosphere of hopelessness and terror; Mamoulian reinforces a sense of horror, fear, and loss through the nocturnal Hyde. Dressed in black he moves amid rain, mists, and shadows. When he first emerges from Jekyll's laboratory, he momentarily savors the rain, then draws his cape about him and walks quickly toward us, coming so close that he completely blocks out all but his own black presence (RM, 76-78). A similar visualization of the menacing, desperate Hyde takes place after he has killed Carew. As he flees down dark labyrinthian streets he rushes toward us, and his shadow, at first normal size, grows to such huge proportions it appears to envelope all that is before it (RM, 229).

Lamps punctuate but do not disperse the darkness Hyde walks in; they create the shadows that give Hyde his larger-than-life appearance, and suggest the trap Jekyll's willfulness and society's repressiveness have led him into. Reinforcing the feeling of entrapment is the expressionistic composition. Pillars, roofs, a hitching post, diagonal staircases, archways, drapes, bedposts, fences, and grills reduce the space within frames while increasing the complexity of the images. A nightmare world is created. The flow, warmth, and quiet of Muriel's presence are capable initially of dispelling this world for Jekyll (RM, 29-40), but once Hyde has gained control even Muriel loses her incandescence and exchanges her radiant white for black (RM, 200-06).

Change is also evident in Ivy as a result of her contacts with Jekyll and Hyde. In her first meeting with Jekyll Ivy responds with charm and flirtatious lambency to his attention and Jekyll's amused reaction briefly sustains the light-hearted mood. However, after only a few moments of sexual sparring with Hyde, Ivy is overcome with fear. She is trapped and made vulnerable by her sexuality and beauty, the attributes she initially regarded as assets. The change is seen in the apartment Hyde furnishes for her. It is an apartment filled with fetishistic statues and pictures of nudes as well as with plush, baroque drapes and heavy ornate furniture, an apartment from which there is no escape (RM, 103-20, 152-166). The despair created there for Ivy parallels that experienced increasingly by Jekyll.

Though Stevenson and Mamoulian work within the limits of distinct art forms, Stevenson relying on graphic and suggestive language, Mamoulian combining vivid dialogue with an effective *mise-en-scène*, they create similar imagery, landscapes, and moods. They differ greatly, however, in the structure of their respective Jekyll/Hyde stories and in the kind of audience involvement their works evoke. Stevensons wrote his novel as a mystery as well as a horror story, using a somewhat dry, detached observer, the lawyer Mr. Utterson, as his investigator. Being Dr. Jekyll's friend and his lawyer, Utterson becomes the reluctant repository of information leading to the horrifying discovery that the respected Dr. Jekyll and the disreputable Mr. Hyde are one. Slowly, at times casually, over a period of some ten or twelve years, Utterson gathers clues, not realizing they are clues, until another client, Sir Danvers Carew, another friend, Dr. Hastie Lanyon, and Dr. Jekyll himself are dead. Only when Lanyon's and Jekyll's final letters are read is the Jekyll and Hyde mystery resolved.

Stevenson suggests rather than specifies the horror that defines and surrounds Hyde as we move closer to Jekyll's secret with Utterson. Curiosity and a fascination with the indescribable and horrifying Hyde keep us interested despite Utterson's reserve and Jekyll's distance. Often Utterson's information comes to him from someone else, from eyewitnesses who tell of their encounters with Hyde. Thus Enfield tells the story of his meeting him when Hyde trampled a child (RLS, 350-53), and the narrator recounts the story of Carew's murder as it was described by the maid who saw it (RLS, 374-76). These stories within stories keep us at some distance from all the characters and have the effect of a series of Chinese boxes which must be successively opened to get to the heart of the mystery. The last two such boxes are Lanyon's and Jekyll's letters, the most personal and subjective narratives within the novel. Jekyll is the focus of the novel but the last person to be given an opportunity for a hearing. He is not an admirable man, his motive for releasing Hyde being his desire to enjoy every imaginable license while still being able "to carry [his] head high, and wear a more than commonly grave countenance before the public" (RLS, 428).[5] In the end he loses control over Hyde and refuses to accept responsibility for his actions. The two are consumed ultimately by their hatred of one another.

Jekyll's experiment is a failure and the Victorian society to which he belonged is left with the problem he tried to solve. As with other pioneers Jekyll failed because he undertook too much; because he lost sight of the essential unity of man; because he mistook the

5. Edwin M. Eigner, *Robert Louis Stevenson and Romantic Tradition* (Princeton: Princeton University Press, 1966), pp. 153-54.

dichotomy between the spiritual and the physical for the dichotomy between good and evil; and because his motives ultimately were selfish. His became a Faustian endeavor. Though Jekyll seems unwilling to admit it, his pride and self-delusion function within his spiritual self as well as within Hyde. He has not separated good from evil but the animal from the spiritual, and while his animal nature craves complete freedom to indulge itself, his spiritual side seeks recognition and respectability, the approbation and, perhaps, even the adulation of his fellows. Given this portrait it is not surprising that Stevenson does not seek reader identification with Jekyll. Stevenson seems more interested in a critique of the Victorian sense of division which prompted Jekyll's experiment.[6] He keeps readers involved through his emphasis on the mystery of Hyde's identity and through his ability to create with language a world at once fascinating and terrifying.

Stevenson's focus on the uncovering of Hyde's identity is not Mamoulian's focus. The filmmaker not only introduces Jekyll earlier and Hyde later, he very carefully leads his audience to identify with Jekyll from the opening moments of the film. He dispenses with Utterson and Enfield and with Stevenson's investigative approach. He adds new characters, most significantly Muriel and Ivy with whom we are encouraged to identify, and he alters the roles of Dr. Lanyon and of Sir Danvers Carew, giving each more weight. As a result the overall thematic interest of the narrative is shifted and audience response is changed. Jekyll is made not only the center of the film's narrative but the primary vehicle for the development of the action. Viewers are invited to identify with him as he first articulates his theory of the separation of the good and evil within men, then experiments with the drugs that eventually effect the separation, and finally lives out the consequences of his work. The narrative follows a chronological sequence and depicts action that occurs within the span of six or eight weeks.

While none of Stevenson's characters, not even our interested but dispassionate guide, Utterson, provides a strong identification figure, Mamoulian encourages audience identification with several major characters, most importantly, with Dr. Jekyll. In the very first

6. Irving S. Saposnik, *Robert Louis Stevenson* (New York: Twayne, 1974), pp. 88-89.

shots of the film we share Jekyll's point of view and to an extent his experience through the use of subjective shots (RM, 11-15). Later, a subjective camera graphically and immediately captures Jekyll/ Hyde's daring and exhilaration, even his motivational dilemma, as the doctor releases Hyde for the first time (RM, 69-74). That we, and no film character, are in on this secret from the beginning furthers our identification, as does Mamoulian's positive presentation of Jekyll as a capable, generous, and concerned physician (RM, 21, 22-23), ardent lover (RM, 29-43), and courageous adventurer (RM, 46-48, 61-74), especially when placed against the pedestrian and self-righteous Lanyon. Jekyll does get carried away in the course of his experimentation; he does go too far; he does lose control—and he does pay the price. He has not thought through the idea of man's dual nature and the consequences of separation. He is vague on essential points: the relationship of man's natural impulses that bind "him to some dim animal relation with the earth," and the bad, or evil; and the fulfillment of this evil once it is liberated (RM, 17-19). Because of their identification with him audiences forgive Jekyll for his lack of patience, care, and clarity in thinking through his theory and they even seem to overlook the fact that his early reactions to Hyde are never known.

After Hyde is freed there is a period of a month or so during which Jekyll gives himself over entirely to Hyde and Hyde moves from "exuberance and joy and freedom"[7] to sadism and lechery (RM, 74-127). There is no word whatever of Jekyll. When the doctor again emerges it is with the resolve to be rid of Hyde forever (RM, 122-23, 126-28), but by this time it is too late. Hyde emerges, murders Ivy, and must appeal to Lanyon for help. Jekyll resolves to banish Hyde, fails, and, as Hyde, murders Carew and subsequently is killed himself. By avoiding any record of that crucial month when Hyde establishes his right to an independent existence, Mamoulian skirts the question of Jekyll's motivation as he learns how dangerous his experiment is. Mamoulian also avoids the possible loss of audience sympathy for the doctor: Jekyll ultimately becomes a tragic hero.

The inclusion of Muriel (Rose Hobart) and Ivy (Miriam Hopkins)

7. Rouben Mamoulian, "Style Is the Man," in *Discussion*, ed. James R. Silke (Washington, D.C.: American Film Institute, 1971) p. 22.

in Mamoulian's film, along with that of a female charity patient, is another major departure from Stevenson's work. We have seen above how Ivy's presence is used to underscore Hyde's bestiality and how Muriel's world of calm and comfort set off the murder and mayhem of Jekyll and Hyde's nightmare worlds. The scene in which the charity patient silently pleads for Jekyll's attention and care serves to make Jekyll's dedication to his profession evident and to contrast his response to human need with Dr. Lanyon's interests in wealthy patients and social status (RM, 22-23). In fact, Jekyll's interest in individuals, no matter what their social or economic status, is responsible for his initial meeting with Ivy, who at the time was being physically assaulted.

Ivy and Muriel are both major characters in Mamoulian's film and as such they function as more than foils for Jekyll and Hyde. Their presence shifts the primary and initial manifestation of evil from hypocrisy to lust. Stevenson's Jekyll acts out of pride and hypocrisy; Mamoulian's Jekyll is an energetic and dedicated but impatient and sexually frustrated man. He is asked to sublimate his sexual desires in order to comply with societal conventions and traditions: "There is such a thing as decent observance, you know" (RM, 43). Yet Jekyll insists to Lanyon that his response to sexual stimuli is natural, "not a matter of conduct but of elementary instincts" (RM, 59). As Jekyll he suppresses a desire to act on them but as Hyde he immediately seeks out Ivy in order to gratify them.

Perhaps is is because Jekyll has suppressed his natural instincts for so long that, when released, Hyde crosses every boundary of propriety and gives full reign to every savage impulse. "An animal . . . is never so wild and dangerous as when it is wounded."[8] Jekyll's instincts have been wounded by a society which prefers to pretend they do not even exist, a society that values punctuality and propriety over charity. When he finally indulges himself through Hyde it is without any kind of restraint. The moment of exhilaration in the rain lasts only a moment; then Hyde is off to find Ivy. When he does find her, he tells her, "I want you. What I want I get. . . . Do you suppose I'd let anybody stand in my way? I love you. I love you. Do you understand? You'll come with me . . ." (RM, 101). He

8. Aniela Jaffe, "Symbolism in the Visual Arts," in *Man and His Symbols*, ed. Carl G. Jung (New York: Dell Publishing, 1964), pp. 265-66.

makes this declaration of love as he brutally holds her head in his hands and brings her face to within inches of his.

That Hyde has his way with Ivy is evident when we see her in a new apartment. Hyde comes in, crudely dismisses the landlady with whom Ivy has been talking, and questions the frightened girl, with the threat, "If I ever catch you lying, these (pointing to scratches on her arm) are a trifle of what you'll get" (RM, 106). Sex has become linked to violence; Hyde's behavior has become masochistic as well as sadistic. He can't get Jekyll out of his mind: "I'm not good enough for you. I'm not a nice kind gentleman like that nice kind gentleman who was so good to look at. And so . . . cowards, weaklings!" He goes on: "Tell me you hate me. Please my lamb. Please my dear sweet pretty little bird. Tell me that you hate me" (RM, 110-11). Later, after Ivy has gone to Jekyll for help, Hyde reemerges and again accosts her physically and verbally: "You took the word of that snivelling hypocrite Jekyll against mine. . . . You went down on your knees to the man I hate more than anybody else in the world. . . . You wanted him to love you, didn't you? Well, I'll give you a lover now. His name is death" (RM, 157-58). Ivy tries desperately to escape but is finally cornered and strangled as Hyde goes on with his torments. "There, my sweet," he says as his huge, hairy hands close about her throat, "There, my love. There my little bride. Isn't Hyde a lover after your own heart?" (RM, 158-65).

Hyde's hatred of Jekyll is directed toward Ivy at the same time Hyde seeks her out to satisfy his lust. He cannot fully possess her as he is, given his monstrous looks and his crude, violent manner; but he refuses to don the gentlemanly attributes which might draw her to him but which he detests, because to him they are linked with hypocrisy, with Jekyll, with all the refined men of culture who strive to keep him repressed or try to deny his very existence. When he sees Muriel Carew his response is essentially the same as it was with Ivy. He wants her sexually and he goes after her; it is only his sense of self-preservation and confrontations with General Carew and the butler that prevent him from having her.

Muriel and Ivy have beauty in common. On other levels they differ. Muriel is a self-assured member of the elite—privileged, pampered, and deeply in love with Dr. Jekyll, whom she admires for his professional dedication and daring as well as his impatience with social form and manners. When Jekyll and she are in her father's garden their world takes on the appearance of a shimmering fairyland; they live, if only for a moment, in a romantic dream where all is light, laughter, and love. The moment is brilliantly captured through Karl Struss's photography. Not only are Jekyll and Muriel radiant but the garden sparkles with magical charm (RM, 32-39). For Jekyll, Muriel is a goddess, the Unknown, the idealized woman. She is kept, however, in a gilded cage by an ever watchful Father who periodically places her on a pedestal to be admired and desired. She remains unattainable.

Ivy, on the other hand, is a member of the lower class, a woman of the world, and on her own. There is no doting father or pedestal for her. Her beauty and sexuality are accessible. From her point of view it is Dr. Jekyll who is unattainable. He is the "angel" that offers hope for escape from a life that has become hell. For him, she is linked to those uncontrollable animal impulses he would like to satisfy but cannot without breaking the taboos of his social group. Of course, he does satisfy them in Hyde. As Hyde he goes far beyond the normal satisfaction of sexual drives and through a perversion of love creates the hell that Ivy is trying to escape. Jekyll/Hyde is at once Ivy's potential deliverer and her destroyer. As a woman Ivy is initially spunky, tough, flirtatious, and ready to take chances. Hyde breaks her through cruelty, both physical and mental: he tortures her until the reality of her world is completely shattered.[9] That romantic moonlit garden scene shared by Jekyll and Muriel is totally reversed in the scene depicting Ivy's murder by Hyde.[10]

Ivy, though poor and desirous of higher social status, is comfortable with her sexuality, and Muriel, though attracted by what is unconventional and spontaneous in Jekyll, is at ease in the asexual role society has imposed on her. Jekyll is suspended between the two. He wants to share Ivy's easy acceptance of her sexual impulses as well as Muriel's high-minded spirituality. Under pressure from a puritanical society he wrongly identifies the former with evil and

9. Luhr and Lehman, p. 236.
10. Mamoulian reminds us of the earlier scene via the statue of Cupid and Psyche we see as Hyde bends over Ivy. The sensual aspects of male/female relationships are present in the nude paintings flanking the statue.

the latter with good. Like Victorian man he strives for a perfectly ordered world in which his impulses as well as his thoughts and actions are understood and systematized. He would rid himself of that dark side of his nature which is associated with primitive man, with instinct, with the unscientific, the unclassifiable. He does not seek integration or annihilation of these natural impulses, but separation and fulfillment of what he asserts is evil. Clearly, his is a dangerous path and clearly he fails. He becomes a Beast, whose instincts are corrupted and debased because they are tainted by human faults, by hatred, jealousy, and pride, while he remains also a man of reason whose instincts and animal impulses are still active. As Hyde he destroys the sensual Beauty that is Ivy, and together with Jekyll he wrecks the happiness of Muriel, the personification of spiritual Beauty.

As presented by Stevenson, Jekyll experiments in order to enjoy more fully and without fear of discovery pleasures forbidden by a restrictive society, while continuing also to maintain an approved and honorable position. Mamoulian's Jekyll experiments in order to "be clean not only in [his] conduct but in [his] innermost thoughts and desires" (RM, 60). After Stevenson's Jekyll recognizes the danger of possible involuntary transformations into Hyde, his short period of abstinence is followed by "throes and longings, as of Hyde struggling after freedom; and at last, in an hour of moral weakness, [he] once again compounded and swallowed the transforming draught" (RLS, 443). He consciously decides to resume his life of self-indulgence under cover of Hyde's identity. When he does so he murders Sir Danvers and is thereafter forced to hide under Jekyll's identity, a situation which leads to mutual hatred and disgust and ultimately to suicide. Once the chemicals needed to effect the change are gone Jekyll succumbs to Hyde completely and it is as Hyde that he kills himself to avoid capture and death on the scaffold. It is an act of cowardice interpreted by Jekyll as courage. Jekyll's own last act is a final disavowal of responsibility, a refusal to face the enormity of his act: "what is to follow concerns another than myself" (RLS, 454).

In Mamoulian's film Jekyll allows Hyde free reign for a time but upon Muriel's return to London he resolves to give up his dual existence, reinforcing his decision by throwing away the key to the back door of his laboratory (Hyde's means of entry) and by sending his servant Poole to Ivy with restitutory money. He reestablishes contact with Muriel and her father and is in the process of resuming his respectable place in society when, involuntarily, Hyde emerges. Ivy's murder follows, as do renewed resolutions and pleas for help. When Jekyll goes to Muriel to break their engagement, he does so as an act of penance. The emphasis is on Jekyll's repentance and on his desire but inability to stop the chain of events he has started rather than on his submission to and hatred of Hyde or on Hyde's hatred and need of him. When he is trapped after Carew's murder, however, his instinct of self-preservation proves stronger than any allegiance to truth or justice and he attempts to divert the police in their pursuit. When Lanyon accuses him, Hyde spontaneously takes over, and it is as this now pitiable creature that he is killed. Lanyon, Poole, and the police witness his resumption of Dr. Jekyll's form. The last image of the doctor is one of tranquillity but as we move back from the body, Jekyll is lost to view and we are left with an image of his experimental apparatus, the representatives of society who surround his body, and the rising flames that remind us of his tragic and ill-advised but not ignoble venture.

On Adapting " The Most Audacious Thing in Fiction "

JIM BECKERMAN

With the exception of Walt Disney's cheerfully bastardized *Jungle Book* (1967), the works of Rudyard Kipling were ignored as movie material for more than twenty years before John Huston was able to make *The Man Who Would Be King* in 1975. Huston, who fell in love with Kipling's writings when he was fourteen, had been making periodic attempts to film the story throughout his career—Clark Gable and Humphrey Bogart were originally to star; when that fell through it was to be Richard Burton and Peter O'Toole. Eventually, John Foreman, the producer of *Butch Cassidy and the Sundance Kid* (1969)—who no doubt saw something trendy and marketable in Kipling's male cameraderie—took an interest in the project, and *The Man Who Would Be King* was finally made, with two fine, expansive performances by Sean Connery and Michael Caine.

Perhaps inevitably, the Huston film suffered in comparison with the Kipling-inspired adventure movies of the 1930s—it was not visceral or "stirring" like *Four Feathers* (1939) or *Gunga Din* (1939), and Huston's reserve was interpreted as an attempt to be fashionably cynical at Kipling's expense. Although there *is* an emotional and visual distance in the film (Oswald Morris's photography, in particular, tends to be formal and godlike—the cinematic equivalent of what in epic form would be called high style), this is perfectly appropriate for a story which is, after all, not about a triumphant

180

quest but an ironic one. And the irony is Kipling's; a look at the original confirms that Huston has been wholly faithful to the spirit of his source.

The Man Who Would Be King was written in 1886, when Kipling was only twenty-one, and it made its first appearance in print two years later. Briefly, it concerns Peachy Carnehan and Daniel Dravot, two engaging soldiers turned confidence men, who decide that colonial India "isn't big enough for such as us" and set out to conquer Kafiristan, a remote and mysterious corner of Afghanistan. Their scheme is to supply arms and military expertise to native chieftains, win their allegiance, and then nudge them off the throne. Once in Kafiristan, the plan works splendidly for a short time—the natives even take the two men to be gods—but eventually they are found out. Danny is killed and Peachy, mutilated and half mad, returns to India to recount the adventure.

This crazy yarn has always had admirers, and it was extravagantly praised by Kipling's contemporaries, among them H. G. Wells, Somerset Maugham, Sir Edmund Gosse, and J. M. Barrie. If today the story seems less than great, it is, at least, admirably constructed. There is a fearful symmetry in the design: Peachy goes forth as a mad priest and returns as a madman; the two scoundrels come to Kafiristan "as though we had tumbled from the skies" but eventually "tumble from one of those damned rope bridges"; the story begins with the newspaper editor writing obituary notices for kings, and ends with the severed head of Daniel Dravot the King being laid upon his desk—the tale itself becomes his obituary. Beyond this, there is something childish and appealing about Kipling's mixture of incongruous elements—heathen idols and lost kingdoms are impossibly thrown together with Masonic rituals and slangy rogues.

Although the whimsical side of the tale no doubt attracted Barrie, he probably didn't call it "the most audacious thing in fiction" on this account.[1] The term "audacious" suggests an affront. And although Michael Caine, who plays Peachy in the film, has offered a genial warning against seeing the story as a "great vast tome about something or other," the larger ironies in *The Man Who Would Be*

1. Brown, Hilton, *Rudyard Kipling*. (New York: Harper, 1945), p. 224.

King are too delicious to neglect.[2] Peachy and Danny, who indulge their wildest fantasies of power and wealth and are destroyed by their own audacity, are merely following the code of their culture; they are Victorian Everymen, and their methods of conquest are a parody of imperialist policy. To readers like Barrie, at the height of the colonial movement, the story must have been a slap in the face. This is not the familiar take-up-the-white-man's-burden Kipling so much as it is the concerned, cynical Kipling who wrote "If, drunk with sight of power, we loose/Wild tongues that have not Thee in awe . . . Thy mercy on Thy people, Lord!" For Kipling, power without responsibility is a form of blasphemy, and Danny's downfall is the direct result of his impersonating a god. If *The Man Who Would Be King* is essentially a schoolboy adventure story like Rider Haggard's *She* (1885), it also has affinities to such grotesque fables of imperialism as Wells's *The War of the Worlds* (1897) and Conrad's *Heart of Darkness* (1899).

The screenplay for the film, which was cowritten by Huston and Gladys Hill, stays surprisingly close to its model. Large chunks of dialogue are lifted intact from the original—for instance, the scene in which Peachy (Caine) and Danny (Connery) sign their "contrack" is an almost verbatim transcription. Kipling, like Damon Runyon, had a fondness for low-life lingo, and Huston retains Peachy and Danny's arsenal of eccentric phrases, e.g., "Well *and* good" and "it's hugeous great." The hymn in the story, which comments on the transience of Danny's conquest—"The Son of God goes forth to war . . . who follows in His train?"—is not only preserved but becomes a satiric leitmotif in Maurice Jarre's score, to the tune of "The Minstrel Boy." For the most part, Huston was successful in finding visual equivalents even for Kipling's more outré conceits. In terms of film adaptation, there is an almost insurmountable difficulty built into the work—the Peachy who recounts the adventure is almost insane, and much of his narrative is rendered in psychotic, fragmented imagery. If the montage of clashing mountains in the film is not quite up to Peachy's anthropomorphic narration ("these mountains, they never keep still . . . Always fighting they are, and don't let you sleep at night"), other

2. Kaminsky, Stuart, *John Huston, Maker of Magic.* (Boston: Houghton-Mifflin, 1978), p. 198.

The Man Who Would Be King (1977). The paths of glory lead but to the grave. Sean Connery is Daniel Dravot in this tale that has affinities to Conrad's *Heart of Darkness*. (Photo courtesy of the Museum of Modern Art)

passages are improved: where Kipling writes, "Old Dan fell, turning round and round and round twenty thousand miles, for it took him half an hour to fall till he struck water," Huston shows us Dan slowly twisting through the air while the crown he fought to possess falls ahead of him, eluding him forever—an image at once more powerful and absurd.

There are alterations and embellishments. The nameless editor who narrates the story is replaced in the film by "Rudyard Kipling"—a benign and bewhiskered Christopher Plummer. The film's Kipling, (like other outsider-narrators in literature) is attracted to the life of the protagonists but remains a slightly amused nonparticipant. Although straightlaced, he has his subversive side, and is secretly delighted when Peachy and Dan flout authority and ridicule a pretentious government official. (Kindly, stuffy Kipling, though hardly the "singularly robust" twenty-one-year-old *enfant terrible* described by Henry James, is nevertheless effective in terms of the film—he becomes the necessary link between the heroes and the government bureaucracy that has no place for them.) Some of the changes are purely structural. Peachy's dramatic entrance into the newspaper office, scarred and limping, occurs about a third of the way through Kipling's story; the incident is sensibly used to open the film. (Though this means that Peachy, for our benefit, has to recount information that "Kipling" would already know.) The Holy City of Sikandergul, with its fabulous Greek temple perched above mud houses, is a Huston contribution; so is the treasure of Alexander which is eventually scattered like the gold dust in Huston's *The Treasure of the Sierra Madre* (1948). Billy Fish (Saeed Jaffrey), the heroes' companion in Kafiristan, is provided with a much more plausible genesis—originally one of the conquered Kafiri tribesmen (who improbably spoke perfect English), he becomes in the film a Gurkha soldier who wandered from his British regiment, a wonderful innocent whose self-sacrifice, in a cynical reversal of "Gunga Din," does *not* save the day for his English comrades.

The real Kipling, apart from his perennial fascination with secret societies and ritual law (see, for instance, the animal laws in his *Jungle Books*, 1895) was a dedicated Mason, and both story and film contain a number of explicit references to Freemasonry. When it appears in the story, however, it is largely as a mischieveous comment on the background of the heroes. Peachy and Danny, who are Masons, have the military experience to conquer a country, but they lack the political experience to run it; their methods of civilizing the natives are mostly improvisational. Thus when Dan discovers that the Kafiris are also Masons, he bases his entire Kafiri government on the degrees of Freemasonry, obviously the only comparable system he can think of. "It's a master stroke of policy," he decides, "it means running this country as easy as a four wheeled bogy on a down grade." Huston rightly assumes that this episode was too complicated to use on screen, but he retains the Masonry for other reasons.

> I use a Masonic emblem to symbolize a universal connection between men, and my protagonists' lives are saved in a remote mountain town because the unfriendly high priest recognizes in the emblem on Sean Connery's chest an old holy insignia he believes belonged to Alexander the Great.[3]

Masonry unites the three classes of people in the film—the respectable bourgeois (Kipling), the outcast-adventurers (Peachy and Danny), and the Kafiri natives. Moreover, the Masonic ideal becomes a device to tie the whole adventure together. Early in the film, "Kipling" describes Masonry as "an ancient order dedicated to the brotherhood of man under the all-seeing eye of God." All too briefly, the prophecy is fulfilled—Peachy and Danny bring the warring tribes of Kafiristan together under the leadership of Danny Dravot, the bogus god. When Danny is exposed, it is because he has disobeyed the command of Imbra, the cyclops-idol, whose "all-seeing eye" matches with the master-Mason insignia.

Peachy and Danny, as Huston has pointed out, are really antithetical halves of one man. At the beginning of the film, their personalities are almost indistinguishable—they even finish each other's sentences—and it is only later on, in Kafiristan, that a division occurs. "One half of 'him,' as one half of ourselves often does, falls prey to that illness that attacks us when we get to high places, *folie de grandeur*. Imagining that we are more than we are.

3. Bachmann, Gideon, "Watching Huston," *Film Comment*. Jan-Feb, 1976, p.22.

Gods, in fact. The other one is that half of ourselves that chides us and says that we are absurd."[4]

The later rift between the two men becomes, for Huston, also a distinction between two kinds of imperialists. Peachy and Danny start out as old-fashioned adventurer-plunderers being driven out of India by what Conrad, in *Heart of Darkness,* called "the new gang—the gang of virtue": the idealists, pious crooks, and white-man's-burden bearers. (The mature Kipling was of course the literary spokesman for the new movement, and it may have been Huston's concern for historical context that prompted him to include the character in the film.) Peachy remarks that India was once a great country "until the bureaucrats took over and ruined it," and when a lofty district commissioner (Jack May) calls Dan and Peachy "detriments to the dignity of the Empire," Peachy is quick to remind him that "it was *detriments* like us that built this bloody Empire." The two men, honest frauds, are an intolerable embarrass-ment to the sanctimonious government frauds—small wonder the commissioner wants to see them deported.

In Kafiristan, the cycle of empire is repeated in miniature: Peachy and Danny set out intending to loot and run, but when Dan is crowned King he develops some sanctimonious ideas about his people and his "destiny," and he snubs Peachy, the simple, sane crook. The allegory may be more explicit in the film version, but Huston and Kipling ultimately arrive at the same point: Danny's delusions are those of a whole culture that began to view exploita-tion and plundering as a moral imperative. Danny is no longer after mere wealth, and when he builds bridges to tie his kingdom together, it is in the same spirit of "progress" that made the British run railroads through India. It is appropriate that Dan should spend his last moments poised on such a bridge—monument to colonial expansion and the meeting of East and West—while the natives hack away at the supports. His great plunge into the ravine is more than a fall from power. The myth of Empire has collapsed from under him.

4. *Ibid.*

The Time Machine (1895), H.G. Wells
George Pal, 1960

Myths of the Future

RICHARD WASSON

Films and novels are separate entities, not to be compared; yet the temptation remains irresistible, particularly when we are confronted with popular works of science fiction. This literary mode has come to be a vehicle through which our culture does much of its political and social speculating, much of its public mythmaking. Both H. G. Wells's novel *The Time Machine* and George Pal's film are closely tied to the social problems of their respective eras, to an identifiable archetype and, more importantly, to an anonymous myth related to the roles of classes in society.

Wells's novel, published in 1898, is organized around Victorian class struggle and its interpretation through Social Darwinist rhetoric. Pal's film, released in 1960, is organized around the rhetoric of atomic holocaust and technological humanism. Wells, employing a rhetorical strategy the French critic Roland Barthes has called "ex-nomination," shifts from the language of class to the language of myth and makes the archetype of Everyman-facing-Death central to his novel. The film puts the language of class and of concrete politics through a further process of ex-nomination to establish the archetype of Prometheus. Yet each work shares a common twentieth-century myth of the classless outsider—the man apparently without social and economic ties is the true perceiver of social reality.

In comparison to the film, the rhetoric of the novel is remarkable for its open naming, its nomination, of classes and of political systems. Arriving in the year 802,701 Wells's Traveller discovers the Eloi, a group of small, delicate creatures living in what at first seems an Edenic environment. Free from labor, these people engage in sensuous play in a lush garden. The Traveller admires their fair beauty, their blond hair, their red lips and delicate chins as well as their gentle manners and musical voices. He feels himself somewhat rough and crude, perhaps too aggressively masculine in comparison to their refined ways. But soon his admiration turns to contempt because he discovers them to be physically weak, intellectually uncurious, without creative culture and perhaps a trifle diseased. In short he finds their combination of virtues and vices to be entirely too feminine and childlike for him. When one of their numbers, Weena by name, is about to drown, no one moves to rescue her, a fact which not only morally offends him, but leads him to contempt for their pale indifference.

Interestingly enough, the Traveller names the social order which produces such effete creatures "Communism." From Social Darwinist rhetoric he concocts the hypothesis that the human species won a victory over nature, thus abolishing scarcity and therefore exploitation. But rather than fulfillment of the Social Darwinist prediction of racial improvement, degeneration sets in. Here, as Darko Suvin pointed out, Wells ironically attacks the complacent bourgeois audience's belief "in linear progress, Spencerian Social Darwinism and such."[1] Victory over scarcity saps the moral virtues which lead to progress—"Hardship and Freedom; conditions under which the strong and subtle survive and the weaker go to the wall"[2]—and devolution is the consequence.

However the Time Traveller, having journeyed forward through history to the world of the future, soon discovers the existence of the Morlocks, and his historical thesis has to be discarded. Two varieties of creature now inhabit what was once England: above ground, the Eloi; below ground, the Morlocks. Unlike the description of the

1. Darko Suvin, "*The Time Machine* vs. *Utopia* as a Structural Model for Science Fiction," *Comparative Literature Studies* X, 4 (Dec. 1973), p. 335.
2. H. G. Wells, *The Time Machine* (New York: Charles Scribners Sons, 1924), p. 41. Hereafter all references will be to this edition and included in parentheses in the body of the text.

Eloi, that of the Morlocks is almost entirely negative. Though they have the rudimentary capacity to maintain mechanical operations, they are hairy, apelike, soft, and cold to the touch, and the traveller compares them to spiders, worms, vermin, rodents, etc. In contrast to the feminine and childlike Eloi, the Time Traveller characterizes the Morlocks as savage, instinctive, and animallike.

Relying on Social Darwinist rhetoric, the Traveller now postulates that these two groups are the biological descendents of the Victorian Working and Capitalist classes. Winning a permanent victory, the Capitalist-Eloi forced the Morlock-Workers underground, killed off their more intelligent and rebellious leaders, and, freed from the necessity to labor, pursued education, refinement, pleasure, and luxury above ground while the hapless Morlocks, continually adapting to the conditions of their labor, turned into repulsive creatures below ground.

Again Wells satirizes Social Darwinism, pointing out that a victory of the strongest does not mean victory of the fittest, that devolution is as possible as evolution. More significant than the satire, however, is the open naming of classes and class warfare. As Darko Suvin has pointed out, Wells creates through this nomination a biopolitical division: where for Darwin man was a unitary species, Wells's rhetoric creates a mankind divided by two diverent gene pools contained within the major classes. Such rhetoric, Suvin has shown, resembles "a curious hybrid of Deterministic or Malthusian pseudo-Darwinism and bourgeois, or indeed imperialist, social theory (and practice)."[3]

Of equal interest with this biopolitical nomination is the class anonymity of the Traveller. While communism, capital and labor, and class warfare are openly nominated, the Traveller's class goes unnamed. But as most critics understand, and Suvin has clearly stated, the Traveller is "isotopic with the petty bourgeois Wells who is disdainful of the decadent upper class, but horrified and repelled by a crude lower class."[4] To explicitly name the Traveller's class would make obvious the bias of his descriptions and response to the Morlocks and the Eloi: neither the overly refined, self-indulgent, pleasure-seeking, and finally childlike and feminine upper class nor

3. Suvin, p. 339.
4. Suvin, p. 347.

the instinctive, animallike, and savage working class should be entrusted with the future of humanity. By creating a pattern of nomination which leaves the Traveller's class anonymous, Wells fosters the fictional illusion that his descriptions represent both a scientifically objective report and a statement of values representing the fully human.

Class anonymity becomes even more crucial to the motivation of the only public act the Traveller commits in the future—his war against the Morlocks. The rhetoric at this point in the novel is particularly interesting because it combines the rhetoric of class with that of a typically Victorian antifeminism. Having discovered that the Morlocks have reversed the usual power relationship between Capital and Labor and now raise the Eloi as cattle, as a food supply, the Traveller gives way first to despair, then to fear, and finally to hatred. His hopes for progress dashed, his efforts for the improvement of the species in his own time proven futile, he comes to a desperate rage against the Morlocks.

Recognizing that such hatred is less than justified by the aeons of oppression which produced the Morlocks' cannibalism, the Traveller rationalizes his action by claiming the Eloi are more human. But it is the rhetoric of feminine dependence on the male which justifies his action. Having rescued Weena, he takes more than a little comfort in her feminine Eloi ways—her childlike playfulness, her singing, her dancing, her unquestioned admiration and love for him, and even her somewhat cloying dependence. Yet he is annoyed because she tires easily, takes him from his work, and, most of all, because she fails to understand the seriousness of his mission: "I had not come into the future to carry on a miniature flirtation," (pp. 55, 56) he tells his audience. However, loyal to the values of Victorian masculinity, he recognizes that as a dominant male he must defend her against the Morlocks. Though objectively he knows that there is no reason for him to choose between the Eloi and the Morlocks, he decides, watching "little Weena sleeping . . . her face white and starlike under the stars," that he cannot maintain a "Carlyle-like scorn for this wretched aristocracy in decay. However great their intellectual degradation, the Eloi had kept too much of the human form not to claim my sympathy and to make me perforce a sharer in their degradation and fear" (pp. 79, 80). To the Traveller, the Morlocks now become "the inhuman sons of men" and finally he finds it impossible to feel "any humanity in the things" (p. 87). The rhetoric of class nomination is now complete. The childlike and feminine Eloi, descendants of the Capitalist class, are named "human," the Morlockean Working class is "inhuman." Not for the first time in history, the aggressive male, defined anonymously as the representative of the fully human, goes to war to protect the dependent female against a biologically inferior group. Were such rhetoric used about Jews and Aryans in Hitler's Germany, about Europeans and Colonials in Orwell's Burma, Forster's or Kipling's India, blacks and whites in Faulkner's Mississippi, we should recognize immediately the esthetic and political terrain. The strategy of class anonymity here submerges the Traveller's obvious petty bourgeois masculine bias and creates the illusion that he is acting in a fully human way.

Immediately after the Traveller kills a Morlock or two, enjoying the crunch of bones under his blows, the rhetoric of the novel changes, and the language of biological and physical determinism moves to the fore. Flying off to the reaches of outer time, the Traveller discovers that entropy has set in: the earth revolves more slowly, descending into a cooling sun; plant life devolves into rudimentary ferns; animal life into hugh amphibian forms, for whom he is legitimate prey. Analyzing this rhetoric of devolution, Suvin has correctly pointed out that Wells departs significantly from Darwin's schemata to create a stark set of oppositions between the Traveller as the last representative of the species and the powers of negation and death. Put briefly, Darwin's seriation gives a privileged position to both the force of existence and man, where Wells's variations award that position to the force of negation, nonexistence, and death; man is a dispensable species. Suvin convincingly argues that the Traveller sheds his class identity to become a "a generic representative of *homo sapiens*, an Everyman defined in terms of biological rather than theological classification, as a species-creature and not a temporarily embodied soul."[5]

The rhetoric of natural determinism, then, produces the myth that turns the Traveller into Everyman facing death. Suvin's analy-

5. Suvin, p. 346.

The Time Machine (1960). George (Rod Taylor) and Weena (Yvette Mimieux) in Futureworld. The childlike and feminine Eloi are descendants of the Capitalist class and named "human." (Photo courtesy of the Museum of Modern Art)

sis, correct as it is, overlooks the strategy of ex-nomination of class, and therefore misses the specific social content of the archetype. The full implications of the rhetorical shift in the novel can only be seen after an analysis of the film. For George Pal, the language of class is never relevant and though the film is concerned with the destructive power of war and "the bomb," concrete political terms never appear in the work. The Time Traveller, here named George, is presented as a technological idealist, a man who feels he has been born in the wrong time. On his journey to the year 802,701 he stops in 1917, 1940, and in the mid-1960s to witness the increasing destructive power of war, which, because of atomic air raids, increasingly drives Londoners to live underground. Arriving at his destination he finds the Eloi, full-sized, living in what at first appears to be Edenic ease. Soon he discovers that paradise is not only in decay, but subject to the cannibalistic brutalities of the Morlocks—bulky blue brutes with contorted but not particularly apelike faces. Unlike Wells's Time Traveller, George offers no explanation for this state of affairs, but learns from taped voices that as a result of a long war between "East and West" the earth's atmosphere became so polluted that human life was everywhere threatened. At that point, the recordings tell him, "each made his own decision; some chose to take refuge in the great cavern . . . others decided to take their chances in the sunlight." The Morlocks then became masters over the Eloi, but no explanation is given of how they rose to power. George discovers that the Morlocks control the Eloi simply by blowing air raid sirens; the Eloi, conditioned by millennia of war, move toward the caves as they moved toward air-raid shelters in early 1940s and mid-1960s.

Unlike the Traveller, George decides the situation is not irrevocable. When Weena comes into the night to warn him of Morlockean dangers, he tells her "you came out of your safe house to protect me. The one characteristic which distinguished man from the rest of the animal kingdom was the spirit of self-sacrifice." Her people all have that quality, he explains, "it just needs someone to re-awaken it." Thus, his rhetoric is abstract and moral, not political, social, or Darwinist. Later he explains to Weena that mankind's past was "mainly a grim struggle for survival. But there have been a few moments when a few voices have spoken up. And these moments have made the history of mankind a glorious thing."

George never specifies the particularity of these voices; they have no existence in time or place, use no particular medium, have no specified message, no identifiable politics, and, obviously, never mention class; they exist as disembodied voices, apparently speaking to something like an Arnoldian "better self." George decides to add his voice to theirs, and when the air-raid sirens wail again, he urges the Eloi to recognize that the war is over and to throw off the yoke of their Morlock oppressors. His voice goes unheeded until a Morlock nearly throttles him, and then an Eloi youth, his spirit of self-sacrifice apparently awakened, strikes down the brute with a well-aimed rabbit punch. Under George's leadership the Eloi destroy the Morlockean underground. Unfortunately, the time machine almost goes up in flames. Though George gets to his machine, he is separated from Weena. He returns to his own time, again raises his voice to explain the coming millennia of suffering, but his contemporaries pay him little heed. With cautious optimism, he decides to return to 802,701 when he hopes to lead the Eloi to a restored humanity.

The rhetoric of the film affirms that a class anonymous technician, without specific politics, can morally spark a people conditioned to indifference into a new phase of human development. Unlike Wells's biological Everyman-facing-Death, George is a cautious Prometheus bringing a new technology, a spirit of self-sacrifice, and the right to overthrow an oppressor.

Film and novel then each confirm a familiar archetype. While the novel is rooted in an identifiable class, political and social rhetoric, which Wells then ex-nominates, the movie from the beginning avoids not only the language of class, but the language of specific politics as well. The Morlocks and Eloi represent neither class, nor even "east and west," but rather cartoon figures of the most abstract oppressor and oppressed. But the strategy of ex-nomination carried out in both works contains a common social content. The class anonymity accruing to the Traveller at the end of the novel, and of George throughout the movie, barely conceals a social myth defined by Roland Barthes in *Mythologies*. Such anonymity is hardly accidental but is, rather, the cornerstone of bourgeois mythology and ideology. According to Barthes, the bourgeoisie is the *"class which does not want to be named."*[6] While that class will name itself in the economic realm, in the political realm it grows wary: there are no parties in the French Chamber (or the British Parliament or American Congress) with the name Bourgeois, while left-wing groups compete for the names Socialist, Workers, Labor. In the cultural realm, the bourgeoisie seeks to make itself completely anonymous by creating an unceasing hemorrhage of meaning in class terms. The main aim of this strategy, Barthes explains, is to transform the qualities of bourgeois man into the qualities of human nature, to make bourgeois man Eternal Man. As Barthes points out, this strategy takes the once revolutionary ideology of the bourgeoisie, with its emphasis on the power of mankind to transform nature and direct history, its emphasis on the new, free individual, and turns it into its opposite, emphasizing the permanent quality of nature, of human nature, of bourgeois social organization. The consequence is the creation of a sense that mankind can do little to influence or change historical development. In this sense, Barthes says that bourgeois "Eternal Man" turns out to be "Irresponsible Man," or, as he finally terms him, "Derelict Man."

Both film and novel confirm a variant of this central myth. Neither the Traveller nor George belongs to either the Capitalist or the Working Class, but to an anonymous technical and professional middle sector. Caught between two powerful contending class forces, each character experiences a genuine sense of frustration because neither he nor the class to which he belongs can influence the development of the race. They must ally with one of the two dominant groups. Where the central bourgeois myth of anonymity is designed to conceal class responsibility for both the present and future, the variant in these two works, particularly in Wells's, is based on the concrete powerlessness of the petty bourgeoisie.

However, the two versions of *The Time Machine* move in different directions. In Wells, the mythic structure creates the sense that the powerlessness of the Traveller and of the class he represents is a fixed quality of human experience. The Traveller learns that the laws of nature and the mistakes of the other two classes make it

6. Roland Barthes, *Mythologies*, tr. Annette Lavers (New York: Hill and Wang, 1972), p. 138. Emphasis Barthes'.

impossible for him and his class to change the course of history. George, however, clings to the slim hope that history can be changed by technology, by a morality of self-sacrifice leading to resistance to oppression, and by the memory of those voices which have spoken, however abstractly, against barbarism and oppression. Such hope hinges, of course, on an absence of concrete politics or precise analysis of the nature of "oppression," and certainly on the absence of any sense of class conflict. They are, of course, almost entirely abstract and idealist in nature. The film stakes out a claim for the progressive nature of the petty bourgeoisie by appealing only on this higher plane and at the sacrifice of concrete political and class analysis.

Film and novel, then, despite their differences, rhetorically carry out a strategy which ex-nominates class as a significant term in the discussion of human historical development; each work creates, in a different way, a class anonymous hero who gives voice to petty bourgeois feelings of powerlessness, of frustration of its hopes, of its sense of its own idealism. Behind the two very different sets of contents, behind the two different archetypes, both works rest in and serve to keep alive the social myth that only those outside of class fully appreciate and understand reality. In this sense there is a remarkable continuity between Wells's novel, written out of representative nineteenth-century concerns over class struggle, and George Pal's film released in 1960 reflecting mid-century anxiety over the atom bomb and the cold war.

Dracula (1897), Bram Stoker

Werner Herzog, 1979: *Nosferatu the Vampyre*

The Class-ic Vampire

JANET M. TODD

Chafing under the arrogance of the noble Lord Byron, Dr. Polidori revenged himself by making his employer's unfinished vampire tale a study of an aristocratic monster; so began a tradition of world-weary, noble blood-suckers that continues to haunt both film and fiction.[1] Years later, the male vampire was given definitive life by another middle class writer, the Irish Bram Stoker. In *Dracula* (1897) he welded the noble vampire onto a nasty East European princeling, Vlad the Impaler from Transylvania, a land always mythical to Anglo-Saxon ears.[2] His fictional Count, feeding on the historical Vlad and vampire superstitions in general, was also sustained by a memory of Stoker's mother about a cholera epidemic. Its silent, anarchic spreading became the image of the vampire's progress. Werner Herzog's *Nosferatu* (1979), out of F. W. Murnau (*Nosferatu* 1922), out of Stoker, continues the themes and images of Stoker. His undead is flamboyantly vampire and pestilence. But for

1. John Polidori, *The Vampyre* (1819; London: J. Clements, 1840). The tradition of the female vampire in literature and film stems largely from Sheridan LeFanu's tale "Carmilla" in *In A Glass Darkly* (1872; London: Peter Davies, 1929).
2. A full account of Vlad occurs in Radu Florescu and Raymond T. McNally's *Dracula: A Biography of Vlad the Impaler 1431-1476* (London: Robert Hale & Co., 1973). The Romanians have recently made a patriotic film about the historical Vlad, treating him as one of their foremost freedom fighters.

the dialectic of the film and the inevitable dialogue with the film's progenitor, *Dracula*, he is most crucially a count.[3]

In Stoker's late nineteenth-century fictional world, two groups oppose each other to the death and beyond. One is headed by Dracula, noble, anti-social, alienated, and bestial. He leads a miscellaneous grouping of female vampires, a few Slavs, an assortment of wolves, and a host of rats, all completely at his command. Against him range the forces of the ordinary decent middle class, a band of equal and gallant men (though one becomes a lord) and chaste and serious women. Their ideals are domestic, romantic, scientific, and social; where the Count is self-communing and hierarchical, they are obsessively companionable, gluttons for communication. Their created scheme eschews the animal and anarchic and pursues the human and ordered, the social and enlightened.

The vampire belief derives from sex and death and their confusion. Of the plethora of twentieth-century vampire films inspired by Stoker, the majority concentrate on sex—the 1977 BBC production, for example, has Louis Jourdan as a suave and handsome Dracula, whose sucking inevitably titillates.[4] Yet the book is not especially erotic and it gains its thrills less from eros than from thanatos, a fin-de-siècle preoccupation. Stoker's Count Dracula is an old man with the courtliness of the elderly rather than the gallant. His heavy breathing, inevitably sexual, is predominantly deathly, and the passivity he foists on women, though sensual of course, suggests also a longing for easeful death. When the sexual aspect is stressed in a work, the vampire is usually unchanging, lewd and repulsively attractive throughout. But Stoker's Dracula endlessly transforms himself, undermining his sexual character and underlining his

3. Since I am following a theme through Stoker and Herzog, I am not concerned here with judging *Nosferatu*. Nonetheless it is worth pointing out that it is a very flawed work which, by exaggerating effects, frequently falls into bathos. The audience among whom I watched it often tittered at the climatic moments.

4. There are numerous vampire films based on Stoker's *Dracula*. The major ones are F. W. Murnau's *Nosferatu* (Prana Films 1922); *Dracula* (Universal 1931), directed by Tod Browning from a script by Garret Fort, based in turn on a play by Hamilton Deane and revised by John L. Balderston (Dracula was played by Bela Lugosi); and *The Horror of Dracula* (Hammer Films, 1958), directed by Terence Fisher with script by Jimmy Sangster (Dracula was played by Christopher Lee). The 1977 BBC production was directed by Philip Saville, with script by Gerald Savory.

deathliness through reversals of human decay. When he gluts himself on his prey, for example, his profuse white hair turns gray and black, a mockery of human mortality.[5]

Dracula's three female vampires are concubines of an imperious master, who treats them carelessly and arrogantly. They are unequal, voluptuous, animal, and so ravishingly beautiful that the upright Jonathan and the wise professor, Van Helsing, are both wickedly drawn to them. Yet the good men of the book stress the female vampires' distinction from their own women. Although momentarily enthralled by them, Jonathan insists they have nothing in common with a real woman, his beloved Mina. When Lucy, the lesser heroine, becomes vampiric, she is termed "a devilish mockery" of the sweet pure woman they all knew.[6]

The opposing bourgeois group of social men and women exists against a background of ordinary fallible decency. Officials do their jobs scrupulously and beer-drinking laborers work independently and are not intimidated. The townspeople of Whitby are eager to honor the brave dead captain who tied himself to his helm while Dracula raged against his crew, and they turn out in force for the funeral. The daily newspaper assumes its readership will respond in its own decent manner to the horror of child-molesting.

The individual opposers of the vampire—the heroines Mina and Lucy, Lucy's three suitors, Mina's husband Jonathan and the fatherly vampire-expert, Van Helsing—are connected with their wider communities, concerned and fearful for others. But they are especially connected with each other. They talk, write in longhand and shorthand, typewrite, dictate into phonographs, send letters and telegrams, and keep journals, all to ensure that each of them knows the minutest detail in another's experience and thoughts. Communication is indeed the essence of their fellowship. When they do not tell all, they fail. Lucy dies because she cannot speak her suffering though she may write it, while a hint of "morbid

---

5. *Dracula* (1897; New York: Dell, 1978).

6. The BBC production goes against Stoker by juxtaposing and connecting the three female vampires and three good women (Mina, Lucy, and her mother). Just before the credits, over the trio of vampires, the three women wave rather ominously to Jonathan.

reticence" immediately endangers Mina. To protect Mina and keep her pure, the men resolve to keep her ignorant. It is then that she falls prey to the vampire.

Stoker's men are upright and true, living in each other's congratulatory prose. They are bourgeois lovers, husbands and fathers, emotionally intense and strong; their active leader is Lucy's American suitor Quincey, who dies for the concept of pure womanhood, while their philosophical spokesman is the courtly Van Helsing, who binds them with science and religion—the two go hand in hand in the novel—and gives the philosophical message of the book, that evil in oneself must be strenuously battled. It is he too who organizes the communal transfusion to Lucy in which the four men donate their blood in healing parody of Dracula's deadly sucking.

The women are male ideals, domestic if wed and romantic if unwed, pure in spirit and chaste in body, true intelligent helpmates to men. Lucy, destined for a vampire, is more flirtatious than Mina, her three suitors inevitably paralleling Dracula's three vampires; nonetheless she remains moral and good, safe when protected by good men. Mina, the main heroine, lives for her husband, Jonathan. She strives to be useful to him, typing his notes and even learning train times in case he might need them. Her constant service inspirits her and keeps her husband to the mark; beside her ruthless femineity, Jonathan must be staunchly masculine and in her company he dare not flinch. When Mina enters a house, it becomes a home and the men of the novel vie with each other to praise her. After Lucy dies, Mina in a way inherits her three suitors and her fatherly friend. She mothers them all in turn and encourages them in their chivalrous quest. Yet she, like Lucy, is primarily victim and receptacle, and her use to the vampire-hunting men is as an ideal, the flower of their culture.

Against the powerful and coherent forces of the enlightened middle class, of community, decency, and marriage, Count Dracula is not man enough to stand, He is too old-fashioned and haughty. Conquered in his aristocratic lair by this bourgeois fellowship, he dies before he can see his desolate castle become a sight for touring couples. Despite the lurid sensationalism of the subject matter, then, Stoker's novel tells of a serious struggle between human systems. The ending is a paean not only to the good and moral but also to the enlightened, social, domestic, and scientific culture of late nineteenth-century England.

Herzog's *Nosferatu* follows Stoker in stressing the place and culture his Count defiles—the film was shot in Delft in Holland, epitome of all that is prosperous, bourgeois, rational, and dull. Stoker's characters are simplified, stylized, and reduced to four. Mina, Lucy, and the female vampires coalesce in Lucy (played by Isabella Adjani), wife of Jonathan (Bruno Ganz). The other men disappear, leaving only Van Helsing, declined from philosopher to doddering fool. On the other side of course remains the Count (Klaus Kinski), without even a female vampire for company.

In *Dracula*—written in naturalistic mode despite its supernatural subject—Jonathan can enter the Transylvanian castle and believe for a moment that he encounters an eccentric nobleman. No such possibility exists for Herzog's wanderer—nor for the audience since the camera juxtaposes shots of the ruined castle and its gaping windows with Jonathan's view of closed and finished rooms.[7] Herzog's Count, inspired by Murnau, is a cadaverous fetus with bald white head, twitching elfin ears, bruised, quivering mouth, crimson and black eyes, and the most Chinese fingernails. He is agonized and deathly; like Stoker's Dracula he avoids blatant sexuality (transposed here onto a large sensuous bat, shot in slow motion). Dense, intense music separates him from the light, bright tones of ordinary life. A Tithonus figure, he laments his bloody hunger and his inability to die. Nosferatu is vampire through and through and there is sadness but little subtlety in his portrait.

But, like Stoker's Dracula, he is also an aristocrat. All Herzog heroes speak little, but the Count utters just enough to boast of his ancient lineage. The meal he offers his guest is opulent, the spoil of privilege, and it contrasts with the cool austere meal Lucy provides her husband. The Count is big and alone, heir to enormous ruins, and his immense and menacing shadow grows against the neat rows of gabled houses, symmetrical dwellings of common folk.[8] In

---

7. *Nosferatu* eschews the realistic style of *Dracula* and achieves its effects by exaggerating and making literal what is suggested and left metaphorical in Stoker.

8. Herzog follows Murnau in playing much with his vampire's shadow. Stoker stays with tradition when he makes his vampire neither appear in a mirror nor cast a shadow.

Stoker's novel, the fearsome Count Dracula is strangely reduced when he leaves the hierarchical Transylvanian mountains to enter the flat democracies of the West. In London he seems almost vulnerable, more lonely than aloof, and Mina even pities him. In the novel, his reduction foreshadows his defeat; in Herzog's film his enlargement in the bourgeois town looks to the ultimate victory of the vampire.

The human bourgeois world that Herzog's Count ravages is a poor affair. The old dotard Van Helsing has a face as dead as the vampire's but denied its crimson gashes. He is a caricature of a moribund society and personification of the film's distrust of science and rationality. Where in Stoker he headed a league of dedicated men and women, in Herzog's film he refuses to act, lead, join, or communicate. Yet his vision ultimately dominates the nonvampiric world for the viewer. When Lucy sacrifices herself to destroy the vampire he arranges her arms in death—the only hint we have that she has died—and he alone drives the stake through the Count—though the action is hidden from us. At the end he becomes the vehicle for the film's mockery of the bourgeois social order: he resignedly faces the ordinary implications of his extraordinary act—the impaling of the Count—and is arrested for murder.

Jonathan is coopted early in the film. He is black in the creamy female environment of Lucy and he leaves her hurriedly for the darker masculine world of street and office. Like the Count, he is associated with animals: he intrudes his horse's rump into the foreground of the picture and picks up one of the cats playing with Lucy's miniature. (In the Transylvanian castle Jonathan and the Count will echo this play when they squabble over the same miniature.) Told of the lucrative business trip to the Count, Jonathan responds in proper bourgeois style—he will be able to buy Lucy a better house—but he adds that he is sick of a town with canals turning back on themselves. Already the antibourgeois world-weariness of the Count—legacy of the Byronic pose—is foreshadowed in this strange discordant remark.

Jonathan leaves the little domestic haven of Lucy and its clear folksy music for the extreme world of Transylvania. The loud Wagnerian noise—common in Herzog films of obsessive quest—thickens and intensifies. Black mists and quickened clouds turn the natural supernatural, while lingering shots of huge hypnotic torrents stress the inhumanness of the landscape, obverse of the narrow placid canals of home. The extreme images and the sheer difficulty of the journey—few estate agents clamber over boulders and waterfalls to reach a client—suggest that Jonathan is on a psychological voyage into alienation. The camera stresses this by deserting the subjective viewpoint and making him one among many objects in its sweep. The audience is given immense panoramas hidden from him, as well as glimpses of the ruin he is struggling to reach. Only when he enters the castle, broken in spirit and almost wandering in wits, does the camera reidentify with him, jerking with him as he walks or spiraling upwards as his eyes travel the walls. But by now we have grown used to seeing through him, not with him, and we can note how animal he has become in his eating habits and how relatively indifferent he is to the striking horror of the Count. When he is vampirized, it is fitting that the distant Lucy, not he, responds in terror, for he is already a man estranged from himself.

Jonathan arrives home wrecked, ashen, and old, not recognizing Lucy and shunning the sun. Unlike Stoker's primarily heterosexual vampire, the Count has sucked Jonathan and taken his soul, thus giving the man a role reserved for women in *Dracula*'s polarized scheme. So he sits in the white house he has darkened, a dormant danger, until his wife acts for him and destroys the Count. Then he takes possession of his vampire kingdom, announcing his entry by a trivial but imperious act: caught in Lucy's circle of holy wafer, he cannot move until he has sharply ordered a maid to sweep away the "dirt."

In Stoker's novel, it was of course the men who acted to safeguard threatened womanhood and it was Van Helsing who put the holy wafer round the heroine. The ending saw Mina a wife and mother in a pious bourgeois scheme that justified all the horror and death. In *Nosferatu*, however, the men are weakened or subverted and the sexual roles are reversed. Jonathan, not Lucy, becomes the vampire and Lucy not Jonathan the vampire-killer. Yet this is no feminist statement and female failure remains constant. In Stoker's novel the woman is saved through the man; in Herzog's film the woman's act cannot save the man.

Lucy begins as an exaggerated version of Stoker's passive but intelligent bourgeois heroine, neither liberated woman nor submissive vampire. She has a white tragedienne's mask of a face and a pre-Raphaelite beauty that insists on purity. She lives in a world of pallid, luminous, porcelain colors and sleeps in a white tomblike bed draped in white. By all the laws of female symbolism, she is fated to die.

The men's inaction forces her into action: because Jonathan is drained of emotion, it is she who must suffer and, because he is passive and willing, she must scream in protest as the black bat tugs at her crimson and white curtains.[9] Since Van Helsing stupidly believes in science and method, she must act on superstition and impulse and, since he refuses to philosophize, she must speak the lines on universal madness and study vampire lore. Her growing activity is reflected in her dress, at first white, then pastel pinks and greens, and finally dark blue as she loses the husband who valorized her purity. Only when she wishes to betray the Count does she put on white again, enticing him into death with the purity he, like any bourgeois man, has learned to covet.

Lucy believes in the ideals of wedded and romantic love and of social communion. Yet the film mocks her, for as she bends over the maddened husband who should head her home, and as she stands beside the senile patriarch who should advise it, she is framed by the black figure of Dracula before the window. So too, while she speaks to the Count of her everlasting love for Jonathan, she bares her neck for the vampire's bite and it is he who withdraws. Finally of course it is by acting on her romantic bourgeois ideals of sacrifice, purity, and love that she makes her husband a vampire. Her noble act slays the aristocrat, releasing the poison into her own class and rejuvenating evil.

In *Nosferatu*, middle-class society breaks down before the Count; In *Dracula* it is reaffirmed. Two incidents in particular declare this difference: the central linking episode of the Count's sea voyage to the West and the coming of the rats. In both book and film, a boat sets sail with the Count and his coffins deep in its hold. On the voyage the crew is sucked or frightened to death until only the captain remains to record the horror in his log. Anticipating his own

9. Herzog agrees with most film directors in downplaying male emotion. In Stoker's book, the men are overtly and loudly emotional.

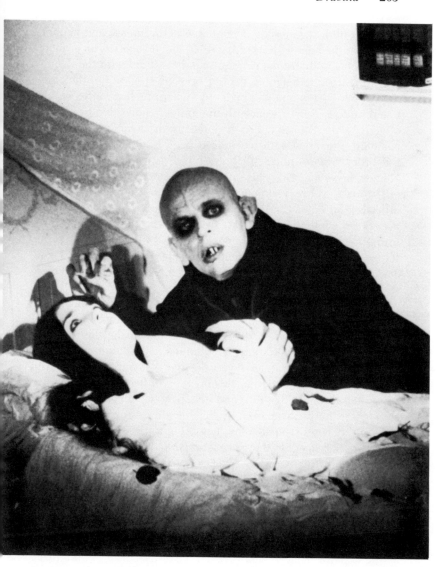

Nosferatu the Vampyre (1979). In Werner Herzog's version of Bram Stoker's *Dracula*, Klaus Kinski as the dying aristocratic vampire feasts on Lucy (Isabelle Adjani). (Photo courtesy of the Museum of Modern Art)

end, he straps himself to the helm where he too is murdered. In Herzog's film, the episode is presented in an intense and haunting sequence; the boat with its sails a dried blood color sits on a smooth blue sea while the camera circles round (as it did with the doomed raft in *Aguirre*) to heighten the isolation and futility. But the end of the episode severs film and book. In Stoker, the boat, after arriving in a disorderly storm, is decently and properly unloaded by efficient officers, while the captain is honored by the whole town at at an elaborate funeral. Death has indeed been introduced into society, but order and restraint still prevail and can mitigate the horror. Herzog, however, moves his ship of death quietly into the very heart of the town, as heavy ominous music deadens ordinary sounds. The officials who enter the boat are aged and incompetent, muttering over boxes while the plague rats swarm down the gangplank. Later in the town hall, as the captain's log is read in front of his corpse, the neat ranks of men fragment at the mere mention of a plague. The order of the community breaks and the Count is master before even a bite.

Rats in *Dracula* are a minor prop, used sparingly to suggest the vampire's bestial control, while the plague remains merely a metaphor for Count Dracula's silent progress. But in the film they are prominent. Herzog declared, "My film is about a community that is invaded by fear, the rats are a very decisive element, almost a key to the film because they signify this invasion of fear."[10] The Count is expressed through the rats and the plague, which break down society and hurl it back from the nineteenth century to the Middle Ages and beyond. The anarchy they bring is presented in the film's most striking images: the central square, the heart of the town, crossed by coffins borne by black-suited men—former symbols of the stable bourgeois order; an old woman sitting like Whistler's mother but alfresco on a dining room chair, surrounded by smouldering fires, coffins, and pigs; the dance of death when the contaminated fill their last hours with merrymaking, eating and drinking in opulent, almost aristocratic style (reminiscent of Jonathan's fatal eating with the Count), while myriad rats swarm close by and finally devastate the table. Loud music, mostly the Mass, dissociates sound

10. Quoted in the *Morning Star* review, May 18, 1979.

and image, both belittling the action and giving it an awesome supernatural context.[11] By the end of the film, the plague has destroyed and trivialized social order, propriety, and civic morality: when Van Helsing is arrested for murder, there remains no officer alive to detain him.

The whole bourgeois edifice, threatened by the arrogant, aristocratic, and anarchic vampire, collapses in Herzog's *Nosferatu*, where in *Dracula* it was more firmly reestablished. (That Herzog's Count himself is destroyed in the end is due not to his evil, antisocial ways but to a fatal falling from his aloof, imperious state into a bourgeois yearning for wedded purity and companionship.) Communication, the essence of community, is prevented, and only silent violence and command gain results.[12] Dependent women act as men, while independent men fail to act at all. Caught by society's idea of pure womanhood and sacrifice, the chaste heroine destroys herself for her love, but her sacrifice does not lead to tearful memory and gratitude, as Quincey's does in *Dracula*; instead it liberates a new cruelty in her husband. Where Stoker's novel ends like so many Victorian works in the domestic tableau of middle-class community—husband, wife, child, and faithful friends—*Nosferatu* has the typical modern ending of film and fiction—the alienated hero walking or riding out of society alone, perhaps superior like the aristocrat but certainly different and apart. In short, bourgeois domestic love is judged a fragile affair, civic order a mockery, and science a ludicrous hoax. *Nosferatu* becomes a jaundiced twentieth-century look at the progressive ideals of an earlier age—of community, love, duty, sacrifice, and science—part of our own fin-de-siècle weariness.

My subject so far has been exclusively Herzog's *Nosferatu* in the context of Stoker's *Dracula*. But two other works inevitably shadow the film and require at least brief mention here: Murnau's *Nosferatu* of 1922 and Paul Monette's book of 1979. Both in different ways illuminate the conflicting messages of Stoker and Herzog.

11. The cleanness of the rats also dissociates the plague idea from the image. Herzog is said to have used small, tame laboratory rats, and on the instructions of the Dutch authorities to have had each of the 10,000 sterilized in case any should escape. In general, *Nosferatu* seems a very hygienic film, notably lacking in blood.

12. *Nosferatu* tends toward a clipped speech. In English this portentous imperious speech appeared ridiculous and a dubbed German version was released. I saw only the dubbed version.

Murnau's filmscript, written by Henrik Galeen, was loosely based on Stoker's book (not loosely enough, however, since Murnau was successfully prosecuted by Stoker's widow). It makes the man (Hutter) into the victim and the woman into the active vampire-killer. The heroine responds as her husband's blood is sucked and finally sacrifices herself to expose the vampire to the sun.

Clearly Murnau's film provides Herzog's plot. It also provides many of the images of menace. Murnau's Count Orlick (Max Schreik) is twin to Herzog's Count, an ambiguous, corpselike, weary old man throwing expressionist shadows and emerging threateningly from the depths of the shot. He brings the plague in his cloak and inhabits a world of jagged scudding clouds and ghostly light. Like Herzog's vampire, he is splendidly noble, surrounded in his castle by ancestral portraits, massive Renaissance furniture, and mounds of delicacies.

If the menacing, wearied Count keeps his state in Murnau, Hutter (Jonathan) is much reduced in rank. Perhaps 1922 was not a time to praise the social status quo, but nor was it the moment to sneer at affluence and civic order. It is no prosperous bourgeois who flees like Herzog's questor from too much peace and plenty; instead Hutter is a poor man who endangers his soul to feed himself and his wife. If Stoker's Jonathan is driven to the Count by professional duty and Herzog's by ennui, Murnau's Hutter goes for money.

Ellen (Lucy-Mina) is similarly placed between extremes. Unlike Stoker's Mina, she acts independently to save her husband and community, but, unlike Herzog's Lucy, she is justified by the narrative and supported by her society. The professors and town authorities she helps are neither ridiculous nor inept and her ailing husband is still a sentient, loving man who holds her hand as she dies. And her death destroys the vampire. Losing complete faith in the bourgeois social scheme, then, Murnau and Galeen have produced a tragic version of Stoker's story, not a parody of it.[13]

Paul Monette wrote his *Nosferatu* immediately after Herzog's

---

13. Murnau's film evidently left some people with a desire for a happy ending, for there exists a German version (made probably without Murnau's knowledge) in which the heroine comes to life again at the end and lives happily ever after. This miracle was achieved by transferring the happy domestic sequences from the beginning to the end. See Lotte H. Eisner's *Murnau* (London: Secker & Warburg, 1973) for a full account of the *Nosferatu* versions.

screenplay and so his book interests not for any temporal dialogue with its source but for its qualification of the film.[14] It is a kind of metatext that throws into relief the harsh message of its original.

Monette's *Nosferatu* panders to our present liking for the vague and portentous and it avoids much social statement. Yet even here Dracula cannot altogether deny his rank, and, like Herzog's and Stoker's vampires, he makes much of his nobility. But much more is made of his yearning for romance and companionship, ideals of Stoker eschewed in Herzog's scheme. Dracula desires a companion not a slave in the servile estate agent, and sighs for a wife and equal friend in Lucy. He dies partly because he tries to save his new vampire and he dies happy because he believes he has tasted love. Jonathan on the contrary grows into nobility and is quickly corrupted and bestialized. He is aristocratically arrogant, wanting privilege (as the Count wants equality) and sneering at the envy of the wretched. Yet he returns to the town to love his Lucy again and only at the conclusion wanders off (for no clear reason) to the vampire's haunts. Lucy herself, the exquisite inhabitant of the pretty town in Herzog, is an outsider and visionary romantic in Monette. She alone understands that the town deserves a plague for keeping its gardens too neat and its citizens too tidy, and she sacrifices to send the pestilence away and return everything to dreary normality.

Clearly Monette avoids Stoker's (and Murnau's) scheme, in which bourgeois order, love, and purpose face aristocratic evil, isolation, and nihilism. Yet he also avoids Herzog's harsh pitting of a false ideal against a weary evil. Instead he takes the romantic way out, elevating love above community and order and in its service removing his characters from their class. Dracula is here denobled and humanized by love, while Lucy is isolated from her community. The ending is that of a romance with the vampire dying happily with his love.

In his *Nosferatu*, Monette has sentimentalized Herzog's film and largely avoided the social issues to which Herzog still attends; his wicked Count is more romantic outsider than privileged potentate. Herzog keeps something of a class division, mocking the bourgeois

---

14. *Nosferatu the Vampyre* (London: Picador, 1979).

ideals his vampire threatens and yet refusing to romanticize the anarchic, hierarchical world of the Count; his ending is a wry comment on Murnau's tragic vision of the price of bourgeois ideals. Murnau in turn qualifies Stoker's stolid belief in middle-class values and the need to hold firmly to them against the powerful and unambiguous darkness of might and bestiality. His poverty-stricken hero suffers from as well as for his society, and a social ideal does not keep his heroine alive.

Inevitably each of the four vampire works, *Dracula* and the three *Nosferatus*, speaks to the others and each is commentator on its fellows. In a way they themselves have entered a vampiric relationship: each takes its predecessor's story, sucks out the message, then forces new life into plot and character. And each work is at the same time a victim of Dracula, for each resurrects the noble cadaver and pumps into him contemporary blood.

Heart of Darkness (1902), Joseph Conrad

Francis Coppola, 1979: *Apocalypse Now*

Coppola Films Conrad in Vietnam

DIANE JACOBS

Critics have traditionally felt uneasy with anything that might be construed as intellectualism in the American cinema. So it is no surprise that even as astute a critic as Michael Wood should chortle a bit at Francis Ford Coppola's bald allusions to "The Hollow Men" in Colonel Kurtz's weird Cambodian haven in the final scenes of *Apocalypse Now* (1979). (T. S. Eliot himself is rarely chided for excerpting Conrad's "Mistah Kurtz—he dead" for his poem's epigraph.) "I would like to think Kurtz is drawn to this poem by Coppola's sense of humor," writes Wood in the *New York Review of Books*. "... But I am afraid the attraction is purely pedantry."[1]

There *is* a touch of not unpleasing pedantry and seductive virtuosity to *Apocalypse Now*, as there is to its uncredited source, Joseph Conrad's *Heart of Darkness* (1902). Still, the issue is not Coppola's literariness, but whether his borrowing from Eliot and more especially from Conrad are decorative or organic. What relevance has Conrad's Victorian allegory to Coppola's contemporary vision of soldiers water-skiing through combat zones, of sailors shooting heroin, of officers sniffing napalm for the scent of victory, and of the sort of gnarled genius who would think to sever the recently innoculated arms of enemy children?

Coppola himself broached this issue of decoration versus sub-

1. Wood, Michael, *"Apocalypse Now"*, *New York Review of Books*, October 11, 1979, Volume XXVI.

stance when discussing his more abstracted film *The Conversation* (1974). Because he could not identify with his protagonist, Coppola told Brian De Palma, he decided to "enrich"[2] him: to embellish the wiretapper Harry Caul with his own childhood polio, his love for music, his Catholicism, etc. Unfortunately, that "enrichment" shows, and despite a nuanced performance by Gene Hackman, Harry remains a skein of quirks and obsessions. He plays the saxophone, suffers a pesky guilt, and clings tenaciously to his privacy. These details add up to a fascinating concept, but the character and ultimately the film itself lack sinew.

A number of critics insist that a similar esthetic decoration is at work in *Apocalypse Now*, that *Heart of Darkness* is little more than "enrichment," neatly appended to John Milius's genre script and no more essential to the film than polio is to Harry. To my mind, this is not the case: *Heart of Darkness* is the spine of *Apocalypse Now*. The film succeeds as an updated interpretation of Conrad because author and filmmaker share uncannily similar goals; because Coppola's thoughts on American involvement in Vietnam and on power and the compulsion to vanquish the enemy are compatible with Conrad's thoughts on avarice and colonialism, with its "strange commingling of desire and hate"[3]; because Marlow's up-river journey, in the novel, to the "horror" of colonial Africa is a fittingly ironic paradigm for Captain Willard's (Martin Sheen's) penetration of Asia; because Mr. Kurtz's lust for something beyond ivory is a fitting correlative for Colonel Kurtz's yen for the ineffable beyond victory; and, finally, because Marlon Brando's murky, corpulent, "unsound" Kurtz is very much Conrad's Kurtz: a superior individual "on the threshold of great things," "exalted," and not just "hollow at the core" but unreal and sometimes unbelievable. There is a crucial difference between the novel and the film, but more on this later.

Like the novel, the film opens with its narrator anxiously awaiting a mission. Captain Willard prowls his Saigon hotel room, gulping booze, muttering about how uncomfortable he felt on his leave at home, and finally splintering a mirror with his fist and bloodying

---

2. De Palma, Brian, "The Making of *The Conversation*", *Filmmakers Newsletter*, May 1974, Volume 7, number 7.

3. Conrad, Joseph. *Heart of Darkness* 1902 (rpt. London: Penguin, 1975), p. 101.

himself. When two men usher him off to receive orders for a top-secret mission, Willard's reaction could be summed up in Marlow's pre-existential musing: "I don't like work,— no man does—but I like what is in the work—the chance to find yourself. Your own reality—for yourself, not for others. . . ."

Marlow is a seaman, Willard an intelligence officer. Marlow, in the employ of a Belgian trading company in colonial Africa, sets off up the Congo to discover what has happened to one of his predecessors, the legendarily successful ivory trader, Mr. Kurtz. Willard, in the employ of the government, sets off not only to find but to kill his Kurtz, the Army's erstwhile favorite son Colonel Kurtz, who has taken the war effort into his own hands. Against orders, Kurtz has crossed the Cambodian border and (like his Congo counterpart) has set himself up as a god/king to the willing natives. As a commanding officer points out to Willard, "what Lincoln calls 'the better angel of our nature' " has lost out in the battle for Kurtz's soul.

Like *Heart of Darkness, Apocalypse Now* is on one level an adventure tale. Conrad sends Marlow off to do battle with inclement weather, unfriendly geography, cannibals, inefficient Europeans, and unsympathetic natives with deadly weapons. Coppola dispatches Willard on a mission that will pit him against the NLF, tigers, and routine carnage as well as his "choice of nightmares" (p. 89).

Yet very little actually happens, either to Marlow or to Willard. They wait, and they watch. Marlow waits for a mission, and, once he has it, observes the coast of Africa ("smiling, frowning, inviting, grand, mean, insipid or savage and always mute with an air of whispering, come and find out") from the deck of a French steamer (p. 19). Arriving at his company's Central Station, he discovers his boat sunk and wrecked and waits for the rivets with which to mend it. By the time he encounters Kurtz, the novel is nearly two-thirds finished: Marlow's intellect has digested the quiddities of Africa and the human soul, and he has done almost nothing.

Similarly, Willard anticipates and endures and, most importantly, scrutinizes: a helicopter attack, the ravaging of a village, playboy bunnies teasing the sex-starved troops, a bridge reconstructed every day to be demolished nightly. He observes carefully, but only rarely—when he shoots a Vietnamese woman, for instance—is he called upon to participate or to make decisions.

Coppola's "heart of darkness," like Conrad's, is a triumph of style over story. Or rather, the description—words for Conrad, *mise-en-scène* for Coppola—is the story's *raison d'être*. Marlow confronts the particulars of Africa in order to expatiate on the "flabby, pretending, weak-eyed devil of a rapacious and pitiless folly" (p. 23), or to explore "the fascination of the abomination" (p. 9). Marlow is not really concerned with rivets. The rivets are so diaphanously a pretext for him to ruminate on man's relation to work that he never bothers to inform us where the rivets ultimately came from. One moment he is stuck, the next he is on his way, with no explanations offered.

The day-to-day, arduous reality of combat is equally irrelevant to Coppola, who is no more concerned with the little man in the trench than Conrad is with rivets. He is out to forge a vision of War, of the Vietnam War, and—less convincingly—of related horrors through dense, multilayered cinematography (by Vittorio Stovaro) and sound (by Walter Munch).

Neither Conrad nor Coppola really succeeds in fathoming "the horror" because neither succeeds in rendering Kurtz palpable. Conrad describes him as "very little more than a voice" (p. 69) and his "horror" as "the strange commingling of desire and hate" (p. 101). But what, after all, is this? For Coppola, "the horror" is a similarly elliptical distance between superiority and madness. Like Conrad, Coppola is at his best when circling that horror, when presenting it a few rungs down on a recognizable, pedestrian level. Thus, *Apocalypse Now* is most effective when describing not Kurtz himself but the world surrounding him.

Like Conrad's language, Coppola's *mise-en-scène* at once batters and soothes. While the Dolby sound whooshes at us from myriad speakers, the limpid images attract us with their sensual beauty and repel us with their content. Similarly, the cinematography renders us both victim and perpetrator of numerous horrors. In the film's most spectacular scene, for instance, we watch Lieutenant Colonel Kilgore (Robert DuVall) and his fire-spitting helicopters swoop down from the skies as if we were the bewildered Vietnamese on the ground. Kilgore has ordered that his tapes of "The Ride of the

Valkyries" be played, and the Wagner meshing with the helicopter descent and the splaying of bomb fire is at once terrifying and absurd—clearly a lesser Conradian "nightmare." But in the next shot, the tables are suddenly turned. Now, the camera places us in the plane with Kilgore and directly behind the helicopter controls, thus affording us the arrogant, shameful exhilaration of power—yet another "nightmare."

Contrary to much critical opinion, *Apocalypse Now* gets into trouble not in its allegiance to Conrad, but when it veers away from the book's assumptions. Indeed, the one serious problem with this often brilliant film is the character of Willard. Like Harry Caul and unlike Marlow, Willard is too idiosyncratic, too much the unknown variable to sustain the complexities of the work we perceive through his eyes. He is not an Everyman to *Apocalypse Now* the way that Marlow is to *Heart of Darkness*.

We can identify with many of Willard's traits and impulses. He is an efficient officer, for instance, and his judgments on such matters as Kilgore's bizarre helicopter descent—"If that's how Kilgore fought the war, I began to wonder what they had against Kurtz"— would surely be ours and Marlow's. But in other respects, Willard is inscrutable and perhaps malevolent, for example when he abruptly kills a Vietnamese woman in order to get on with his up-river journey. Willard's companion has capriciously wounded the woman for the sin of harboring a small dog in her boat. She is badly injured and in pain, and she will almost certainly die; yet, if given proper medical care, she might possibly live. To his credit, Willard will not have the woman suffer, but neither will he deflect his mission in order to find her a proper doctor. Shooting her is a half-merciful, half-murderous compromise.

It is useful to compare Willard's reaction to the woman with Marlow's response to the "too fleshy" man with the "exasperating habit of fainting" who accompanies him on a two-hundred-mile hike through thickets and ravines. Clearly, he is a bungling albatross, and Marlow admits as much: "Annoying, you know, to hold your coat like a parasol over a man's head while he is coming-to" (p. 29). Still, hold that coat he does. Marlow is a moral quantity we know; Willard is an enigma.

As a rule, there is no reason to cavil about the idiosyncratic

Apocalypse Now (1979). Kurtz (Marlon Brando) in Coppola's version of Joseph Conrad's *Heart of Darkness* became an American colonel serving in Vietnam. (Photo courtesy of the Museum of Modern Art)

protagonist, but *Apocalypse Now*, like *Heart of Darkness*, demands a narrator we can trust. Coppola is flirting with myth, not debunking it (as Altman was, for instance, in his irreverent adaptation of Chandler's *The Long Goodbye*). He is dealing with characters who are larger and situations that are, on the whole, more sweeping and less delineated than life. To lead us through this mythic world and, more importantly, to render that world credible, he needs a guide whose quirks we recognize and understand. We need someone to make sense of bridges that are destroyed every night and rebuilt each dawn to keep up the *appearance* of an open waterway. We need a sensibility capable of observing the particular lunacy of soldiers ordered to surf while a town explodes around them and to take that lunacy a step further. Willard is not quite that man. He is too shifty, too reticent with his ideas. Thus the horror he glimpses not only in Kurtz, but in himself, is not as universal as Marlow's, and the film is not as powerful as it might have been.

Despite this weakness, *Apocalypse Now* is the most successful interpretation of Conrad to date. While its flaws are numerous, Coppola has achieved a felicitous welding of literary structure and genre subject: no mean accomplishment.

Conrad and Hitchcock: Secret Sharers

JAMES GOODWIN

Though different in many significant aspects, Conrad's *The Secret Agent* and Hitchcock's screen adaptation *Sabotage* (1936) are remarkably comparable in terms of theme and narrative technique. To speak of the dissimilarities first, it should be explained that the novel's title was not available to Hitchcock since he had used it for his previous film, which was based on Somerset Maugham's stories about the British agent Ashenden. The Conrad novel, published in 1907, is set in London of the 1880s, a historical period of "dynamite outrages" by anarchists, as the preface explains. Secret agent Adolf Verloc (a name obviously derived from the German *verlocken*, which means to mislead, to tempt) is in the employ of a foreign embassy whose home government finds the British police and courts permissive in their treatment of political extremists. Verloc is instructed to instigate a terrorist bombing of the Greenwich Observatory that will prompt a public outcry and coerce British authorities into greater political vigilance. As with his later novel *Under Western Eyes* (1911), Conrad is deeply interested in the complicated personal and political factors that influence government decision-making, such as the Assistant Commissioner's concern to ingratiate himself in upper-class society and to rise within the bureaucracy, a concern that interferes with his duties as a police official. Hitchcock and his screenwriter Charles Bennett leave aside the contradictions and ambiguities of both domestic and international politics as depicted in the novel. The only political overview made explicit in the film is the comment by a Scotland Yard chief that foreign elements are causing internal disturbances to distract the British from events taking place abroad. Hitchcock makes the foreign threat distinctly German through the characterization of Verloc (played by Oscar Homolka) and his superior. This suggestion of Nazi international intrigue is consistent with Hitchcock's *The Man Who Knew Too Much* (1934), which features Peter Lorre as a German agent.

What apparently most intrigued Hitchcock about the original material is Conrad's depiction of life in the Verloc household. The novel's Verloc lives at the back of a stationer's shop, where he deals in pornographic magazines and books and other "shady wares." The shop is a useful front for Verloc's activities as a foreign *agent provocateur*. Assisting Verloc in the sale of these illicit goods, which Conrad describes as "poor expedients devised by a mediocre mankind for preserving an imperfect society from the dangers of moral and physical corruption," is his wife Winnie. Completing the family are her retarded brother Stevie and, for a period, her ailing mother. All four live on the premises of Verloc's grubby shop. Though she cannot help but be aware of her husband's involvement in political matters, Winnie does not question his motives for she leads an essentially unconscious existence according to an instinctive conviction that "things do not stand looking into very much." For her, marriage to Verloc has meant a home and security for Stevie, whom she protects with maternal devotion and passion. In their seven years together, Winnie has grown to view Verloc as a father to Stevie. Over twenty years old and physically a man, Stevie possesses the mind of a child. He is a person of pure, unreasoned feeling and has absorbed the political rhetoric of the anarchists who meet in the Verloc home. When Winnie's mother is transported to the almshouse, Stevie rides with the cabman and looks on in horror as the man whips his horse. Stevie identifies the animal with all of society's victims and, after a long struggle to articulate his feelings, he blurts out: "Bad world for poor people." One of the novel's greatest ironies is that Stevie amounts to no more than a dumb creature himself as far as Verloc is concerned, though he keeps such thoughts secret from Winnie in an effort to preserve the order and comfort of life at home. Described as at heart a man of incalculable "idolence," Verloc prizes simple domestic pleasures above all else in the world.

Conrad, then, portrays the Verloc family in an unrelentingly grotesque vein. The Verlocs' ambition to enjoy a secure, comfortable, middle-class life is perhaps the novel's most chilling irony. Hitchcock has maintained the book's cruel parody of bourgeois existence, but in the film's first half he deflects irony somewhat away from the Verlocs in an effort to encourage audience identification with them. For probably similar reasons, the film eliminates the character of Winnie's mother. The Professor—in the novel a lone explosives expert obsessed by fantasies of "the perfect detonator"—becomes in the film a petshop owner who lives with his daughter and her illegitimate child. He stores his deadly wares in a kitchen cupboard, and we see the child's toys alongside sauce bottles that contain explosives. In order to compress the action and heighten dramatic tension, the film does not fully portray Verloc's other political associates. At least two of these, the "ticket-of-leave apostle" Michaelis and the ex-medical student Ossipon, figure prominently in the complex series of events Conrad presents. The film's most radical alteration of the original material is in the characterization of Stevie, who is an altogether normal and likable lad of twelve or thirteen. Our first glimpse of him is in the Verloc kitchen where, in taking a roast from oven to sideboard, he encounters several obstacles, burns his fingers, and breaks a serving plate. The slapstick humor in this scene establishes Stevie as a sympathetic character and prepares viewers for the boy's more hazardous journey across London later in the film.

In another major alteration, the film condenses the activities and personalities of the police (which the novel details and speculates upon at length) into the new character Ted Spencer, an undercover man from Scotland Yard who has been added also for romantic interest. Disguised as a clerk in the greengrocery located next door to the Verlocs, Ted is able to observe his suspect's movements. In the process, he befriends Stevie and takes an interest in Verloc's wife (who is never called by first name in the film). To develop a plot line that will alter Winnie's ultimate fate (in the novel she commits suicide), the film adds a scene in which Ted takes Stevie and Winnie to lunch at Simpson's in the Strand. Here and on other occasions the camera presents this set of characters as a threesome and thus offers them to the audience as an alternate, and more "natural," family unit. Ted appears to take more of a fatherly interest in the boy than does Verloc, whom Hitchcock shows sneaking about in his own household. The Verlocs live at the back of the neighborhood movie theater they own and operate. This transposition from the novel in regard to Verloc's ostensible occupation is shrewdly calculated for effect. As with many of Hitchcock's and Bennett's revisions, it modernizes and intensifies leading themes in the novel.

Through Hitchcock's reflexive references to cinema, *Sabotage* suggests the pervasiveness of secrecy and murderous instincts within bourgeois society, among legitimate and criminal elements alike, a theme that preoccupies Conrad in *The Secret Agent* as well as in other novels. The film's references to other motion pictures range from sensationalistic fare such as *Bartholomew the Strangler* to seemingly innocent entertainments like the drawing room melodrama we glimpse and the Disney cartoon "Who Killed Cock Robin?" In an early scene Ted is in the Verloc apartment when a transom window suddenly opens and we hear a screech that sounds like a woman's scream. To Ted's remark "I thought someone was committing murder," Verloc replies without hesitation: "Someone probably is—on the screen." The films to which *Sabotage* refers are like the novel's "shady wares" in that both satisfy appetites that ordinary reality does not readily satisfy and both give expression to antisocial drives latent among their audiences. The difference, of course, is that cinema is a widespread and socially accepted cultural matter. The nature of film's secret appeal to audiences is made clear by the early scene in which Verloc's patrons are inconvenienced when London suffers a power failure (caused by his act of sabotage) and the program is interrupted. The movie audience quickly becomes loud and unruly. Displaying no concern for the general situation, the patrons crowd around the box office and demand that the program be resumed or their money be refunded. Asked by his wife what to do, Verloc advises her to return their money, explaining: "It doesn't pay to antagonize the public." Before she can do so, power is restored; the audience drops its protest and files back into the auditorium. The episode reveals the extent to which cinema acts as a control over audiences and channels off their disruptive energies. As one would expect, the explosion that demolishes the movie theater in the closing scene draws a hugh crowd of curiosity seekers.

Sabotage (1936). The calm before the storm in Hitchcock's adaptation of *The Secret Agent*. Sylvia Sidney is Mrs. Verloc, Oscar Homolka is Verloc, and Desmond Tester is the doomed Stevie. (Photo courtesy of the Museum of Modern Art).

Sabotage visibly and audibly links cinema and anarchy through a sequence in which Ted, spying on Verloc and his colleagues, slips behind the movie screen that separates the auditorium from Verloc's living quarters. Looking through the transom window into the Verloc parlor, Ted overhears discussion of the plot to plant a bomb in Piccadilly Circus. On one side of the wall we hear the anarchists' conversation, on the other a movie soundtrack. In terms of filmic space, the movie screen in Verloc's theater cloaks the murderous deeds planned in his back rooms. Indeed, as Verloc's earlier comment indicates, the movie screen itself is often the scene of mayhem and chaos. Hitchcock himself is notorious for making concerted assaults on audience sensibilities. *Sabotage* commits its own public outrage in having Stevie and a busload of innocent people destroyed by the time bomb the boy unwittingly carries. In a masterfully edited sequence of suspense, Stevie carries a rigged package, along with two film tins containing *Bartholomew the Strangler*, across London. Verloc has instructed him to take these items by foot since nitrate film is not permitted on public conveyances, due to its highly combustible properties. This fact lends a perverse irony to the situation, which Hitchcock of course does not hesitate to emphasize. Stevie saunters on his errand, delayed first by the sights of a Saturday city market, then by the Lord Mayor's annual parade. In the market Stevie is detained by a street vendor who demonstrates brands of toothpaste and hair oil on the unwilling boy. His demonstration is performed to the delight of gathered shoppers and onlookers. Since we, the film's audience, know the full circumstances of Stevie's situation, the scene appears somewhat sadistic. Stevie tries to leave so that he can be on time, But the crowd encourages the vendor to continue. Thus we perceive Stevie as the victim of the showman and his audience.

Told to deliver the package by 1:30 that afternoon (the detonator is in fact set for 1:45), Stevie tries to take a shortcut across the parade route but is turned back by a policeman. Once he realizes how late it is, Stevie hops aboard a municipal bus. A friendly conductor makes an exception to the regulations and allows the boy to remain. Then, in a tightly edited sequence, we see a montage of close shots taken inside the bus (of Stevie, a kindly woman, her playful puppy, back to Stevie and intercut shots of clock faces as the minutes tick off. When 1:44 arrives the bus is stopped at an intersection, the traffic light changes to green, the bus moves forward, 1:45 passes without incident, a clock hand advances a minute and—the bomb explodes! In interviews Hitchcock has expressed regret that he depicted the boy's death on screen and made it an occasion for suspense, but not that he had the boy killed. This visualized story element, however, is perfectly in keeping with later films like *Psycho* (1960), where the viewer is encouraged to identify with the film's leading lady only to see her killed within the first reel, and *The Birds* (1963), which becomes a virtual slaughter of the innocents.

In the film, Mrs. Verloc learns of Stevie's death through the afternoon paper she buys from a newsboy who wears advertising boards announcing the bus explosion. The previous sequence details the steps by which senseless mass murder is converted into a screaming headline and sensational news story for the arousal of public interest. Ted, at the scene of the disaster, finds a label to the film cans amidst all the rubble and is questioned by a newsman. A close shot of the reporter writing down this information in shorthand dissolves into a shot of the full-page headline on the explosion. Once again, then, *Sabotage* suggests the extent to which the public thrives on incidents of destruction and death. Confronted with what he has done, Verloc casually protests to his wife, "I didn't mean any harm to come to the boy," and soon resumes the routines of home life as if nothing had happened. In her grief and confusion Mrs. Verloc walks into the auditorium, where a matinee is in progress. Her attention drawn to the screen by the laughter of children in the audience, she sits down to watch the Disney cartoon with them. For a moment she joins in the laughter but abruptly stops when, onscreen, Cock Robin falls to his death. The song "Who Killed Cock Robin?" ringing in her ears, Mrs. Verloc is told by the help that supper is ready.

In the dining room, Verloc complains that the vegetables are once again overcooked. Still in shock, the wife begins the familiar motions of serving the meal as her gaze falls on Stevie's unoccupied chair. Unconsciously, she uses the carving knife to lift a boiled potato onto her husband's plate. She suddenly realizes what she is doing and her hesitation attracts Verloc's attention. Without a word of dialogue, the sequence combines close-ups of wife, knife, and husband to develop the intensity of their confrontation and to reveal Mrs. Verloc's murderous impulses. Verloc rises from the table and toward the knife, moves close to his wife and, in the next instant, is fatally stabbed in the stomach. In a 1937 essay entitled "Direction," Hitchcock discusses this particular sequence as an example of audience manipulation and of visual characterization. In the first regard, the editing structure forces crucial details on viewers' attention and makes them vicarious participants in the drama. In regard to the presentation of Mrs. Verloc's unpremeditated action, Hitchcock explains, people "often don't show their feelings in their faces: so the film treatment showed the audience her mind through her hand, through its unconscious grasp on the knife." Hitchcock's technique here is entirely nonverbal, but a similar scene in his first sound film, *Blackmail* (1929), uses subjective sound to emphasize the visual imagery. The scene takes place the morning after a woman has stabbed a man in self-defense. Seated at the family breakfast table, her attention obsessively returns to a butter knife and the family conversation fades until only the word *knife* is heard.

In similar fashion, Conrad depicts the murder scene through concentration on a few amplified details. The carving knife is made prominent from the outset, with the ravenous Verloc using it to cut thick slices of roast beef laid out, the novel specifies, "in the likeness of funereal baked meats for Stevie's obsequies." When the knife is next mentioned it is in Winnie's hand, then in Verloc's breast. The scene's most horrifying detail, however, is Verloc's hat. Arriving home that evening, Verloc removes his coat and makes himself comfortable, "disregarding as usual the fate of his hat." The chapter ends with Winnie's flight from the apartment; the last paragraph describes the hat slightly rocking in the breeze caused by her movement. Soon after, Ossipon enters the apartment and discovers Verloc's body and his hat; the hat, not the body, reveals to the anarchist "the true sense of the scene." Our last glimpse of the hat is of it on the floor, engulfed by a "beastly pool" of blood.

Beyond their use of concrete detail for psychological effect, Conrad and Hitchcock both employ irony extensively in the handling of characters and action. In the author's preface to *The Secret Agent*, Conrad explains that only through ironic treatment was he able to write all that he wished to say "in scorn as well as in pity." His contempt for the anarchists' hypocrisy is everywhere evident. Their political activism is sheer absurdity. Michaelis, the legendary leftist, is a lethargic, wheezing man only five-foot-five or-six tall and weighing over 250 pounds. For Verloc, in both novel and film, politics have become a matter of employment, not of principle.

The deeper irony the two works share is an insistence on the affinities between police and criminals. Conrad's Professor, who numbers himself apart from all other terrorists in his goal of total destruction, views revolution and legality as "counter moves in the same game." Chief Inspector Heat, the novel's main representative of the police, finds the Professor and anarchists generally an impossible breed to fathom. Heat far prefers dealing with burglars, for they are a class of criminal that acts according to the same rules as the police. The novel further indicates that there is a social dialectic that binds police and criminals. From the perspective of legitimate society, the superiority of policeman over criminal satisfies both "vanity of power" and "vulgar love of domination over our fellow creatures." Elsewhere, notably in *The Secret Sharer*, Conrad develops the theme of a law-abiding (indeed, law-making) individual's criminal double, as in the bond of the ship captain to the murderer Leggatt.

Hitchcock, for his part, presents the police as a social force every bit as dangerous as the criminal world. They are apt to identify suspects mistakenly, as in *The Thirty-Nine Steps* (1935) and *North by Northwest* (1959). In the process, victims are branded criminals and innocent lives are jeopardized, all in the name of social order and justice. In *Sabotage*, it is expressly Ted's intrusion into the Verloc family that leads to Stevie's death. Unable to hire someone to carry the explosive device, Verloc is ready to take it himself, until he discovers Ted's identity and realizes the place is under surveillance. What follows is a series of comic and cruel ironies. The Professor had delivered the bomb earlier in a birdcage containing two parakeets and the message: "The birds will sing at 1:45." Verloc makes a present of the songbirds to Stevie. Soon after, hearing the boy whistling to them in the other room, Verloc hits upon the solution of sending him. In giving the boy the film tins along with the package to deliver at Piccadilly Circus, Verloc smiles and tells him that in taking both he "can kill two birds with one stone." The parting words of Mrs. Verloc to Stevie are a warning to be careful crossing the city streets. These macabre touches of humor are, to be sure, typical of Hitchcock.

Lastly, Conrad and Hitchcock share a vision of the murderous secrets that lie at the heart of respectable society. Presenting its story in both psychological and political terms, *The Secret Agent* (which is subtitled *A Simple Tale*) reveals that "simple" domestic life is more complex and deadly than the operations of international terrorism. Its description of the dead husband, in fact, makes murder seem right at home in the Verloc apartment. To Winnie, the corpse seems "so homelike and familiar. . . . Mr. Verloc was taking his habitual ease. He looked comfortable." Conrad is unsparing in his ironic attack on the supposed decencies of bourgeois life. In *The Secret Agent*, as in *Heart of Darkness*, he uncovers the murderous nature of such "civilized" existence.

Hitchcock, with customary relish, summarizes his estimation of the family in modern society with the following statement, made in 1974: "Some of our most exquisite murders have been domestic; performed in simple, homey places like the kitchen. . . ." The awful, and often comic, truth in many Hitchcock films is that no one, least of all an innocent person, is safe from the evil that respectable society unleashes and even, at a distance, enjoys. Apparent models of respectability, such as the well-dressed, pleasant-mannered young man in *Frenzy* (1972), may well be mass murderers. *Frenzy*'s often-cited sequence shot—which takes the viewer from a murder scene set in a walk-up apartment, down a long, steep stairway, and out onto a busy London street—is not simply a piece of camera virtuosity. More importantly, the sequence discloses that murder and ordinary reality virtually adjoin one another. At the close of *Sabotage* the movie house explosion destroys the evidence that incriminates Mrs. Verloc. The one person who knows that she has committed murder, Ted Spencer, convinces her to flee to the Continent with him. In the last shot they disappear into the crowd drawn by the blast. As do characters in Conrad, these two share an intimate knowledge of the secrecy and crime at the heart of society.

Of Human Bondage (1915), W. Somerset Maugham
John Cromwell, 1934; Ken Hughes, 1964

Variations on a Theme

TRISHA CURRAN

In *The Pattern of Maugham, A Critical Portrait*, Anthony Curtis describes his subject as a "mediator who reflected the current of ideas within the traditional form."[1] The same description is equally applicable to John Cromwell and Ken Hughes, directors of the 1934 and 1964 film versions of Maugham's *Of Human Bondage* (1915). Each director reflects Maugham's current of ideas within the traditional form of the film of 1934 and 1964. Thus the differences between the films are determined more by the date of the film than by the director; more by the styles of filmmaking of the 1930s and 1960s than by the particular styles of Cromwell and Hughes (although Hughes's art background is evident in the artistic beginning of his version); and more by the current of ideas, especially the ideas of movie morality, that prevailed in the Breen Code 1930s and the rebellious 1960s than by the ideas that prevailed in Maugham's pre-World War I reflections.

Like literature, film is both art and artifact. However, unlike the art and artifact of the novel, the art and artifact of film are always in the present tense. Even with the dated stylistics (wipes and dissolves in the 1934 version) and even more obviously dated settings (the 1930s in the 1934 film and the 1890s in the 1964 film), the viewer experiences Maugham's characters in the present. Although

1. Anthony Curtis, *The Pattern of Maugham, A Critical Portrait* (New York: Taplinger Publishing Co., 1974), p. 80.

228

Maugham's story is followed in both film versions of *Of Human Bondage*,[2] the films are not narratives in Scholes's and Kellogg's definition of narrative as "a story told by a storyteller."[3] Whereas storyteller Maugham could tell his reader: " 'I can do nothing more,' he said to himself. That was the end. He did not see her again,"[4] directors Cromwell and Hughes have to show Mildred die on screen (even though Maugham does not have her die in the novel) so the viewer will know that Philip does not see her again. In this sense film is closer to Scholes's and Kellogg's definition of drama as "a story without a storyteller,"[5] but neither is it drama, for as Langer notes, drama is history coming, destiny,[6] and film is present.[7] Were *Of Human Bondage* to be adapted for the stage the action would build toward the climax, the future, the destinies of Philip and Mildred as opposed to the filmic presence of Philip and Mildred in the film and the narrator's (Maugham's) memory of them in the novel. Philip and Mildred are present in the films. The actors and actresses provide their images and their acting reflects different aspects of Philip and Mildred on the screen in the present.

In the later film version, the two main characters' more appealing aspects are presented by Laurence Harvey and Kim Novak, and intensified by the immediacy of Hughes's images, the movement of his camera, and the three-dimensionality of his cinematography. Indeed, Laurence Harvey and Kim Novak are Maugham's Philip and Mildred. In image and acting they far outdistance Leslie Howard and Bette Davis, their counterparts in the 1934 film. Unfortunately Howard's 1934 Philip is limited by the self-consciousness of such lines as "I have my limitations" with an accompanying tilt down to his club foot, and by the extremely limited cinematog-

2. Actually there have been three films, 1934, 1946, and 1964, but only the first and last are available for screening, and, according to the critics, worth screening.

3. Robert Scholes and Robert Kellogg, *The Nature of Narrative* (New York: Oxford University Press, 1966), p. 4.

4. W. Somerset Maugham, *Of Human Bondage* (New York: The Modern Library, 1915), p. 679.

5. Scholes and Kellogg, p. 4.

6. Susanne K. Langer, *Feeling and Form* (New York: Charles Scribner's Sons, 1953), pp. 306-25.

7. Trisha Curran, *A New Note on the Film, A Theory of Film Criticism Derived from Susanne K. Langer's Philosophy of Art*, to be published by The Arno Press, pp. 36-57.

Of Human Bondage (1964). Kim Novak as Mildred and Laurence Harvey as Philip share a moment of recognition in this remake of W. Somerset Maugham's 1915 novel. (Photo courtesy of the Museum of Modern Art)

raphy—a preponderance of close-ups of his feet, completely out of place in a film composed of medium and medium long shots.

Happily, Hughes spends much less time on Philip's handicap with much greater success. His first shot of Philip is a long shot of him as a child wearing an orthopedic shoe, silent when asked "What's the matter with your foot?" Only when he is walking down the medical school corridor as an adult and a colleague asks "Something wrong with your leg?" does he say "I've a club foot." Thus Hughes mirrors Maugham's gradual revelation of Philip's deformity. On page four of the novel Maugham writes:

> Knowing she would not be allowed to keep the child much longer, the woman kissed him again; and she passed her hand down his body till she came to his feet; she held the right foot in her hand and felt the five small toes; and then she slowly passed her hand over the left one. She gave a sob.

And on page eight: "Yes, he's got a club foot. It was such a grief to his mother." Instead of Cromwell's incessant shots of Philip's feet, Hughes uses a single scene to illustrate both Philip's handicap and Mildred's lack of compassion—they are running for the train and Mildred, far ahead of Philip, keeps turning around and calling "come on," "hurry up," as she runs toward the train and Philip tries desperately and painfully to catch up.

The story told by storyteller Maugham is the long, heavily autobiographical saga of Philip Carey from age nine, shortly before his mother's death, through his unhappy youth at his uncle's vicarage, his early education at boarding school, his young adulthood at art school in Paris and medical school in London, and his bondage to Mildred through most of medical school. Whereas Maugham's bondage throughout the first part of his life is the theme of the novel, only Philip's bondage to Mildred is represented by the plots of the films. Thus, they only include those details that are pertinent to Philip vis-à-vis Mildred. No mention is made of Philip's Paris friends or of his aunt, and little of his uncle. Indeed, contrary to the novel, Hughes has Philip's uncle dead by the beginning of the 1964 film. With the exception of Hughes's precredits introductory scene of the young Philip being harassed by his classmates at boarding school, both films begin halfway through the novel with Philip in Paris, unsuccessful as an art student, and hampered by a club foot; and then both follow the same basic chronology—Philip leaves Paris, goes to medical school in London, and falls hopelessly in love with Mildred. She scorns him, becomes pregnant with the child of Philip's former friend, Miller, and comes to Philip for help. He helps her, she hurts him; he continues to help, she continues to hurt, thus ruining his attempts at a normal relationship first with Norah and then with Sally Athelny.

Unlike Maugham's Norah, who was very young, very short, and very poor, Cromwell's Norah (Kay Johnson) is older, tall, stately, and affluent, a beautiful refined gentlewoman, much more pleasing to look at than Hughes's much older and much too theatrical Norah (Siobhan McKenna). Movies are not Miss McKenna's medium. Nor is Hughes's Sally (Nanette Newman) as real, as pretty, or as well developed a character as Cromwell's 1934 Sally (Frances Dee). In a dated, but then-delightful montage sequence, Cromwell superimposes Sally, growing older and more beautiful on pages of a calendar to indicate Sally's increasing maturity and Philip's repeated visits to the Athelny home. Both Sally and her father, Thorpe Athelny (Reginald Owen), are more appealing and play off each other far more effectively in the 1934 film than in the 1964 film. Although Sally is more central than Athelny in the 1934 film than in the novel, Sally is still Maugham's Sally and Athelny, Maugham's Athelny. Hughes's Athelny (Roger Livesey) is Hughes's Athelny, and is completely out of character when he comes to Philip and says "What about my daughter?" as is his daughter in going to the cemetery to confront Philip.

Although both films are very similar in content, they differ widely in form. The form of the 1934 film is functional—bright lighting, distinguishable rather than distinguished images, sparse studio sets, self-conscious use of sound, and extreme faithfulness to the letter of the novel, with the obvious exceptions of Mildred's death, disease (tuberculosis rather than syphilis), and extremely disagreeable personality. Maugham's dialogue does not Maugham's Mildred make. What Maugham creates with words, Hughes creates with movement and images. His form, like Maugham's form, is organic, "a whole resulting from the relation of mutually dependent factors."[8] The

8. Susanne K. Langer, *Problems of Art* (New York: Charles Scribner's Sons, 1957), p. 16.

mutually dependent factors that make the 1964 Mildred magnetic, Philip believable, and *Of Human Bondage* memorable are Hughes's moving camera, close-ups, silences, rich backgrounds, location shooting, realistic lighting, abrupt cutting, and sexual suggestiveness—Philip's nude drawing of Mildred and her "I'll have to confirm it for you some day, won't I"; her "I'll do anything you say. I owe it to you don't I?," followed by his removing his coat; and her lying naked on the bed as she tries unsuccessfully to seduce him. Voluptuousness does Maugham's Mildred make. And Hughes's moving images of Novak are voluptuous. She is Maugham's Mildred, "more Mildred than Maugham ever dared imagine."[9] Hughes's Philip is Maugham's Philip with one major exception. Whereas Hughes's Philip packs his bags to run away after Mildred's death, Maugham's Philip was able to go from bondage to Mildred, while she was still alive, to a stable, guilt-free, romantic relationship with Sally. Indeed Hughes, in his concentration on Mildred omits most of Philip's interaction with Sally, making his ending appear contrived and justifying *Variety*'s quip of "period meller."[10] Although more faithful to Maugham, Cromwell's ending is cryptic and corny. Sally's "'I don't want to stand in your way'" does not make sense unless the viewer knows, as the reader does, that Sally and Philip believe she is pregnant, necessary information prohibited in 1934 by the Breen Code.

Would that purple prose were prohibited instead. Both Cromwell and Hughes out-Maugham Maugham in their reiterations of human bondage. Thus, in the 1934 film, Norah looks straight ahead and says dramatically, "It's just as though you were bound to her in some way, as I am to you, and she was to Miller"; and Philip, "I had to be free to realize that all these years I've dreamed of escape. I was limping through life, and I was bound up with a person who was intolerable to me." Perhaps the 1964 Norah is referring to the above, when, in the same farewell scene with Philip she asks "What decided you to take her back? Isn't there a saying somewhere about human bondage?" and he answers solemnly over the mood music, "If there isn't, there ought to be." More period meller. And more Cromwell and Hughes than Maugham. On finding Mildred outside

9. *Newsweek*, 28 September 1964.
10. *Variety*, 1 July 1964.

his door, Maugham's Philip asked angrily and earthily, "What the hell do you want?"[11]

The trend, technique, and technology of the times limited the richness of expansive forces in the 1934 film that we find in the 1964 film. Thus in terms of Goethe's forces, the vertical or directive forces of doing and happening (and talking) are more obvious in the 1934 film, and the spiral or expansive forces, the embodying, digressing, resolving aspects of mood and setting are more opulent in the 1964 film. A simple shot of Philip against dark drapes, following, as it does, lustrous close-ups of Philip and Mildred making love, subtly conveys Philip's sadness when Mildred tells him she is going to marry Miller, as an earlier shot of him sinking in the frame conveyed his sinking spirits when Mildred broke their theater date. Later Philip's power to help Mildred and her powerlessness, alone and pregnant, are emphasized by low angle shots of Philip and high angle shots of Mildred, as he tells her to "Go to Griffiths. Let him keep you in the manner you've been accustomed to," portray Philip's freedom from Mildred's bondage and her precarious economic situation without Philip's continued support. A moving camera accentuates Mildred's movement and the all-pervasiveness of her taunting as she walks around Philip calling him "cripple."

The details are subtle and somewhat subliminal, expansive rather than expressive, an appropriate cinematic mirroring of Maugham's literary form. As Ortega has noted, "a work of art lives on its form, not on its material. The essential grace it emanates springs from its structure, from its organism."[12] The difference in structure, in organism, is the difference between the 1934 and the 1964 films. Whereas the 1934 film is mostly Maugham's material, the 1964 film mirrors Maugham's expressive form and is thus the more powerful of the two, for "ultimately the greatest source of emotional power in art lies not in any particular subject matter, however passionate, however universal. It lies in form."[13]

11. Maugham, p. 409.
12. José Ortega y Gasset, *The Dehumanization of Art and Notes on the Novel* (Princeton: Princeton University Press, 1968), p. 57
13. Susan Sontag, *Against Interpretation* (New York: Dell Publishing Co., 1966), p. 179.

All Passion Spent

D E N N I S   D E N I T T O

The viewer who has read the original of a film adaptation is apt to be confronted with the disturbing phenomenon of "memory reverberation": the memory of the world created by the author intrudes during the viewing of the film. This dual perspective can, however, be turned into a critical advantage. Comparing a motion picture and its source can reveal aspects of a narrative not developed by the filmmakers or dimensions added by the transformation from one medium into another. The problem is to distinguish between potentialities inherent in one medium and lacking in the other and so to avoid the fallacy of criticizing a film for not preserving a quality that only a literary work can realize. For example, a viewer should not expect in a two-hour motion picture the complexity of characterization to be found in a novel that requires eight hours to be read. Furthermore, filmmakers must be granted the right to exercise their own creative freedom. Viewing a film adaptation is a *different* experience from reading its original, but not necessarily a more or less moving or significant experience. Fidelity of a film to its source is not in itself a virtue. Michelangelo Antonioni's freewheeling version of Julio Cortazar's short story "Blow-Up" is as valid an approach as Robert Bresson's steadfast rendering of Georges Bernanos's novel *Diary of a Country Priest*.

These considerations make the process of comparing a film adaptation to its source a sort of intellectual highwire act. At each step the critic keeps his balance by maintaining an equilibrium between two different works in two different media joined together by corresponding narratives. I have attempted to achieve such an equilibrium in this essay devoted to comparing Jack Cardiff's film version of *Sons and Lovers* (1960) and D. H. Lawrence's classic novel (1913). In particular I have focused on the problems faced by filmmakers in representing on a screen the inner realities of character.

The most obvious starting point for a comparison of a film and novel is their respective narratives. The following is a summary of the major events, characters, and relationships as condensed into the film. Paul Morel, an aspiring painter in his early twenties, lives at home in the mining village of Bestwood, near the town of Nottingham, in central England. He is passionately attached to his possessive mother, Gertrude, and resentful of his crude, forceful father, Walter, a miner. Although his mother disapproves, Paul maintains a warm, intellectual friendship with Miriam Lievers, who lives on a farm outside the village. Miriam is in love with Paul, but she is also emotionally demanding and has had instilled in her by her religious mother a fear of sexual relations with men.

In a mining accident, Paul's brother Arthur is killed. Soon after the funeral, a painting by Paul is included in an exhibition. This leads to a crotchety old man offering to support the young man while he studies art in London. A violent argument between Gertrude and Walter, however, convinces Paul that he cannot leave.

He begins work at a surgical appliances factory in Nottingham. Here he meets Clara Dawes, a few years older than himself, a suffragette, and separated from her husband. Sometime later, he insists that Miriam give herself to him physically; the sexual experience is for both a complete failure. At Christmas time, William, Paul's older brother living in London, comes home for a visit with his fiancée, Lily, an attractive but flighty young woman. William believes that his sensual relationship with Lily compensates for any of her deficiencies of character. A consequence of this visit is that Paul stops seeing Miriam. Paul and Clara become lovers, but she feels he never gives himself completely to her and, furthermore, still considers herself bound to her husband. After a fight between

Baxter Dawes and Paul, the former becomes ill and Clara insists that she must take care of him. She and Paul agree to separate.

Mrs. Morel dies. After a period of despair, Paul meets Miriam for the last time. He declares that he is going to be free and manage his own future as an artist. In the concluding shot of the film, Paul leaves for London.

Gavin Lambert and T. E. B. Clarke have fashioned a neat, carefully structured screenplay for *Sons and Lovers*. They have of necessity condensed the time scope of Lawrence's work and eliminated secondary characters (for example, Paul's sister, Annie, and Miriam's older brothers). The novel begins with the meeting and marriage of Gertrude and Walter and encompasses decades of life in the Morel family, whereas the film opens with Paul as a young man and is confined to events within a year's time.

The screenwriters have also simplified the narrative. Paul's affairs with Miriam and Clara are in sequence rather than concurrent. The friendship that develops between the young man and Baxter Dawes is not included. One minor and two major revisions are notable. The showing of Paul's painting in an art gallery and the appearance of a patron are added, making more concrete an alternative for him to life in Bestwood. More radical are changes in the fate of the two older Morel sons. In Lawrence's fiction, Arthur goes into the army and marries. William lives in London and becomes engaged to Lily, but dies of pneumonia. In the streamlined cinematic version William's death would have added an unnecessary complication. The same holds true of Paul's illness after his brother's death. Mrs. Morel's conviction that Paul must never enter the mines is more dramatically reinforced here by the death of Arthur than, as in the original, Walter Morel's accident.

The most controversial departure from Lawrence's plot is the manner of Mrs. Morel's death. In the novel, Paul cannot endure his mother's suffering from cancer and kills her with an overdose of morphine. Again simplification appears to be the dominant factor influencing this omission; for the same reason Mrs. Morel can more easily be dispatched in the film with a heart condition than a lingering cancer. Moreover, an act that in the novel is justified during two chapters would be unconvincing and melodramatic if presented in a few moments of a motion picture.

In addition to condensing and simplifying the plot of Lawrence's work, the screenwriters have applied another technique often used in film adaptations. An interaction between two characters is explored in dozen of pages of a book and during many incidents. An individual scene in a film can, at the expense of carefully developed motivations and revelations of shades of feelings, more directly and concretely summarize an aspect of a relationship. For example, in the screen *Sons and Lovers,* the source of Miriam's sexual frigidity is indicated in a brief conversation with her mother. Clara's doubts about Paul's ability to give himself entirely to a woman while his mother lives are exposed in only one conversation in a bedroom at the seashore.

Throughout all these revisions in plot, however, the screenwriters have retained the two major themes of the novel: a young man unnaturally attached to his mother cannot become an independent human being until he emancipates himself from her; and a satisfactory relationship between a man and woman requires not only fulfilling sexual experiences and emotional commitments, but also the respect of each partner for the individuality of the other. The two themes are interrelated in both novel and film; for instance, it is a lack of physical responsiveness yet spiritual possessiveness on Miriam's part, as well as the invisible presence of Mrs. Morel that stands between Miriam and Paul.

Although plot and themes determine the fundamental structure and function of a film, they are only stages in the development of a narrative and do no more than hint at the means available to filmmakers to transform the architectonics and ideas inherent in a screenplay into a vivid, authentic film experience. Before examining these components of *Sons and Lovers,* however, we should be aware, for purposes of comparison, of the approaches and techniques Lawrence used in his novel, beyond the mere sequence of events, to implement his themes.

Lawrence's *Sons and Lovers* is sometimes described as being essentially "realistic." There is, at least in one respect, validity in this view, for the writer accurately depicts the texture of life in a mining village with its grime, poverty, and economic insecurity. However, impressive as Lawrence is in recreating the soul-destroying milieu of the mining village and its people, he is not simply a realist like Arnold Bennett or John Galsworthy, two writers he heartily castigated as narrow and shallow in vision. His paramount interest is in the psychological forces that permeate human relationships and especially in those feelings so deeply embedded in an individual's psyche that he or she is barely aware of their existence except in moments of great tension when they well up and determine his or her actions.

Lawrence devised a number of techniques to convey to readers the inner realities of his characters. He enters into their psyches and reveals not only what they are thinking, but also their basic desires and needs, much as Conrad, Joyce, and Dorothy Richardson were doing. What makes Lawrence distinctive, however, is the intensity with which he probes shades of feeling and the perceptivity with which he discloses the ebb and flow of emotions, especially the self-contradictions that belie what he condemned as the conventional portrayal of "the old stable *ego* of the character."

By the time Lawrence completed *Sons and Lovers* in 1913, he had developed a prose style flexible enough to communicate both the concrete reality of place and the overtones of the flux of intangible human feelings. Two brief examples illustrate his range of style. These are the first three sentences of the novel:

> "The Bottoms" succeeded to "Hell Row." Hell Row was a block of thatched, bulging cottages that stood by the brook-side of Greenhill Lane. There lived the colliers who worked in the little gin-pits two fields away.

In Chapter XIII, Paul is with Clara as they lie on a bank near a canal:

> He lifted his head and looked into her eyes. They were dark and shining and strange, life wild at the source staring into his life, stranger to him, yet meeting him; and he put his face down on her throat, afraid. . . . They had met, and included in their meeting the thrust of the manifold grass-stems, the cry of the peewit, the wheel of the stars.

As the latter quotation demonstrates, Lawrence's style at its most intense is fervent, metaphorical, often fusing inner feelings with external nature.

Lawrence also depended on incidents with symbolic significance to penetrate beneath the surface of events. In Chapter VII, Paul is with Miriam in the barn of the Lievers' farm. The young man rides

Sons and Lovers (1960). In Cardiff's adaptation of Lawrence's novel the Morels—Gertrude (Wendy Hiller), Paul (Dean Stockwell) and Walter (Trevor Howard)—seem isolated in the community. (Photo courtesy of the Museum of Modern Art)

on a swing. We share his joy in the freedom and exultation of its movement. He insists Miriam take a turn and pushes her. She is afraid of freedom and the insistent rhythm of swinging. As Paul continues to push her, the ride begins to connote sexual intercourse: "Down to her bowels went the hot wave of fear. She was in his hands. Again, firm and inevitable came the thrust at the right moment. She gripped the rope, almost swooning." A commonplace incident is transformed into an epiphany that gives us insights into two contrasting personalities.

In recreating *Sons and Lovers* for the screen, the filmmakers had to contend with this daunting richness of expression. Restricted by the screen time of the film, they had to decide what to ignore in the novel's form and content, and what to attempt to translate into images and sound.

The medium of cinema excels, as Siegfried Kracauer and André Bazin have insisted, in its ability to present definite physical realities, which include settings and human beings. The film *Sons and Lovers* successfully reconstructs the major settings of the novel, particularly the contrast between the open countryside and the restrictive mining village of Bestwood and town of Nottingham. The first shot of the film is brilliant in epitomizing this contrast: a view of sheep in a field, then a slow pan to the right that reveals the surface mining structures.

What the filmmakers have obviously decided not to focus on is the mining community itself. The Morels seem strangely isolated, which may be appropriate for Mrs. Morel and Paul, but even Walter Morel has but a shadowy existence outside of the house in the Bottoms. This is an important lack in the film, for Mrs. Morel's sense of superiority and Paul's rebellion against the world of his father are unconvincing unless we apprehend, through more than shots of houses and surface mine structures, the crude, emotionally vitiating atmosphere of the community as well as its positive qualities that support Walter. The one scene that gives us a sense of people drawn together by common bonds and needs—when Arthur is killed in the mines—is too brief (approximately four minutes) to do more than inform us that a community exists.

The physical reality of the characters in a film is tangibly present so long as actors appear on the screen. The appropriateness of their appearances, however, is another matter. The casting for *Sons and Lovers* from this perspective is commendable. Athough Wendy Hiller looks exceptionally young for a woman in her middle fifties, none of the actors has physical characteristics that clash with the role he or she is playing.

It is in projecting to an audience the inner worlds of the characters, however, that the film is open to major criticism. There are few techniques of and approaches to filmmaking that cannot be used expressionistically, going beyond the merely functional to convey either the feelings of the characters or those of the filmmakers toward their subject. Four categories of such techniques and approaches in *Sons and Lovers* can be postulated: the plot (already considered); the dialogue and interpretations of the actors; what I designate as "camera-editing dynamics" (effects achieved with a camera and through the process of editing); and "elements of presentation" (sound, lighting, settings, costumes, and props).

Much of the dialogue in the film was lifted directly from the book. Nonetheless it is, by definition, confined to just those words the characters speak, without the qualifications and contradictions Lawrence could indicate through additional descriptions of inner thoughts and desires. The actor can add nonverbal overtones by means of facial expressions, gestures, and the intonation of lines. The more spontaneous and uncomplicated the emotions expressed by a character, the easier the task of the actor and the more effective can be the dialogue. Walter Morel's rage and frustration at the critical attitude toward him of his wife and Paul are the most unambiguous and dramatically forceful feelings in the film. The antecedent sources of his alienation from his family are less clearly presented, being principally confined to Mrs. Morel's description to Paul, after the confrontation between son and father, of the beginning of the marriage and her making Walter "face himself."

Actually Walter Morel is more sympathetically portrayed in the film than in the novel. His grief at the death of Arthur is obviously genuine; he makes gestures toward reconciliation with his wife by bringing her a coconut after spending the night at a pub and by serving her tea in bed the morning after locking her out of the house; he carries himself with impressive dignity when walking through the living room clothed only in a towel when William and

Lily arrive; he sings at the Christmas party with appealing gusto. For all his rages and excessive drinking, he is the most stoic and clear-sighted member of the family. The morning after his argument with his wife and son he says to Paul, "It happened before; it'll happen again. . . . Stop being a softy." While Paul is with Clara at the seashore, he honestly tells his wife what her possessiveness has done to their son. After her death, it is Walter who prods Paul into facing life without his mother, into grasping an opportunity for freedom (a scene not in the novel).

It is the excellent acting of Trevor Howard that makes credible the two sides of Walter's nature. The character's rages and crudity are imbued with passion, but Howard is even better in projecting the underlying warmth of the man. While this interpretation creates a more appealing person than in the novel, it also weakens the justification for the resentment his wife and son bear toward him.

Wendy Hiller gives the finest performance in the film. She is able to portray Gertrude Morel's selfishness and self-pity without making a monster of the woman. Her lines articulate her fear of losing dominance over Paul and William. She has authority when she cruelly rejects Miriam as a wife for her son in the art gallery or when she battles with her husband. In the scenes with Walter and Paul before she dies, Hiller infuses her role with dignity. The film's Gertrude is less zealous in her possessiveness, less savage in attacking Walter, less crafty in approving of Clara as a woman who cannot completely take Paul from her as might Miriam, than the Mrs. Morel of the novel. A fuller, more complex character could only have been achieved with additional incidents demonstrating her reactions to others.

The least realized major character in the film is Miriam. This is not entirely the fault of Heather Sears, who projects the young woman's love of Paul and the pain of her sexual frigidity. She is also outstanding when Paul breaks off their relationship after William's visit. On the other hand, the young actress is too passive and unimaginative in expressing Miriam's feelings in the crucial scene with Paul after they have had sexual intercourse.

Most reprehensible is the failure of the screenplay to dramatize two essential characteristics of Miriam: her spirituality and her compulsive need to suffocate Paul with her love. Mrs. Morel, Mrs.

Radford (Clara's mother), Clara, and even Paul himself *state* that the farmgirl is otherwordly and possessive, but both qualities are never demonstrated on the screen. Mention is made of her reading Shelley under Paul's tutelage and for a brief moment we observe her effusiveness in imposing her feelings on her little brother. This is insufficient, however, to convince us that Miriam is as much a danger as Mrs. Morel to Paul's development as an independent human.

Mary Ure is a lovely Clara Dawes, carrying herself with dignity and self-assurance. She nicely suggests Clara's coolness turning into physical passion in the scene in her mother's house. The restrictions of the screenplay require her to declare her intuitive sense that Paul could never give himself completely to her, without showing the development of her doubts. What a viewer has most difficulty in comprehending is her relationship with her husband. From what we learn of Clara in the film, we do not understand why she feels Baxter "belongs" to her. For this reason the scene in which she breaks off with Paul and returns to her husband seem contrived. The ease with which she makes the decision and the ease with which Paul accepts it cast doubt on the depth of their feelings toward each other. In the novel, Clara is a more ambiguous character, and the friendship that develops between Baxter and Paul gives us insights into the struggle for dominance preoccupying husband and wife, which contains echoes of the conflict between Walter and Gertrude Morel.

It is Paul who is the central figure of the novel. Dean Stockwell (the only American in the British cast) gives an intelligent if somewhat overly restrained performance. What one feels most lacking in his interpretation is the insecurity and self-doubts of a growing young man. Especially in his seduction of Clara, he appears far too sure of himself. Paul's lines point to feelings we can easily identify: attachment to his mother, resentment and jealously of his father, disappointment in Miriam, ardor for Clara. There is, however, insufficient subtlety and uncertainty in what he says; we feel shut out from the turmoil of his innermost emotions. Stockwell adds little through the nonverbal means available to him to give us insights into Paul's seeking, confused psyche.

The actor's moments of anger carry conviction but are interchangeable, not molded to context. After sex with Miriam, he appears merely disappointed, nor feeling the anguish his words indicate. Stockwell is more effective in the scenes of his mother's death and in his later conversation with his father. Even in the latter, however, we find it hard to believe this is a young man in such despair that he is contemplating suicide. In short, Stockwell conveys only the surface of Paul's character and fails to suggest a complex, three-dimensional young man undergoing experiences that test the mettle of his selfhood.

Camera-editing dynamics, when manipulated by a Renoir, Bergman, or Antonioni can provide indications of inner feelings beyond the screenplay and the interpretations of actors. The least one can expect from a competent professional director is fluency and grace of style. Jack Cardiff eminently fulfills the latter function of a director in *Sons and Lovers* but appears incapable of the former. That he enhances the visual excitement of the film comes as no surprise, for he is known in Great Britain and the United States as a superb director of photography. His work as a director has been less outstanding. Although Freddie Francis is credited with the photography for *Sons and Lovers*, we can assume Cardiff played a decisive role in the shooting and editing of the film.

Sons and Lovers consists of individual scenes basically joined together by dissolves. Cardiff's transitions are often imaginative. Some examples: After Paul tells Miriam their sexual experience has only separated them further, the scene ends with a close-up of the young woman's features and a slow dissolve that becomes a superimposition of her face on the town and snow at Christmas time. From Paul and Clara ardently kissing, there is a dissolve to twirling bobbins in the factory. After Mrs. Morel's death and Paul's conversation with his father, a shot of daffodils on a canvas Paul painted for his mother dissolves to real ones in a field. There are also many memorable shots. In the first scene the camera moves from the miners coming up from the pit to their row houses, and then through the door of the Morel house into the interior. Later that morning, Paul is with Miriam beside a pond; there is a rumbling sound; cut to the surface of the pond, where ripples appear; back to Paul, who realizes an accident has occurred at the mine. The montage of shots of people running to the mine, especially those through the wheel of the mine elevator, is exceptional.

However, while the refinement and sensitivity of Cardiff's photography for *Sons and Lovers* is impressive, his camera-editing dynamics only grace the surface of the film, without reaching the inner realities of the characters. The director did not find a cinematic style that communicates the fervor of Lawrence's literary style and the psychological depths of his characterizations. This is not to say that baroque camera-editing dynamics constitute the best approach. Ken Russell utilized this style in his version of Lawrence's *Women in Love* (1969), with uneven results. Some scenes, such as the death of Gerald Crich, are masterful; others, such as the wrestling scene between Gerald and Rupert Birkin approach the ridiculous. A more consistently effective compromise was achieved by Christopher Miles in *The Virgin and the Gypsy* (1970), based on Lawrence's novella of the same title. Miles managed to combine visual lyricism with revelations of character motivation and feelings without the affected flourishes to which Russell is prone. In all fairness, it must be pointed out that *The Virgin and the Gypsy* is a less complex work than either *Sons and Lovers* or *Women in Love*.

Cardiff is not incapable of creating an ambience rich in emotional reverberations that do not depend solely on dialogue. He demonstrates this in the sequence that takes place in Mrs. Radford's home. A palpable sensuality builds up as Clara and Paul wait for the older woman to retire to bed. There is a fine subjective shot from Clara's point of view of Paul's hands shuffling cards. Equally telling is the scene in Clara's room where Paul is to spend the night. At the climax of the sequence, Paul stealthily descends the stairs to join Clara before the fireplace. Rhythm and tone reinforce each other as they rarely do elsewhere in the film.

For some reason Cardiff has insistently kept his camera objective and distant from the characters. He definitely favors the *mise-en-scène* approach to that of montage. In this way he avoids the excesses of a Russell but places the burden of psychological insights on a screenplay that is inadequate in this respect. Occasionally the director does indulge in close-ups or close shots of the characters. Generally, however, the camera is too discreet, as though embarrassed by emotional displays and tensions.

Visual symbols are also avoided, while those that do appear are either patently obvious or undeveloped. The one exception is the shot of rotating bobbins after the one of Paul and Clara embracing.

The empty stool that reminds Walter of the dead Arthur, the snowdrop flowers that Paul and Clara discuss, and the painting of the daffodils are more signs than symbols. An instance of an opportunity lost is the swing scene in the barn at Miriam's farm. Earlier in this essay, this incident was used as an illustration of the way in which Lawrence imbues a simple event with symbolic overtones. In the film, this scene consists basically of three shots that convey Miriam's caution in contrast to Paul's adventurousness; however, sexual associations are muted. That Cardiff and his colleagues had this possibility in mind is demonstrated by the fact that after Paul kisses the young woman and implores her to give herself to him physically, she walks over to the swing, stands next to it for a moment, then returns and says, "you shall have me." It is, however, knowledge of the scene in the novel and not the camera-editing dynamics, and surely not the dialogue, that give the swing incident special significance. A director is not required to invest events with symbolic implications, but in the case of *Sons and Lovers* this technique could have compensated, in this story of complex feelings, for a psychologically passive use of the camera.

The elements of presentation are generally conventional. The background music is rather mundane, functioning primarily to underscore dramatic moments. Natural sounds are used more imaginatively. For example, we hear the heavy steps of Walter Morel before we are introduced to him visually. The lighting is used expressionistically only in the scene in which Paul is upstairs in Clara's room and a shadow eliminates Baxter in a photograph of Clara and her husband.

Weighing the strengths and weaknesses of a film inevitably results in a subjective evaluation. I feel that on the whole the screen *Sons and Lovers* is an admirable work. My chief criticism obviously is of potentials unrealized. Even within the limitations of less than two hours, the film could have been made more intense and could have contained greater psychological depth. D. H. Lawrence was bold and experimental when it came to creating art. *Sons and Lovers* is a cautious film. It is unlikely Lawrence would have approved.

Russell's Images of Lawrence's Vision

J O S E P H   A .   G O M E Z

Both D. H. Lawrence and Ken Russell have been described as self-indulgent, extravagant, and excessive.[1] In his fiction, essays, and poetry, Lawrence uncompromisingly and intemperately assaulted his readers in an attempt to radically alter their attitudes. He overemphasized the power of the body and the "blood" because he claimed this aspect had been denied by twentieth-century man's overdependence on abstraction reasoning. His purpose, however, was not to tip the scales in favor of flesh at the expense of spirit. Instead, he used extremes to compensate for man's dominant preoccupations and to assist in the development of the total self. Russell's methods of assaulting his audience are strikingly similar. He, too, resorts to extremes to bring an audience to his position, which often rests somewhere between their conventional pieties or indifference and the argument on the screen.

Early in his career, Lawrence discovered the theme ("the relation between men and women") that would dominate his writing, and, as a result, he quickly transcended the limitations of social realism and sought entirely new modes of characterization. Through highly charged symbolic language, such as that employed in *The Rainbow* (1915) and *Women in Love* (1920), Lawrence sought to delve into the "core" of his characters, to touch them where they did not even

1. Some of the material contained in this essay appeared in a different form in my book, *Ken Russell: The Adaptor as Creator* (London: Frederick Muller, Ltd., 1976).

know themselves. Like Lawrence, Russell also eschewed realism early in his career and embraced metaphorical and symbolic techniques, which although highly successful, can never rival the depths of Laurentian characterization. Russell's chief method of characterization is visual. He is consumed by images, and his entire career could be analyzed in terms of his attempts to transform other people's words into his unique images. Appropriately, one of his most successful efforts was his adaptation of *Women in Love* (1969).

For some film critics, like Pauline Kael and John Simon, Lawrence's novel was best left alone because it in no way lent itself to the movement from word to image. While it must be acknowledged that Russell's film does not capture all the dimensions of Lawrence's prose, the film is not the simplistic rendering of the novel that Kael and Simon make it out to be. Russell uses much of the actual dialogue from the novel to accompany his visuals, but he also forms a new structure appropriate to the medium of film and creates often overpowering images which reveal the nature of the relationships depicted in the novel and his own attitudes toward them.

Lawrence's novel is built on counterpointing and follows the typical pattern found in most of his fiction. The central characters find themselves trapped in a symbolic limbo, in which they must choose between a death-in-life submission to a machinelike existence or a radical, new kind of resurrected life of reintegration into "being." The work traces the development and outcome of two intense, combatative relationships: between Gudrun and Gerald, which degenerates and ends in symbolic and finally literal death; and between Ursula and Birkin, which emerges out of conflict into what Lawrence saw as a new synthesis, and perhaps as a model in the modern world.

In the novel, through creating a series of tensions, variations, repetitions, and richly symbolic set scenes delineating the two contrasting love affairs, Lawrence weaved together material into a complex fabric in which every conversation, slight detail of description, and minor character assisted the development of his major themes. Novelist Angus Wilson has even suggested that the thematic interplay of *Women in Love* has a form as strict as a court dance. Although unfamiliar with this comment, Russell also sensed the dancelike variations which served as the backbone of Lawrence's novel, and he created a film patterned after the structure of dance rhythms. In fact, in a jocular comment to critic John Baxter, he indicated that he "should have turned the whole thing into a musical; it wasn't far off in some ways." Indeed, even on the most literal levels, Russell uses dance as a means of character development, as a counterpointing device, and as a dominant image which assists in providing a pattern of unification. Background music also functions in this way, as well as providing Russell with yet another way of commenting on the characters and on Lawrence's particular vision.

Most of Lawrence's novels revolve around the conflict between what might simplistically be described as life forces and a death-in-life quest for dominance and possession, and the use of dance in Russell's film reflects this dichotomy. Hermione's "Greek ballet" concerns women who have become widows, and almost all of Gudrun's dances reveal a quest for domination. The most obvious example, of course, is Gudrun's dance before the herd of Highland cattle, which finally succeeds in putting them to flight. Lawrence's prose makes it clear that this act symbolizes Gudrun's reaction to Gerald, but Russell achieves the same feeling in visual terms through the choreography of the sequence. It begins simply enough with Gudrun's spontaneous dance improvisations, as the lake and trees provide a natural backdrop proscenium. With the appearance of the cattle, however, both the music and the dance become sinister. Finally, with the arrival of Gerald and Birkin, the nature of the relationships between the men and the women are revealed through dance, gesture, music, and cross-cutting. Birkin dances up to Ursula as he sings "Oh, You Beautiful Doll" and exclaims "pity the world isn't madder." Russell then cuts to dissonant music accompanying Gudrun's pursuit of the cattle and Gerald's response. The masterful dissolves and moving camera shots, taken by Russell himself, capture the feeling conveyed by Lawrence's prose description of the scene. Gudrun's gestures to Gerald as she "dances" before him parallel her movements when teasing the cattle.

Gerald declares his love for Gudrun at the end of this dancing episode, and the beginnings of Loerke's affair with Gudrun, toward the end of the work, occur during a dance at the mountain lodge. The perverseness of the relationship between Gudrun and Loerke is

Women in Love (1970). Gudrun's (Glenda Jackson) dance before the herd of cattle is one way in which Russell projects her quest for domination. (Photo courtesy of the Museum of Modern Art).

also underscored by their pantomime-dance of Nina and Peter Tchaikovsky's honeymoon journey to a recording of the homosexual composer's *Pathetique Symphony*. This sequence, as well as the one depicting Herr Leitner in Loerke's bed, helps to dispell, through contrast, any label of homosexuality that some viewers might attach to Gerald's relationship to Rupert. Loerke is the bisexual to whom Gudrun finally abandons herself when, dancing before the highest mountain and ironically humming "I'm Forever Blowing Bubbles," she decides to follow her "rat-like" mentor to Dresden. Finally, in contrast to these dances of domination are the spontaneous Charlestons and roughhouse, comical polkas which usually involve Birkin and Ursula.

The dancelike rhythms of *Women in Love* are also suggested in a number of other ways, including vivid visual counterpointing, parallel sequences, and parallel shots with slight but meaningful variations. Part of this method is simply exhibited in the editing, as in the combination of close-ups and close middle shots during the wedding sequence which, like Lawrence's opening chapter, clearly links Ursula with Birkin and Gudrun with Gerald. Other examples are more subtle and include the now famous cut from the nude bodies of the drowned Laura and Tibby to the entangled bodies of Birkin and Ursula immediately after making love. Such parallels abound throughout the film. The discussion of catkins, for instance, should come to mind when Rupert lectures on the ways in which to eat a fig, and both of these incidents provide the backdrop for the scene in which Rupert and Ursula argue in the cornfield and finally achieve harmony through Ursula's gift of the wild flowers. Gudrun sees a miner with his woman embracing in an underground passageway early in the film and later returns to the same location to act out the scene with Gerald.

The rhythmic structure is also evident in the complex use of mirrors and reflections throughout the film, and in the frequent repetition of objects such as fireplaces, statues, and cups in the *mise-en-scène* of the shots depicting the discussion between Gerald and Birkin. The use of parallelism and variations also extends to Shirley Russell's costuming for the film. In many sequences, for instance, Gerald wears dark trousers and a striped sports jacket, while Birkin wears his straw hat and white suit; yet his tie is exactly the same color and pattern as Gerald's jacket.

It is the manner in which Russell visually captures Lawrence's characters and themes while also reflecting his own responses, however, that makes the film a significant adaptation. His approach to his material is obvious even in the prologue to the film which appears before the titles. The emotional coldness of Mr. and Mrs. Brangwen is visually manifest through the economical use of two medium close shots, while the more or less unconventional attitudes of the sisters, Ursula and Gudrun Brangwen, are made known by their clothing, which sets them off from the townspeople. The visuals that accompany their discussion also exemplify Russell's approach. When Ursula suggests, for instance, that marriage might very well be the end of experience, Russell presents a shot of a couple pushing a baby carriage. The musical background of "I'm Forever Blowing Bubbles" comments ironically on the major characters' idealistic hopes for love, since so much of the film, as Russell presents it, concerns illusion.

In the novel, Lawrence simply has Ursula and Gudrun watch the Crich wedding from the low stone wall of the grammar school just outside the churchyard, whereas Russell places the girls in the church graveyard. Thus as Gudrun complains that "*Nothing materializes*! Everything withers in the bud," she falls back on a bench and folds herself up in the position of a corpse. The image at this point in the film is not obvious because as yet we know so little about the characters, but like the terrifying cuttlefish image in Gudrun's Chinese lantern (described by Lawrence in the "Water-Party" chapter), it suggests that Gudrun is a doomed character long before the journey to the continent.

The movement from sequence to sequence in the film frequently involves paralleling of events and consistency of imagery. For instance, the episode of Gerald holding the white mare (changed from Lawrence's account in which the horse is red) at the crossing gate near the loud but slowly moving locomotive is followed by scenes of Gerald at the mines, and the ride with his father in the spotless white car through the throng of coal-dust-covered men establishes a visual link between the two areas (sexual and economic) of Gerald's dominance. Also, Gerald's remark that the miners' hatred for him is better than his father's so-called love for them recalls Birkin, who in a previous sequence attacked the minister's sermon on brotherhood by claiming that one might as well say that hate is the greatest thing the world has ever known. "In the name of righteousness and love, you shall have hate."

These patterns and textures exist throughout the film, but as in Lawrence's novel, they demand a different means of approach from the usual event-oriented structure that too many readers and filmgoers expect. For instance, just as "Water-Party" (Chapter XIV) is the center of the symbolic structure of the novel, the party sequence at Shortlands in the film ends the delineation of the early relationship between the sisters and their respective lovers. It also looks back to the death-in-life relationship of Hermione and Birkin in the beginning of the film and ahead to the will to power, destructive relationship of Gerald and Gudrun. More than anything else, however, the sequence allows Russell to express his own attitudes toward the views of the characters, especially those of Birkin and Ursula, through editing and the shifting of events. The conversation between Birkin and Ursula after the drowning of Laura and Tibby is drawn directly from the novel (though there the couple does not make love). In the film, the seduction is both erotic and comic, but through the intercutting shots of Birkin and Ursula in the same position as the drowned victims, Russell successfully punctures Birkin's philosophical attempt to transcend himself through a kind of selfless love.[2]

Certainly, the love affair between Birkin and Ursula is meant to contrast sharply with the sinister, dark and morbid relationship of Gerald and Gudrun. But Russell still mocks the pretensions of Birkin and Ursula by picturing them making love in slow motion in a wheat field, and filming them with a swirling, tilted camera amidst an overly lush, conventionally lyrical music score. The difficulty here is that too many critics and film viewers have accepted conventional advertising's vision of lyricism and therefore miss the irony in this sequence.

In contrast to the pseudolyricism of Birkin and Ursula stands the

2. Ana Laura Zambrano makes a similar observation in "*Women in Love*: Counterpoint on Film," *Literature/Film Quarterly*, 1 (January 1973), p. 51.

subdued, almost dismal, atmosphere associated with Gerald and Gudrun. After the death of his father, Gerald tries to flee from his past by journeying to Gudrun's house to make love to her for the first time. In the novel, Lawrence underscores the failure of this relationship by showing that it stems directly from death and involves no real reciprocity. In fact, it is described as a kind of perverse union between mother and child rather than as an encounter between lovers. Russell's visuals for this sequence communicate the same idea, but again in a manner appropriate to the film medium. Shots of Gerald's mother, Mrs. Crich, laughing uncontrollably at her husband's funeral are intercut with shots of Gudrun and Gerald making love.

Russell comments both on Lawrence's ideas and on the characters' illusions. The failure of Gerald and Birkin to establish the kind of relationship Birkin so ardently seeks is visually underscored by Russell, who thinks that what Lawrence desires through Birkin is impossible. When Birkin discusses "the additional perfect relationship between man and man," the *mise-en-scène* of the shots undercuts his entire argument. A statue of two dancing women, which separates the men, looms forward in the frame. In the background, the chalice and fireplace from previous sequences are replaced by mirrors, reflections of a woman's portrait, and a sculpture of a woman's head.[3]

With the shift of the scene to the Swiss Alps, the film "opens up" visually, but while light and whiteness seem ever present, there is no heat—no fireplaces, for example, which are Russell's most obvious and significant symbol of communion. This last section of the film is also a final working out of parallels found in the first section. The relationship between Loerke and Gudrun is established through close-ups, in much the same way they were used initially to link the sisters with Gerald and Birkin; and just as Birkin and Ursula argued over Hermione, Gerald and Gudrun discuss Gudrun's attraction to the German sculptor who believes that art should interpret industry. Also, just as Hermione revealed her limited nature through her lifeless dance, Loerke presents his true depths through his little esoteric games of sensual dominance. Finally, just as Hermione's

3. See Zambrano, p. 47.

quest for dominance resulted in the attempted murder of Birkin, Gerald's inability to construct a meaningful union with the willful emasculating Gudrun results in his attempt to kill her. Unlike Birkin, who found communion with nature, Gerald's excursion into nature ends in his death in the snow-covered mountains.

Like Lawrence's novel, Russell's film ends with Birkin and Ursula back in the warmth and comfort of the mill house, seated on each side of a fireplace. Russell satirizes Ursula to a much greater degree than found in Lawrence's account, and at no point does he suggest that she has freely grown to accept Birkin's Laurentian attitudes. Instead, with Jennie Linden's unfortunate resemblance to Debbie Reynolds, Ursula emerges as a somewhat conventional figure who ultimately accepts conventional ideals. It is Ursula, however, who receives the final emphasis, differing from Lawrence's ending. In the novel, the discussion ends in the following manner:

> "You can't have two kinds of love. Why should you?"
> "It seems as if I can't," he said. "Yet I wanted it."
> "You can't have it, because it's false, impossible," she said.
> "I don't believe that," he answered.

The film ends with this same exchange, but the final shot returns to a close-up of Ursula giving her, not Birkin, the equivalent of the last word.

For Russell, adaptation has nothing to do with translation; it is a process of creation. Thus, even in the adaptation of works like *Women in Love*, in which he respects the artist's methods and seeks to find appropriate visual equivalents to the techniques used by the writer, he must also emphasize his own personal vision. In his best adaptations, he manages to achieve a balance between fidelity to the theme and tone of the original work and fidelity to the expression of his own conceptions.

The Virgin and the Gypsy (1930), D. H. Lawrence
Christopher Miles, 1970

An English Watercolor

S. E. GONTARSKI

When Christopher Miles first showed his and Alan Plater's screen-play of *The Virgin and the Gypsy* to executives at Columbia pictures they were horrified because it essentially followed the book. Colum-bia decided that if the gypsy were not in the first reel, that is, in the first ten minutes at least, they would not put up the money. Miles, to his credit, argued artistic integrity:

> The whole point of the film was to establish the virgin in relationship to her family and the rectory, to establish the frustration of the young people. The gypsy must be discovered . . . about half-way through. Unless this structure was kept to, the film would collapse, the story would collapse. I mean, I think it's a very delicate story, it's a watercolor, if you like. . . . And it was this particular element that I was not prepared to change.[1]

Miles's stand against commercial interests cost him his original backers and started him on a two-year search for new financing. The film which Miles eventually shot (released in 1970) suffers neither from a rigid dependence on Lawrence's original tale (one wonders how carefully the Columbia executives had read either novella or screenplay) nor from a capitulation to commercial inter-

1. Unpublished interview of present author with Christopher Miles, London, Summer 1978. All quotations from Miles are from this interview. Lawrence actually spells gypsy as "gipsy."

ests. It is a film which, while significantly different in theme and structure from Lawrence's novella, is a delicate period piece, which, despite its departures, is often more fully developed, and its texture is often more Lawrentian than Lawrence's own unfinished tale.

It is difficult to guess how Lawrence might have revised *The Virgin and the Gypsy* had he lived. Perhaps sketchy characters like Uncle Fred may have been more roundly drawn, or the suddenness of the ending prepared for more carefully. Written in 1928, published posthumously in 1930, the work lacks the author's final revisions. And one suspects that it has not received the critical attention it might partly because of its incomplete state, partly because some critics like Graham Hough see it as essentially an early, unsuccessful attempt at *Lady Chatterley's Lover*,[2] and partly because "the tale of the lady and the raggle-taggle gypsies is so little novel."[3] Indeed the story contains a fairy-tale element which causes it to perch precariously at the edge of cliché. But Lawrence saves the piece in good part by the complexity of his central character, Yvette, and her search for some significance to her English, middle-class life, a significance supplied neither by the Anglican Christianity of her father nor by the social values of her community. Her most frequent question is, "Why is nothing important?" (59).[4]

After a continental education, the two young daughters of an Anglican minister, whose passionate wife Cynthia had deserted him and the children years earlier, return home to the small Derbyshire community to find their place within the local social structure. Lucille, the elder sister, fits into the family circle and the community more easily than does Yvette, who has vague emotional stirrings which she does not quite understand. Yvette finds herself uncomfortable in the social structure of both rectory and community. But Lawrence's tale is not only, perhaps not even primarily, one of social restrictions. She and her friends are also free in a curious way, carefree, free not to work, free to motor about the countryside with the local upper-middle class:

2. *The Dark Sun: A Study of D. H. Lawrence*, (New York: Octagon Books, 1973), p. 50.

3. Hough, p. 89.

4. Quotations are from the Bantam edition (New York: Bantam Books, 1968); page numbers in parentheses.

. . . young rebels, they sat very perkily in the car as they swished through the mud. Yet they had a peaked look too. After all, they had nothing really to rebel against, any of them. They were left so very free in their movements. Their parents let them do entirely as they liked. There wasn't really a fetter to break, nor a prison-bar to file through, nor a bolt to shatter. The keys of their lives were in their own hands. And there they dangled inert. It is very much easier to shatter prison-bars than to open undiscovered doors to life (21).

For Lawrence, the principal restrictions were not on Yvette's social movement, but on her development as a woman, on her emotional and, in Lawrence's mythical sense of this term, spiritual growth. The matriarchy under which she lives and which produces the sort of pettiness seen in Aunt Cissie and the hypocrisy seen in the Rector, who is concerned only with the appearance of family unity and love, inhibit Yvette's budding womanhood, her natural life force. The Rector's Christianity is sterile, a series of passionless rituals, a theme which is effectively developed in the film with the opening church sequence. The stone houses and fences of the English countryside serve Lawrence and Miles as symbols of this emotional and spiritual restriction. Yvette lives in a society which encourages control and restriction of emotions, not their development; hence the rector, in all his social and religious hypocrisy, is acceptable, while she-who-was-Cynthia (the rector's former wife) the contrasting couple in the novel, the nearly divorced Mrs. Fawcett and the rakish Major Eastwood, in all their emotional honesty are not.

The gypsy, that dark mythic force, the outlaw who lives outside of stone houses and can scale stone walls, who camps primitively on the edge of the domestic and the civilized, offers an alternative or egress, albeit a temporary one. The gypsy is perhaps an underdeveloped character in both novel and film, finally more mythic than real, but not, thankfully, the story-book figure for Yvette he might have been. Her attitude toward him is complex and reflects another of Lawrence's dualities. On the one hand "the thought of the gypsy had released the life of her limbs, and crystallised in her heart the hate of the rectory; so that now she felt potent, instead of impotent" (43). Another time she is indifferent: "She never even thought of the gypsy. He was a perfectly negligible incident" (59). What he represents is a natural force like the flood which occasionally rises within her and through which Yvette can establish her own sexual identity; he is not necessarily someone to whom one makes a lasting attachment: "She wanted him to hold her in his arms, if only *for once, for once*, and comfort and confirm her. She wanted to be confirmed by him, against her father, who had only a repulsive fear of her" (94-95, italics added). What the Rector fears is Yvette's sexual potential which can manifest itself in behavior which is not socially approved, as it did with his wife. But Lawrence is not concerned with the social implications of Yvette's rebellion. In fact, quite the contrary: "she liked comfort, and a certain prestige. Even as a mere Rector's daughter, one did have a certain prestige. She liked that. Also she liked to chip against the pillars of the temple, from the inside. She wanted to be safe under the temple roof"(99).

This duality, this attraction and lack of interest, this fascination for adventure coupled with the need for security is Yvette's character. The most serious and fundamental change which Christopher Miles makes in his film version is to simplify the central character, to deal with her rebellion but not with her counter need for security. It is the change from which most of the significant plot alterations begin. For Miles the story of the virgin is one of female liberation, and he sees Lawrence's ending as dishonest:

> She lost her virginity and I also think that she gained her womanhood, and I was not prepared to let her snivel in bed with a terrible chill while the remainder of the family came around and consoled her, in bed. She would then revert back to being captured by the rectory, in her own bed. Therefore, she had gone right back to the family in escape of herself. They're going to have the last word; poor, poor little girl with a cold. . . . I'm saying that I wanted to give her complete freedom. I don't like Lawrence's dishonesty. I did not want to trap her back under the family wing in the movie. I wanted to give her total freedom to go off with this fun couple, the Eastwoods, to London or wherever they were going, if they weren't going to London. And let her find her liberation with this charming couple.

This is the sort of change which lead at least one critic to complain, unfairly, that Miles did not understand Lawrence. Moreover, "the real trouble with *The Virgin and the Gypsy*," complains G. B. Crump, "is not only that Christopher Miles and Alan Plater were guilty of errors in judgment. To borrow Wayne Booth's term, there is a rhetoric of fiction, and it is, by its very nature, different from the rhetoric of film. This movie particularly illustrates that it is not always possible to duplicate the effects of one medium in another."[5] This is the sort of reasoning, however, which leads to the cul-de-sac called Simon's Law, that anything worth filming shouldn't be filmed. Crump first assumes that the filmmaker's function is to duplicate the novel on celluloid, and then he carefully points out how this was not done with *The Virgin and the Gypsy*. Once we admit, however, that film, like every other medium, has limitations, that it does not, for example, translate exposition well (short of direct narration), once we have admitted that director and screen-writer have made (indeed must make) fundamental alterations, what have we said of the film and the director's achievement? The more useful approach is the one offered by Julian Smith, even though he assumes a very reductive role for film and fails to examine the film's strengths as fully as he might: "In a sense, Miles's vision is critical as well as creative, for he has tended . . . to show only what he wants us to see, thereby singling out just one of the many possible films within the novella."[6] Once we grant Miles his fundamental decision, his view of Yvette's character, which, inciden-tally, does not wholly belie Lawrence's, once we grant Miles his own rhetorical stance and acknowledge both the limitations and strengths of the medium, we are in a better critical position to judge the final artistic achievement.

If Miles slights the duality within Yvette's character, that is, her psychological complexity, he does follow and extend Lawrence's tendency to develop her character by contrast to those around her. In addition to seeing Yvette against Lucille, the Rector, Aunt Cissie, and the Mater, Miles further expands the roles of two characters, Uncle Fred and Mary, the maid. Some of this expansion is necessi-tated by the medium itself. "Uncle Fred is poorly portrayed," Miles notes. "He is given a couple of lines and then dismissed. He is always around in the room, but a novelist can do this. He will dismiss a character that he introduced, won't give him anything to

5. "Gopher Prairie or Papplewick?: *The Virgin and the Gypsy* as Film," *D. H. Lawrence Review*, 4 (Summer 1971), 150.

6. "Vision and Revision: *The Virgin and the Gypsy* as Film," *Literature/Film Quarterly*, 1 (Winter 1973), 28.

do at all. But a filmmaker knows that Uncle Fred can't just stand there." And Miles created thematically-integrated action for Uncle Fred, a closet lecher. Uncle Fred adjusts to the community because he has releases. We see him picking up a girl at a bus stop and singing a bawdy song at the benefit show. If Aunt Cissie has destroyed her life, forfeited her womanhood in the name of social and familial responsibility, and the Reverend has dealt with his passion, his loss of his wife, and his fundamental religious doubts with hypocrisy, Uncle Fred has developed a playful schizophrenia.

Miles also fleshes out a second relationship barely mentioned in the novella, that between Yvette and the servant, Mary. Almost from the moment Yvette enters the house Mary is visually set up as a foil against whom we see Yvette and her struggle more clearly. The homecoming scene is significant not only because it introduces Yvette's relationship to her family, but also to the servant. When Yvette and Lucille enter the house, the family is arranged in the hallway in imitation of a set Victorian family photograph; Lucille moves into the family circle easily, while Yvette hesitates, needs to be coaxed to perform the formal greetings. The homecoming scene then initiates the contrast between Yvette and Mary. Once we cut to Yvette, we see Mary standing unobtrusively behind her, and Miles continues to use that background/foreground relationship throughout the film. As G. B. Crump has pointed out in his generally complete comparison of the film and novel, Mary functions as a counterpoint to Yvette. She performs useful work— washing clothes, scrubbing dishes, emptying chamber pots—while Yvette has nothing significant to do. She is "vague," to use Lawrence's term, and drifting; the sisters "were . . . two poor young rudderless lives moving from one chain anchorage to another" (10). But Crump has missed the full import of Mary's expanded role and the skill with which Miles uses her. It is Mary, without the restrictive walls of middle-class Victorian culture, who could approach the gypsy as Yvette never could. The servant is again used as background in the film as Yvette prepares to depart for the gypsy camp. As she moves to the kitchen to cut a piece of cake, Mary works in the background washing and wringing the family's laundry. But Mary's most important role is as sexual foil, and Miles handles this contrast with scenes wholly of his own creation which, if, not visually, are at least thematically parallel.

In a scene which allows Miles and Plater to develop some of Lawrence's suggestions, Yvette (played by Joanna Shimkus) cycles out to the gypsy camp on a rainy afternoon. Yvette's potential earthiness is established as she fights her way through the mud, a scene that stands in sharp contrast to the delicate pastel tone of most of the film, Miles's watercolor quality. She gives the window-fund money to the young, fertile gypsy woman, who has been breastfeeding her child, and, on her way home, meets the gypsy (Franco Nero) returning from a search for her, to tell her the dream his wife (in the novella, "the old gypsy") has had: "Be braver in your body or your luck will leave you." In this meeting Miles develops the gypsy's sexual virility. He is vigorously riding a horse, a stallion as he points out to Yvette, in the rain, and is thereby associated with the sexuality of the horse and the fertility of the rain which eventually causes the flood. In this scene, much altered and more sexually charged than the chance second meeting of the novella (see p. 99), the gypsy makes his most direct proposition to Yvette, to go riding into the hills. When she complains about the rain, he responds, "I know the right places, warm places." She, dressed in raincoat and rainhat to protect herself from the rain, standing on a road with a stone wall on only one side so that the *mise-en-scène* suggests the possibility of escape, refuses him by erecting a second wall of social responsibility: "I'm expected home for tea, and there's no more to be said." He again warns her to be braver with her body. The scene, if not subtle, is at least fully developed and consistent with Lawrence's description of Yvette's vagueness: "She had a curious reluctance, always, towards taking action, or making any real move of her own. She always wanted someone else to make a move for her, as if she did not want to play her own game of life" (103). Even in her fantasies she is passive. The gypsy takes the sexual initiative in his caravan.

The demure Yvette stands then in sharp contrast to Mary. When the gypsy comes to the rectory to sell his wares, Yvette watches him pull into the courtyard from a second-floor landing, through a leaded-glass window. The shot establishes the barrier of class, her

The Virgin and the Gypsy (1976). The stone wall on only one side suggests the possibility of escape for Yvette (Joanna Shimkus) in her encounter with the Gypsy (Franco Nero). (Photo courtesy of the Museum of Modern Art)

own elevated position, and the restrictions of the house, as the lead in the windows takes on the quality of prison bars. When Yvette later handles the candlesticks, the gypsy delivers one of his double entendres. Asked the price of his wares, he says, "People usually make me offers." This line, which is not strictly part of the novel, further highlights Yvette's inability to take the initiative. Mary, however, is not so hampered. Once the gypsy departs, Mary leaves for the shops, runs after him, and jumps on his wagon. Yvette again observes the scene through the leaded glass of the second floor bedroom window, and the social superiority, restrictions caused by the house, and the emptiness of her bedroom are all reestablished. This is all very effective cinematagraphy, the sort of meticulous *mise-en-scène* for which Miles has not been given adequate credit.

Mary further figures prominently in the climactic portion of the film when Yvette sees her and the gypsy making vigorous love in what is presumably one of the abandoned local mills. The symbols of horse and water are mixed with a fecund nature to suggest a natural vitality, and the abandoned building suggests the depressed state of the community's vitality. Mary, free of the class barrier and social restrictions, is capable of human relations that Yvette, again separated by a stone wall, can only fantasize about. This discovery, a scene wholly created by Miles and Plater, is brilliantly cross-cut with Leo's plunging a knife into a cake at his twenty-first birthday party, a scene whose phallic implications not only throw the gentility of the party into high relief, but show us Leo's sexual limitations. The birthday party, as Miles reshapes it, provides Yvette with an opportunity to test Leo. She has just seen the gypsy making love to the maid: "the next thing is he's [Leo is] plunging his own knife into a cake and that is as far as he can go. And she knows it and that is when she slaps him to make something happen." But nothing happens; Leo's passions are not stirred.

Mary's affair with the gypsy further establishes the latter's sexual vitality and reduces suggestions of an ambiguous ending to inconsequence. While neither the novel nor the film shows directly a sexual consummation, the critical attitude that film or fiction communicate meaning only directly is naive. The gypsy's virility has been established with the addition of the love scene with Mary, and even if Yvette had second thoughts about fulfilling her fantasies, the gypsy would certainly have no such inhibitions; his horse can easily jump stone fences. And if we insist too strongly on an essential ambiguity surrounding the lovemaking scene, we miss much of Lawrence's playful irony. It is love (that is, making love) which warms Yvette and hence saves her life, physically and spiritually. As Lawrence has the Christ figure in *The Man Who Died* tell us, "virginity is a form of greed," and Yvette is learning "to give ungreedily." She is learning to grow out of the selfishness of which she had earlier been accused. Furthermore, the lovemaking scenes reestablish Yvette's essential passivity, her inability to make the conscious choice. The consummation occurs as much through chance, through an accident of nature, through the undeniable power of nature in both the flood and the gypsy, as by design. And this is the theme which fascinated Miles. As he suggests, Lawrence uses "natural forces to wipe away this passive hypocrisy; in the same way, the gypsy himself and the forces of nature cannot be controlled. A very small crocus . . . forces its way through a tennis court . . . a tar-top or a road. . . . [it] cannot be stopped by the Rector and she's going to win." This view of a natural imperative is reinforced by the addition to the film of the very Darwinian line which Yvette speaks to her family: "One day I'll be alive and you will be dead."

Miles's contribution to *The Virgin and the Gypsy* goes beyond these reinterpretations however. He has also managed to capture the writer's texture and the poetic tempo on film. For one, simply the delicate recreation of the period in muted tones has added a visual dimension to the tale and added what Miles has called the delicate English watercolor quality to the film. That quality is achieved in good part by the visual development of Lawrentian fecundity in nature, a fecundity that is explicit in the major novels but only implicit in *The Virgin and the Gypsy*. The development of the water imagery in the film not only helps prepare for the catastrophic flood much more fully than Lawrence does, but also gives the director an opportunity to focus on the natural lushness of the English countryside. But perhaps the most important development of Lawrentian texture can be found in the poetic rhythms the film captures. If we turn again to the ending we see Miles heighten the sexual tension and rhythms of the film by having the gypsy make a direct sexual offer to Yvette, then having Yvette come across the gypsy and Mary *flagrante delicto*, followed by the cross-cut to Leo's plunging his knife into the cake. Each of these scenes adds another dimension to Yvette's mounting internal struggle. The tensions of the party are then followed by the pastoral serenity before the flood, the idyllic scenes of Yvette walking to the river, which suggest nineteenth-century paintings. The serene scenes throughout the film are set up as counterpoint to the sexual tension symbolized by horses, fire, rain, knife, and, finally, the flood. Through most of the film then, the water imagery suggests the harmony of nineteenth-century painting, but always latent is the raw libidinous power which is artificially dammed up.

Through all of this buildup the filmmakers have been considerably more obvious than Lawrence; that in part is due to the medium itself and to the real fact that film is usually a a popular art form. Yvette, for instance, tells Leo that she is like her mother, he like her father; what Cynthia did to the Reverend, Yvette would to do Leo. And during the flood, the sinking Bible is almost embarrassingly explicit. But Miles's major achievement is of a more subtle nature. He restructures the shape of Lawrence's novella around his own vision, and he develops the implicit level of Lawrence's work with explicit visuals that create the almost fragile quality of the film under which lies latent a natural power. Miles may assert, "there is not to me any similarity between films and novels," but his film is, in part, testimony to the contrary. While Christopher Miles's *The Virgin and the Gypsy* is not a visual reproduction of the novel, it is finally a faithful transformation of Lawrence's story and, more important, spirit.

Lady Chatterley's Lover (1928), D. H. Lawrence

Marc Allegret, 1955

Sensuality and Simplification

LINDLEY HANLON

It is the way our sympathy flows and recoils that really determines our lives. And here lies the vast importance of the novel, properly handled. It can inform and lead into new places the flow of our sympathetic consciousness, and it can lead our sympathy away in recoil from things gone dead. Therefore, the novel, properly handled, can reveal the most secret places of life: for it is in the *passional* secret places of life, above all, that the tide of sensitive awareness needs to ebb and flow, cleansing and freshening.

—D. H. Lawrence, *Lady Chatterley's Lover* (1928)[1]

Marc Allegret's film of *Lady Chatterley's Lover* (France, 1955) is in no sense pornographic. There is no reference to or mention of Lawrence's erotic personifications John Thomas and Lady Jane. Sexuality and sensuality vibrate just below the surface of the film's form. It is through Allegret's implications and our inferences that the erotic subtext is conveyed. "The secret places of life" are not visually revealed, but the "flow of sympathetic consciousness," the "tide of sensitive awareness" travel from shot to shot, from character to character via the all-important "connections" of sight line, musical commentary, objective correlative, spatial proximity, and ellipsis. Although the erotic is sublimated and displaced, graciously and politely, many of Lawrence's central themes are given elegant

1. D. H. Lawrence, *Lady Chatterley's Lover*, ed. and intro. Ronald Friedland (New York: Bantam Books, Inc., 1968), p. 106, hereafter cited as LCL.

film form, in particular the persistent dichotomy of the natural and the mechanical, around which Allegret centers his imagery.

The savage tone, direct analysis of character and situation, and lengthy discourses of the novel's narrator are absent from the film, which is a straightforward, classical, dramatic narrative. The novel's omniscient narrator allows each character to speak and interact dramatically, but never hesitates to provide us with his lengthy interpretations of the "real" meanings of words, inclinations, gestures, and actions. Further, we know from the narrator's previous thematic and philosophical expositions when he is speaking in a character's voice, a type of indirect discourse via a delegated speaker. The history of Lady Chatterley's consciousness evolves as she herself begins to be aware of and to articulate what Lawrence has been telling us all along in his narration. After her last and shocking encounter with Michaelis, in which Michaelis denigrates her assertive sexual role and spurns her, Lady Chatterley meets the gamekeeper and his daughter, an incident which occasions a typical example of Lawrence's transparent indirect discourse via a character-mediator:

> . . . All the great words, it seemed to Connie, were cancelled for her generation: love, joy, happiness, home, mother, father, husband, all these great, dynamic words were half dead now, and dying from day to day. (LCL, p. 63)

Lawrence, free to manage a character's thoughts and dialogue as he would a puppet, tells us about and interprets his or her past experiences and their significance. The greatest freedom of the literary narrator resides in the all-important past tenses and in particular the "imperfect" tense of the verb wherein a whole series of habitual actions can be summed up and named: "Sometimes she wept bitterly." The filmmaker who chooses a strictly linear narrative must depict one such instance and suggest, probably through the dialogue of that character, that the action is typical. Or he must leave out all such character-developing incidents or condense them into one. His "narration" must be temporally and spatially specific.

In the film then the burden of "narration" or "meaning conveyal" is on showing, on the visual style and presentation. Without recourse to flashbacks, voice-over narration, or internal monologue, we view the film's characters from outside and listen to them as they interact with others. Our one privilege, as viewers of a classical narrative film, is to be able to see them when they are alone, away from the other characters in the story. In these moments of privacy we, as voyeurs, are given access to their faces and emotions with the mask of socially acceptable conduct removed. We infer from a variety of these contexts what their glances, words, and actions mean. The development of characters is gradual, with no narrator to tell us "over the shoulder" as it were what they are *really* like.

As a result of the filmmaker's inability to tell us what we do not see and to interpret for us "in so many words" what we do see, our knowledge of characters tends to be more superficial in the film than in the novel. For example, Clifford is the central focus of first sequences which show him directing the rituals of a boar hunt and a rescue operation at the mine. Lady Chatterley watches and tends to him dutifully. There is no hint of Lady Chatterley's rather interesting background as related by the sociointellectual historian we have as our narrator in the novel:

> . . . Her father was the once well-known R. A., old Sir Malcolm Reid. Her mother had been one of the cultivated Fabians in the palmy, rather pre-Raphaelite days. Between artists and cultured socialists, Constance and her sister Hilda had what might be called an aesthetically unconventional upbringing. They had been taken to Paris and Florence and Rome to breathe in art, and they had been taken also in the other direction, to the Hague and Berlin, to great Socialist conventions, where the speakers spoke in every civilised tongue, and no one was abashed. (LCL, p. 2)

This analysis of the intellectual energy and independence of the girls' youth is Lawrence's way of logically preparing us for the sexual energy and liberation of Lady Chatterley. "The spasm of self-assertion" becomes highly developed in Lady Chatterley as the novel progresses.

Although Sir Clifford at one point in the film refers to Lady Chatterley's student-days lover, we never know much of Constance as a thinker. We see her caring for Clifford and wittily dismissing the advances of Michaelis, but these seem signs of sophistication typical of the French upper classes of which she is a part in this French film. Her conversion from loyalty to secession seems very much more sudden in the film. There is no intellectual debate in the film, no statement of the deep existential problems of sexuality, humanity, consciousness, and existence which Lady Chatterley mediates in the novel. In the film she is a more domesticated lady who suddenly finds herself attracted to her husband's gamekeeper. In lengthy passages of dialogue in the film the gamekeeper and Lady Chatterley do discuss some of these issues, such as her inability to "love" him caused by her offense at his verbal familiarity and his assessment of what women want from men, but these "dialogue-dependent" sequences seem to a certain extent a disruption of the flow of images and action. In the novel, of course, descriptive "images," narrative action, and intellectual debate take place across a continuous and coherent fabric of language. The novel's infinite capacity for intellectual nuance through language and extended development in time are telescoped in the film's linear series of incidents.

The arrangement of those incidents is one of the tasks of the "invisible" and "inaudible" narrator in the film art. The first sequence in the film condenses much thematic material and information about characters in one very elegant hunt episode which visually "quotes" and in the dialogue alludes to Renoir's *Rules of the Game* (1939). The major thematic opposition of the "natural" and the "mechanical" is made clear in the first shot as the camera pans left from a medium shot of a mechanical mill wheel to the forest behind. The shot is initially underscored by the "love theme" which will slip in unnoticed to represent Lawrence's "tide of sensitive awareness" throughout the film. The opposition of natural and mechanical motifs continues in sharp visual contrasts between the solemn procession of shiny cars through the forest and the hectic chase of the boar by hounds baying through the woods. The yelping of dogs and the formal trumpet fanfares of the hunters pierce the knowing silence of the forest. Allegret's clear-cut long shots of towering trees with mists hanging low beneath them perfectly evokes Lawrence's description of the powerful symbolic presence of the forest.

In the woods all was utterly inert and motionless, only great drops fell from the bare boughs, with a hollow little crash. For the rest, among the old trees was depth of grey, hopeless, inertia, silence, nothingness.

Connie walked dimly on. From the old wood came an ancient

melancholy, somehow soothing to her, better than the harsh insentience of the outer world. She like the *inwardness* of the remnant of forest, the unspeaking reticence of the old trees. They seemed a very power of silence, and yet a vital presence. They, too, were waiting: obstinately, stoically waiting, and giving off a potency of silence. Perhaps they were only waiting for the end; to be cut down, cleared away, the end of the forest, for them the end of all things. But perhaps their strong and aristocratic silence, the silence of strong trees, meant something else. (LCL, p. 67)

The insignificance of man among these giants and man's willful rape of them for industrial profit are specified in the film. The hollow putter of Clifford's mechanical chair echoes in the deep wood which seems to dwarf him despite his strong sense of ownership conveyed as he terms them *his* forest. The forest and industrial landscape are portrayed as the microcosm within which transpires the primeval contest of man and nature, war and peace, maiming and procreation, social formality and natural passion, social rank and natural equality, and finally corporeality and rationality. Rain, mud, thunder, sunlight, forest, fire, heat, plants, and animals are allied with the gamekeeper against the sterile, formal, severe world of Sir Clifford's wheelchair, books, household, cars, mines, and the "forest of steel" which he hopes to erect as an emblem of his mental powers and control. The foreboding siren from the mines parallels the threatening sound of nature's thunder which seems to warn Lady Chatterley as she enters the natural world of the gamekeeper.

The transfer from novel to film of objective correlatives is accurate and extensive. The meaning of those objects is in many ways more elusive in the film. The surroundings are first of all a realistic setting in which "real" human beings must live according to the conventions of realism. The transformation of ordinary object into symbolic object is less direct in the film than in the novel, where Lawrence analyses in words the extra significance, for example, of the forest.

In film the symbolic function of an object evolves from repetition, parallels with other similar objects or with conventional iconography, specific reference to the object as a symbol in the dialogue, musical underscoring, and special cinematic treatment or context. The dramatic scale of the forest, its stillness and extraordinary beauty, and its use as the location of their love affair set it off and encourage us to think of it as more than a set location which could be substituted for any other setting. The chopping down of trees becomes Allegret's symbol for the sexual act itself. Phallus-shaped trees falling to the ground as they are cut are intercut between shots of the gamekeeper unbuttoning Lady Chatterley's blouse and shots of them lying together with naked shoulders visible above the blanket. In the tree-cutting image Allegret's major implication is sexual fulfillment and release rather than castration which such a description might imply. In film symbolic meaning exists as a special luminescence visible across the lighted surfaces of the everyday. We can see the object as symbolic, but in this film at least, the symbolic meaning exists comfortably alongside the ordinary sense of the object, two sides of the same coin.

The contrasts between the mechanical and natural, the rational and the passional, are expressed on the level of voice, accent, and dialogue as well. Allegret's transformation of the characters and their dialogue from English to French is an interesting cross-cultural aspect of Allegret's adaptation. The setting of the film is England, but all of the characters are French-speaking (and one must add French-acting) with the exception of Sir Clifford (Leo Genn), who speaks French with a marked and appropriate British turgidity. The sensual sounds of the French language as spoken by Lady Chatterley (Danielle Darrieux), the slurring connections and pert, witty intonations are contrasted effectively with Sir Clifford's slow, drawn-out, nonallided way of speaking French. His voice conveys his cold, businesslike, self-absorbed bitterness, for example when he repeats what he had heard the miners say about him after the mine disaster: "Dom-mage qu'il-ne-soit-pas cre-vé-au-fond. . . ." ("Too bad he wasn't crushed to death at the bottom.") Clifford goes on to state that the miners wish he were dead so that they could take over the mine. His motivation for a son and heir is then made clear: if he had a son, his family's future control of the mines would be assured. His desire for a son in the film is part of an economic management scheme, far from the realm of passion, tenderness, and desire into which Lady Chatterley wanders.

In contrast to the novel, in the film Mellors, the gamekeeper (Erno Crisa), is consistently aristocratic in bearing and attitude with

Lady Chatterley's Lover (1955). Phallus-shaped trees falling to the ground are intercut with shots of Constance (Danielle Darrieux) and Mellors (Erno Crisa) making love. (Photo courtesy of the Museum of Modern Art)

no lapse from his French into what in the novel is (I find) an annoying dialect. He is very tall and magisterial, expressing his disdain and pride without hesitation, and gently and tenderly guiding Lady Chatterley in her discovery of physical love.[2] These aspects of his character conform to several descriptions in the novel: "He had a natural sort of quiet distinction, an aloof pride, and also a certain look of frailty" (LCL, pp. 173-4). In a way the film makes Lady Chatterley's transgressions less "offensive" by suggesting that, although social barriers are crossed, the codes of physical type and romantic pairing are maintained.

The symbolic oppositions are systematically represented on the level of shot composition and camera placement as well. The elegant lighting, clear-cut visual contrasts, and glacial formal symmetry of the visual style seem to align elements of visual style with Sir Clifford's domain, although sunlight and implied warmth finally come to represent sensual experience as Lady Chatterley's senses awaken and she savors the sun on her body. There is a definite hierarchy of shot compositions from long shot to close-up which mirrors the emotional dynamics and social strata of the narrative. Most of the sequences take place in long shot, medium shot, or medium long shot which suggest the "proper" distance between people that upper-class conventions, maintained ferociously by Sir Clifford, require, the "rules of the game" so to speak. The camera systematically dollies in to emphasize and underline "important" or "revealing" lines of dialogue, such as when Clifford bitterly describes his return from the war and his resultant dependence on Lady Chatterley. The camera's role as narrator, as interpreter, is most evident in these camera movements. Conversations between Lady Chatterley and Sir Clifford are divided between shots of her (as she powders his paralyzed legs, for example) and shots of him, suggesting their emotional barriers in compositional terms with the shot as private domain. As their discussions become more intense (for example, their discussion of her having a child by another man)

2. It is interesting to note that Allegret wanted Marlon Brando for the part of the gamekeeper, fresh as Brando was from *On the Waterfront*, but could not meet Brando's price, a fact mentioned in Rene Jordan, *Marlon Brando* (New York: Pyramid Publications, 1973), p. 63. Two more opposite personages cannot be imagined.

the camera moves in closer to mirror her surprised reactions to his "plan" and then his rather tragic lack of emotional understanding. They are never united in an "embracing" two-shot close-up. If they do appear in a shot together, it is usually a long shot with other characters looking on as part of their frequent formal social gatherings. In these cases the wheelchair functions as the physical barrier between them.

Similarly, the increasing intimacy of the gamekeeper and Lady Chatterley is registered in closer and closer shot compositions. Allegret invents an episode to bring Mellors and Lady Chatterley closer physically: she falls off her horse and is rescued by the gamekeeper, who places his hands near her breasts to lift off her scarf to make a sling and lifts her up by the waist back on to her horse, holding her for a moment in his arms. The subtly erotic connotation of a woman astride a horse is another invention of Allegret; in the novel she walks about the forest and property. In the scene of her seduction there are two-shots which signify their sexual attraction and intimacy. Their eyes meet as she encounters him preparing sand for nesting pheasant eggs, and he enters the frame from which she has watched him in a separate shot. The deepening of their voices doubles the spatial suggestion of increasing intimacy. Fourteen shots later they are framed in a two-shot close-up as he helps her handle the baby chickens, a shot underscored by the romantic strains of music for flute and harp. In this decisive shot he looks at her hair and eyes appreciatively, as if seeing her as a beautiful woman for the first time.

Eighteen shots later, as the camera moves closer and closer, he enters her shot-space again in a close-up profile two-shot, a sensual, subtle choreography of the awakening of desire. In the next medium shot he moves his strong-looking hand down her back to her waist which he pulls slightly toward him (in the novel his hand travelled significantly further down on its course). They enter the cabin and, in the tree-cutting ellipsis described above, make love for the first time. The progression of events and gestures is swift and understated.

The relentless temporality of the celluloid strip is particularly noticeable in this kind of sequence and suggests a fundamental difference between literature and film. A realistic film adaptation which condenses a great deal of time into a two-hour segment does not allow us that time-between-readings in which to savor the sensuous experience of the narrative and, especially important in erotic works, time to let our imagination and fantasy invent a personal and perhaps parallel narrative with its own cast of characters and scenarios. Nor can we reread the luscious details. Longer, more indulgent takes as Lady Chatterley relishes the light on her hand or as she absorbs every detail of his muscular chest as he sleeps, or as Mellors and she glance at each other suggestively would give the spectator time to search around the frame and absorb the sensual detail more slowly. Perhaps that is why the freeze-frame and slow motion have become the romantic film conventions par excellence whereby we are allowed to suspend the sensuous moment. The visual beauty of Allegret's style give one's eye much to savor, but the temporal organization of a film narrative is necessarily compact and rigid. Only the avant-garde has explored all the possibilities of repetition and lingering in its caressing glances of the erotic. Timelessness, which for Lawrence is the line between consciousness and unconsciousness that characterizes the erotic experience, is difficult to represent in film form:

> . . . It was the stillness, and the timeless sort of patience, in a man impatient and passionate, that touched Connie's womb. She saw it in his bent head, the quick, quiet hands, the crouching of his slender, sensitive loins; something patient and withdrawn. She felt his experience had been deeper and wider than her own; much deeper and wider, and perhaps more deadly. And this relieved her of herself; she felt irresponsible.
>
> So she sat in the doorway of the hut in a dream, utterly unaware of time and of particular circumstances. She was so drifted away that he glanced up at her quickly, and saw the utterly still, waiting look on her face. (LCL, p. 93)

Although an ellipsis implies the temporal and logical extension of a shot or scene, the sensual and temporal experience is firmly left out, absent, modest, veiled. In this important way, then, Allegret does not follow Lawrence in his mission to bring sexual experience in all its forms and details out into the open, to describe, analyse, and discuss unabashedly the transcendent pleasures of the flesh. Sex is implied in naked shoulders, referred to in the dialogue, and implicitly enacted in ellipses, but the overall impression remains with the viewer that *love* is still a somewhat abstract, romantic, pure, and even spiritual thing, tender and elusive, but not as carnal as Lawrence insists. Here history and its laws must be specifically invoked, for this set of implications was enough to enrage the censors, sensitive as they were in 1955 to the theme of adultery (expecially disloyalty of the woman to her husband and to the institution of marriage).[3] Explicit sex was too hot to handle, but commercial filmmakers of the 1960s and 1970s quickly made up for lost time. Showing has far outrun telling, and film's natural predilection for action has given it first place as the vehicle of the voyeur. Yet sensuality of the most provocative kind in the cinema is still perhaps a function of a certain displacement, of subtle visual textures, aural intricacies, and undulating movements which invite us to do the impossible—to touch and be touched. Lawrence was well aware that art condemns us to being once-removed from the "sensual, naked, and unashamed" by sentiment and symbolism:

> . . . What liars poets and everybody were! They made one think one wanted sentiment. When what one supremely wanted was this piercing, consuming, rather awful sensuality. To find a man who dared do it, without shame or sin or final misgiving! (LCL, p. 268)

And for Lawrence the films he saw were a great disappointment:

> Never was an age more sentimental, more devoid of real feeling, more exaggerated in false feeling, than our own. Sentimentality and counterfeit feeling have become a sort of game, everybody trying to outdo his neighbor. The radio and the film are mere counterfeit emotion all the time, the current press and literature the same. People wallow in emotion: counterfeit emotion. They lap it up: they live in it and on it. They ooze with it. (LCL, p. 336)

Allegret's Lady Chatterley is far from this oozing sentimentality. The delicay of his style and the dignity of his characters convey at least in part Lawrence's requirement that tenderness accompany carnal knowledge.

3. Tina Balio, *The American Film Industry* (Madison: The University of Wisconsin Press, 1976), p. 443.

A *Portrait of the Artist as a Young Man* (1914),

James Joyce   Joseph Strick 1978

The "Whatness"
of Joseph Strick's Portrait

ROBERT A. ARMOUR

In the novel A *Portrait of the Artist as a Young Man* (1914), while trying to explain his esthetic theory to his friend Lynch, Stephen Dedalus comes to the concept of *claritas*, the most difficult of the terms Joyce borrowed from Aquinas. In order to explain the word, Stephen asks Lynch to contemplate a basket carried by a passing butcher boy: "You see that it is that thing which is and no other thing. The radiance of which he [Aquinas] speaks is the scholastic *quidditas*, the whatness of a thing."

This concept is important to the young Stephen as the nucleus of his esthetic theory, but it also formed the basis for Joyce's own esthetics. The radiance, or whatness, is the quality of the artistic experience that gives the work of art its peculiar and individual character. It is that which distinguishes it from all else.

Trying to describe the whatness of film is to delve into the deepest mysteries of film esthetics. Film is distinguished from other art forms in that it consists of projected images that give the illusion of movement. Such a distinction is, however, superficial because it fails to account for what it is that film can depict beyond movement. It fails to explain the characteristics of film that allow it to bring together thousands of individual images into an esthetic experience that as a whole affects the viewer in ways that the individual frames cannot.

One of the important elements of the whatness of film is its ability to make visual the inner thoughts or emotions of the characters in

279

the artist's story. Artists in many media have long been trying to discover ways of conveying the complex inner life of people, methods for depicting the ideas, frustrations, and emotions of our inner being. Perhaps, however, no medium is better suited for the attempt than film. One element of the whatness of film is that through a combination of visual and aural images it conveys a character's cognitive and emotional life, which for simplicity I am calling interior space.

Filmmakers have used diverse methods to depict the interior space of their characters. Some methods, such as the voice-over and the flashback, are almost routine in film and simple, but often effective, means of conveying the character's thoughts or feelings. Sometimes the method can be complex, as when Robert Weine uses an expressionistic set to convey the confused and warped sense of reality that festered within Francis, the protagonist in *The Cabinet of Dr. Caligari* (1921). Most often, however, interior space is conveyed through a combination of visual and aural images that are manipulated to indicate that they represent the character's personal view of reality, as when Fritz Lang describes the erotic dance of the robot Maria in *Metropolis* (1927) through the eyes of the hallucinating Freder. Sometimes the entire film is interior space, in the sense that *The Seventh Seal* (1958) is an allegorical presentation of the fear of death that exists in the interior space of Bergman's knight. By trying to penetrate the interior space of a character, filmmakers use the medium's images and movement to permit the audience to share the deepest of esthetic experiences.

In a 1933 article for *Close Up*, Sergei Eisenstein, the Russian film director responsible for much early theory about the nature of his medium, discussed the concept of interior space in film, although he called it "internal monologue." He had come to the United States to film Dreiser's *An American Tragedy*, a project that was aborted; but Eisenstein took the occasion to describe the effect he had wanted to create for the film: "We had to photograph what was going on inside Clyde's mind. We had to demonstrate audibly and visibly the feverish torrent of thoughts, interspersed with external action, with the boat, with the girl sitting opposite, with his own actions."[1] Eisenstein recalls that writers had been attempting to

---

1. S. M. Eisenstein, "*An American Tragedy*," *Close Up*, X (June, 1933), p. 120.

describe what is called here interior space as early as 1887, and he mentions the efforts of Edouard Dujardin, E. T. A. Hoffman, and James Joyce. But according to Eisenstein, literary efforts were doomed to be incomplete when compared to cinematic efforts:

> But only in the film, of course, can it find full expression.
> For only the sound film is capable of reconstructing all the phases and the specific essence of that process of thought. . . .
> Like thought, they proceeded now by means of visual images—with sound—synchronized or non-sychronized. Then, as sound—formless—or with sound images: sounds symbolizing objects.
> Then suddenly, by the coinage of words formulated intellectually—intellectually and dispassionately, and so uttered. With a black film—hurrying, formless visibility.
> Now, by passionate incoherent speech. Only substantives. Or only verbs. Then by interjections. With zigzags of aimless figures, hurrying along with them synchronously. . . .[2]

Eisenstein's verbal montage continues, describing the mental images that he would use to create interior space. He concludes:

> THE TRUE MATERIAL FOR THE SOUND FILM IS, OF COURSE, THE MONOLOGUE.
> And how unexpectedly, in its practical embodiment of the unforeseen particular concrete case of expressiveness, this completely harmonizes with the "last word" about montage form in general, which I had long foreseen theoretically: namely, that the montage form, regarded structurally, is the reconstruction of the laws governing the process of thought.[3]

Eisenstein has discovered what is for him the whatness of film. He shared his ideas of interior space with Joyce when the two met in Paris. There, according to Eisenstein, the writer and the filmmaker "eagerly" discussed Eisenstein's "plans in regard to the inward film monologue, which has far wider possibilities than the literary monologue."[4] Eisenstein says that Joyce, despite his near blindness, was eager to see Eisenstein's films, which depended on an early form of interior space. No evidence that Joyce saw the films has

2. *Ibid.*, p. 121.
3. *Ibid.*, p. 123.
4. *Ibid.*, p. 121.

survived, nor have we Joyce's own version of this meeting. We do know that Joyce did contemplate permitting a filming of *Ulysses*, but he seems to have rejected the idea as too complicated.

Joyce called his central method "interior monologue" as it was an attempt to reproduce through words a character's cognition. This is a method he developed over the years, but even his early stories demonstrate his interest in getting into a character's mind. In *A Portrait of the Artist as a Young Man* the method is not full blown, but it does clearly describe Stephen's thought process as he matures and establishes his independence from his family, his country, and his religion. The progress of Stephen's development as an artist is hesitant, and Joyce's subjective point of view follows him and reveals his mental and emotional growth. This method becomes the key to the whatness of the novel and is the aspect of the novel that is most difficult to translate to film. But since film has the propensity for interior space, a filmed version of *A Portrait* could reflect Joyce's method. Joseph Strick, having filmed *Ulysses* in 1966, brought *A Portrait* to the screen in 1977; and an analysis of his attempt to depict Stephen's interior space is an effort to define the whatness of the film.

A film taken from a novel must strike a balance between showing respect for the source and forcing the viewer to depend on a knowledge of the novel in order to understand the cinematic narrative. The filmmaker has an obligation to make the material his and to create his own work of art; but if he uses a well-known fictional source, his audience—not to mention the novelist himself— will expect the film to reflect the novel. It is quite appropriate for the filmmaker to borrow character, setting, plot, even theme and method; but it is not acceptable to make the viewer fill in plot or character motivation from the novel. If the viewer of the film has to depend on a knowledge of the novel in order to follow the movie, the filmmaker has not achieved whatness. His artistic product is not distinguished from the things around it. At times Strick fails to create his own whatness.

In the novel, for example, the young Stephen goes to the headmaster of Clongowes and tells him that Father Dolan has beaten him unjustly. This moment is a victorious one for Stephen, and his classmates hoist him on their shoulders and cheer his courage. The event is an important contributor to Stephen's self-esteem and maturation. Yet later, Mr. Dedalus describes a meeting with the rector during which the rector with some pleasure told his version of the encounter: "I told them at dinner about it and Father Dolan and I and all of us we had a hearty laugh together over it. Ha! Ha! Ha!" The father and the priest had also shared a good laugh over the incident, and Stephen comes to understand that what had been important to him was a joke to the adults. The two parts of the adventure form one of the major epiphanies of the novel. In the film Strick uses the scene in which Stephen goes in to the rector, but the laughter scene is dealt with in an unsatisfactory manner. There is a cut from the interior of the school to the porch where Mr. Dedalus and the priest are laughing together. We are not told why they are laughing, nor is Stephen when he joins them. Instead there is a conversation about the fact that Stephen is being withdrawn from the school for financial reasons. Neither the viewer nor Stephen ever learns the adults' reaction to his courageous deed. Only those who have read the novel can guess at the cause of the laughter. This is to ask too much of a viewer.

When it comes to the interior space, however, Strick has come closer to creating his own whatness. He has changed the subjective point of view of the novel into an objective one in which the camera presents the exterior of Stephen's life rather than the internal view given in the novel. For example, the story about the "moocow coming down along the road" is related at the opening of the novel through the perceptions of the little boy. It is told in his language and images. In the film, however, the story is told in the voice of Simon Dedalus (T. P. McKenna), while the camera pictures Stephen sitting in his father's lap. This method is quite different from Joyce's method. Joyce's view of the story was internal and subjective; Strick's view is external and objective. Strick's version depicts a cozy moment between a son and his father, but it does put awkward baby talk in the mouth of an adult. This cinematic externalization establishes the method for the entire film which is told mostly from an external point of view. Rarely does Strick penetrate Stephen's thoughts and emotions; but when he does, the effects of those moments are enhanced by the contrast they create with the external parts of the film.

Strick's occasional use of a subjective technique leads to some of the most cinematic moments in the film. The several occasions when Strick has entered into Stephen's interior space suggest Joyce's method and establish Strick's cinematic whatness at the same time. Sometimes the method of creating the interior space in the film is simple: as Stephen walks down a long corridor on his way to talk with the rector about Father Dolan, his voice in a voice-over tells the audience that he has decided not to stand for the mistreatment.

At other times, however, Strick has used more complex means of getting into Stephen's interior space. An analysis of the depiction of major samples of interior space will illustrate the range of Strick's methods.

Guilt is one of the emotions Stephen has instilled in him from the cradle and one of the most difficult for him to deal with as he rejects his family, church, and country. In the novel the first comment on guilt comes when Stephen's mother and Dante agonize over the boy's statement that he is going to marry Eileen, a Protestant. His mother is sure that he will apologize for this heresy, and Dante says that if he does not, eagles will come and pull out his eyes. A simple poem rhyming *eyes* with *apologize* runs through Stephen's head. In the film the source of the guilt is not interfaith marriage but bedwetting, an act mentioned in the novel, but forgotten. The mother and Dante come and stand over Stephen's crib, talking about his wetting the bed. His mother says that Stephen will stop, and Dante assures him that the eagles will come if he does not. At this moment the camera begins a pan of the nursery. It starts with a hobby horse and moves on to other toys, and then to a religious candle. Finally the camera rests on a crucifix of the suffering Christ. A close-up of the anguished face highlights the eyes, reminding the viewer of Dante's threat and establishing one of the visual motifs that runs throughout the film. Stephen's eyes are one of the main means of characterization Strick has borrowed from the novel, but the visuals here also establish the concept of guilt. The adults create guilt in Stephen while the camera reminds us of the guilt of all men.

Further evidence of the guilt in Stephen's interior space is shown later in the film when Stephen has become a teenager. He has experienced the pleasures of the flesh, and during a retreat he is listening to the sermon (the priest is played by John Gielgud) in which fleshly joys are condemned. The methods of interior space here are more complex than in the first example. First the camera comes in on Stephen's face as he listens to the sermon, and the acting of Bosco Hogan conveys what is going on inside the tortured young man. Hogan's face contorts, and his nervous squirming suggests the movements of a teenager regretting his actions of the night before. He drops a flower he has been holding in his hand, the same flower he had taken from the garter of a prostitute during a moment of ecstasy. Then the camera and the editor take over from the actor to extend and expand the depiction of Stephen's guilt. There is a cut to a close-up of Stephen's head with his hands covering the face and eyes. Suddenly blood comes from under the scalp. Then comes a close-up of the face as a slimy, green substance—vomit or excrement, who can tell?—falls on the face. As the camera comes in even closer, a bug crawls from one eye. Then the camera cuts to a medium shot of Stephen on a bed in a fetal position. He pulls a small blanket over him in an effort to retreat more into a private world. Then the camera returns to the face, still covered with the green slime. This time the close-up reveals clearly that this is a plaster model of Stephen's face, but still the bugs crawling on it are revolting. Suddenly a hammer smashes the face, shattering the plaster. The camera cuts to Stephen on the bed, writhing in anguish. The next shot is of Stephen vomiting into a bowl. And then as the camera cuts to Stephen seeking out a priest for confession, the film makes the transition from subjective back to objective. The entire montage sequence has taken only a few seconds, but it has depicted Stephen's mental and emotional anguish caused by his guilt. The combination of acting, camera shots, selected images, and editing has revealed Stephen's interior space.

Stephen's emerging sexuality, the cause of some of this guilt, is described in a similar manner. The camera opens on a shot of Stephen and his parents in a restaurant. A waitress's bust line fills a large part of the screen, and the viewer may well believe this to be an unnecessarily sexist shot. But then the camera records Stephen's shy glances at a female patron's slightly exposed ankle and lovely face. Slowly it becomes obvious that these shots are intended to suggest the sexual beast stirring in the boy/man. Then the camera

A Portrait of the Artist (1978). "Wild spring. Scudding clouds. O life!"
Bosco Hogan as Stephen Dedalus in Strick's film adaptation of the classic
Joyce novel. (Photo courtesy of the Museum of Modern Art)

follows Stephen to his room where he is trying to study. He gives up the effort and retrieves a box hidden up the chimney. As he opens the box and removes some picture cards, the audience comes to realize that Stephen is furthering his sex education with pornography. In this case, simple and straightforward photography has suggested, rather than depicted, Stephen's interior space. There is nothing subtle or original about this method of entering interior space, but it is effective.

A more complex use of interior space comes at the end of the film at the point at which Joyce began Stephen's diary. In the novel the last five weeks of Stephen's stay in Ireland are told through his occasional diary, a technique that is close to the interior monologue of *Ulysses*. Stephen records his thoughts somewhat randomly, but collectively they represent the images and experiences that were part of those final days before he left home. Strick has condensed the diary, but the technique is the best use of interior space in the film. It is not the purpose of this essay to discuss the changes Strick has made in Joyce's monologue; there are many and a comparison of the two versions would be worthwhile under different circumstances.

Strick's version of the diary begins on March 21, an entry in which Stephen talks about being free, while the camera shows him reading in a library but observing Emma with a lover. Stephen's face shows jealousy as he contemplates death: "And let the dead marry the dead," he says.

The next entry is for March 24. Stephen records that he and his mother have discussed religion, a painful subject for both. The visuals are quiet shots of the mother hoeing in a small garden, quite a comedown from the luxury in which she found herself in the opening scenes. One of her daughters combs the hair of another and looks for lice. The warm light of the sun makes this a scene of domestic pleasantries, pleasantries Stephen will have to give up when he leaves. Stephen goes on to say that he had tried to explain to Davin why he was leaving Ireland, and the audience discovers for the first time that the decision has been made. During those lines, the camera presents shots of the Irish sea coast.

The words of the entry for April 5 present a montage of images in Stephen's mind concerning spring. The visuals present an opposite

picture. Instead of photographing spring, Strick photographs Stephen in his study. Strick has in these last two entries used a device
that seems to suggest that however cocky Stephen is about his
mental abilities there is a certain ambivalence about his attitudes.
The March 24 entry verbally describes a confining interior subject
(religion); but the visuals are external, open shots of the mother and
daughters out of doors. The verbal entry for April 5 concerns an
open, exterior subject (spring); yet the visuals are of Stephen in his
study, a closed and confining shot. The visuals contradict and
counterbalance the thoughts and images of the diary. This contrast
suggests cinematically the ambivalence of Stephen's decision to
leave.

In the entry for April 14 Stephen records that Davin has just
returned from a trip into the interior of Ireland and has described
an old man he met in a mountain cabin. Stephen says that he fears
this old man because it is with him that Stephen must "struggle all
through this night till day come, till he or I lie dead. . . ." The old
man, of course, represents the Ireland Stephen is rejecting. The
visuals that accompany this passage begin by showing Davin
walking beside the sea; but as the old man is described the images
change to shots of old men drinking ale in an Irish pub. This is the
first time during this interior space that the visuals have presented
the same images heard in the monologue on the soundtrack; and
even here there is a change: the men are in the pub and not at the
mountain cabin. But the shots are especially effective, even a bit
painful because the grand old men are so hoary they are difficult to
watch.

Then without a switch of date, the technique breaks. Strick
changes from interior space to exterior space, from the interior
monologue with visuals to a dialogue. Stephen meets Emma outside
a shop and they talk. Hers is the first voice other than Stephen's to
break the spell of the diary. Joyce had had Stephen describe the
meeting as part of the diary without dialogue, but in the film
Stephen tells Emma that he is leaving and she wishes him well.
Then Strick returns to the monologue as Stephen writes to himself,
"Now I call that friendly, don't you?"

On April 16 Stephen begins the entry with "Away, away" and
goes on to recall images of the road and ships at sea, images that

pull him from Ireland. There are voices that call to him to make ready to go, voices that invite him to kinship and shake "the wings of their exultant and terrible youth." The words are Joyce's but the visual images are Strick's. To accompany this passage Strick has photographed Stephen walking along a sandbar by the sea. This is an extremely open shot, pulling the eye of the viewer outward and freeing both viewer and Stephen. This openness is in direct contrast to the effect of the shots of Stephen in the library or his study. In the air above him are sea gulls, extending their white "arms" to Stephen; it is their voice that invites Stephen to ready himself for the trip.

And finally on April 26 the diary describes Mrs. Dedalus packing Stephen's suitcase, and Stephen says that she prays for him. Stephen's "amen" puts an end to the prayer and to this part of his life. This passage has been accompanied by visuals of the mother in the bedroom packing the clothes and of both parents seeing Stephen off at the train station. Then as Stephen welcomes his new life in the diary, the visuals cut to passengers, including Stephen, boarding a steamer. As Stephen says, "I go to encounter for the millionth time the reality of experience and to forge in the smithy of my soul the uncreated conscience of my race," the camera shows the steamer as it pulls out of the slip. As Stephen utters his own type of prayer, "Old father, old artificer, stand me now and ever in good stead," the camera is in the stern of the ship, subjectively becoming Stephen's eyes as he looks one more time back at land. The shot is of the rugged and rocky coast of Ireland.

From a Joycean point of view, Strick has noticeably changed the theme of *A Portrait of the Artist as a Young Man*. He has substituted for Joyce's theme of the artist Stephen's guilt as he first discovers sex and then decides that he must leave his family, his religion, and his country—a secondary theme in the novel. The film retains some suggestions of Stephen's decision to devote himself to art, including the dialogue on esthetics, but his struggles with maturation have become central to the film. In making this interpretation of the novel, Strick has stamped on the film as his work of art. He is respectful to Joyce, but he has not been slavish to his source. The fact that he chose to make most of the film external also contributes to the view that Strick was discovering his own whatness. But when he uses the interior monologue from Joyce to create his own version of interior space, he is making the best use of his medium to capture the flavor of the original medium. Even though the idea of entering Stephen's interior space is suggested by the novel, Strick has accomplished this through a combination of visual and sound images that are decidedly cinematic. The fact that most of the scenes in which he uses interior space deal with Stephen's guilt and his final decision to leave despite the guilt supports the view that Strick was consciously changing the theme and using the advantages of his medium to heighten the impact of the change. There are times in the film when Strick is too dependent on the novel, but when he enters Stephen's mind and emotions, he tells the story his own way and the story becomes his. The methods of interior space which he uses to make this his own story constitute the whatness of Joseph Strick's *A Portrait of the Artist as a Young Man.*

When in Doubt Persecute Bloom

RICHARD BARSAM

During his court trial in the "Circe" episode of James Joyce's *Ulysses* (1922), Leopold Bloom is defended by J. J. O'Molloy, a once-promising lawyer, now a "mighthavebeen" (125.13).[1] Faced with a formidable group that accuses Bloom of numerous sins and brings witnesses against him, O'Molloy weakly defends his notorious client. As we first see him in "Aeolus," O'Molloy pretends to more knowledge than he actually commands; in "Circe," his unfamiliarity with Bloom's character confuses the case, which he and his client lose. Pleading for mercy before the verdict, he gasps: "When in doubt persecute Bloom" (464.12).

Joseph Strick has a predilection for literary subjects, especially those that have achieved notoriety through disputes over censorship. His adaptations include such twentieth-century masterworks as Jean Genet's *The Balcony* (1963), Henry Miller's *Tropic of Cancer* (1970), and James Joyce's *A Portrait of the Artist as a Young Man* (1978). Following quarrels with producers, Strick abandoned the production of two films: Carson McCullers's *The Heart Is a Lonely Hunter* (1968), directed by Robert Ellis Miller, and Lawrence Durrell's *Justine* (1969), directed by George Cukor. Quite evidently, Strick views himself as an artist-rebel struggling against the commercial restrictions imposed by the Hollywood moguls. Given this view of himself, it is not difficult to understand his admiration for

1. All references are to James Joyce's *Ulysses* (Vintage Books, 1961).

artists like Joyce and Miller or his relentless public campaign against censorship.

Strick undertook the filming of *Ulysses* (1967) knowing it would be his most challenging project to date. Unfortunately, judging by his interviews, press releases, the controversy involving the British censor, and the ensuing debacle at Cannes, Strick was so preoccupied with the issue of censorship that he consistently placed it before all others, including the difficulties associated with adapting such an intricate and discrete verbal structure to the esthetic demands of a highly visual medium. Strick may have spent his energy in struggling to get Joyce's more controversial scenes of film since there is little evidence of any imaginative rendering of these scenes within the film. Having won the right to make an unexpurgated version of *Ulysses*, Strick appears unable to turn such freedom to his advantage. *Ulysses* fails in almost every way to solve the central problems confronting any director who wants to adapt a modern novel to the screen. Strick's lack of imagination is not surprising in view of Joyce's extraordinary genius. Like J. J. O'Molloy faced with Bloom's complex character, Strick, faced with Joyce's complex novel, was in doubt, and unintentionally persecuted Bloom and Joyce.

With the exception of a few episodes (notably "Circe"), Joyce's novel does not suggest an easy cinematic adaptation. There is no evidence to show that Joyce was influenced by the cinema, although he could have seen D. W. Griffith's *The Birth of a Nation* (1915) and *Intolerance* (1916), the only films of the period (1914-1921) in which he was writing *Ulysses* that correspond in complexity to the novel. We know that he saw many early Italian films and, as his letters indicate, that he appreciated the commercial, if not esthetic, potential of the new medium. In 1909, he was involved in a scheme to open a chain of Irish motion picture theaters, but succeeded only in organizing and managing for a brief while the Volta Cinematograph in Dublin. The theatre opened on December 20, 1909, but within six months it lost money and was sold; moreover, Joyce was increasingly preoccupied with finding a publisher for *Dubliners*. He maintained his interest in cinema, but failing eyesight prevented him from enjoying films.

There are, we recognize, many affinities between the development of cinema and the development of the modern novel. Joyce, the greatest English stream-of-consciousness novelist, knew well the verbal limitations of nonverbal experiences, the difficulties in presenting in words simultaneous actions in time, and the problems inherent in rendering and communicating the unique consciousness of his characters. His verbal language and images, rich in allusiveness, defy the visual transpositions implied by Erwin Panofsky's principle of coexpressibility. But Strick stumbles foolishly where only angels or geniuses dare to tread, stating that his goals were to make a film that would be good enough for those who had read the book and that would create an entirely new experience for those who had not.

The novel and the cinema are different arts, as George Bluestone and others have so persuasively argued, and nowhere is this more evident perhaps than in Strick's attempt to find visual correlatives for Joyce's verbal images. Strick's images are frequently inappropriate. For example, when Stephen thinks about eternal woman, Strick shows us Indian temple sculptures of fecund goddesses; these images might be defensible in Jungian terms, but they are Strick's images, not Stephen's. Nonetheless, there are some moments in the film that give pleasure. The "Cyclops" scene in the pub captures the drunkenness and jingoism that Joyce believed were rotting the Irish character. The "Hades" scene in the cemetery shows a bit of Joyce's humor and something of the Irish funeral ritual. And the "Circe" episode is full of teeming life. However, the continual violations of Joyce's overall characterization and narrative are inexcusable because they are conceived badly, filmed unimaginatively, and thus mislead the viewer.

Strick's *Ulysses* fails from its broad conception to its handling of details. For Bloomsday, Joyce chose Dublin on June 16, 1904, which, in the words of novelist Arnold Bennett, is "nearly the dailiest day possible." Strick was restricted by his $1,000,000 budget from building period sets, so he shot the film in contemporary Dublin. The film lacks the rich municipal activity that Joyce captured and conveyed so well, and for some reason known perhaps only to Strick, Bloomsday in the film has become July 16, 1966 (as revealed to us in a shot of a poster for the Mirus Bazaar scheduled for that day). Strick insisted that there would be "no Hollywood interpolations to bridge sequences," yet he invents dialogue to encapsulate large amounts of information and to provide transitions between scenes. The reduction of the novel to visual images (mostly Strick's visual images, not the characters', not Joyce's) robs the narrative of ambiguity, perhaps the richest of its many qualities. And the images themselves are often composed so badly that in a two-character shot, one character is partially out of the frame. In making his earlier film *Muscle Beach* (1948), Strick had a similar problem in framing (characters were half-in and half-out of the frame), discovered later to have been the result of a defective viewfinder. This unfortunate circumstance seems to have become the controlling cinematographic esthetic of *Ulysses*. The movement of the actors in *Ulysses* is often blocked badly; when coupled with a static, unmoving camera, the result is visual chaos. The scenes are rarely long enough to permit characters to establish themselves within the narrative context, so memorable lines strike the audience as if the characters were not ordinary human beings but witty types from a comedy of manners. The beauty of Joyce's language survives, even though many of the actors read it ponderously. The novel is, after all, about the daily activities of familiar folk, not about the mysteries of hierophantic priests. From the evidence of *Ulysses* alone, Strick has difficulty in directing both the movement and the speech of his actors and actresses.

Many of the roles in the film were taken by ordinary Dubliners, but the major roles were cast with professional actors and actresses: Milo O'Shea, the fine Irish actor who plays Bloom; Barbara Jefford, the English actress, who portrays his wife, Molly; and Maurice Roeves, who plays Stephen Dedalus. Good as he is, Milo O'Shea shows us mostly Bloom's comic side; we rarely see the serious side, and when we do—as in the remembrance of Rudy—the moments are maudlin. This one-sided interpretation ignores the overall complexity of Bloom's character, something that might have been impossible for any actor to convey within the limitations of a relatively short screen adaptation of such a long novel. O'Shea contributes more to the film than perhaps any other actor and has the added advantage of resembling closely the caricature of Bloom that Joyce himself drew. Molly is more important for her presence in Bloom's mind than for her actual presence, and thus the actress playing her has little to do, except in the "soliloquy" that closes both the novel and the film. Strick regards Molly as a slut—an interpretation that most scholars reject—and Jefford, who plays her this way, gives an unbalanced, unsympathetic, and unconvincing performance. However, Jefford could be wonderful as a fully realized Molly, for she is both beautiful and talented, and her other work indicates that she might have given a much richer interpretation of the character than Strick permitted. As the brooding Stephen, Roeves is somewhat tougher than we would expect him to be; in his tender moments—with the schoolboy or Mr. Deasy or his sister Dilly—he understands the full character. The actors and actresses in lesser roles are generally good, especially those who portray Mr. Deasy, The Citizen, and Simon Dedalus. There is good work, too, from T. P. McKenna (who, incidentally, plays Simon Dedalus in Strick's version of *A Portrait of the Artist as a Young Man*) as the mischievous Buck Mulligan, and Anna Manahan, as the domineering Bella Cohen, is appropriately bewitching.

Joyce's love of music is evident throughout the novel, in the fugal structure of "Sirens," in the themes that link music, food, and love, and in his characters who make music. Strick uses music to express emotional states, in much the same way as he uses visual images. However the film's music by Stanley Myers sets moods that are not apparent either in the text of the novel or in Strick's visual interpretations of it, so that it sounds as if it were composed and recorded in a postproduction vacuum. For example, the opening scene is introduced by a chant from the medieval church, a pretentious and incorrect choice, since the novel's opening scene ridicules the Mass. In the film version of the "Sirens" episode, the sentimental strains of "Love's Old Sweet Song" carry the melancholy scene, and the effect seems appropriate, until we remember that it is only in Bloom's mind that we "hear" his old, sweet memories of love. In the novel, Simon Dedalus is actually singing "M'Apari" from Friedrich von Flotow's *Martha* and "The Croppy Boy" by William B. McBurney, both of which are richly suggestive and both of which Strick and Myers fail to use.

Strick's *Ulysses* fails not only as a cinematic adaptation of the novel, but also as cinema. In his desperate attempt to bring great

Ulysses (1967). Milo O'Shea as Bloom and Barbara Jefford as Molly. Rejecting most scholars, Strick shows Molly as a slut and Jefford's performance therefore becomes unbalanced. (Photo courtesy of the Museum of Modern Art)

novels and plays to the screen, he seems to have been unaware of what cinema is and how it differs from literature. The *Ulysses* screenplay, by Strick and Fred Haines, is a series of static episodes connected by a ponderous rhythm rather than by any propulsive energy. Awkward scenes serve in Strick's view to "establish" characters, and equally awkward transitions satisfy his notions of continuity. Strick preserves Joyce's simultaneity of time, so that we see, at the film's opening, the overlap of episodes one, two, and three with episode four. But there is a poor sense of time passing throughout the day, a problem compounded by badly matched cuts of shots taken at different times of day. In addition, numerous static scenes are reduced to lifeless tableaux. As the episodes are dutifully recorded on screen, we feel the presence of an unseen hand turning the pages of the novel, moving from episode to episode.

A greater awareness of cinematography and editing might have lightened and made more fluid this self-conscious adaptation of a novel in which breathtaking literary techniques seldom call attention to themselves. Strick favors the establishing shot, the medium shot, and the close-up, although the composition is frequently uncinematic and the shots in a sequence do not often satisfy rudimentary principles of match-cutting. The camera seldom tracks or pans, and Strick's use of the hand-held camera reveals all the elementary faults to be avoided in its use. The editing throughout is similarly awkward. For example, on the beach in the "Proteus" scene, Stephen Dedalus continually walks out of the frame, only to reappear on the screen in the next shot. And as his off-screen voice reads the beautiful "ineluctable modality" passage, we are asked to suspend our disbelief and accept a young man who can close his eyes and walk across a boulder-strewn beach without stumbling.

The budget for Ulysses was $1,000,000, and considering that all salaries for the crew were deferred, except the cameraman's and minimums for the others, it is impossible to cite lack of funds in explaining these faults. Because of architectural and other changes in Dublin between 1904 and 1966, Strick chose to set the film in contemporary Dublin, and so we accept things, such as automobiles, that would have been out of place on Joyce's Bloomsday. But Strick might have been faithful to details that are familiar to all readers of Joyce and that would not have cost him much, if anything. For example, "Aeolus" takes place in the offices of the *Freeman's Journal and National Press*, not the *Irish Times* as Strick believes; an inexpensive sign would have solved that problem. Denis Breen is seen in the novel with law books, attempting to obtain redress for what he believes is an insult to his character, not, as Strick sees him, carrying a sandwich board for Hely's. The widow Dignam and her children are seen in the film at the funeral of Paddy Dignam, but they remain at home in the novel, a Joycean paradox that Strick unfortunately ignores. It is possible, within the extraordinary bounds of the novel's ambiguities, to assign a homosexual interpretation to Bloom's interest in Stephen. In the novel, Buck Mulligan privately warns Stephen: "Get thee a breechpad" (217.38). But he does not, as Strick would have us believe, publicly sing a ditty alleging a "homosexual crime" while leering at Bloom in the doctors' commons room in the "Oxen of the Sun" episode. To emphasize Stephen's disobedience and inner rebellion at his self-proclaimed servitude, Joyce has him recall his dying mother's bedside, where he refused to kneel. Strick unnecessarily elaborates this theme by having Stephen carry Buck's shaving bowl and spill its soapy contents on his shoes just after they have been discussing the servitude of the Irish artist. In Strick's *Ulysses*, the cuckoo in the clock calls "cuckold," not just "cuckoo," which was enough for Joyce and explained to anyone familiar with traditional poetic imagery that Bloom's married life was in peril. Strick adds his own touch of moral condemnation—something that Joyce never does— by having the bookseller spit in contempt after Bloom has purchased an erotic novel for Molly. These few examples are not picayune indications of Strick's faithlessness, but rather primary evidence that Strick, when in doubt, persecutes Bloom, Stephen, Molly, and Joyce.

In adapting *Ulysses*, Strick has emphasized some episodes over others; in the hands of another director, that approach might have been successful, but Strick imbalances the details of the "dailiest day possible," weakens the narrative, and exaggerates some aspects of character to the neglect of others. A closer examination of three episodes—"Nausikaa," "Circe," and "Penelope"—may help to support those conclusions.

The complex ambiguity and balance of Joyce's "Nausikaa" is

reduced in Strick's film to a tawdriness that almost completely obscures the mutual eroticism of this scene between Gerty Mac-Dowell and Leopold Bloom. Joyce used Mirus Bazaar fireworks to heighten what he called this moment of tumescence and detumescence, but Strick omits the pyrotechnics, leaving just the lame Gerty and the aroused Bloom. Strick emphasizes the point that Gerty arouses Bloom, not that she is equally aroused, yet we do not actually see him masturbating as he does in the novel. By emphasizing Bloom's reactions to Gerty, and not hers to Bloom, Strick destroys the delicate balance achieved in the novel.

"Circe" is the longest episode in the novel as well as the longest in the film (approximately forty minutes). "Circe's" instantaneous shifts in space and time are perfect for cinematic adaptation, and Joyce's stage directions ("Circe" was written for the novel as dramatic script, not screenplay) provide a careful guide for the director. Strick is more successful here than elsewhere, especially in conveying Bloom's motivating sense of guilt, but the static tableaux and the overacting diminish the effect of the long scene that is central to our understanding of Bloom and Bloomsday.

"Penelope," the episode of Molly Bloom's pure stream-of-consciousness, is photographed with Molly in bed, as she is in the novel; she scans the room and the camera eye sees her in places that she remembers, as well as in those about which she has fantasies. Strick invents visual images to "explain" her words (for example, an African mask symbolizes masculine sexual strength). Again, there is little connection between his weak visual images and her rich verbal text. Barbara Jefford does the best that she can under the circumstances, but she looks uncomfortable, lying in bed and listening to her own voice read Molly's words. By providing his own images for Molly's (and for Joyce's), Strick intrudes upon the private, evocative domain of her memories and fantasies. Thus, the richest interior monologue in English literature becomes an almost interminable bore, a long scene of exterior action, photographed by an omniscient camera.

The titles preceding the film include this assertion: "The book makes new demands on the reader, and this film attempts to make new demands on the moviegoer." The demands that it makes are not those that Strick intended. The film demands that the audience accept Strick instead of Joyce, ignore continual violations of the elementary principles of cinematic theory and practice, and sit impassively while a complex, ambiguous comic masterpiece is interpreted clumsily in a one-sided manner. One has the disheartening feeling that Strick has presented what he feels to be a rich and evocative visual correlative for Joyce's language, but his complete inability to do other than simplify the novel leaves the viewer with the impression that he has seen a highly abridged version of the original. The film does not encourage viewers to read the novel, but it leaves indelible, unreliable images for those who might still have some enthusiasm for Joyce after seeing it. Finally, the film does not succeed as a work of art in its own right. In the novel, Bloom escapes his persecution, finds a friend in Stephen, surprises Molly with his boldness, and drifts peacefully to sleep in the ultimate ambiguity of the void that ends "Ithaca" and introduces "Penelope." But in Strick's film, neither Bloom nor the audience can escape the persecution that is the result of the director's lack of literary and cinematic sensibility.

The Word Made Celluloid:
On Adapting Joyce's Wake

SARAH W.R. SMITH

It is probably true that artistic success should interest us more deeply than failure; failure is a general enough condition of artistic attempts, while artistic success is always unique. But occasionally a film that fails to do what it attempts can tell us something profound about the nature of cinema. Mary Ellen Bute's *Passages from Finnegans Wake* is one of those films. As simply a "Bute" film, an exercise in rhythmic variations in sound and image track, it has moments of extraordinary beauty. However, while retaining ideas and images from Joyce's *Finnegans Wake*, it gives them a radically different, indeed opposed meaning; it misrepresents the work. The question is whether Bute could have done otherwise. After every allowance is made for the difference in artistic preoccupation between her work and Joyce's, there still remain basic differences in the nature of the two forms, the novel as Joyce has modified it and the film. Can the film do what Joyce has made the novel do? That is, can Joyce's view of the world in *Finnegans Wake* be expressed *at all* in film?

Finnegans Wake (1939) takes as its subject the history of the world, past, present and to come. Joyce, influenced by Giambattista Vico, finds history to be circular, developing not linearly from a beginning to an end, but going round and round in endless cycles of birth, growth, decay and death—death which by fertilizing the materials of growth leads to birth again. At all times, at some place,

301

all moments of the cycle are occurring—and, since all Humankind exists as a single whole in the cycle, at all times the great single organism of Humankind is at all points of the cycle, its height of summer, its dead of winter, its autumn and spring.

The Eternal Masculine and Eternal Feminine are the basic "characters" of the "history" of the cycle, emanations of the single Humankind. Joyce calls them Humphrey Chimpden Earwicker, HCE, and Anna Livia Plurabelle, ALP. HCE and ALP "have" three children, two boys, Shem and Shaun, and a girl, Iseult, who, since there is only one masculine and one feminine, are emanations or alternative versions of their parents. Among these five characters are played out all possible combinations of jealousy and love, war, peace, life, death. Shem and Shaun are locked in eternal battle for Iseult or ALP; each wishes to destroy the other and/or their father. Iseult flirts with her brothers and father, who is obscurely accused of having raped her in a park. All history reflects their loves and battles. Caesar and Brutus, Napoleon and Wellington, Helen of Troy, the "All-father" ("Haveth Childers Everywhere"), Jove, Proserpine, and Cleopatra, with many other historical figures, and more obscure emanations like the rainbow and the days of the week, are shadows of the Masculine and Feminine. HCE is the land, "Howth Castle and Environs"; ALP is "Amnis Livia," the River Liffey, which flows through Dublin, and by extension all rivers including the Liffey's tiny tributary, the River Dodder, "the river's daughter," Iseult.

Illustrating this continually changing order are a number of universal psychic events. Among these are the incident in the park, mentioned above, which may be a rape of daughter/sister/mother by father/brother/son or a seduction by ALP/Iseult of HCE/Shem/Shaun; like most events in the book, it is both creative and destructive. This creation/destruction is incarnate also in other events, including the writing of a book by Shaun or a letter by ALP, the making of tea, and (apparently "destructive" or cycle-ending events) the making of water, urination, or defecation. Apparently disparate events blend into each other, so that from an infinite series of incidents emerges one Event, the act of destruction that begets the act of creation that begets destruction that begets creation. The incident that gives the book its name, HCE's fall to his death, his wake, and his resurrection, is the only incident in the book in the sense that it exemplifies the Event; but in the Event is everything, from the Wall Street crash to the story of Humpty Dumpty and the creation of the world.

Finnegans Wake is simple enough in conception, though fairly complicated in effect. What has given it its reputation for inscrutability is not the story, but the language: the *Wake* is not written in ordinary English. Ordinary English, like any ordinary European language, entails with it certain preconceptions, which we do not object to or even notice because they are the rules under which our minds customarily operate. In ordinary language, one word usually stands for one object, person, or conception. The word "apple" represents a class of roundish tart-sweet fruit, red or green or yellow, thick-skinned, with internal seeds (*you* know what an apple is), and represents only that. To say another thing, we use another word. The principles of grammar in ordinary language contain similar preconceptions. The categories of "subject," "verb," and "object" presume that certain rules of causation apply. The subject influences or causes the object, but the object does not at the same time influence or cause the subject, and subject and object are not the same.

These are very useful rules, but obviously they do not apply to *Finnegans Wake*, where we have already seen that one event may have several identities, that a person may be both acting and acted upon, and that events are the result of multiple and conflicting causes. Obviously, Joyce thought that he had to create a new language that embodied at least some of these rules. Here it is, as he describes Finnegan's fall on the first page of *Finnegans Wake:*

> The fall (bababadalgharaghtakamminarronnkonnbronntonnerronn-tuonnthunntrovarrhounawkskawntoohoohoordenenthurnuk!) of a once wallstrait oldparr is retaled early in bed and later on life down through all christian minstrelsy. The great fall of the offwall entailed at such short notice the pftjschute of Finnegan, erse solid man, that the humptyhill-head of humself prumptly sends an unquiring one well to the west in quest of his tumptytumtoes. . . .

Confusing but not impossible. As we would expect, the text is full of puns and allusions. "Erse," for instance, sounds like "erst," previously, but also refers to "erse," Irish, while "erse solid" refers to one of Finnegan's physical traits, a hefty rear. Finnegan rumbles down in a huge polyglot word suggesting, among other things, Jove's creating thunder, Vico's destroying thunder, the Word of Creation, and the destruction of language (as in the fall of the Tower of "bababadal"). Allusions to the patriarch Old Parr, to Humpty Dumpty, and to Wall Street enrich the passage through their associations. This is "description" in Joyce's most extended sense, in which to "describe" an event is to show that it contains the universe.

Filmic theory, drawing on linguistics, provides an exact description of what Joyce is doing, through a principle called "double articulation." The word "apple," our example of a moment ago, can be taken in two senses: as a convenient shorthand for the fruit, the thing, and purely as a word, "apple." The word is quite different from the thing, though we often think of them together; the word can be stored indefinitely without going mushy, takes up no room at all, and can be applied to paper using conventionalized signs, like this:

apple

—which cannot be done with the thing, apple.

We confuse them because there is a one-to-one relationship between them and we think of them as interchangeable. In a Joycean word the one-to-one relationship between a word and its thing is replaced by a relationship between a word and two or more things. We have already seen such a relationship with "erse." Another, more substantial example is "flyday," which Joyce refers to, early in the book, as one of the days of the week. "Flyday" occurs in a religious context and thus may mean the traditional Catholic day of penitence, Friday, or a day of bad omen (perhaps associated with the Lord of the Flies, Satan), or possibly the Day of Resurrection when saints, angels, and redeemed souls "fly" upward to God. These three quite disparate meanings become reassociated as the Day of Judgment or Good Friday (which Joyce not surprisingly conflates). "Flyday" might also be the day when Adam and Eve were forced to "fly" from Eden (after the Event in the Park); it could refer to the obsolete slang sense of "fly," criminal or sexually abnormal, as well as to the "fly" of a man's trousers. The one-to-many relationship that the Joycean word evokes calls up a little image of the book.

Christian Metz was the first to note that cinematic visual "language" has no double articulation.[1] That is, in the images of cinema it is impossible to tell the thing from its word. In the cinema, we see a picture of an apple. Does it mean the thing, apple, or the word, "apple"? Impossible to know. The thing is represented by its picture, the word, likewise by its picture. It is thus difficult to use a cinema image in a purely "verbal" sense, for instance as a metaphor, because the metaphor functions in a world of words, while the image of an apple functions in both the world of words and as a literal apple; it is fixed to a literal meaning. Because of the lack of double articulation in visual images, because there is no separation between thing and word, there is an often inescapable one-to-one relationship between the thing that is meant and the way it is expressed. The primary function of Joycean language, to serve as a mediating element through which ideas are yoked, has no analogue in the language of cinema.

There is another major difference between the experience of reading *Finnegans Wake* and that of seeing any movie—a difference so great that, in all likelihood, no adaptation, however sensitive, could overcome it. *Finnegans Wake* is not necessarily to be read like most ordinary novels, front cover to back cover. A paragraph like the one quoted above may send the reader on to the next paragraph, but it might also send him to a passage several pages away, behind or before it, to the dictionary, or to his own cultural or personal experience. The very constitution of the words breaks down "consecutivity": one word develops in two or three directions.

But consecutivity is in the nature of film. Unless we are blessed with a viewer and limitless time, we cannot roll the film back and forth before our eyes, looking and wandering at will through the landscape of symbol and meaning Bute has given us. Nor does she expect us to do so; it is certainly her idea that the "proper" viewer of this film will start at the beginning of Reel One and end at the end of Reel Three. Joyce's *Wake* is genuinely circular; the sentence

1. See his "Some Points in the Semiotics of the Cinema," *Film Language* (London and New York: Oxford University Press, 1974), pp. 92-107.

Passages from Finnegans Wake (1969). In Mary Ellen Bute's film version of Joyce's fantasia Martin Kelley plays H.C. Earwicker and Jane Reilly is ALP. (Photo courtesy of the Museum of Modern Art)

that ends on page 1 begins on page 628, inviting the ideal reader to read eternally. Bute's *Wake* gives only a nod toward circularity, beginning with the first words of Joyce's text and ending with his "the" but also conceiving of her first sequence as a traditional beginning (with, for example, title credits, including a scholarly explanation) and her last as a traditional ending, showing that her film has ended by using conventional signs such as "finale" music over the "the" and the presence of end-titles.

It is not impossible to conceive of some approximate version of the circularity of the *Wake*. Nothing prevents us from showing Reels One, Two, Three, One, Two . . . forever, except the presence of conventional cinematic signs for "The End." A film, or more likely a videotape or videodisc, can be designed to be "read" slowly and nonconsecutively by an individual on a viewer. An infinite number of tiny reels, show on an infinity of tiny projectors in aleatory order in innumerable separate pictures on every surface of a white room, conjures up some of the simultaneity for which circularity is a clumsy sign. Lighting and the soundtrack, as well as camera angles, add overtones and might add different meanings. But we are talking about another film, not Bute's.

Passages from Finnegans Wake (1969) represents probably the closest approach possible to Joyce's book using standard filmic language. Bute's previous films with Ted Nemeth, such as *Anitra's Dance* (1936) and *Tarantella* (1941)

> were all composed upon mathematical formulae depicting in ever-changing lights and shadows, growing lines and forms, deepening colours and tones, the tumbling, racing impressions evoked by the musical accompaniment. Their compositions were synchronized—sound and image following a chromatic scale, or divided into two themes—visuals and aurals developing in counterpoint.[2]

There are elements of these earlier films in *Finnegans Wake*, particularly in the splendid resurrection scene at the end of the film, a scene which has no exact counterpart in the book. But the "elements of theatrical power such as comedy, suspense, pathos and

2. Roger Manvell, *Experiment in the Film* (London: Gray Walls Press, 1949), p. 131.

drama . . . which lifted [the work of Bute and Nemeth] above the usual abstract films"[3] drag down the two when they attempt to adapt Joyce's work. Theatrical power and the concept of "patterning" and constructing "passages" depend on development through time and on separation of certain elements of the universe of the work from others; these concepts are antithetical to the spirit of *Finnegans Wake*. Bute's film gets around the problem it has created for itself by simplifying the organic original into dualities and contradictions and by inventing a kind of historical optimism to substitute for Joyce's achronological history. The "explanation" prefixed to the film asserts that

> [*Finnegans Wake*] deals with the nightworld, with the subconscious, and with dreams. Joyce felt that during the night man must redeem himself by means of a quest; must refresh his powers through sleep, which takes him beyond himself into a world without definition. Man's goal is lucidity, a fresh awakening. The quest carries him through all history, which seems to be a constant process of waking . . . Finnegan must come to terms with . . . parts of himself [his sons, daughter, wife], realize the dangers inherent in their extreme forms, and experience his "reunited selfdom," in order to "WAKE" up.

There is a creeping morality here, a sort of Horatio Algerism, no less admirable, perhaps, than Joyce's theory of history, but certainly more naive and more conventional.

To see the extent of Bute's changes, let us look, as briefly as possible, at two extracts, one from the book, one from the film. About a third of the way through the film, the Guests in the living-room of the Earwicker house/saloon gather around the coffin where HCE lies.

1. ¼ shot, back of waiter carrying wine bottle and glasses; Waiter turns L toward . . .

   VO GUESTS: Grampupus has fallen down but Grinny sprids the boord.
2. MS of Guests, gathered around coffin, midground; two candles burn near head. ALP background, dressed in black, long black veil. Waiter passes L with tray. Guests follow L.

   VO GUESTS: . . . and will again if so be sooth.

3. *Ibid.*, p. 132.

3. CU of ALP. Face bare, sadly sensual. She looks L and turns . . .

VO GUESTS: . . . by elder to youngers shall be said.

4. Extreme high angle of tray with glasses being filled; Guests surround tray. A hand moves L, passes a glass to a Guest, returns, begins to fill another.

VO GUESTS: Have you whines for my wedding?
                      Did you bring bride and bedding?

5. MS ALP, R, and Shaun, L, behind coffin. Two candles near head. ALP looks L, Shaun R; Shaun moves R to stand protectively behind ALP.

(Background Noise from Guests)

6. CU of ALP's face, Shaun's blurrily behind hers in extreme UR. He moves R and his face comes into focus.

SHAUN: Do you not must want to go somewhere on the present? ALP drops her eyes, replying:

ALP: Yes! O pity! At earliest moment!

SHAUN: Here we shall do a far walk. . . .

[In two shots, ALP and Shaun move into a corridor and play out an ambiguous scene; looking like a nun, ALP addresses him tenderly, almost like a lover. "I am not sighing, I assure, only I am soso sorry about all in my saarasplace." Both walk through a dark door; Shem, coming into the scene, follows them angrily.]

9. 3/4 shot of Guests looking R, slightly apprehensive; they stand round a table holding two candles, flowers, food, and drink; this is either the coffin itself or meant to suggest the coffin. The tray is now being held, waiter-style, by an Undertaker, L.

10. From R, ALP, now seen to be holding a candle, and Shaun enter a bright Hall with a staircase. They begin to climb the stairs, Shaun behind ALP, past a portrait of a soldier dressed in the uniform of the Napoleonic era.

VO SHAUN: Annah, the Allmaziful—

Shem enters behind them, R, and follows them L as Shaun and ALP continue to climb the stairs.

VO SHAUN: —the Everliving,

11. High angle CU, from R, of ALP's face as she continues to climb.

VO SHAUN: the Bringer of Plurabilities,

She turns to look down the stairs.

12. 1/4 shot, high angle, of Shem (L) and Shaun (R), from POV of ALP on stairs.

VO SHAUN: —haloed be her eve, her singtime sung, her rill be run, unhemmed as it is uneven! Her untitled mamafesta memorializing the Mosthighest has gone by many names—

13. As 11. ALP is shown in CU from above, the stair-rail between her and the camera. She turns R and climbs the stairs.

VO Shaun: the primal sacrament of baptism or the regeneration of all man . . .

Camera pans and tilts R and up as ALP climbs past; we see her face, then her body and R hand on the baluster

VO Shaun: —by affusion of water.

Camera pans R as ALP moves R and toward camera, until her black clothing turns the screen almost completely dark.

VO ALP: YES

In double exposure, against the darkness of ALP's clothes (we still see two white triangles of neck and shoulder) there is the sparkle of light on dark water. Camera pans L and

Dissolves to

14. Semi-abstract shot of light dancing on dark water. High contrast. Camera zooms (?) in and slightly blurs focus.

(music)

15. Water pours from L and meets an obstruction center screen; it foams and splashes. Camera pans L and tilts up to show similar obstructions in an energetic rapids; continues to tilt up and pans R over creamy whites and deep blacks of rocks and water. We see the farther shore. Like 14, a long-continued and beautiful shot.

(*music*)

blending into

VO Guests: Wake! Wake!

[. . . and HCE wakes, as the guests shout "Wake! Usqueadbaugham!"][4]

The scene is obviously well stocked with Freudian puns. The tray with glasses and a bottle—round tray and glasses, vaguely phallic bottle pouring liquid into and onto them—contains the "water of life", *usquebaugh*, the whiskey drunk at the Wake (though in another manifestation, wine and/or holy water). That fluid is connected with the act of creation, the fluid (excretory or sexual) produced by ALP. The sexual overtones are insistent. It is unclear whether ALP is leaving the Wake to urinate or to have sex; Shaun's invitation is ambiguous, and we know only that the water that resurrects her husband has come from inside ALP. We see through, or into, her body and find a river. The sexual image is given greater potency by shots 14 and 15, in which the energetic play of light over

4. Described from the film as distributed by Grove Press.

darkness manifests again the union of male (light) with female (darkness). (Note also the omnipresent phallic candles.) The two sons, HCE's split doubles, recognize the act of creation that ALP is initiating and pray to her, a typical Joycean comment on the relationship between man and his deities. The imagery of the Eucharist applies to both ALP (the wine) and HCE (the bread, the food on the coffin-table), and the act of communion becomes that of consummation; with typical Joycean mockery, the presiding "priest" is an undertaker/waiter. The guests combine the functions of congregation, Greek chorus, and gossip-pandars. The fighting brothers are referred to by the Napoleonic portrait on the stairs; in pursuit of ALP, both brothers enter doorways and climb stairs, two familiar symbols of religious enlightenment and sexuality. HCE lies in a womb/tomb, surrounded by candles and flowers that may come from a well-set table, an altar, or a set of mythological attributes: HCE's phallic candles, Iseult's flowers. ALP is bride, Bride of Christ, and widow.

All this is rich and far from completely unsuccessful, but its success is not filmic. Bute's work is a classic case of the difficulty of making metaphors in a language without double articulation; we "see" the metaphors clearly only by abstracting them from Bute's form, clothing them with their literary and cultural overtones, and then treating the overtones as though they were the entire filmic experience. We do not really *see* the connection between the fluid in the bottle and the river inside ALP—in fact, we cannot even read the dissolve between shots 13 and 14 as a statement of equivalence or of "inside-ness"; we read such meanings into the film because we previously know, from the book, that they are valid. The candles are phallic in a metaphorical context, but the film does not, and perhaps cannot, provide such a context; in the film they relentlessly remain candles. Joyce's form makes no distinction between literal nature and metaphor; Bute's finds their differences awkward.

Bute's form similarly has trouble expressing simultaneity. We see that HCE's coffin is also an altar and a dining-room table, not by a simultaneous realization, but by seeing it as a coffin first and a table later. Jane Reilly, as ALP, indicates that she is both widow and nun by looking first like one, then like the other. Some statements about simultaneous identity may be made simultaneously; the staircase is both a religious and a sexual symbol. However, these images are allusive, not original, and certainly not specifically cinematic. Bute's form encourages separation of identities by following their permutations through times. Joyce's unifies them by ignoring temporal sequence.

Complex as it is, Joyce's writing has both great intelligence and great beauty. The reader need only compare the scene above with its major parallels in the novel[5] to see the gain in both compression and beauty—particularly in the dizzying description of the event in the Park, in which ALP/Iseult urinates, seduces, is raped, gives a history lesson, spells out the Letter by/to/and perhaps on her brother/ father, as she possibly becomes him (like HCE, she stutters), while the male in the event turns to feminine water.[6] How could such heterogeneous material become poetry? Never mind; it is. The writing expresses exactly what it must, exploding with the simultaneity of all the events in the book, words crisscrossing each other in infinitely varied geometries of meaning. *Finnegans Wake* is simple, as the Bute film is not, because form is substance in it; Bute must call on material outside the basic formal resources of her art to illuminate Joyce's world, but Joyce has no need of anything but his form. The form contains the world.

We are left with the question that the Bute film originally posed,; unanswered, perhaps unanswerable. Is the film form *by its nature* unable to adapt a book like *Finnegans Wake?* Do the twenty-four frames a second to which we are tied imply some necessary relationship to time? Mary Ellen Bute's classical Hollywood grammar of editing and rhythmic progression does not answer the question, but neither do such time-oriented films as *Citizen Kane*, Connors's *A Movie*, Snow's *Wavelength*, or multiple-screen films; all filmmaking, so far, seems tied to some concept of development either through chronological time or within the psyche of the viewer. Must film always be tied to an esthetics of consecutivity, development, and change through time? Until it can escape, there will remain important ideas of the twentieth century that it cannot express—and the world of the *Wake* will never be adapted to film.

5. The Wake itself, the prayer to ALP and naming of the book, and the Park episode described here—Section I, pp. 104-5, and pp. 570-571 of the revised Viking text.

6. See pp. 570-571.

ROBERT A. ARMOUR is Associate Professor of English at Virginia Commonwealth University where he teaches courses in fiction into film, film for the classroom, and film history. His continuing interests are in poetry and film and in the history of the Biograph Studio. He has published articles on film in *Literature/Film Quarterly*, the *Journal of the University Film Association*, and the *English Journal*. He contributed a chapter on film bibliography to the recent *Handbook of American Popular Culture*. He is the author of two books: *Fritz Lang*, and *Film: a Reference Guide*

RICHARD BARSAM is Professor of Cinema Studies at the College of Staten Island of the City University of New York, where he has for many years taught a course on James Joyce. His books include *Nonfiction Film: A Critical History, Nonfiction Film Theory and Criticism, Filmguide to Triumph of the Will*, and *In the Dark: A Primer for the Movies*. He is currently preparing a critical study of the films of Robert Flaherty.

JIM BECKERMAN is an undergraduate, majoring in English. He is himself a filmmaker, and recently won an award for his adaptation of Poe's *The Fall of the House of Usher*, with Tim Johnston.

H. PHILIP BOLTON is Associate Professor of English, Mount Vernon College, Washington, D.C. His particular interest is the theory of narrative, especially dramatic narrative of the nineteenth century. His dissertation was concerned with the essential differences between fiction and theater as revealed by dramatic adaptations of prose fiction.

NOEL CARROLL teaches film at New York University, is a coeditor of *Millennium Film Journal*, and is a staff critic for *Soho Weekly News*.

313

RITA COSTABILE is a doctoral candidate in English at Columbia University.

TRISHA CURRAN is Director of Film at Fordham University, an award-winning documentary filmmaker, and a free-lance film critic. The Arno Press will be publishing her dissertation, *A New Note on the Film: A Theory of Film Criticism Derived from Susanne K. Langer's Philosophy of Art* in their Distinguished Dissertations on Film Series. Her film criticism appears regularly in *Films in Review*.

DENNIS DeNITTO teaches film history and theory at the City College of New York and is Coordinator of the Film Program at City College's Theatre Arts Department and the Leonard David Center for the Performing Arts. He is coauthor of *Film and the Critical Eye* and has just completed *Film: Form and Feeling*, which is being published next year. His latest article is "Jean Cocteau's *Beauty and the Beast*."

KATE ELLIS is Associate Professor of English, Livingston College, Rutgers University, where she teaches Creative Writing, English Literature, and Women's Studies. She has written articles on film for *Jump Cut* and wrote an article on *Little Women* in Gerald Peary and Roger Shatzkin's *The Classic American Novel and the Movies*. She writes poetry and lives in Manhattan with her son.

LESTER D. FRIEDMAN teaches English at the Upstate campus of the State University of New York and Film at the College of Visual and Performing Arts, Syracuse University. His articles have appeared in *Millennium, Literature/Film Quarterly, The English Record,* and *Film Criticism*. Currently he is at work on two books, one examining the image of Jews in the American cinema, and the other a series of interviews with film personalities such as Arthur Penn, David Newman, Peter Watkins, Peter Wollen, and Verna Fields.

JOSEPH A. GOMEZ is an Associate Professor at Wayne State University where he teaches film courses in the English Department. He is the author of two books: *Ken Russell: The Adaptor as Creator* and *Peter Watkins*. He has also written articles for *Film Quarterly, Literature/Film Quarterly, The Velvet Light Trap, Film Heritage, Film Criticism,* and *Movie Maker*.

S. E. GONTARSKI has published essays and reviews in journals including *Modern Fiction Studies, Journal of Modern Literature, Modern Drama, Journal of Beckett Studies, Perspectives on Contemporary Literature,* and *James Joyce Quarterly*. He has published a study of the genesis of Beckett's play, *Beckett's Happy Days: A Manuscript Study* and is currently at work on a booklength study of D. H. Lawrence tentatively entitled *Lawrence on*

Film. He is also American Book Review editor for the *Journal of Beckett Studies* and editor of *The Beckett Circle: Newsletter of the Samuel Beckett Society.*

SHARON GOODMAN studies film at Yale and is currently a reader at Warner Bros.

JAMES GOODWIN teaches modern literature and film at the University of California, Los Angeles, where he is an Assistant Professor of English. He has published essays on literary subjects in *Genre, ESQ,* and *Denver Quarterly.* His essays on film have appeared in *College Literature, Praxis,* and *Quarterly Review of Film Studies.* He is also a contributor to the section of the *Dictionary of Literary Biography* devoted to screenwriters.

LINDLEY HANLON has a Ph.D. in Cinema Studies from New York University and is currently writing a book on the American avant-garde 1960-1980 for the Twayne theatre arts series. She has an article on Bresson's *Une Femme Douce* in Andrew Horton and Joan Magretta's *Modern European Literature and the Art of Adaptation* and has written widely on French film.

JOHN HARRINGTON has published widely on film, and is the author of *The Rhetoric of Film* and *Film and/as Literature.* He teaches film at California State University at San Luis Obispo.

ANNETTE INSDORF, author of *François Truffaut,* is an Assistant Professor at Yale University where she teaches "Literature into Film." She has written film criticism for the *New York Times, American Film, Take One,* and *French Review.* She has translated for François Truffaut and Abel Gance at film symposia, and she recently conducted a seminar on François Truffaut for the American Film Institute Center for Advanced Studies.

DIANE JACOBS is the author of *Hollywood Renaissance,* a study of contemporary American directors including Cassavetes, Altman, Coppola, and Scorcese. She writes on film for the *Soho Weekly News, New York Times, Film Comment,* and *Village Voice.*

E. ANN KAPLAN teaches film, literature, and women's studies. She writes extensively on film and has recently published two books, *Women in Film Noir,* a British Film Institute publication and *Fritz Lang: A Research and Reference Guide.* She is Film Editor for *Marxist Perspectives.*

LESTER J. KEYSER is an Associate Professor in the Department of English, Speech and World Literature at the College of Staten Island (City University of New York), where he teaches courses in film and literature. He recently coauthored *The Cinema of Sidney Poitier* with Canadian sociologist André Ruszkowski and is now completing a book on *Hollywood in the Seventies*.

LAWRENCE F. LABAN is an Assistant Professor of English at Virginia Commonwealth University where he teaches courses on the British novel, literature and film, and methods of literary criticism.

GEORGE LELLIS, Assistant Professor in Communications at Mount Vernon College, Washington, D.C., has written criticism for *Sight and Sound, Film Quarterly, Film Heritage*, and *Take One*. He is a coauthor of *The Film Career of Buster Keaton*, and is completing *Film: Form and Function*.

WILLIAM LUHR is Assistant Professor in English and Film at St. Peter's College. He is the coauthor of *Authorship and Narrative in the Cinema: Issues in Contemporary Aesthetics and Criticism*, and is completing two forthcoming books, one on Blake Edwards, the other on Raymond Chandler and film.

JULIAN MOYNAHAN has written four novels, the latest being *Where the Land and Water Meet*, and critical studies of D. H. Lawrence (*The Deed of Life*), V. Nabokov, Dickens, and Hardy. He teaches English at Rutgers in New Brunswick and is writing a book on Anglo-Irish themes and authors, 1800–1939.

SARAH W. R. SMITH has taught at Harvard and currently teaches English and Fim at Tufts University. She is a field editor for Twayne's English Authors Series. Her translation of *Colette at the Movies*, a collection of the French novelist's film criticism and screenplay, was published this year. She is currently working on a book on film theory.

JANET M. TODD, editor of *Women and Literature*, recently spent a year at Oxford on an ACLS fellowship, where she wrote, among other things, her chapter for this volume. She has written critical studies of John Clare (*In Adam's Garden*) and Mary Wollstonecraft; her most recently completed work, *Women's Friendship in Literature*, is being published at the end of the year.

RICHARD WASSON has published numerous articles and reviews on topics related to modern literature in *College English, Partisan Review, Journal of Modern Literature*, and elsewhere; he is currently at work on a book on the rhetoric of class in modern fiction.

JANICE R. WELSCH teaches film courses at Western Illinois University. She is the author of *Film Archetypes: Sisters, Mistresses, Mothers and Daughters* (1976) and is currently coediting a collection of essays on the theory of film and literary narrative that will be published as a special issue of *Essays in Literature*.

THE EDITORS

MICHAEL KLEIN was educated in the United States (University of Rochester and University of California Berkeley) and England (Sussex University) where he received his Ph.D. A member of the English Department of Rutgers University, he has written on film and literature, the French New Wave (particularly Truffaut and Godard), and American documentary film in *Film Quarterly, Film Comment, Film Heritage, Cinéaste,* and *Jump Cut.* He has contributed articles to Lewis Jacobs's *The Emergence of Film Art,* John Harrington's *Film and/as Literature,* Gerald Peary and Roger Shatzkin's *The Modern American Novel and the Movies,* and Karyn Kay and Gerald Peary's *Women in Film: A Critical Anthology.* He is currently completing a novel, working on a study of F. Scott Fitzgerald and film, and teaching as a visiting Professor at the University of Warwick.

GILLIAN PARKER, Assistant Professor of English at Rutgers University, comes from England. She has published articles on film in *The Velvet Light Trap, Cinéaste* and, most often, *Film Quarterly.* Her central literary interest in the prophetic tradition as it emerges in English writing is reflected in a recently completed study of Margaret Drabble's novels, *And Was Jerusalem Builded Here?*, and in her current work on Milton.

FILM CREDITS

Films are listed in alphabetical order.
CODE: *Dir*: director. *Prod*: producer. *Scr*: screenplay.
Photo: director of photography.
(Rental sources are included in the filmography.)

Apocalypse Now (1979). *Prod-Dir* Francis Coppola. *Scr* Francis Coppola, John Milius. *Photo* Vittorio Storaro. *Music* Carmine Coppola, Francis Coppola. Cast: Marlon Brando (*Capt. Kurtz*), Robert Duvall (*Kilgore*), Martin Sheen (*Willard*).

Barry Lyndon (1975). *Prod-Dir* Stanley Kubrick. *Scr* Stanley Kubrick. *Photo* John Alcott. Cast: Ryan O'Neal (*Barry Lyndon*), Marisa Berenson (*Lady Lyndon*), Patrick Magee (*Chevalier*), Hardy Kruger (*Capt. Potzdorf*), Marie Kean (*Barry's mother*), Murray Melvin (*Rev. Runt*), Frank Middlemass (*Sir Charles Lyndon*), Leonard Rossiter (*Capt. Quin*), Leon Vitali (*Lord Bullingdon*). *Narrator*: Michael Hordern.

Becky Sharp (1935). *Dir* Rouben Mamoulian. *Scr* Francis Edward Farragoh. *Photo* Ray Rennahan. *Music* Roy Webb. Cast: Miriam Hopkins (*Becky Sharp*), Sir Cedric Hardwicke (*Marquis of Steyne*), Frances Dee (*Amelia Sedley*), Billie Burke (*Lady Bareacres*), Nigel Bruce (*Joseph Sedley*), Alan Mowbray (*Rawdon Crawley*), Colin Tapley (*William Dobbin*), G. P. Huntley, Jr. (*George Osborne*).

A Christmas Carol (1951). *Prod-Dir* Brian Desmond Hurst. *Scr* Noel Langley. *Photo* C. Pennington-Richards. *Music* Richard Addinsell. Cast: Alastair Sim (*Scrooge*), Kathleen Harrison (*Mrs. Dilber*), Jack Warner (*Mr. Jorkins*), Michael Hordern (*Jacob Marley*), Mervyn Johns (*Bob Cratchit*), Hermione Baddeley (*Mrs. Cratchit*), George Cole (*young Scrooge*), Patrick McNee (*young Marley*), Hattie Jacques (*Mrs. Fezziwig*).

David Copperfield (1935). *Dir* George Cukor. *Prod* David O. Selznick. *Scr* Howard Estabrook. *Photo* Oliver T. Marsh. *Music* Herbert Stothart.

Cast: Freddie Bartholomew (*young David*), W. C. Fields (*Mr. Micaw-ber*), Lionel Barrymore (*Mr. Peggotty*), Maureen O'Sullivan (*Dora Spenlow*), Madge Evans (*Agnes Wickfield*), Edna Mae Oliver (*Betsey Trotwood*), Lewis Stone (*Mr. Wickfield*), Frank Lawton (*David Copper-field*), Elizabeth Allen (*Mrs. Copperfield*), Roland Young (*Uriah Heep*), Basil Rathbone (*Mr. Murdstone*), Elsa Lanchester (*Clickett*).

Dr. Jekyll and Mr. Hyde (1932). *Prod-Dir* Rouben Mamoulian. *Scr* Samuel Hoffenstein, Percy Heath. *Photo* Karl Struss. Cast: Fredric March (*Dr. Henry Jekyll/Mr. Hyde*), Miriam Hopkins (*Ivy Pearson*), Rose Hobart (*Muriel Carew*), Holmes Herbert (*Dr. Lanyon*), Edgar Norton (*Poole*), Halliwell Hobbes (*Carew*), Arnold Lucy (*Utterson*).

Far from the Madding Crowd (1967). *Dir* John Schlesinger. *Scr* Frederick Raphael. *Photo* Nick Roeg. Cast: Julie Christie (*Bathsheba Everdene*), Terence Stamp (*Troy*), Peter Finch (*Boldwood*), Alan Bates (*Gabriel Oak*), Prunella Ransome (*Fanny*), Fiona Walker (*Liddy*).

Finnegans Wake (1969). *Prod-Dir* Mary Ellen Bute. *Scr* Mary Ellen Bute, T. J. Nemeth, Jr., and Romana Javitz. *Photo* Ted Nemeth. *Music* Otis MacLay. Cast: Martin J. Kelley (*Finnegan/ H.C. Earwicker*), Jane Reilly (*Anna Livia Plurabelle/ALP*), Peter Haskell (*Shem*), Page Johnson (*Shaun*), Ray Flanagan (*young Shem*), Maura Pryor (*young Iseult*), Jo Jo Selvin (*young Shaun*). *Commentator:* John V. Kelleher.

Frankenstein (1931). *Dir* James Whale. *Prod* Carl Laemmle, Jr. *Scr* Garrett Ford and Francis Edwards Farragoh. *Photo* Arthur Edeson. Cast: Colin Clive (*Henry Frankenstein*), Mae Clarke (*Elizabeth*), John Boles (*Victor Moritz*), Boris Karloff (*The Monster*), Edward Van Sloan (*Dr. Waldman*), Frederick Kerr (*Baron Frankenstein*), Dwight Frye (*Fritz*).

Great Expectations (1946). *Dir* David Lean. *Prod* Ronald Neame. *Scr* David Lean, Ronald Neame, Anthony Havelock-Allen. *Photo* Guy Greene. *Music* Walter Goehr. Cast: Anthony Wager (*young Pip*), John Mills (*Pip*), Bernard Miles (*Joe Gargery*), Freda Jackson (*Mrs. Joe*), Hay Petrie (*Pumblechook*), Martita Hunt (*Miss Havisham*), Jean Simmons (*young Estella*), Valerie Hobson (*Estella*), Finlay Currie (*Magwitch*), Francis L. Sullivan (*Jaggers*), Ivor Barnard (*Wemmick*), Alec Guinness (*Herbert Pocket*).

Jane Eyre (1944). *Dir* Robert Stevenson. *Scr* Aldous Huxley, Robert Stevenson, and John Houseman. *Photo* George Barnes. *Music* Bernard Herrman. Cast: Orson Welles (*Edward Rochester*), Joan Fontaine (*Jane Eyre*), Margaret O'Brien (*Adele Varens*), Peggy Ann Garner (*young Jane*), Elizabeth Taylor (*Helen Burns*), John Sutton (*Dr. Rivers*), Sara Allgood (*Bessie*), Henry Daniell (*Brocklehurst*), Agnes Moorhead (*Mrs. Reed*).

Jane Eyre (TV, 1970). *Dir* Delbert Mann. Cast: George C. Scott (*Edward Rochester*), Susannah York (*Jane Eyre*).

Joseph Andrews (1978). *Dir* Tony Richardson. *Scr* Allan Scott and Chris Bryant. *Photo* David Watkin. *Music* John Addison. Cast: Ann-Margret (*Lady Booby*), Peter Firth (*Joseph Andrews*), Michael Hordern (*Parson Adams*), Beryl Reid (*Mrs. Slipslop*), Jim Dale (*Pedlar*), Natalie Ogle (*Fanny*), Karen Dotrice (*Pamela*), Norman Rossington (*Gaffes Andrews*), Patsy Rowlands (*Gammes Andrews*), Murray Melvin (*Beau Didapper*), Peggy Ashcroft (*Lady Tattle*), Bernard Bresslaw (*Parson Trulliber*), John Gielgud (*Doctor*), Hugh Griffith (*Squire Weston*).

Lady Chatterley's Lover (1955). *Dir* Marc Allegret. *Scr* Marc Allegret. Cast: Danielle Darrieux (*Constance Chatterley*), Erno Crisa (*Mellors*), Leo Genn (*Sir Clifford Chatterley*), Berthe Tisson (*Mrs. Bolton*), Janine Crispin (*Hilda*), Gerard Sety (*Michaelis*).

The Man Who Would Be King (1975). *Dir* John Huston. *Prod* John Foreman. *Scr* Gladys Hill and John Huston. *Photo* Oswald Morris. *Music* Maurice Jarre. Cast: Sean Connery (*Daniel Dravot*), Michael Caine (*Peachy Carnehan*), Christopher Plummer (*Rudyard Kipling*), Saeed Jaffrey (*Billy Fish*), Karrovin Ben Bouih (*Kafu-Selim*), Shakira Caine (*Roxanne*).

Nosferatu the Vampyre (1979). *Prod-Dir* Werner Herzog. *Scr* Werner Herzog. Cast: Klaus Kinski (*the Count*), Isabelle Adjani (*Lucy*), Bruno Ganz (*Jonathan*).

Of Human Bondage (1934). *Dir* John Cromwell. *Scr* Lester Cohen. Cast: Leslie Howard (*Philip Carey*), Bette Davis (*Mildred*), Frances Dee (*Sally*), Kay Johnson (*Norah*), Reginald Denny (*Griffiths*), Reginald Owen (*Athelny*), Desmond Roberts (*Dr. Jacobs*).

Of Human Bondage (1964). *Dir* Ken Hughes. *Scr* Brian Forbes. Cast: Laurence Harvey (*Philip Carey*), Kim Novak (*Mildred*), Nanette Newman (*Sally*), Siobhan McKenna (*Norah*), Roger Livesey (*Athelny*), Jack Hedley (*Griffiths*), Robert Morley (*Dr. Jacobs*).

A Portrait of the Artist as a Young Man (1978). *Dir* Joseph Strick. *Scr* Judith Rascoe. *Photo* Stuart Hetherington. *Music* Stanley Myers. Cast: Bosco Hogan (*Stephen*), T. P. McKenna (*Simon Dedalus*), John Gielgud (*the Preacher*), Rosaleen Linehan (*Mrs. Dedalus*), Maureen Potter (*Dante*), Niall Buggy (*Davin*), Brian Murray (*Lynch*), Desmond Care (*Cranly*).

Pride and Prejudice (1940). *Dir* Robert Z. Leonard. *Scr* Aldous Huxley and Jane Murfin. *Photo* Karl Freund. Cast: Greer Garson (*Elizabeth Bennet*), Laurence Oliver (*Mr. Darcy*), Mary Boland (*Mrs. Bennet*), Edna May Oliver (*Lady Catherine de Bourgh*), Maureen O'Sullivan (*Jane Bennet*),

Frieda Inescort (*Miss Bingley*), Edmund Gwenn (*Mr. Bennet*), Bruce Lester (*Mr. Bingley*), Edward Ashley (*Mr. Wickham*), Melville Cooper (*Mr. Collins*).

Robinson Crusoe (1953). *Dir* Luis Bunuel. *Scr* Luis Bunuel and Philip Roll. *Photo* Alex Philips. *Music* Anthony Collins. Cast: Dan O'Herlihy (*Robinson Crusoe*), Jaime Fernandez (*Friday*), Felipe da Alaba (*Captain Oberzo*).

Sabotage (1936). *Dir* Alfred Hitchcock. *Prod* Michael Balcon. *Assoc, Prod.* Ivor Montague. *Scr* Charles Bennett. *Photo* Bernard Knowles. Cast: Sylvia Sidney (*Mrs. Verloc*), Oscar Homolka (*Carl Verloc*), Desmond Tester (*Stevie*), John Loder (*Ted Spencer*), William Dewhurst (*the Professor*).

Sons and Lovers (1960). *Dir* Jack Cardiff. *Scr* Gavin Lambert and T. E. B. Clarke. *Photo* Freddie Francis. *Music* Lambert Williamson. Cast: Wendy Hiller (*Gertrude Morel*), Trevor Howard (*Walter Morel*), Dean Stockwell (*Paul Morel*), Mary Ure (*Clara Dawes*), Heather Sears (*Miriam Lievers*), Donald Pleasence (*Mr. Pappleworth*), Rosalie Crutchley (*Mrs. Lievers*).

The Time Machine (1960). *Prod-Dir* George Pal. *Scr* David Duncan. *Photo* Paul Vogel. *Music* Russell Garcia. Cast: Rod Taylor (*George*), Alan Young (*Philby*), Yvette Mimieux (*Weena*), Sebastian Cabot (*Doctor*), Tom Helmut (*man*).

Tom Jones (1963). *Prod-Dir* Tony Richardson. *Scr* John Osborne. *Photo* Walter Lassally. *Music* John Addison. Cast: Albert Finney (*Tom Jones*), Susannah York (*Sophie Western*), Hugh Griffith (*Squire Western*), Edith Evans (*Miss Western*), Joan Greenwood (*Lady Bellaston*), Diane Cilento (*Molly Seagrim*), George Devine (*Squire Allworthy*), David Tomlinson (*Lord Fellamar*), Joyce Redman (*Mrs. Waters/Jenny Jones*), Angela Baddeley (*Mrs. Wilkins*), Wilfrid Lawson (*Black George*), Jack Mac-Gowran (*Partridge*), David Warner (*Blifil*), Lynn Redgrave (*Susan*). *Narrator*: Michael MacLiammoir.

Ulysses (1967). *Prod-Dir* Joseph Strick. *Scr* Joseph Strick and Fred Haines. Cast: Milo O'Shea (*Leopold Bloom*), Barbara Jefford (*Molly Bloom*), Maurice Roeves (*Stephen Dedalus*), T. P. McKenna (*Buck Mulligan*), Anna Manahan (*Bella Cohen*).

The Virgin and the Gypsy (1970). *Dir* Christopher Miles. *Scr* Alan Plater. Cast: Joanna Shimkus (*Yvette*), Franco Nero (*the Gypsy*), Honor Blackman (*Mrs. Fawcett*), Mark Burns (*Major Eastwood*), Fay Compton (*the Mater*), Maurice Denham (the Rector), Kay Walsh (*Aunt Cissie*).

Women in Love (1969). *Dir* Ken Russell. *Scr* Larry Kramer. *Photo* Billy Williams. *Music* George Delerue. Cast: Alan Bates (*Rupert Birkin*),

Oliver Reed (*Gerald Crich*), Glenda Jackson (*Gudrun Brangwen*), Jennie Linden (*Ursula Brangwen*), Eleanor Bron (*Hermione Roddice*), Vladek Sheybal (*Loerke*), Michael Gough (*Mr. Brangwen*).

Wuthering Heights (1939). *Dir* William Wyler. *Scr* Ben Hecht and Charles MacArthur. Cast: Laurence Olivier (*Heathcliff*), Merle Oberon (*Cathy*), David Niven (*Edgar*), Flora Robson (*Ellen Dean*), Hugh Williams (*Hindley*), Geraldine Fitzgerald (*Isabella*), Miles Mander (*Lockwood*).

SELECTED   FILMOGRAPHY:

Film Adaptations of English Novels, 1719–1930s

The sheer number of novels made into films and the fact that the literary and cinematic "canon" is invariably in flux has forced us to make this a very "selected," if eclectic, listing. Our general principle has been to include those novels and films we think will be of immediate interest to film and literary scholars, to archivists and librarians. At present, there are no comprehensive reference guides for filmed adaptations, although the eventual completion of the American Film Institute Catalogues may help fill that gap. In the meantime, further information can be culled from A. G. S. Enser, *Filmed Books and Plays 1928–1974*, London: Andre Deutsch, 1975 (though Enser's reliance on British publishing sources and dates of film release creates some problems); Richard B. Dimmit, *A Title Guide to the Talkies*, 2 vols., Metuchen, N.J.: Scarecrow Press, 1970, 1971, 1973, supplemented by Andrew A. Aros, *A Title Guide to the Talkies, 1964–1974*, Scarecrow Press, 1977; *The American Film Institute Catalogue of Motion Pictures, Feature Films 1960–1970*, ed. by Richard P. Krafsur, 2 vols., N.Y.: R. R. Bowker, 1976; *The New York Times Film Reviews 1913–1968*, 6 vols., N.Y.: Arno, 1970, and the four subsequent volumes covering 1969–70 (Arno, 1971), 1971–72 (1973), 1973–74 (1975), 1975–76 (1977); *Contemporary Authors: A Bio-Bibliographical Guide to Current Authors and Their Works*, 69 vols. to date, Detroit: Gale Research Co.

This introduction reprinted with permission from *The Modern American Novel and the Movies*, Edited by Gerald Peary and Roger Shatzkin (New York: Frederick Ungar, 1978) p. 349.

323

Author—Title	Film Version: Title (if changed) Production Company, Release Date Director (d)	Rental Source(s)
Austen, Jane (1775–1817)		
Pride and Prejudice (1813)	MGM, 1940 (d) Robert Z. Leonard	FNC
Barrie, James M. (1860–1937)		
The Little Minister (1891)	*The Story of . . .* Vitagraph, 1912	
	Neptune, 1915 (d) Percy Nash	
	Famous Players, 1921 (d) Penrhyn Stanlaws	
	Vitagraph, 1921 (d) David Smith	
	RKO, 1934 (d) Richard Wallace	
Bennett, Arnold (1867–1931)		
Buried Alive (1908)	*The Great Adventure* Turner Films, 1915 (d) Larry Trimble	
	The Great Adventure Whitman Bennett, 1921 (d) Kenneth Webb	
	His Double Life (Br) Eddie Dowling Pictures, 1933 (d) Arthur Hopkins	UNF
	Holy Matrimony Fox, 1943 (d) John M. Stahl	FNC

Author—Title	Film Version: Title (if changed) Production Company, Release Date Director (d)	Rental Source(s)
The Card (1911)	*The Promoter* (USA) British Film Makers, 1952 (d) Ronald Neame	WRS
Mr. Prohack (1922)	*Dear Mr. Prohack* Pinewood Films-Wessex, 1949 (d) Thornton Freeland	
B_{RONTE}, Charlotte (1816–55)		
Jane Eyre (1847)	Thanhouser, 1910	
	Whitman Features, 1914	
	Biograph, 1915	
	Woman and Wife Select Pictures, 1918 (d) Edward Jose	
	Hugo Ballin Productions, 1921 (d) Hugo Ballin	
	Monogram, 1934 (d) Christy Cabanne	CIN
	Fox, 1944 (d) Robert Stevenson	FNC
	Omnibus-Sagittarius, 1970 (d) Delbert Mann	BUD, FNC, ROA, TWY
B_{RONTE}, Emily (1818–48)		
Wuthering Heights (1847)	Ideal, 1922 (d) A. V. Bramble	
	Samuel Goldwyn, 1939 (d) William Wyler	AB

Author—Title	Film Version: Title (if changed) Production Company, Release Date Director (d)	Rental Source(s)
	Cumbres Borrascosas/Abismos de Pasion Mexico, 1953 (d) Luis Bunuel	
	American International, 1970 (d) Robert Fuest	
Butler, Samuel (1835–1902)		
The Way of All Flesh (1903)	Paramount, 1940 (d) Louis King	UNI
Carroll, Lewis (1832–98)		
Alice in Wonderland (1865)	Hepworth, 1903 (d) Cecil Hepworth, Percy Stow	
	Alice's Adventures in Wonderland Edison, 1910	
	Maienthau, 1914	
	Nonpareil, 1915 (d) W. W. Young	BUD
	Pathe, 1927	MOG
	Paramount, 1933 (d) Norman McLeod	UNI
	Souvaine Selective, 1951 (d) Dallas Bower	
	Disney, 1951 animated	AB, FNC
	Alice's Adventures in Wonderland Fox, 1972 (d) William Sterling	AB, BUD, CWF, UNF,

Author—Title	Film Version: Title (if changed) Production Company, Release Date Director (d)	Rental Source(s)
Cleland, John (1709–89)		
Fanny Hill (1749)	Gala, 1965 (d) Russ Meyer	
	Sweden, 1972 (d) Mac Ahlberg	WSA
Collins, W. Wilkie (1824–89)		
The Moonstone (1868)	World Film Corp., 1915	
	Monogram, 1934 (d) Reginald Barker	MOG
	British television production	
The Woman in White (1860)	Gem, 1912	
	The Dream Woman Blaché Features, 1914 (d) Alice Blaché	
	Tangled Lives Fox, 1917 (d) J. Gordon Edwards	
	British and Dominions, 1929 (d) Herbert Wilcox	
	Warners, 1948 (d) Peter Godfrey	UAS
Conrad, Joseph (1857–1924)		
Heart of Darkness (1902)	*Apocalypse Now* Omni Zoetrope, 1979 (d) Francis Coppola	
Lord Jim (1900)	Paramount, 1925 (d) Victor Fleming	

Author—Title	Film Version: Title (if changed) Production Company, Release Date Director (d)	Rental Source(s)
	Columbia-Keep, 1964 (d) Richard Brooks	AB, BUD, CCC, AB, CHA, CWF, ROA, SWA, TWY
Outcast of the Islands (1896)	British Lion, 1951 (d) Carol Reed	WRS
The Secret Agent (1907)	*Sabotage* (Br) *A Woman Alone* (USA) Gaumont, 1936 (d) Alfred Hitchcock	BUD, JAN, MMA
The Secret Sharer (1909)	*Face to Face* Huntington Hartford, 1953 (d) John Brahm	
Victory (1915)	Paramount-Artcraft, 1919	
	Dangerous Paradise, Paramount, 1930 (d) William Wellman	UNI
	Paramount, 1941 (d) John Cromwell	UNI
Within the Tides (1916)	*Laughing Anne* Imperadio, 1953 (d) Herbert Wilcox	IVY
DEFOE, Daniel (1659–1731)		
Robinson Crusoe (1719)	Bison, 1913 (d) Otis Turner	
	Henry W. Savage, 1916	
	Universal, 1917	
	Universal, 1924	

Author—Title	Film Version: Title (if changed) Production Company, Release Date Director (d)	Rental Source(s)
	Epic, 1927	FCE
	Guaranteed Pictures, 1936 (d) M. A. Wetherell *The Adventures of Robin- son Crusoe* Mexico, 1953 (d) Luis Bunuel	AB,
	Australia, 1970 animated	CWF, ROA, TWY
	Man Friday England, 1975 (d) Jack Gould	
Moll Flanders (1722)	*The Amorous Adventures of . . .* Winchester, 1965 (d) Terence Young	FNC
DICKENS, Charles (1812–70)		
A Christmas Carol (1843)	*Scrooge; or, Marley's Ghost* R. W. Paul, 1901 (d) W. R. Booth	
	Essanay, 1908	
	Edison, 1910	
	Scrooge Zenith, 1913 (d) Leedham Bantock	
	London Film Company, 1914 (d) Harold Shaw	
	The Right To Be Happy Bluebird Photoplays, 1916 (d) Rupert Julian	

Author—Title	Film Version: Title (if changed) Production Company, Release Date Director (d)	Rental Source(s)
	Scrooge Master Films, 1922 (d) George Wynn	
	Scrooge British and Colonial, 1923. (d) Edwin Greenwood	
	Scrooge British Sound Film, 1928 (d) Hugh Croise	
	Scrooge Twickenham, 1935 (d) Henry Edwards	BUD, FCE
	MGM, 1938 (d) Edwin L. Marin	FNC
	Renown, 1951 (d) Brian Desmond Hurst	AB
	CBS, 1956 (d) Ralph Levy	AB, BUD, TWY
	Alpha, 1960 (d) Robert Hartford-Davis	
	. . . with Mr. Magoo UPA, 1965 animated	KER,
	Australia, 1970 animated	AB, BUD
	Scrooge Waterbury, 1970 (d) Ronald Neame	SWA
David Copperfield (1849–50)	Thanhouser, 1911	
	Hepworth, 1913 (d) Thomas Bentley	
	Associated Exhibitors, 1923	

Author—Title	Film Version: Title (if changed) Production Company, Release Date Director (d)	Rental Source(s)
	MGM, 1935 (d) George Cukor	FNC
	Omnibus, 1969 (d) Delbert Mann	
Dombey and Son (1847–48)	Ideal, 1917 (d) Maurice Elvey	
	Rich Man's Folly Paramount, 1931 (d) John Cromwell	
Great Expectations (1860–61)	Paramount, 1917	
	Universal, 1934 (d) Stuart Walker	UNI
	Cineguild, 1946 (d) David Lean	BUD, CON
	Encyclopaedia Britannica, 1959	EBE
	Two Cities, 1974 (d) Joseph Hardy	SWA
Hard Times (1854)	British television production	
Little Dorrit (1857–58)	Thanhouser, 1913	
	Progress 1920 (d) Sidney Morgan	
Martin Chuzzlewit (1843–44)	Edison, 1912	
	Biograph, 1914	
The Mystery of Edwin Drood (1870)	Gaumont, 1909 (d) Arthur Gilbert	
	Ideal, 1914 (d) Herbert Blaché	
	Universal, 1935 (d) Stuart Walker	UNI

Author—Title	Film Version: Title (if changed) Production Company, Release Date Director (d)	Rental Source(s)
Nicholas Nickleby (1838–39)	Ealing, 1947 (d) Albert Cavalcanti	JAN
The Old Curiosity Shop (1841)	Thanhouser, 1911	
	Britannia Films, 1912 (d) Frank Powell	
	Hepworth, 1914 (d) Thomas Bentley	
	Welsh-Pearson, 1921 (d) Thomas Bentley	
	Wardour, 1934 (d) Thomas Bentley	FCE, JAN
Oliver Twist (1837–38)	Hepworth, 1912 (d) Thomas Bentley	
	Paramount, 1916	
	Oliver Twist, Jr. 1921 Fox, 1921 (d) Millard Webb	
	Nancy/Fagin Master Films, 1922 (d) H. B. Parkinson	
	First National, 1922 (d) Frank Lloyd	IVY, TWY
	Monogram, 1933 (d) William J. Cowen	FCE
	Cineguild, 1948 (d) David Lean	JAN
	Oliver! Warwick-Romulus, 1968 (d) Carol Reed	CWF, ROA, SWA
Our Mutual Friend (1864–65)	British television production	

Author—Title	Film Version: Title (if changed) Production Company, Release Date Director (d)	Rental Source(s)
The Pickwick Papers (1836–38)	Vitagraph, 1913 (d) Larry Trimble	
	Renown, 1952 (d) Noel Langley	BUD, ROA, UNF
A Tale of Two Cities (1859)	Vitagraph, 1911 (d) William Humphreys	
	Fox, 1917 (d) Frank Lloyd	
	Master Films, 1922 (d) W. C. Rowden	
	The Only Way United Artists, 1926 (d) Herbert Wilcox	
	MGM, 1935 (d) Jack Conway	FNC
	Rank, 1958 (d) Ralph Thomas	TWY, WRS
DOYLE, Arthur Conan (1859–1930)		
The Hound of the Baskervilles (1902)	Pathé, 1915	
	Stoll, 1921 (d) Maurice Elvey	
	R—C Pictures, 1922	
	Gaumont, 1931 (d) V. Gareth Gundrey	
	Fox, 1939 (d) Sidney Lanfield	BUD, FNC, ROA, TWY
	Hammer, 1959 (d) Terence Fisher	UAS
The Sign of Four (1890)	Stoll, 1923 (d) Maurice Elvey	

Author—Title	Film Version: Title (if changed) Production Company, Release Date Director (d)	Rental Source(s)
	Associated Talking Pictures, 1932 (d) Rowland V. Lee, Graham Cutts	
A Study in Scarlet (1887)	Pathé, 1914	
	G. B. Samuelson, 1914 (d) George Pearson	
	Worldwide, 1933 (d) Edwin L. Marin	BUD
Eʟɪoᴛ, George (1819–80)		
The Mill on the Floss (1860)	Mutual, 1915	
	Morgan, 1937 (d) Tim Whelan	BUD
Romola (1863)	Inspiration Metro-Goldwyn, 1924 (d) Henry King	
Silas Marner (1861)	Thanhouser, 1911	
	Edison, 1913	
	Mutual, 1916	FCE
	Associated Exhibitors, 1922 (d) Frank Donovan	
Fɪᴇʟᴅɪɴɢ, Henry (1707–54)		
Joseph Andrews (1742)	Woodfall, 1978 (d) Tony Richardson	
Tom Jones (1749)	Ideal, 1917 (d) Edwin J. Collins	
	Woodfall, 1963 (d) Tony Richardson	UAS

Author—Title	Film Version: Title (if changed) Production Company, Release Date Director (d)	Rental Source(s)
GALSWORTHY, John (1867–1933)		
The Man of Property (1906)	*The Forsyte Saga* (Br) *That Forsyte Woman* (USA) MGM, 1949 (d) Compton Bennett	FNC
	The Forsyte Saga British television production	
GOLDSMITH, Oliver (1728–74)		
The Vicar of Wakefield (1766)	Thanhouser, 1910	
	Britannia Films, 1912 (d) Frank Powell	
	Hepworth, 1913 (d) Frank Wilson	
	Planet Films, 1913 (d) John Douglas	
	Thanhouser, 1917 (d) Fred Paul	FCE
GRAVES, Robert (1895–——)		
I, Claudius (1934)	British television production	
HARDY, Thomas (1840–1928)		
Far from the Madding Crowd (1874)	Turner Films, 1915 (d) Larry Trimble	
	MGM, 1967 (d) John Schlesinger	FNC
Jude the Obscure (1896)	British television production	

Author—Title	**Film Version:** **Title (if changed)** **Production Company,** **Release Date** **Director (d)**	**Rental** **Source(s)**
The Mayor of Casterbridge (1886)	Progress, 1921 (d) Sidney Morgan	
	British television production	
Tess of the D'Urbervilles (1891)	Famous Players, 1913	
	Metro-Goldwyn, 1924 (d) Marshall Neilan	
	Tess Columbia (1981) (d) Roman Polanski	
JOYCE, James (1882–1941)		
Finnegans Wake (1939)	*Passages from James Joyce's . . .* Continental, 1969 (d) Mary Ellen Bute	CAL, GRO
A Portrait of the Artist as a Young Man (1914–15)	Ulysses/Mahler Films, 1978 (d) Joseph Strick	TX
Ulysses (1922)	Walter Reade-Joseph Strick, 1967 (d) Joseph Strick	CWF, TWY, WRS
KIPLING, Rudyard (1865–1936)		
Captains Courageous (1897)	MGM, 1937 (d) Victor Fleming	FNC
The Jungle Book (1894)	United Artists, 1942 (d) Zoltan Korda	CWF, MOG, ROA
	Disney, 1966 animated	
Kim (1901)	MGM, 1949 (d) Victor Saville	FNC
The Light that Failed (1890)	Pathe, 1916	

Author—Title	Film Version: Title (if changed) Production Company, Release Date Director (d)	Rental Source(s)
	Famous Players-Lasky, 1923 (d) George Melford	
	Paramount, 1939 (d) William A. Wellman	UNI
The Man Who Would Be King (1888)	Allied Artists, 1975 (d) John Huston	CIN
Soldiers Three (1888)	MGM, 1951 (d) Tay Garnett	FNC
Toomai of the Elephants (1894)	*Elephant Boy* London Film Production, 1937 (d) Robert Flaherty, Zoltan Korda	BUD, ROA
Wee Willie Winkie (1888)	Fox, 1937 (d) John Ford	FNC
LAWRENCE, David Herbert (1885–1930)		
The Fox (1923)	Raymond Stross/M.P.I., 1968 (d) Mark Rydell	WSA
Lady Chatterley's Lover (1928)	France, 1957 (d) Marc Allegret	AB
The Rocking Horse Winner (1926)	Two Cities, 1949 (d) Anthony Pelessier	JAN
Sons and Lovers (1913)	Two Cities/Company of Artists, 1960 (d) Jack Cardiff	FNC
The Virgin and the Gypsy (1930)	Kenwood, 1970 (d) Christopher Miles	KER
Women in Love (1920)	Brandywine, 1969 (d) Ken Russell	UAS

Author—Title	Film Version: Title (if changed) Production Company, Release Date Director (d)	Rental Source(s)
MAUGHAM, W. Somerset (1874–1965)		
Ashenden (1928)	*The Secret Agent* Gaumont, 1936 (d) Alfred Hitchocock	
Cakes and Ale (1930)	British television production	
Christmas Holiday (1939)	Universal, 1944 (d) Robert Siodmak	
The Hour before the Dawn (1942)	Paramount, 1944 (d) Frank Tuttle	UNI
The Moon and Sixpence (1919)	United Artists, 1942 (d) Albert Lewin	BUD, IVY
Narrow Corner (1932)	Warners, 1933 (d) Alfred E. Green	UAS
Of Human Bondage (1915)	RKO, 1934 (d) John Cromwell	BUD, NYF
	Warners, 1946 (d) Edmund Goulding	
	MGM, 1964 (d) Ken Hughes	FNC
The Painted Veil (1925)	MGM, 1934 (d) Richard Boleslawski	FNC
	The Seventh Sin MGM, 1957 (d) Ronald Neame	FNC
The Razor's Edge (1944)	Fox, 1947 (d) Edmund Goulding	FNC
Vessel of Wrath (1933)	The Beachcomber (USA) Paramount, 1938 (d) Erich Pommer	AB, BUD

Author—Title	Film Version: Title (if changed) Production Company, Release Date Director (d)	Rental Source(s)
Mᴵʟɴᴇ, Alan Alexander (1882–1956)		
Winnie the Pooh (1926)	*. . . , and the Honey Tree* Disney, 1965 animated	
Mᴏᴏʀᴇ, George (1852–1933)		
Esther Waters (1894)	Wessex, 1948 (d) Ian Dalrymple, Peter Proud	
Rɪᴄʜᴀʀᴅsᴏɴ, Samuel (1689–1761)		
Pamela (1740–41)	*Mistress Pamela* Fanfare, 1973 (d) James O'Conally	FNC
Sᴄᴏᴛᴛ, Sir Walter (1771–1832)		
The Bride of Lammermoor (1819)	Vitagraph, 1909	
The Heart of Midlothian (1818)	Hepworth, 1914 (d) Frank Wilson	
	A Woman's Triumph Famous Players, 1914	
Ivanhoe (1819)	Independent, 1913 (d) Herbert Brenon	
	Rebecca the Jewess (USA) Zenith, 1913 (d) Walter and Frederick Melville	
	MGM, 1951 (d) Richard Thorpe	FNC
Quentin Durward (1823)	*Adventures of . . .* MGM, 1955 (d)Richard Thorpe	FNC
Rob Roy (1818)	United Films, 1911 (d) Arthur Vivian	
	Eclair, 1913	

Author—Title	Film Version: Title (if changed) Production Company, Release Date Director (d)	Rental Source(s)
	Gaumont-Westminster, 1922 (d) W. P. Kellino	
	. . . , *the Highland Rogue* Disney, 1953 (d) Harold French	AB, FNC, ROA, SWA, TWY
The Talisman (1825)	*King Richard and the Crusaders* Warners, 1954 (d) David Butler	
SHELLEY, Mary Wollstonecraft		
Frankenstein (1818)	Universal, 1931 (d) James Whale	CWF, SWA, TWY, UNI
	The Curse of . . . Hammer-Clarion, 1957 (d) Terence Fisher	BUD, CON
STEVENSON, Robert Louis (1850–94)		
Black Arrow (1889)	Columbia, 1948 (d) Gordon Douglas	BUD
	Australia, 1972 animated	
The Body Snatcher (1884)	RKO, 1945 (d) Robert Wise	FNC
Catriona (1893)	Rank, 1972	
Dr. Jekyll and Mr. Hyde (1886)	Selig, 1908	
	Independent, 1913 (d) James Cruze	
	Famous Players-Lasky, 1920 (d) John S. Robertson	BUD, UNI
	Pioneer, 1920	FCE, MOG

Author—Title	Film Version: Title (if changed) Production Company, Release Date Director (d)	Rental Source(s)
	Paramount, 1932 (d) Rouben Mamoulian	FNC
	MGM, 1941 (d) Victor Fleming	FNC
	The Two Faces of Dr. *Jekyll* (Br) *House of Fright* (USA) Hammer, 1959 (d) Terence Fisher	
Kidnapped (1886)	Edison, 1917 (d) Alan Crosland	
	Fox, 1938 (d) Alfred M. Werker	FNC
	Monogram 1949 (d) William Beaudine	CIN
	Disney, 1959 (d) Robert Stevenson	AB, CWF, FNC, ROA, SWA, TWY
	Omnibus 1972 (d) Delbert Mann	
	Australia, 1972 animated	ICS
The Master of Ballantrae (1889)	Warners, 1953 (d) William Keighley	WSA
St. Ives (1894)	*The Secret of . . .* Columbia, 1949 (d) Phil Rosen	CCC
The Sire de Malétroit's Door (1878)	*The Strange Door* Universal, 1951 (d) Joseph Pevney	UNI
The Suicide Club (1878)	*Trouble for Two* MGM, 1936 (d) J. Walter Ruben	FNC

Author—Title	Film Version: Title (if changed) Production Company, Release Date Director (d)	Rental Source(s)
Treasure Island (1883)	Vitagraph, 1908	
	Edison, 1912 (d) J. Searle Dawley	
	MGM, 1934 (d) Victor Fleming	FNC
	Disney, 1950 (d) Byron Haskin	AB, CCC, SWA, TW
	UPA, 1965 animated	ICS, SWA
	Australia, 1970 animated	BUD, ICS, ROA, SW
Treasure of Franchard (1884)	*Treasure of Lost Canyon* Universal International, 1952 (d) Ted Tetzlaff	UNI
STEVENSON, Robert Louis and OSBOURNE, Lloyd (1868–1947)		
Ebb Tide (1893–94)	*Adventure Island* Paramount, 1947 (d) Peter Stewart	AB, CWF
The Wrong Box (1889)	Salamander, 1965 (d) Bryan Forbes	AB, BUD, COL, CWF, SWA, TWY
STOKER, Bram (1847–1912)		
Dracula (1897)	*Nosferatu*, /Prana, 1922 (d) F.W. Murnau	CON, BUD, MMA
	Vampyr, 1931 (d) Carl Dreyer	AB, BUD
	Universal International, 1931 (d) Tod Browning	CWF, SWA, TWY, UNI

Author—Title	Film Version: Title (if changed) Production Company, Release Date Director (d)	Rental Source(s)
	Dracula's Daughter Universal, 1936 (d) Lambert Hillyer	UNI
	Horror of Dracula (USA) Hammer-Cadogan, 1958 (d) Terence Fisher	BUD, CON, CWF, SWA
	. . . , *Prince of Darkness* Hammer, 1965 (d) Terence Fisher	FNC
	. . . *Has Risen from the Grave* Hammer, 1968 (d) Freddie Francis	AB, ICS, SWA, TWY
	Andy Warhol's Frankenstein, 1974 (d) Andy Warhol	SWA
	Young Frankenstein, 1975 (d) Mel Brooks	FNC
	Nosferatu the Vampyre, 1979 Werner Herzog, (d) Werner Herzog	
Jewel of the Seven Stars (1903)	*Blood from the Mummy's Tomb* MGM, 1971 (d) Seth Holt	UNF
Swift, Jonathan (1667–1745)		
Gulliver's Travels (1726)	A New Gulliver U.S.S.R., 1935 (d) Alexander Ptushko	
	Paramount, 1939 animated	

Author—Title	Film Version: Title (if changed) Production Company, Release Date Director (d)	Rental Source(s)
	The Three Worlds of Gulliver Columbia, 1959 (d) Jack Sher	AB, BUD, CWF
THACKERAY, William Makepeace (1811–63)		
The Luck of Barry Lyndon (1844)	*Barry Lyndon* Peregrine, 1975 (d) Stanley Kubrick	
Vanity Fair (1847)	Vitagraph, 1911 (d) Charles Kent	
	Edison, 1915 (d) Eugene Howland	
	Master Films, 1922 (d) W. C. Rowden	
	HOL, 1932 (d) Chester M. Franklin	FCE, MOG
	Becky Sharp RKO, 1935 (d) Rouben Mamoulian	IVY, MOG
	British television production	
TRESSELL, Robert (1870–1911)		
The Ragged Trousered *Philantropists* (1914)	British television production	
TROLLOPE, Anthony (1815–82)		
"Barsetshire novels," 6 vols. (1855–67)	*The Pallisers* British television production	

Author—Title	Film Version: Title (if changed) Production Company, Release Date Director (d)	Rental Source(s)
W<small>ALPOLE</small>, Hugh (1884–1941)		
Mr. Perrin and Mr. Traill (1911)	Two Cities, 1948 (d) Lawrence Huntington	
Vanessa (1933)	. . . : *Her Love Story* MGM, 1935 (d) William K. Howard	
W<small>AUGH</small>, Evelyn (1903–66)		
Decline and Fall (1928)	. . . *of a Birdwatcher!* Foxwell, 1968 (d) John Krish	FNC
The Loved One (1948)	MGM, 1965 (d) Tony Richardson	FNC
W<small>ELLS</small>, Herbert George (1866–1946)		
The Door in the Wall (1895)	British Film Institute, 1956 (d) Glenn H. Alvey, Jr.	
The First Men in the Moon (1901)	Gaumont, 1919 (d) J. L. V. Leigh	
	Columbia, 1963 (d) Nathan Juran	AB, BUD, CWF, TWY
The History of Mr. Polly (1910)	Two Cities, 1949 (d) Anthony Pelessier	
The Invisible Man (1897)	United Artists, 1933 (d) James Whale	SWA, UNI
The Island of Dr. Moreau (1896)	*Island of Lost Souls* Paramount, 1932 (d) Erle C. Kenton	SWA, UNI
	Eros, 1959	
	Wetherly, 1977 (d) John Taylor	

Author—Title	Film Version: Title (if changed) Production Company, Release Date Director (d)	Rental Source(s)
Kipps (1905)	Stoll, 1921 (d) Harold Shaw	
	The Remarkable Mr. Kipps (USA) Fox, 1941 (d) Carol Reed	
The Man Who Could Work Miracles (1899)	London Films, 1937 (d) Lothar Mendes	BUD, MOG
The Passionate Friends (1913)	Cineguild, 1949 (d) David Lean	
The Shape of Things to Come (1933)	*Things to Come* London Films, 1936 (d) William Cameron Menzies	BUD, MOG, UNF
The Time Machine (1895)	MGM, 1960 (d) George Pal	FNC
The War of the Worlds (1898)	Paramount, 1953 (d) Byron Haskin	FNC
WILDE, Oscar (1854–1900)		
The Canterville Ghost (1891)	MGM, 1944 (d) Jules Dassin	FNC
Lord Arthur Savile's Crime (1891)	*Flesh and Fantasy* Universal, 1943 (d) Julien Duvivier	TWY, UNI
The Picture of Dorian Gray (1891)	Barker-Neptune, 1916 (d) Fred W. Durrant	
	MGM, 1945 (d) Albert Lewin	FNC
	The Secret of . . . American International, 1970 (d) Massimo Dallamano	IVY, UNF

Author—Title	Film Version: Title (if changed) Production Company, Release Date Director (d)	Rental Source(s)
	Dorian Gray Hemdale, 1973 (TV Film) (d) Dan Curtis	
W ODEHOUSE, Pelham Grenville (1881–1975)		
A Damsel in Distress (1919)	RKO, 1937 (d) George Stevens	FNC
The Girl on the Boat (1922)	Knightsbridge, 1962 (d) Henry Kaplan	
My Man Jeeves (1919), et al.	*Thank You, Jeeves* Fox, 1936 (d) Arthur Greville Collins	
Piccadilly Jim (1918)	MGM, 1936 (d) Robert Z. Leonard	
Summer Lightning (1929)	British and Dominions, 1932 (d) Maclean Rogers	

RENTAL SOURCES FOR FILMS
LISTED IN FILMOGRAPHY

AB
Audio Brandon Films (Macmillan)
34 MacQuesten Parkway South
Mount Vernon, New York 10550
(914) 664-5051
or 1619 North Cherokee
Los Angeles, California 90028
(213) 463-0357
    or
Branch offices in Oakland,
Dallas, and Brookfield, Illinois

BLA
Blackhawk Films
Eastin-Phelan Corp.
Davenport, Iowa 52808
(319) 323-9736

BUD
Budget Films
4590 Santa Monica Blvd.
Los Angeles, California 90029
(213) 660-0187

° Denotes archive.

CAL
University of California
Extension Media Center
2223 Fulton Street
Berkeley, California 94720
(415) 845-6000

CCC
Cine-Craft Company
709 SW Ankeny
Portland, Oregon 97205
(503) 228-7484

CHA
Charard Motion Pictures
2110 E. 24th Street
Brooklyn, New York 11229
(212) 891-4339

CIN
Hurlock Cine World, Inc.
13 Arcadia Road
Greenwich, Connecticut 06870
(203) 637-4319

CIV
Cinema 5-16mm.
595 Madison Avenue
New York, New York 10022
(212) 421-5555

CLA
Classic Film Museum, Inc.
4 Union Square
Dover-Foxcroft, Maine 04426
(207) 564-8371

COL
Columbia Cinemateque
711 Fifth Avenue
New York, New York 10022
(212) 751-4400

CON
Contemporary/McGraw Hill Films
Princeton Road
Hightstown, New Jersey 08520
(609) 448-1700
or
828 Custer Avenue
Evanston, Illinois 60202
(312) 869-5010
or
1714 Stockton Street
San Francisco, California 94133
(415) 362-3115 or 997-1221

COR
Corinth Films
410 East 62nd Street
New York, New York 10021
(212) 421-4770

CSV
Cine Service Vintage Films
85 Exeter Street
Bridgeport, Connecticut 06606
(203) 372-7785

CWF
Clem Williams Films, Inc.
2240 Noblestown Road
Pittsburgh, Pennsylvania 15205
(412) 921-5810
or
Branch offices in Atlanta,
Chicago, and Houston

EBE
Encyclopaedia Britannica
Educational Corp.
425 N. Michigan Ave.
Chicago, Illinois 60611
(312) 321-6800

EMG
Em Gee Film Library
4931 Gloria Avenue
Encino, California 91316
(213) 981-5506

FCE
Film Classic Exchange
1926 South Vermont Avenue
Los Angeles, California 90007
(213) 731-3854

FNC
Films Incorporated
4420 Oakton Street
Skokie, Illinois 60076
(312) 676-1088
or
440 Park Avenue South
New York, New York 10016
(212) 889-7910
or
5625 Hollywood Boulevard
Hollywood, California 90028
(213) 466-5481
or
Branch offices in Atlanta, Boston,
Salt Lake City, and San Diego

FIM
Film Images
(a Division of Radim Films, Inc.)
71 West 60th Street
New York, New York 10023
(212) 279-6653
    or
1034 Lake Street
Oak Park, Illinois 60301
(312) 386-4826

GRO
Grove Press Film Division
214 Mercer Street
New York, New York 10012
(212) 989-6400

ICS
Institutional Cinema Service
915 Broadway
New York, New York 10010
(212) 673-3990

IVY
IVY Film
165 West 46th Street
New York, New York 10036
(212) 765-3940

JAN
Janus Films
24 W. 58th Street
New York, New York 10023
(212) 753-7100

KER
Kerr Film Exchange
3034 Canon Street
San Diego, California 92106
(714) 224-2406

KPF
Kit Parker Films
Box 227
Carmel Valley, California 93924
(408) 659-4131

°LOC
Library of Congress
E. Capitol and Independence
    Avenue S.E.
Washington, DC 20540
(202) 783-0400

°MMA
Museum of Modern Art
11 West 53rd Street
New York, New York 10019
(212) 956-4205

MOG
Mogull's
235 West 46th Street
New York, New York 10036
(212) 757-1414

NY
New Yorker Films
43 West 61st Street
New York, New York 10023
(212) 247-6110

NYF
New York Review Presentations
250 W. 57th Street
New York, New York 10019
(212) 265-1690

ROA
Roa's Films
1696 N. Astor St.
Milwaukee, Wisconsin 53202
(414) 271-0861

SWA
Swank Motion Pictures
201 S. Jefferson Avenue
St. Louis, Missouri 63166
(314) 531-5100
   or
333 Front Street
Hempstead, New York 11550
(516) 538-6500

TFC
"The" Film Center
915 12th Street, N.W.
Washington, D.C. 20005
(202) 393-1205

TMC
The Movie Center
57 Baldwin Street
Charlestown, Massachusetts 02129
(617) 242-3456

TWY
Twyman Films
321 Salem Avenue
Dayton, Ohio 45401
(513) 222-4014

TX
Texture Films
1600 Broadway
New York, New York 10019
(212) 586-6960

UAS
United Artists Sixteen
729 Seventh Avenue
New York, New York 10019
(212) 575-3000

UNF
United Films
1425 South Main
Tulsa, Oklahoma 74119
(918) 583-2681

UNI
Universal Sixteen
445 Park Avenue
New York, New York 10022
(212) 759-7500
   or
2001 South Vermont Avenue
Los Angeles, California 90007
(213) 731-2151
   or
Branch offices in Atlanta,
Chicago, and Dallas

WCF
Westcoast Films
25 Lusk Street
San Francisco, California 94107
(415) 362-4700

WRS
Walter Reade 16
241 E. 34th Street
New York, New York 10016
(212) 683-6300

WSA
Warner Brothers
Non-Theatrical Division
4000 Warner Blvd.
Burbank, California 91503
(213) 843-6000

Note: for further information on film rental sources see James L. Limbacher, ed., *Feature Films on 8mm. and 16mm.*, 5th ed., N.Y.: R. R. Bowker, 1977; and Kathleen Weaver, ed., *Film Programmer's Guide to 16mm. Rentals*, 2nd ed., Berkeley, California: Reel Research, 1975.

SELECTED BIBLIOGRAPHY

I / Individual Films and Novelists

Anderegg, Michael A. "Conrad and Hitchcock: *The Secret Agent Inspires Sabotage*," *Literature/Film Quarterly*, 3, No. 3 (Summer 1975), pp. 215-225.

Anobile, Richard, ed. *Dr. Jekyll and Mr. Hyde*. New York: Avon, 1975.

Baldanza, Frank. "*Sons and Lovers*: Novel to Film as a Record of Cultural Growth," *Literature/Film Quarterly*, 1, No. 1 (January 1973), pp. 64-70.

Barrett, Gerald R. and Thomas L. Erskine. *From Fiction to Film: D. H. Lawrence's "The Rocking-Horse Winner."* Encino, California: Dickenson Publishing Co., 1974.

Battestin, Martin C. "Osborne's *Tom Jones*: Adapting a Classic," *Virginia Quarterly Review*, 42 (Summer 1966), pp. 378-393.

Becker, Henry. " 'The Rocking Horse Winner': Film as Parable," *Literature/Film Quarterly*, 1, No. 1 (January 1973), pp. 55-63.

Brooks, Richard. "Forward to Lord Jim," *Movie*, 12 (Spring 1965), pp. 15-16.

————. "On the Thematic Visual Action in 'Lord Jim,' " *Cinema*, 2, No. 5 (March-April 1965), pp. 4-5.

Buscombe, Edward. "Dickens and Hitchcock," *Screen*, 2, Nos. 4-5 (1970), pp. 97-114.

Calder, Robert L. "Somerset Maugham and the Cinema," *Literature/Film Quarterly*, 6, No. 3 (Summer 1978), pp. 262-273.

Canby, Vincent. "Kubrick's Latest has Brains and Beauty" [*Barry Lyndon*], *New York Times* (Dec. 21, 1975), II, 1:7.

Cardiff, Jack. "Lawrence: . . . and the Camera" [*Sons and Lovers*], *Films and Filming*, 6, No. 8 (May 1960), p. 9.

Clarke, T. E. B. "Every Word in Its Place" [*A Tale of Two Cities*], *Films and Filming*, 4, No. 5 (February 1958), pp. 10+.

Curry, George. *COPPERFIELD '70* [film script]. New York: Ballantine, 1970.

DeNitto, Dennis, ed. *Media for Our Time* [film script of "The Secret Sharer"]. New York: Holt, Rinehart and Winston, 1971.

Dewey, Lang. "Ulysses," *Film*, No. 49 (Autumn 1967), pp. 23-26.

Disney, Walt. "How I Cartooned *Alice*," *Films in Review*, 2 (May 1951), pp. 7-11.

Doniol-Valcroze, Jacques and André Bazin. "Conversation with Buñuel" [*Robinson Crusoe* and *Wuthering Heights*], *Sight and Sound*, 24, No. 4 (Spring 1955), pp. 181-185.

Durgnat, Raymond. "Loved One," *Films and Filming*, 12, No. 5 (February 1966), pp. 19-23.

Edwards, Roy. "Movie Gothick—A Tribute to James Whale" [*Frankenstein*], *Sight and Sound*, 27, No. 2 (Autumn 1957), pp. 95-98.

Eisenstein, Sergei. "Dickens, Griffith, and the Film Today," *Film Form*. Ed. by Jay Leyda. New York: Harcourt, Brace, 1949.

Ellin, Stanley. "Mr. Dickens and Mr. Pichel," [*Great Expectations*], *Hollywood Quarterly*, 3, No. 1 (Fall 1947), pp. 87-89.

Garcia-Abrines, Luis. "Rebirth of Buñuel" [Robinson Crusoe], *Yale French Studies*, 17 (Summer 1956), pp. 54-66.

Gassner, John and Dudley Nichols, eds. *Twenty Best Film Plays* [*Wuthering Heights*]. New York: Crown, 1943.

Gerard, Lillian N. "Of Lawrence and Love" [*Women in Love*], *Film/Literature Quarterly*, 3, No. 4 (Fall 1970), pp. 6-12.

————. "*The Virgin and the Gypsy* and 'D. H. Lawrence in Taos," *Film/Literature Quarterly*, 4, No. 1 (Winter 1970-71), pp. 36-42.

Gill, Brendan. "The Man Who Would Be Kipling," *Film Comment*, 12, No. 1 (January-February 1976), pp. 23+.

Glut, Donald F. *The Frankenstein Legend: A Tribute to Mary Shelley and Boris Karloff*. Metuchen, N.J.: Scarecrow Press, 1973.

Goulding, Edmund. "The Razor's Edge," *Life*, 21 (August 12, 1946), pp. 75-83.

Hamill, Pete. "Lord Jim," *Saturday Evening Post*, 237 (November 21, 1964), pp. 24-29.

Hanson, Curtis Lee. "The Loved One," *Cinema*, 2, No. 6 (July-August 1965), pp. 9-11.

Harrington, John and David Paroissien. "Alberto Cavalcanti on *Nicholas Nickleby*," *Literature/Film Quarterly*, 6, No. 1 (Winter 1978), pp. 48-56.

Hitchens, Gordon. " 'A Breathless Eagerness in the Audience . . .': Historical Notes on Dr. Frankenstein and His Monster," *Film Comment*, 6, No. 1 (Spring 1970), pp. 49-51.

Houston, Penelope. "Barry Lyndon," *Sight and Sound*, 45, No. 2 (Spring 1976), pp. 77-80.

Hutchins, Patricia. "James Joyce and the Cinema," *Sight and Sound*, 21 (August-September 1951), pp. 9-12.

"In Wonderland," *Time*, 22 (December 25, 1933), pp. 20-22.

Jensen, Paul. "Frankenstein," *Film Comment*, 6, No. 3 (Fall 1970), pp. 42-46.

──────. "H. G. Wells on the Screen," *Films in Review*, 18, No. 9 (November 1967), pp. 521-527.

Joyce, Paul. "Richard Brooks and Lord Jim," *Film*, No. 42 (1965), pp. 27+.

Kestner, Joseph A. "Stevenson and Artaud: 'The Master of Ballantrae,'" *Film Heritage*, 7, No. 4 (Summer 1972), pp. 19-28.

Kirschner, Paul. "Conrad and the Film," *Quarterly of Film, Radio, and Television*, 11, No. 4 (Summer 1957), pp. 343-353.

Knoll, Robert F. "Women in Love," *Film Heritage*, 6, No. 4 (Summer 1971), pp. 1-6.

Lambert, Gavin. "Lawrence: The Script" [*Sons and Lovers*], *Films and Filming*, 6, No. 8 (May 1960), p. 9.

──────. "Shadow upon Shadow upon Shadow: Hugh Walpole in Hollywood" [*David Copperfield*], *Sight and Sound*, 23, No. 2 (October-December 1953), pp. 78-82.

McCabe, Bernard. "Ulysses in the Reel World," *New Catholic World*, 204 (March 1967), pp. 346-351.

Mellen, Joan. "Outfoxing Lawrence: Novella into Film" [*The Fox*], *Literature/ Film Quarterly*, 1, No. 1 (January 1973), pp. 17-27.

Moore, Harry T. "D. H. Lawrence and the Flicks," *Literature/Film Quarterly*, 1, No. 1 (January 1973), pp. 3-11.

"New Art Medium for 'Alice' . . . Animated Cartoons," *Design*, 53 (October 1951), pp. 10-11.

Oares, Phillip. "Ken & Glenda & Peter & Nina" [*Women in Love*], *Show* (March 1970), pp. 56-59+.

Osborne, John. *Tom Jones: A Film Script Based on the Novel by Henry Fielding*. New York: Grove Press, 1965.

Palmer, James W. "Fiction into Film: Delbert Mann's *Jane Eyre* (An Edited Interview)," *Studies in the Humanities*, 5 (October 1976), pp. 3-8.

Phillips, Gene D., "Big Screen, Little Screen: Adaptations of Evelyn Waugh's Fiction," *Literature/ Film Quarterly*, 6, No. 2 (Spring 1978), pp. 162-170.

Pichel, Irving. " 'This Happy Breed' and *Great Expectations*," *Hollywood Quarterly*, 2, No. 4 (July 1947), pp. 408-411.

Riley, Michael. "Gothic Melodrama and Spiritual Romance: Vision and Fidelity in Two Versions of *Jane Eyre*," *Literature/Film Quarterly*, 3, No. 2 (Spring 1975), pp. 145-159.

Roman, Robert C. "Dickens' *A Christmas Carol*," *Films in Review*, 9 (December 1958), pp. 572-574.

Rosenberg, Harold. "Notes on Seeing *Barry Lyndon*," *New York Times* (Feb. 29, 1976), II, 1:1.

Scott, James F. "The Emasculation of *Lady Chatterley's Lover*," *Literature/Film Quarterly*, 1, No. 1 (January 1973), pp. 37-45.

Silver, Alain. "The Untranquil Light: David Lean's *Great Expectations*," *Literature/Film Quarterly*, 2, No. 2 (Spring 1974), pp. 140-152.

Silver, Alain and James Ursini. *The Vampire Film* [*Dracula*]. Cranbury, N.J.: A. S. Barnes, 1975.

Silverstein, Norman. " Movie-Going for Lovers of *The Wasteland* and *Ulysses*," *Salmagundi*, 1, No. 1 (Fall 1965).

Smith, Julian. "Vision and Revision: *The Virgin and the Gypsy* as Film," *Literature/Film Quarterly*, 1, No. 1 (January 1973), pp. 28-36.

Solecki, Sam. "D. H. Lawrence's View of Film," *Literature/Film Quarterly*, 1, No. 1 (January 1973), pp. 12-16.

"Sons and Lovers," *Sight and Sound*, 29, No. 2 (Spring 1960), pp. 54-55.

Stephenson, William. "The Wodehouse World of Hollywood," *Literature/Film Quarterly*, 6, No. 3 (Summer 1978), pp. 190-203.

Tarratt, Margaret. "An Obscene Undertaking" [film adaptations of Lawrence's fiction], *Films and Filming*, 17, No. 2 (November 1970), pp. 26-30.

Thomaier, William. "Conrad on the Screen," *Films in Review*, 21, No. 10 (December 1970), pp. 611-621.

Tupper, Lucy. "Dickens on the Screen," *Films in Review*, 10 (March 1959), pp. 142-152.

"Ulysses," *Life*, 62 (March 31, 1967), pp. 54-58.

Wald, Jerry. "Scripting *Sons and Lovers*," *Sight and Sound*, 29 (Summer 1960), p. 117.

Weichtman, John. "Trifling with the Dead" [*Women in Love*], *Encounter*, 34, No. 1 (January 1970), pp. 50-53.

──────. "This Is Why We'll Film James Joyce," *Films and Filming*, 4, No. 12 (September 1958), pp. 9+.

Weinberg, Gretchen. "An Interview with Mary Ellen Bute on the Filming of 'Finnegans Wake,' " *Film Culture*, 35 (Winter 1964-65), pp. 25-28.

Wykes, Alan. *H. G. Wells in the Cinema.* London: Jupiter Books, 1977.

Zambrano, Anna Laura. "*Great Expectations*: Dickens and David Lean," *Literature/Film Quarterly*, 2, No. 2 (Spring 1974), pp. 154-161.

Zambrano. A. L. *Dickens and Film.* New York: Gordon, Press, 1976.

————. "*Women in Love*: Counterpoint on Film," *Literature/Film Quarterly*, 1, No. 1 (January 1973), pp. 46-54.

II / Selected Directors of Film Adaptations

Agee, James. "Agee on Huston," *Films and Filming*, 9, No. 11 (August 1963), pp. 35-38.

Allegret, Yves. "Notes of a Film Maker—'Why I Choose the Unusual' " *Films and Filming*, 2, No. 1 (October 1955), p. 12.

Atkins, Thomas R., ed. *Ken Russell.* New York: Monarch Press, 1976.

Aubry, Daniel and Jean Michel Lacor. "Luis Buñuel," *Film Quarterly*, 12, No. 2 (Winter 1958), pp. 7-9.

Bachmann, Gideon. "The Films of Luis Buñuel," *Cinemage*, 1 (1955), pp. 10-17.

————. "How I Make Films: An Interview with John Huston," *Film Quarterly*, 19, No. 1 (Fall 1965), pp. 3-13.

————. "Watching Huston," *Film Comment*, 12, No. 1 (January-February 1976), pp. 21-22.

Batten, Mary. "The Cinematic Use of Scientific Machines: Actuality on Abstraction" [Bute], *Vision*, 1, No. 2 (Summer 1962), pp. 55-59.

Bergman, Ingmar. *Bergman on Bergman.* Trans. by Paul Britten Austin. New York: Simon and Schuster, 1973.

Bernstein, Jeremy. "Profiles: How About a Little Game" [Kubrick], *New Yorker*, 42, No. 38 (November 12, 1966), pp. 70-110+.

Braudy, Leo and Morris Dickstein, eds. *Great Film Directors: A Critical Anthology.* New York: Oxford University Press, 1978.

Buache, Freddy. *The Cinema of Luis Buñuel.* Trans. by Peter Graham. New York: A. S. Barnes, 1973.

Buñuel, Luis. "A Statement," *Film Culture*, 21 (No date), pp. 41-42.

Carey, Gary. *Cukor & Co.* New York: Museum of Modern Art, 1971.

Cowie, Peter, ed. *Fifty Major Film-Makers.* Cranbury, N.J.: A. S. Barnes, 1976.

De La Roche, Catherine. "Conversation with Hitchcock," *Sight and Sound*, 25, No. 3 (Winter 1955-56), 157-158.

————. "Man with No Message" [Reed], *Films and Filming*, 1, No. 3 (December 1954), p. 15.

Dempsey, Michael. "The World of Ken Russell," *Film Quarterly*, 25, No. 3 (Spring 1972), pp. 13-25.

DeVries, Daniel. *The Films of Stanley Kubrick*. Grand Rapids, Michigan: William B. Erdmans Publishing Co., 1973.

Durgnat, Raymond. *The Strange Case of Alfred Hitchcock*. Cambridge, Massachusetts: The M.I.T. Press, 1974.

Feldmann, Hans. "Kubrick and His Discontents," *Film Quarterly*, 30, No. 1 (Fall 1976), pp. 12-19.

Geduld, Harry M., ed. *Filmmakers on Film Making*. Bloomington: Indiana University Press, 1967.

Gillett, John and David Robinson. "Conversation with George Cukor," *Sight and Sound*, 33, No. 4 (Autumn 1964), pp. 188-193.

Gomez, Joseph A. *Ken Russell: The Adaptor as Creator*. New York: Pergamon Press, 1977.

Hanson, Curtis Lee. "William Wyler," *Cinema*, 3, No. 5 (Summer 1967), pp. 22-28.

Higham, Charles. "Hitchcock's World," *Film Quarterly*, 16, No. 2 (Winter 1962-63), pp. 3-16.

Hochman, Stanley, ed. *American Film Directors*. New York: Frederick Ungar, 1974.

Houston, Penelope. "The Figure in the Carpet" [Hitchcock], *Sight and Sound*, 32, No. 4 (Autumn 1963), pp. 159-164.

Hughes, Ken. "Those Nutty Intellectuals," *Films and Filming*, 9, No. 4 (January 1963), pp. 9-10.

Isaacs, Hermione R. "William Wyler, Director with a Passion and a Craft," *Theatre Arts*, 31, No. 2 (February 1947), pp. 20-24.

Jensen, Paul. "James Whale," *Film Comment*, 7, No. 1 (Spring 1971), pp. 52-57.

Jones, DuPre. "Beating the Devil: Thirty Years of John Huston," *Films and Filming*, 19, No. 4 (January 1973), pp. 26-32.

Kanesaka, Kenji. "A Visit to Luis Buñuel," *Film Culture*, 41 (Summer 1966), pp. 60-65.

Kubrick, Stanley. "How I Learned to Stop Worrying and Love the Cinema," *Films and Filming*, 9, No. 9 (June 1963), pp. 12-13.

———. "Words and Movies," *Sight and Sound*, 30, No. 1 (Winter 1960-61), p. 14.

Lane, John Francis. "Young Romantic" [Young], *Films and Filming*, 13, No. 5 (February 1967), pp. 58-60.

Lambert, Gavin. *On Cukor*. New York: Putnam's, 1972.

Lellis, George. "Recent Richardson—Cashing the Blank Cheque," *Sight and Sound*, 38, No. 3 (Summer 1969), pp. 130-133.

Madson, Axel. *William Wyler: The Authorized Biography.* New York: Thomas Y. Crowell, 1973.

Markopoulos, Gregory. "Beyond Audio Visual Space" [Bute], *Vision*, 1, No. 2 (Summer 1962), pp. 52-54.

McVay, Douglas. "Lean—Lover of Life," *Films and Filming*, 5, No. 11 (August 1959), pp. 9-10+.

Mellen, Joan, ed. *The World of Luis Buñuel: Essays in Criticism.* New York: Oxford University Press, 1978.

Millar, Gavin. "Hitchcock Versus Truffaut," *Sight and Sound*, 38, No. 2 (Spring 1969), pp. 82-88.

Milne, Tom. "How I Learned to Stop Worrying and Love Stanley Kubrick," *Sight and Sound*, 33, No. 2 (Spring 1964), pp. 68-72.

———. *Mamoulian.* Bloomington: Indiana University Press, 1970.

———. "The Mexican Buñuel," *Sight and Sound*, 35, No. 1 (Winter 1965-66), pp. 36-39.

Overstreet, Richard. "Interview with George Cukor," *Film Culture*, 34 (Fall 1964), pp. 1-16.

Pett, John. "A Master of Suspense" [Hitchcock], *Films and Filming*, 6 No. 2 (November 1959), pp. 9-10+.

Phillips, Gene. "George Cukor: An Interview," *Film Comment*, 8, No. 1 (Spring 1972), pp. 53-55.

———. "An Interview with Ken Russell," *Film Comment*, 6, No. 3 (Fall 1970), pp. 10-17.

———. "John Schlesinger, Social Realist," *Film Comment*, 5, No. 4 (Winter 1969), pp. 58-63.

———. "Kubrick," *Film Comment*, 7, No. 4 (Winter 1971-72), pp. 30-35.

Pratley, Gerald. *The Cinema of John Huston.* New York: A. S. Barnes, 1977.

Prouse, Derek. "Interviewing Buñuel," *Sight and Sound*, 29, No. 3 (Summer 1960), pp. 118-119.

Reisz, Karel. "Interview with Huston," *Sight and Sound*, 21, No. 3 (January-March 1952), pp. 130-132.

"Richard Brooks," *Movie*, 12 (Spring 1965), pp. 2-17.

Richardson, Tony. "The Films of Luis Buñuel," *Sight and Sound*, 23, No. 3 (January-March 1954), pp. 125-130.

———. "The Man Behind an Angry-Young-Man," *Films and Filming*, 5, No. 5 (February 1959), pp. 9+.

———. "The Two Worlds of the Cinema," *Films and Filming*, 7, No. 9 (June 1961), pp. 7+.

Riley, Michael M. " 'I Both Hate and Love What I Do': An Interview with

John Schlesinger," *Literature/Film Quarterly*, 6, No. 2 (Spring 1978), pp. 104-115.

Robinson, David. "Rouben Mamoulian: Painting the Leaves Black," *Sight and Sound*, 30, No. 3 (Summer 1961), pp. 123-127.

Rohmer, Eric, and Claude Chabrol, *Hitchcock*. New York: Frederick Ungar, 1979.

Sarris, Andrew. "Alfred Hitchcock—Prankster of Paradox," *Film Comment*, 10, No. 2 (March-April 1974), pp. 8-9.

————. "Carol Reed in the Context of His Time—Part One," *Film Culture*, 2, No. 4 (1956), pp. 14-17; "Part Two," 3, No. 1 (1957), pp. 11-14+.

————, ed. *Interviews with Film Directors*. New York: Bobbs-Merrill, 1967.

Sherman, Eric. *Directing the Film: Film Directors on their Art*. Boston: Little, Brown, 1976.

Sonbert, Warren. "Alfred Hitchcock: Master of Morality," *Film Culture*, 41 (Summer 1966), pp. 35-38.

Spoto, Donald. *The Art of Alfred Hitchcock*. New York: Hopkinson and Blake, 1976.

Truffaut, Francois. *The Films in My Life*. Trans. by Leonard Mayhew. New York: Simon and Schuster, 1978.

————. *Hitchcock*. New York: Simon and Schuster, 1967.

Walker, Alexander. *Stanley Kubrick Directs*. New York: Harcourt, Brace, 1971.

Wood, Robin. *Hitchcock's Films*. New York: A. S. Barnes, 1965.

Young, Colin. "Tony Richardson: An Interview in Los Angeles," *Film Quarterly*, 13, No. 4 (Summer 1960), pp. 10-15.

III / *On Film and Literature*

Admussen, Richard L., Edward J. Gallagher and Lubbe Levin. "Novel into Film: An Experimental Course," *Literature/Film Quarterly*, 6, No. 1 (Winter 1978), pp. 66-72.

Asheim, Lester. "From Book to Film." Four articles in *Hollywood Quarterly*, 5, No. 3 (Spring 1951), pp. 289-304; 5, No. 4 (Summer 1951), pp. 334-349; 6, No. 1 (Fall 1951), pp. 54-68; 6, No. 3 (Spring 1952), pp. 258-273.

Astre, Georges Albert, et al. *Cinéma et roman*. Special issue of *Révue des lettres modernes* , 5, (Summer 1958), pp. 36-38.

Bates, H. F. "When the Cinemagoer Complains That—'It Isn't Like the Book'—Who's to Blame?" *Films and Filming*, 5, No. 8 (May 1959), p. 7.

Bauer, Leda V. "The Movies Tackle Literature," *American Mercury*, 14 (July 1928), pp. 288-294.

Bergman, Ingmar. "Film Has Nothing to Do with Literature." Introduction to *Four Screenplays of Ingmar Bergman*. Trans. by Lars Malmstrom and David Kushner. New York: Simon and Schuster, 1960.

Bluestone, George. *Novels into Film*. Berkeley: University of California Press, 1957.

————. "Time in Film and Fiction," *Journal of Aesthetics and Art Criticism*, 19, No. 3 (Spring 1961), pp. 311-315.

————. "Word to Image: The Problem of the Filmed Novel," *Quarterly of Film, Radio, and Television*, 11, No. 2 (Winter 1956), pp. 171-180.

Bodeen, DeWitt. "The Adapting Art," *Films in Review*, 14 (June-July 1963), pp. 349-356.

Bond, Kirk. "Film as Literature," *Bookman*, 84 (July 1933), pp. 188-189.

Brownell, Baker. "Drama, the Novel, the Movie Review." In *Art Is Action*. New York: Harper, 1939, pp. 159-170.

Buchanan, Andrew. *Film-Making from Script to Screen*. Rev. ed. London: Phoenix House, 1951.

Burgess, Anthony. "On the Hopelessness of Turning Good Books into Films," *New York Times* (April 20, 1975), 2:1,15.

Burton, T. "Books into Pictures," *Saturday Review of Literature* (March 30, 1940), p. 20; (April 13, 1940), p. 21; (May 11, 1940), p. 21; (June 8, 1940), p. 21.

Butcher, M. "Look First upon this Picture; Books into Film" *Wiseman Review*, 238 (Spring 1964), pp. 55-64.

Cahiers du Cinéma, 185 (December 1966). Issue devoted to novels and film.

Chatman, Seymour. *Story and Discourse: Narrative Structure in Fiction and Film*. Ithaca: Cornell University Press, 1978.

Cohen, Keith. *Film and Fiction: The Dynamics of Exchange* New Haven: Yale, 1979.

Conger, Syndy, and Janice Welsch, eds. *Narrative Strategies: Essays in Film and Prose Fiction*. Macomb: Western Illinois University Press 1981.

Connor, Edward. "Of Time and Movies," *Films in Review*, 12, No. 3 (March 1961), pp. 131-143.

Dick, Bernard F. "Narrative and Infra-Narrative in Film," *Literature/Film Quarterly*, 3, No. 2 (Spring 1975), pp. 124-130.

Durgnat, Raymond. "The Mongrel Muse," *Films and Feeling*. Cambridge, Massachusetts: M.I.T. Press, 1971, pp. 13-30.

————. "This Damned Eternal Triangle," *Films and Filming*, 11, No. 3 (December 1964), pp. 15-19.

Edel, Leon. "Novel and Camera." In *The Theory of the Novel: New Essays*. Ed. by John Halperin. New York: Oxford University Press, 1974, pp. 177-188.

Eidsvik, Charles. "Soft Edges: The Art of Literature, the Medium of Film," *Literature/Film Quarterly*, 2, No. 1 (Winter 1974), pp. 16-21.

————. "Toward a 'Politique des Adaptations,'" *Literature/Film Quarterly*, 3, No. 3 (Summer 1975), pp. 255-263.

Eisenstein, Sergei. "Lessons from Literature." In *Film Essays and A Lecture*. Ed. by Jay Leyda. New York: Praeger, 1970.

Enser, A. G. S. *Filmed Books and Plays*. Rev. ed. London: Deutsch, 1974.

Fadiman, William. "But Compared to the Original," *Films and Filming*, 11, No. 5 (February 1965), pp. 21-23.

Fell, John. *Film and the Narrative Tradition*. Norman: University of Oklahoma Press, 1974.

Geduld, Harry M., ed. *Authors on Film*. Bloomington: Indiana University Press, 1972.

———— and Ronald Gottesman. "Adaptation [Annotated Bibliography]," *Guidebook to Film*. New York: Holt, Rinehart, 1972, pp. 30-35.

Godfrey, Lionel. "It Wasn't Like That in the Book," *Films and Filming*, 13, No. 7 (April 1967), pp. 12-16.

Gow, Gordon. "Novel into Film," *Films and Filming*, 12, No. 8 (May 1966), pp. 19-22.

Greene, Graham. *Graham Greene on Film*. New York: Simon and Schuster, 1972.

Guzzetti, Alfred. "The Role of Theory in Films and Novels," *New Literary History*, 3 (1972), pp. 547-558.

————. "Narrative and the Film Image," *New Literary History*, 6 (1975), pp. 379-392.

Harrington, John, ed. *Film and/as Literature*. Englewood Cliffs, N.J.: Prentice-Hall, 1977.

Hartley, Dean Wilson. " 'How Do We Teach It?' A primer for the Basic Literature/Film Course," *Literature/Film Quarterly*, 3, No. 1 (Winter 1975), pp. 60-68.

Hulseberg, Richard A. "Novels and Films: A Limited Inquiry," *Literature/Film Quarterly*, 6, No. 1 (Winter 1978), pp. 57-65.

Jahiel, Edwin. "Literature and Film," *Books Abroad*, 45 (1971), pp. 259-261.

Jinks, William. *The Celluloid Literature: Film in the Humanities*. Riverside, N.J.: Glencoe Press, 1971.

Kawin, Bruce F. *Telling It Again and Again: Repetition in Literature and Film.* Ithaca, N.Y.: Cornell University Press, 1972.

Koch, Stephen. "Fiction and Film: A Study for New Sources," *The Saturday Review* (December 27, 1969), pp. 12-14.

Limbacher, James L. *Remakes, Series and Sequels on Film and Television.* 2nd ed. Dearborn, Michigan: Dearborn Public Library, 1969.

Lindsay, Vachel. *The Art of the Moving Picture.* New York: Macmillan, 1952 (reprint of 1915 ed.).

Luhr, William and Peter Lehman. *Authorship and Narrative in the Cinema: Issues in Contemporary Aesthetics and Criticism.* New York: Putnam, 1977.

Marcus, Fred H., ed. *Film and Literature: Contrasts in Media.* Scranton, Pa.: Chandler Publishers, 1971.

Mason, Ronald. "The Film of the Book," *Film*, 16 (March-April 1958), pp. 18-20.

McConnell, Frank. "Film and Writing: The Political Dimension," *Massachusetts Review*, 13, No. 4 (Autumn 1972), pp. 543-562.

Mitry, Jean. "Remarks on the Problem of Cinematic Adaptation," *MMLA Bulletin* (Spring 1971), pp. 1-9.

Monaco, James. *How to Read a Film.* New York: Oxford University Press, 1977.

Moreno, Julio L. "Subjective Cinema: And the Problem of Film in the First Person," *Quarterly of Film, Radio, and Television*, 7, No. 4 (Summer 1953), pp. 341-358.

Morrissette, Bruce. "Post-Modern Generative Fiction: Novel and Film," *Critical Inquiry*, 2 (1975), pp. 253-262.

Murray, Edward. *The Cinematic Imagination: Writers and the Motion Pictures.* New York: Frederick Ungar, 1972.

Nathan, Robert. "A Novelist Looks at Hollywood," *Hollywood Quarterly*, 1, No. 2 (1945), pp. 146-147.

Nicoll, Allardyce. "Literature and the Film," *English Journal*, 26 (January 1937), pp. 1-9.

Ortman, Marguerite Gonda. *Fiction and the Screen.* Boston: Little, Brown, 1935.

Panofsky, Erwin. "Style and Medium in the Moving Pictures," *Critique*, 1, No. 3 (January-February 1947).

Peary, Gerald and Roger Shatzkin, eds. *The Classic American Novel and the Movies.* New York: Frederick Ungar, 1977.

Pingaud, Bernard. "The Aquarium," *Sight and Sound*, 32, No. 3 (Summer 1963), pp. 136-139.

Praz, Mario. *Mnemosyne: The Parallel between Literature and the Visual Arts.* Princeton, N.J.: Princeton University Press, 1967.

Probst, Robert E. "Visual to Verbal," *English Journal,* 61, No. 1 (January 1972), pp. 71-75.

Purdy, Strother B. "Can the Novel and the Film Disappear?" *Literature/Film Quarterly,* 2, No. 3 (Fall 1974), pp. 237-255.

Quesnoy, P. F. *Literature et cinéma.* Paris: Gallimard, 1928.

Richardson, Robert. *Literature and Film.* Bloomington: Indiana University Press, 1969.

Riesman, Evelyn. "Film and Fiction," *Antioch Review,* 17 (Fall 1957), pp. 353-363.

Roud, Richard. "Novel Novel; Fable Fable?" *Sight and Sound,* 31, No. 2 (Spring 1962), pp. 84-88.

Ruhe, Edward. "Film: The 'Literary' Approach," *Literature/Film Quarterly,* 1, No. 1 (January 1973), pp. 76-83.

Schickel, Richard. *The Disney Version.* New York: Simon and Schuster, 1968.

Schneider, Harold W. "Literature and Film: Making Out Some Boundaries," *Literature/Film Quarterly,* 3, No. 1 (Winter 1975), pp. 30-44.

Seldes, Gilbert. "Fiction Influenced by the Movies," *Scribners Magazine,* 100 (November 1936), 71-72.

————. "Vandals of Hollywood: Why a Good Movie Cannot Be Faithful to the Original Book or Play," *Saturday Review of Literature* (October 17, 1936), pp. 3-4.

Smith, Julian. "Short Fiction on Film: A Selected Filmography," *Studies in Short Fiction,* 10 (1973), pp. 397-409.

Sobchack, Vivian. "Tradition and Cinematic Allusion," *Literature/Film Quarterly,* 2, No. 1 (Winter 1974), pp. 59-65.

Sontag, Susan. "A Note on Novels and Films." In *Against Interpretation.* New York: Dell, 1972, pp. 245-250.

Spiegel, Alan. *Fiction and the Camera Eye: Visual Consciousness in Film and the Modern Novel.* Charlottesville: University of Virginia Press, 1975.

Symposium, 27, No. 2 (1973). Issue devoted to the relationship of literature to film.

Taylor, John R. *Graham Greene on Film: Collected Film Criticism, 1935-1939.* New York: Simon and Schuster, 1972.

Thorp, Margaret. "The Motion Picture and the Novel," *American Quarterly,* 3, No. 3 (1951), pp. 195-203.

Tiessen, Paul. "A Comparative Approach to the Form and Function of

Novel and Film: Dorothy Richardson's Theory of Art," *Literature/Film Quarterly*, 3, No. 1 (Winter 1975), pp. 83-92.

Wagner, Geoffrey. *The Novel and the Cinema*. Rutherford, N.J.: Fairleigh Dickinson University Press, 1975.

Weinberg, Herman G. "Novel into Film," *Literature/Film Quarterly*, 1, No. 2 (April 1973), pp. 99-102.

Winston, Douglas Garrett. *The Screenplay As Literature*. Rutherford, N.J.: Fairleigh Dickinson University Press, 1973.

Woolf, Virginia. "The Film Folio 6: The Cinema," *Sight and Sound*, 23 (April-June 1954), pp. 215-216.

IV / *General Entries*

Agee, James. *Agee on Film*. Boston: Beacon Press, 1964.

Aristotle. *The Poetics*. Several editions available.

Armes, Roy. *A Critical History of the British Cinema*. New York: Oxford University Press, 1978.

————. *Film and Reality: An Historical Survey*. London: Penguin, 1974.

Arnheim, Rudolf. *Film as Art*. Berkeley: University of California Press, 1957.

————. *Visual Thinking*. Berkeley: University of California Press, 1969.

Auerbach, Erich. *Mimesis: The Representation of Reality in Western Literature*. Garden City, N.Y.: Doubleday, 1957.

Balázs, Béla. *Theory of the Film*. New York: Dover, 1970.

Bardèche, Maurice and Robert Brasillach. *The History of the Motion Pictures*. New York: Norton, 1938.

Barnes, John. *The Beginnings of the Cinema in England*. New York: Barnes & Noble, 1976.

Barthes, Roland. *Elements of Semiology/Writing Degree Zero*. Trans. by Annette Lavers and Colin Smith. Boston: Beacon Press, 1968.

Bazin, André. "The Ontology of the Photographic Image." Trans. by Hugh Gray. *Film Quarterly*, 13, No. 4 (Summer 1960), pp. 4-9.

————. *What Is Cinema?* 2 vols. Trans. and ed. by Hugh Gray. Berkeley: University of California Press, 1967, 1971.

Benjamin, Walter. "The Work of Art in the Age of Mechanical Production." In *Illuminations*. Ed. by Hannah Arendt. New York: Harcourt, Brace, 1968.

Berger, John. *Toward Reality: Essays in Seeing*. New York, 1962.

Betts, Ernest. *The Film Business: A History of British Cinema, 1896-1972*. London: Allen and Unwin, 1973.

Bobker, Lee R. *Elements of Film*. New York: Harcourt, Brace, 1969.

Butler, Ivan. *Cinema in Britain: An Illustrated Survey*. New York: A. S. Barnes, 1973.

Casty, Alan. *Development of the Film: An Interpretive History*. New York: Harcourt, Brace, 1973.

Caudwell, Christopher. *Studies in a Dying Culture*. New York: Monthly Review Press, 1971.

Cavell, Stanley. *The World Viewed: Reflections on the Ontology of Film*. New York: Viking, 1971.

Ceram, C. W. *Archeology of the Cinema*. New York: Harcourt, Brace, 1965.

Cowie, Peter, ed. *A Concise History of the Cinema*. 2 vols. Cranbury, N.J.: A. S. Barnes, 1970.

––––––. *Eighty Years of Cinema*. New York: A. S. Barnes, 1977.

Crowther, Bosley. *The Great Films*. New York: Putnam's, 1967.

Denby, David, ed. *Awake in the Dark: An Anthology of American Film Criticism, 1915 to the Present*. New York: Random House, 1977.

de Sayssure, Ferdinand. *Course in General Linguistics*. Trans. by Wade Baskin. New York: McGraw-Hill, 1966.

Dickinson, Thorold. *A Discovery of Cinema*. New York: Oxford University Press, 1973.

Durgnat, Raymond. *Films and Feelings*. Cambridge, Mass.: M.I.T. Press 1967.

––––––. *A Mirror for England: British Movies from Austerity to Affluence*. New York: Praeger, 1971.

Eco, Umberto. *A Theory of Semiotics*. Bloomington: University of Indiana Press, 1976.

Eisenstein, Sergei. *Film Essays and a Lecture*. Ed. by Jay Leyda. New York: Praeger, 1970.

––––––. *Film Form*. Ed. by Jay Leyda. New York: Harcourt, Brace, 1949.

––––––. *Film Sense*. Ed. by Jay Leyda. New York: Harcourt, Brace, 1942.

Fell, John L. *Film: An Introduction*. New York: Praeger, 1975.

Fischer, Ernst. *The Necessity of Art*. Baltimore: Penguin, 1963.

Fulton, A. R. *Motion Pictures*. Norman: University of Oklahoma Press, 1960.

Gans, Herbert J. *Popular Culture and High Culture*. New York: Basic Books, 1974.

Geduld, Harry M. and Ronald Gottesman. *Guidebook to Film*. New York: Holt, Rinehart, 1972.

Gessner, Robert. *The Moving Image: A Guide to Cinematic Literacy*. New York: Dutton, 1968.

Giannetti, Louis. *Understanding Movies.* 2nd ed. Englewood Cliffs, N.J.: Prentice-Hall, 1976.

Gilliatt, Penelope. *Unholy Fools: Wits, Comics, Disturbers of the Peace: Film and Theater.* New York: Viking, 1973.

Gombrich, E. H. *Art and Illusion.* Princeton, N.J.: Princeton University Press, 1969.

————, Julian Hochberg and Max Black. *Art, Perception, and Reality.* Baltimore: Johns Hopkins University, 1972.

Grant, Barry K., ed. *Film Genre: Theory and Criticism.* Metuchen, N.J.: Scarecrow Press, 1977.

Griffith, Richard and Arthur Mayer. *The Movies.* New York: Simon and Schuster, 1957.

Halliwell, Leslie. *The Filmgoer's Companion.* New York: Hill and Wang, 1977.

Hampton, Benjamin. *A History of the Movies.* New York: Dover, 1970.

Hauser, Arnold. "The Film Age." In *The Social History of Art.* Trans. by Stanley Goodman. New York: Knopf, 1951, pp. 927-959.

Hinde, Robert A., ed. *Non-Verbal Communication.* Cambridge: Cambridge University Press, 1972.

Houston, Penelope. *The Contemporary Cinema.* Baltimore: *Penguin, 1963.*

Huss, Roy and Norman Silverstein. *The Film Experience.* New York: Dell, 1968.

Jacobs, Lewis. *The Rise of American Film.* New York: Harcourt, Brace, 1939.

————, ed. *The Emergence of Film Art.* New York: Hopkinson and Blake, 1969.

————, ed. *Introduction to the Art of the Movies.* New York: Noonday Press, 1960.

Kael, Pauline. "Circles and Squares," *Film Quarterly,* 16, No. 3 (Spring 1963), pp. 12-26.

————. *Deeper into Movies.* Boston: Little, Brown, 1973.

————. *Going Steady.* Boston: Little, Brown, 1970.

————. *I Lost It at the Movies.* Boston: Little, Brown, 1965.

————. *Kiss Kiss Bang Bang.* Boston: Little, Brown, 1968.

Kauffmann, Stanley. *Figures of Light.* New York: Holt, Rinehart, 1971.

————. *Living Images.* New York: Harper & Row, 1975.

————. *A World on Film.* New York: Holt, Rinehart, 1966.

Knight, Arthur. *The Liveliest Art.* New York: Macmillan, 1957.

Kracauer, Siegfried. *Theory of Film.* New York: Oxford University Press, 1960.

Kuhns, William. *Movies in America*. Dayton, Ohio: Pflaum/Standard, 1972.

Langer, Susanne K. "A Note on Film" In *Feeling and Form*. New York: Scribners, 1953, pp. 411-415.

Lindgren. Ernest. *The Art of the Film*. New York: Macmillan, 1963.

Lotman, Jurig. *Semiotics of the Cinema*. Ann Arbor: University of Michigan Press, 1976.

MacDonald, Dwight. *On Movies*. Englewood Cliffs, N.J.: Prentice-Hall, 1968.

Mannogian, Haig P. *The Film-Maker's Art*. New York: Basic Books, 1966.

Mast, Gerald. *A Short History of the Movies*. 2nd ed. Indianapolis: Bobbs-Merrill, 1976.

————. and Marshall Cohen, eds. *Film Theory and Criticism*. 2nd ed. New York: Oxford University Press, 1979.

McLuhan, Marshall. *Understanding Media*. New York: McGraw-Hill, 1964.

Metz, Christian. *Film Language: A Semiotics of the Cinema*. Trans. by Michael Taylor. New York: Oxford University Press, 1974.

————. *Language and Cinema*. Trans. by Donna Jean Umiker-Sebeok. The Hague: Mouton, 1974.

Munsterberg, Hugo. *The Film: A Psychological Study*. New York: Dover Press, 1969.

Murray, Edward. *The Cinematic Imagination*. New York: Frederick Ungar, 1972.

Pechter, William. *Twenty-Four Times A Second*. New York: Harper & Row, 1971.

Perkins, V. F. *Film as Film*. London: Penguin, 1972.

Perry, George. *The Great British Picture Show: From the Nineties to the Seventies*. New York: Hill and Wang, 1974.

[Potamkin, Harry Alan] *The Compound Cinema: The Film Writings of Harry Alan Potamkin*. Ed. Jacobs, Lewis. N.Y.: Teachers College Press, 1977.

Read, Herbert. "Towards a Film Aesthetic," *Cinema Quarterly*, 1, No. 4 (Summer 1933), pp. 197-202.

Rhode, Eric. *A History of Cinema*. New York: Hill and Wang, 1976.

Robinson, David. *The History of World Cinema*. New York: Stein and Day, 1974.

Sarris, Andrew. *The American Cinema*. New York: Dutton, 1968.

————. "The Auteur Theory," *Film Quarterly*, 16, No. 4 (Summer 1963), pp. 26-33.

————. *Confessions of a Cultist*. New York: Simon and Schuster, 1970.

————. *The Primal Screen.* New York: Simon and Schuster, 1973.

Schickel, Richard. *Second Sight: Notes on Some Movies, 1965-70.* New York: Simon and Schuster, 1972.

Simon, John. *Acid Test.* New York: Stein and Day, 1963.

————. *Movies into Film.* New York: Dial Press, 1971.

————. *Private Screenings.* New York: Macmillan, 1967.

Solomon, Stanley J. *The Film Idea.* New York: Harcourt, Brace, 1972.

————. ed. *The Classic Cinema.* New York: Harcourt, Brace, 1973.

Spottiswood, Raymond. *A Grammar of Film.* Berkeley: University of California Press, 1950.

Talbot, Daniel, ed. *Film, An Anthology.* New York: Simon and Schuster, 1959.

Tudor, Andrew. *Theories of Film.* New York: Viking, 1974.

Vogel, Amos. *Film as a Subversive Art.* New York: Random House, 1974.

Warshow, Robert. *The Immediate Experience.* Garden City, N.Y.: Doubleday, 1962.

Williams, Raymond. *Keywords: A Vocabulary of Culture and Society.* New York: Oxford University Press, 1976.

Wollen, Peter. *Signs and Meaning in the Cinema.* Rev. ed. Bloomington: University of Indiana Press, 1972.

————, ed. *Working Papers on the Cinema: Sociology and Semiology.* London: British Film Institute, 1969.

Wright, Basil. *The Long View.* New York: Knopf, 1975.

————. *The Use of the Film.* London: Bodley Head, 1948.

INDEX